WAR!

What Is It Good For?

The John Hope Franklin Series in African American History and Culture

WALDO E. MARTIN JR. & PATRICIA SULLIVAN, EDITORS

WAR!

What Is It Good For?

Black Freedom Struggles and the U.S. Military

FROM WORLD WAR II TO IRAQ

Kimberley L. Phillips

THE UNIVERSITY OF NORTH CAROLINA PRESS   *Chapel Hill*

June Jordan poetry in Chapter 6 © 2005 June Jordan Literary Estate Trust;
reprinted by permission. www.junejordan.com.

Library of Congress Cataloging-in-Publication Data
Phillips, Kimberley L. (Kimberley Louise), 1960–
War! what is it good for? : black freedom struggles and the U.S. military from
World War II to Iraq / by Kimberley L. Phillips. — 1st ed.
p. cm. — (John Hope Franklin series in African American history and culture)
Includes bibliographical references and index.
ISBN 978-0-8078-3502-9 (alk. paper)
ISBN 978-1-4696-1389-5 (pbk.: alk. paper)
1. African American soldiers—History—20th century. 2. United States—Armed Forces—
African Americans—History—20th century. 3. Vietnam War, 1961–1975—African
Americans. 4. African Americans—Civil rights—History—20th century. 5. Civil rights
movements—United States—History—20th century. 6. Vietnam War, 1961–1975—Protest
movements—United States. 7. War and society—United States—History—20th century.
I. Title. II. Title: Black freedom struggles and the U.S. military from World War II to Iraq.
UB418.A47P45 2012
355.0089'96073—dc23
2011031531

cloth 16 15 14 13 12   5 4 3 2 1
paper 17 16 15 14 13   5 4 3 2 1
This book has been digitally printed

For my parents,

Don and Myrtle Phillips,

a soldier and a peacemaker

Contents

Illustrations

Acknowledgments

In 1965 I watched a priest bless the tanks and soldiers that the army planned to send to Vietnam. I was a five-year-old army brat who heard my parents talk about Vietnam and the ideals of the nonviolent civil rights movement, but I didn't have a way to question what I saw that day. My father, who was commissioned in 1958 and trained in Fort Benning, Georgia, went to Vietnam in 1966 with the 173rd Airborne. After his tour, he headed the ROTC program at Cal Poly, San Luis Obispo, and my mother worked with other Catholics to help young men evade the draft. We lived in Grover Beach, a small town twenty miles from where my father worked and where my brothers and I went to the Catholic school. Though I loved our large yard where I watched the sun slip into the Pacific Ocean, I knew my parents had tried to buy a home in San Luis Obispo. Local residents' equal disdain for the Vietnam War and the civil rights movement meant no one would sell a black soldier a home.

The few friends I had lived too far away for regular play dates on the weekends and in the summer, so I listened to a lot of music. Along with the murders of Martin Luther King Jr. and Robert F. Kennedy in 1968, the news that my father might return to Vietnam cast shadows in our home. I played Nina Simone's "'Nuff Said" over and over again. In spite of the show's ribald lyrics, my parents let me listen to the soundtrack from *Hair*. I knew every word to Simone's "Backlash Blues" and "Three Five Zero Zero." When my father returned home in 1970, he introduced me to Jimi Hendrix, Edwin Starr, and Curtis Mayfield. With the earphones clasped to my head, I let "War!" and "Machine Gun" thunder. These songs became prayers, and I listened to them for years as I tried to make sense of war and inequality.

I did not plan to write a book about African Americans, war, and civil rights until students in a 2002 Monroe seminar at the College of William and Mary asked me to talk about Jimi Hendrix's brief history in the 101st Airborne and his later antiwar music. Hendrix was like many black men I knew who saw the military as their only opportunity for work. To consider why these men volunteered for war while their communities pressed for their full rights required more than the hour I had with the students.

I have benefited tremendously from the guidance of many scholars, soldiers, and activists. The enthusiastic and demanding questions from participants in the 2003 Davis Center Seminar pushed me to expand my chronology beyond the Vietnam War to include African Americans' demand for the desegregation of the military during World War II. I especially thank Chad Williams, Anthony Grafton, Nell Irvin Painter, and Marc Rodriguez. I completed the first draft of the manuscript while I was at the Warren Center at Harvard University in 2006–7. Nancy Cott and Carol Oja crafted the focus for the workshop "Cultural Reverberations of Modern War" and organized an outstanding year of talks by scholars in art, music, literature, and history. I give deep thanks to Alan Braddock, Susan Carruthers, Suzanne Cusick, Beth Levy, David Lubin, and Susan Zeiger for their questions, comments, and support. Wallace Best, Nadine Cahodas, Lizabeth Cohen, Chris Cappozola, Mary Dudziak, and Werner Sollars offered advice. Anonymous readers for the University of North Carolina Press provided encouragement for the project and important suggestions. They helped make this a much better and different book than I had first imagined.

My colleagues at William and Mary have been with me every step of the way as I talked about this project and presented material. I especially thank Ben Anderson, Chandos Brown, Evan Cordulack, Susan Donaldson, Seth Feman, Mikal Gaines, Arthur Knight, Erin Krutko-Devlin, Lucie Kyrova, Charlie McGovern, Leisa Meyer, Brian Piper, Hollis Pruitt, and Kathleen Scott. Mia Bay, Dan Bender, Samuel L. Black, Fred Carroll, Nancy Cott, Robert Jefferson, Moon-Ho Jung, Kevin Krause, Sherri Linkon, Jacquelyn McLendon, Gayle Murchison, Carol Oja, Hermine Pinson, Dee Royster, and Stephen Tuck have read and commented on all or various sections of the manuscript. Sherri Linkon and John Russo at the Center for Working-Class Studies, my colleagues in the Collegium for African American Research, Dan Bender, Moon-Ho Jung at the University of Washington, Joe William Trotter and his colleagues at the Center for Africanamerican Urban Studies and the Economy, and Maureen Elgersman Lee provided important forums for me to present material.

I thank the many veterans, soldiers, and antiwar activists who attended my talks, where some frequently spoke. I wrote this book in the midst of the nation's longest period at war and when African Americans disproportionately felt the impact of an economic recession. Though they often have been ill-served by the nation, politicians, and fellow citizens, African American men and women have served in the military with courage, honor, and dignity. Their families have endured grief and isolation. While my parents' personal history of war and antiwar have informed me, African Americans' decades of debates about war, peace, and justice form the heart of this book.

I received research support from the College of William and Mary, Wellesley College, and Harvard University, which provided me with the resources to travel to archives, copy documents, and pay for research assistants, including Mikail Gaines, Nadya Jaworsky, Casey Starry, and Peter A. Shmorhun. I am especially grateful for the support I received from the Frances L. and Edwin L. Cummings endowment at the College of William and Mary.

I thank Waldo Martin and Patricia Sullivan, who early on urged me to write the book I needed and wanted to write. The John Hope Franklin series they coedit has an outstanding list, and I am honored to be a participant. I thank Chuck Grench, Beth Lassiter, Rachel Surles, and Stephanie Ladniak Wenzel, who have been unfailingly patient with my questions and needs.

I thank my parents, Don and Myrtle Davenport Phillips, and my brothers, Don A., Michael, and Mark Phillips. My parents have always offered unconditional support for my research, and this project was no different. My father served as an officer in the army for thirty years; my mother has been an activist for social and racial justice. When my parents faced the indignities and terror of segregation, my father went to Vietnam, twice. My mother, Myrtle Davenport Phillips, taught us that only the practice of nonviolence could bring justice. I thank my parents for their love.

Mark, Peter, and Nina Shmorhun endured my work on this book with love and patience. They listened as I talked about the material, sent me off to the archives with good cheer, stayed quiet as I wrote, and applauded when I finished. Mark offered no rebuke as I spent too many months tethered to my desk, and he cheerfully cared for two teenagers as I spent a year in Boston. Our son, Peter, is a gifted researcher, and he read the manuscript and checked every footnote. Nina kept my research materials and books organized. Her passion for justice matches her grandmother's. I thank them for their love and kindness.

Abbreviations and Acronyms

ACLU	American Civil Liberties Union
CAP	Combined Action Platoon
CIO	Congress of Industrial Organizations
CO	conscientious objector
COFO	Council of Federated Organizations
CORE	Congress of Racial Equality
CRC	Civil Rights Congress
FBI	Federal Bureau of Investigation
FEPC	Fair Employment Practices Commission
FOR	Fellowship of Reconciliation
FSA	Farm Security Administration
HUAC	House Un-American Activities Committee
IEDs	improvised explosive devices
MFDP	Mississippi Freedom Democratic Party
MIA	Montgomery Improvement Association
MIICC	Metropolitan Interfaith and Interracial Coordinating Council

MOWM   March on Washington Movement

NAACP   National Association for the Advancement
of Colored People

NCO   noncommissioned officer

OWI   Office of War Information

PTSD   post-traumatic stress disorder

PX   post exchange

ROTC   Reserve Officers' Training Corps

SCLC   Southern Christian Leadership Conference

SNCC   Student Non-Violent Coordinating Committee

SWAT   Special Weapons and Tactics

UMT   universal military training

WACs   Women's Army Corps

WAVES   Women Accepted for Volunteer Emergency Service

WILPF   Women's International League for
Peace and Freedom

WPA   Works Progress Administration

WAR!

What Is It Good For?

INTRODUCTION

"War!" and "Machine Gun" Blues

An immediate hit single, Edwin Starr's 1970 "War!" replicated the urgent debates in the streets, homes, organizations, and churches of black communities where men were compelled into America's wars and military "police actions" while their struggles for freedom remained unfinished. "War!," a minister thundered, "What is it good for?" The congregation roared back, "Absolutely nothin'!" Behatted women attended the frequent funerals for the war's dead and cried, "War can't give life, it can only take it away." Veterans from World War II and the Korean War deliberated how "they say we must fight to keep our freedom, but Lord knows there's got to be a better way." Their sons and daughters goaded from the streets: "Induction, then destruction—who wants to die?" In this neighborhood, like other black neighborhoods, military police went door-to-door and escorted men "from the lowest income groups" into the induction centers in record numbers. Agitated by decades of too little work and barriers to full political participation, and resistant to the disproportionate numbers of black men drafted, injured, and killed in combat, the old and young, women and their daughters, and veterans and their sons debated and asked, How did killing and dying in war make them citizens? How did expensive wars help their struggles for racial and economic justice? How did killing in war bring them freedom?[1]

Starr, whose music career stalled after his induction into the army in 1965, remade Motown's second version of the song.[2] The Temptations,

Protesters in downtown Pittsburgh, January 1967, with signs reading
"Fight Poverty, Not Hanoi," "SAV-CAP in the Hill," and "L.B.J. Where's Your Support?"
for demonstration against curtailment of antipoverty program.
Photo by Charles "Teenie" Harris; Carnegie Museum of Art, Pittsburgh, Heinz Family
Fund. © 2004 Carnegie Museum of Art, Charles "Teenie" Harris Archive.

who recorded the first version in 1969, produced a sound that replicated
the hum of auto factories and the elusive promise of good jobs. Starr's
single simultaneously re-created the din of combat and the cacophony
of the call-and-response between rebellions in black neighborhoods over
too few jobs and high draft rates. Drum rolls mimic the skilled swagger of
men on the front line. A soldier exhales "War! HUNHH!" as he snaps and
thrusts his bayonet. Tambourines replicate the rapid repeat of M-16s, and
horns blast like shrill bombs. At the song's end, the drum paces the precise
and solemn pivot of an honor guard at a soldier's funeral. As more young
men march off to war, machine guns let loose their terrible, infectious
rhythms.

Jimi Hendrix's "Machine Gun," another song released in 1970, organized a complex percussive and electronic dissonance into a soundscape of combat that recovered the menace, fear, and doubt of young men trained to kill other human beings. The twelve-minute-and-thirty-three-second song began with Buddy Miles's snare drum sounding the rapid repeat of the machine gun, with Hendrix's rapid chord changes echoing like return fire. In this sonic firefight, Hendrix, who had trained for the Vietnam War while in the 101st Airborne, distilled a soldier's encounter with the "enemy" into one grim moment: kill or be killed.

> Machine gun, yeah
> Tearing my buddies all apart
> Evil man make me kill ya
> Evil man make you kill me
> Even though we're only families apart.[3]

While "War!" suggested African Americans' doubts that fighting in wars advanced their unfinished quest for full citizenship, "Machine Gun" revealed soldiers' resistances to the racial and class inequalities of the battlefield. As these young soldiers face each other, M-16s in their hands, they recognize they are both brown, one from the poor streets of Chicago, the other from a village in Vietnam, just "families apart." In Hendrix's lamentation, these poor and disfranchised men who do the work of killing, these "children" sent to "fight a war," ask why. Then they audaciously dream of peace:

> No guns, no bombs
> huh, huh
> Let's all just live and live
> You know, instead of killin'.[4]

Hendrix lived this history of young and poor black men who turned to the military for work, learned to kill in U.S. wars, and then asked why. Hungry and unemployed, he twice faced charges of grand theft auto in 1961. Rather than go to jail, he enlisted and volunteered for the 101st Airborne. Like many of his peers, he considered the military steady work, a prospect he did not find elsewhere in American life. As his airborne unit trained for Vietnam, Hendrix deliberately hurt his back and received an honorable discharge in 1962. By 1969, many of his friends had been drafted into combat units, where they actively resisted the war; his younger brother, Leon, had gone AWOL. Even as the changes in the draft policies claimed to mitigate against the class and race inequalities that forced disproportionate numbers of black men into combat, significant numbers of them continued to be drafted. Hendrix's "Machine Gun" and his many incendiary interpretations of the "Star-Spangled Banner" challenged the myth that national regeneration emerged from war. His body contorted and his electric guitar shrieking like bombs and machine gun fire, Hendrix pierced the popular perception that black freedom would arise from carnage on the battlefield.[5]

Starr's and Hendrix's music did not simply replicate the resistances of communities suddenly in confrontation with the draft's inequities and U.S. foreign policy. Since the early twentieth century, African Americans had questioned the logic that linked military service and citizenship, especially when America's wars typically unleashed a nationalism that justified racial violence at home and abroad.[6] This debate became heightened during World War II as blacks were compelled to serve in a segregated military, but it grew more contentious after 1950 as they disproportionately served in the integrated military. This music produced in 1970, then, only hinted at the decades of deliberations between those African Americans who appealed for the "right to fight" as a civil rights goal and a symbol of full citizenship and those who insisted their participation in the nation's wars did not advance their claims for racial justice. By the Vietnam War era, the questions that African Americans had asked for decades presented a dramatic political challenge to mainstream civil rights activists who considered the integration of the military one of their most important successes.

War! What Is It Good For?: Black Freedom Struggles and the U.S. Military from World War II to Iraq considers how African Americans' agitation for the right to fight as an expression of full citizenship and civil rights coincided with the appeals from other African Americans who considered war inimical to their freedom struggles. It examines African Americans' disproportionate participation in the military and the battlefield alongside their protracted and elusive struggles for economic and racial justice. *War!* examines how African Americans who resisted racial violence and critiqued the nation's wars shaped and reshaped the civil rights movement into an antiwar black freedom movement.

This book's focus on African Americans' military experiences within the context of their freedom struggles and antiwar efforts is situated in the scholarship on the social history of the U.S. military, the twentieth-century civil rights movement, and black internationalism. While this book pays particular attention to the contestations surrounding the efforts to integrate the military after World War II, African Americans' experiences within the U.S. military, and their critiques of the nation's many wars abroad, it also engages the scholarship about America's racial hierarchies that shaped and were shaped by wars and militarization since 1940.[7] As Mae M. Ngai notes, while "the construction of racial hierarchies has been, of course, an ongoing project in American history since the colonial period," it is also "historically specific. At times, a confluence of economic, social, cultural, and political factors has impelled major shifts in society's understanding (and construction) of race and its constitutive roles in national identity formation."[8]

U.S. wars consistently have created these times. Depending on the context, differing and competing racial ideologies have operated simultaneously, forcing different nonwhite groups to participate in wars even as their civil rights and human dignity were denied.[9] Before 1950, the military's racial policies for the use of nonwhite troops varied. During World War II, many Mexican Americans and Native Americans served in integrated units, but others served in segregated units. Regardless of assignment, many fared little better than blacks, as their communities lived and worked in unequal circumstances. Other nonwhites were categorized by race and irrespective of citizenship status. The war against Japan led to the internment of Japanese Americans, and only later were they permitted to serve in segregated units. The granting of citizenship to Puerto Ricans in 1917 compelled them to register for the draft and serve in the military. Many Puerto Ricans challenged the U.S. military's classification of them as "Puerto Rican Negroes" and their assignment to separate units in World War I. In the next war, draft boards in Puerto Rico reclassified many Puerto Ricans as white and assigned darker-skinned recruits to separate units, or they served with black troops. When Puerto Ricans served with African Americans, the military typically did not assign them to combat units; commanders considered these troops unfit for anything but labor positions. Like African Americans, all of these groups faced discrimination and racial violence, and they debated the association of military participation with their pursuit of equal rights.[10]

This book also engages the scholarship on the long civil rights movement that has recently focused on the inconsistency between the U.S. resistance to African Americans' struggles for rights at home and its push for democracy abroad. Social and military historians have framed integration of the military and combat as a consequence of those who pointed to the contradictions between policy at home and rhetoric abroad. The desegregated armed forces has been characterized as an advance in blacks' civil rights, but *War!* considers how the roles of African Americans as purveyors of violence in wars and their simultaneous experiences with segregation and violence in the United States shaped their understandings of racial categories and citizenship.[11] Instead of casting the integration of the military as a civil rights victory, this study examines how federal officials calculated African Americans' exclusions from American economic and civic life into the episodic need for combat labor. And it addresses the rich scholarship on black intellectuals' critiques of American imperialism after 1945 by its consideration of how the mass of African Americans who went into the military and went to war against nonwhite nations shaped the rhetoric and tactics of black freedom struggles. As Melani McAlister has noted, "One of the fundamental tensions in African American intellectual and cultural history since World War II [is] how are we to understand the relationship of African Americans to the project of U.S. nationalism and the realities of power in the nation state."[12] Millions of blacks in the military and in combat since 1940 participated in American aggression and violence. This book asks, How did African Americans' overlapping experiences as perpetrators and victims in America's wars and occupations while they also participated in freedom struggles shape their critiques of racial and colonial violence? How did their experiences with militarism and wars reshape their struggles for full citizenship, freedom, and racial justice?[13]

ON THE EVE OF World War II, the nation relegated African Americans to the margins of society, but the War Department and the Roosevelt administration also calculated their labor as essential for victory and enforced their participation.[14] Many African Americans, including intellectuals and members of mainstream civil rights organizations, considered equal participation in the military and combat not only as integral to their struggles for full citizenship but also as a refutation against charges of their incompetency and cowardice as combat troops, charges that had been leveled at black troops since 1898.[15] During World War I, blacks viewed military service as an opportunity to renegotiate and expand their rights as citizens. As they faced segregation, disfranchisement, and violence on the eve of America's entry into the war, many African Americans questioned their nearly half-century association of the battlefield with "race manhood" and citizenship. W. E. B. Du Bois, cofounder of the National Association for the Advancement of Colored People (NAACP) and editor of the *Crisis*, urged blacks to "forget our special grievances" and "close our ranks shoulders to shoulders with white soldiers." As blacks pressed for equal access to jobs, housing, and the ballot, the lynchings of black soldiers and violence against black workers escalated. In the two decades following the war, de facto and rigid segregation expanded beyond the South, and blacks' exclusion or marginalization from the nation's social, economic, and political life, including from the military, continued.[16]

In response to the 1940 Selective Service and Training Act that included them in the draft but limited their representation in the army to 9 percent and compelled them into a segregated military, African Americans called for a "Double Victory" in a two-front war against Jim Crow and fascism. Many African Americans hoped wielding a gun meant "Jim Crow'll be done." Largely relegated to labor units, black men volunteered for combat largely hidden from view and commendation, while the federal government suppressed their resistances to segregation, insisting, instead, that it was necessary for social stability and military victory.[17] While some African Americans described the segregated military as "the most antidemocratic institution in America," they also demanded the "equal right and opportunity to contribute to the welfare and defense of the country" and that "true citizenship" included their equal participation in war. "First-class citizenship" for African Americans, Rayford Logan argued in the last months of World War II, included "equality of opportunity" in the military.[18]

As many Americans believed the democratic ideals espoused during World War II should not extend to African Americans, mainstream civil rights organizations and their leaders argued that blacks' participation in the struggle against communism, especially their participation in an integrated Cold War military, would hasten their political and social inclusions.[19] A diverse coalition of civil rights, labor, and veterans' organizations mobilized and pressed for the military's desegregation. Congress refused, and in 1948 President Harry S. Truman issued Executive Order 9981, which mandated "equality of treatment and opportunity for all persons in the armed services without regard to race, color, religion or national origin." While the order did not explicitly call for integration of the military and the army insisted that "equal opportunity" meant only that blacks had the "right" and "obligation" to be drafted, many African Americans nonetheless hailed it as "the president's desegregation order" and a significant victory for their civil rights agenda. Walter White and others in the NAACP described these changes as American democracy on the battlefield, and they hoped that integration of the armed forces would accelerate the end of segregation elsewhere in American life. Yet the desperate need for combat troops during the Korean War, not the president's order, forced the military to integrate. In the decade after the war, many civil rights leaders compared the seemingly rapid integration of the military with the organized defense of segregation across the nation and insisted "war killed Jim Crow."[20]

The nation's demand for the labor and participation of blacks during wartime occurred within prevailing ideas of racial hierarchies. The military especially used dominant racial stereotypes to limit black men to specific roles, and it used prevailing practices of racial violence to punish and harass them. Even as African Americans' roles in wars expanded, these periods of sustained wars and militarism allowed for the realignment and solidification of racial ideologies in law and culture. Wherever the military appeared, its racial practices followed, and it empowered populations around military bases to police segregation, including in areas where it had not previously existed. Wherever the U.S. military fought or occupied, it established its racial policies.[21]

These practices had deadly consequences. W. E. B. Du Bois observed how wars waged by the United States against other nations arose from and allowed for indiscriminate and systematic violence against its own citizens. The killing of Indians in the West prepared troops, including black troops, to kill civilians in Cuba and in the Philippines, the "Indians of the Caribbean and the South Pacific." During these wars, violence against African Americans in the United States soared. Thousands of lynchings and hundreds of riots occurred during the U.S. wars against Cuba and the Philippines. The subjugation of blacks during the U.S. occupation of Haiti from 1914 to 1934 fueled violence against African American workers in Harlem in 1935 and in Alabama in 1937. The racial rhetoric against the Japanese had its reverberations in the internment of Japanese Americans and in the hundreds of race riots during World War II, including actions against Mexican Americans in Los Angeles and Texas. In the wars in Iraq and Afghanistan, the military has used tactics honed in the black and Latino neighborhoods of the United States and against agricultural workers and illegal immigrants, most of whom are people of color.[22]

Black intellectuals who interrogated the impact of war and violence on their communities drew from their efforts to reconcile their struggles to integrate the military and expand citizenship rights with their struggles against colonialism and efforts for global justice. After urging support for World War I and blacks' full participation in combat, Du Bois considered the paradox of blacks pleading for full citizenship through death on the battlefield in segregated units. He noted that only "when [the Negro] rose and fought and killed" did emancipation "become possible. Nothing else made Negro citizenship conceivable, but the record of the Negro soldier as a fighter." He observed how black troops who liberated themselves and saved democracy during the Civil War faced a paradox—they must murder to claim their manhood and citizenship: "How extraordinary and what a tribute to ignorance and religious hypocrisy, is the fact that in the minds of most people, even those of liberals, only murder makes men. The slave pleaded; he was humble; he protected the women of the South; and the world ignored him. The slave killed white men; and behold, he was a man."[23] As he surveyed blacks' participation in U.S. wars, Du Bois concluded that blacks' murdering for their freedom had yielded little, not in the years after the Civil War and not after World War I. Wars claimed black labor, endangered black communities, and diminished blacks' civil rights. His argument that colored people killing other people, especially other colored people, did not make them free took on a new urgency as Europeans impressed tens of thousands of blacks and Asians from Jamaica to South Africa and India to sustain their empires in the twentieth century. He was not alone in arguing against militarism as a pathway to blacks' full citizenship.

During World War II, poet and writer Langston Hughes wrote articles for the *Chicago Defender* to urge a restive and resentful black America to support the war, but he did not press acceptance of the segregated military. After the United States dropped bombs on Nagasaki and Hiroshima and then reaffirmed its commitment to Jim Crow and racial hierarchies more generally, Hughes's support for the war and black military service dissolved into dissent. He registered dismay and then scorn as Americans resisted full democracy. And he saw no victory in the military's integration as the United States and European nations impressed black men into armies and sent them to defend or expand their colonial reach. These armies of conscripted black and brown men who were forced into wars, he noted, did not expand their rights. Rather, war made them "expendable" in their communities and on the battlefield.[24]

James Baldwin described black Americans turned riotous as their war sacrifices yielded few gains. "You must put yourself in the skin of a man who is wearing the uniform of his country, is a candidate for death in its defense, and who is called 'nigger' by his comrades-in-arms. You must consider what happens to this citizen, after all he has endured, when he returns home: search, in his shoes, for a job, for a place to live; ride in his skin, on segregated buses; see, with his eyes, the signs saying 'White' and 'Colored'; imagine yourself being told to 'wait.'" After World War II, "a certain hope died, a certain respect for white Americans faded." [25] Like Hughes, he drew parallels between the integrated military and blacks' enforced labor. Assessing the menace black people faced in ghettoes during the Korean and Vietnam wars, he concluded America "does not know what to do with its black population now that blacks are no longer a source of wealth, are no longer to be bought and sold and bred like cattle." Young black men, he observed, especially perplexed the nation, for they "pose as devastating a threat to the economy as they pose to the morals of young white cheerleaders. It is not at all accidental that the jails and the army and the needle claim so many." [26] Black Americans' continued "fight for the right to fight" yielded little and, instead, led to "one's murder" and to one's role as a "murderer." [27]

Black antiwar activists like Du Bois who associated racial violence in the United States with its wars abroad acquired new credibility as many African Americans grew alarmed by mainstream civil rights leaders' support for the Cold War and the end of the segregated military. Black pacifists and antiwar civil rights activists who had organized during World War II disagreed with the claim that an integrated battlefield would end segregation and regenerate democracy. Instead, they heard in the inflamed rhetoric that fueled anticommunism and U.S. wars abroad new justification of systematic violence used to suppress their demands for full and equal citizenship.[28] William L. Patterson, Paul Robeson, and others in the Civil Rights Congress (CRC) associated the logic of war abroad with the systematic brutality against African Americans. Writing in 1951, Patterson determined that the nation's "institutionalized oppression and persistent slaughter of Negro people in the United States on a basis of 'race'" met the United Nation's definition of genocide. "White supremacy at home," the CRC charged, "makes for colored massacres abroad. Both reveal contempt for human life in a colored skin. The lyncher and the atom bomb are related." The surge in murders, beatings, burnings, rapes, and false imprisonments of African Americans between 1945 and 1950 correlated "almost in direct ratio to the surge towards war." The petition the CRC submitted to the United Nations asserted that the legal and violent defense of segregation after World War II trained a generation to kill abroad in Asia.[29]

Despite the political efforts to silence them, many black activists continued their agitation against war and the military after 1950. Bayard Rustin, who was a conscientious objector (CO) during World War II, a founder of the Congress of Racial Equality (CORE), and a member of the Fellowship of Reconciliation (FOR), embraced nonviolent direct action as organized resistance to racial and social injustice, violence, war, and colonialism. Claudia Jones wrote repeatedly against war and was deported in the 1950s. Ella Baker, Septima Clark, and Vincent Harding, a veteran, joined pacifist organizations and helped forge the nonviolent philosophy of the Southern Christian Leadership Conference (SCLC), founded in 1957, and the Student Non-Violent Coordinating Committee (SNCC), organized in 1961. They decried militarism, poverty, and racial injustice. They denounced a civil rights agenda that linked black freedom to conscription. Despite censure, deportation, and isolation from mainstream civil rights organizations, these activists insisted that black men who killed and died on a battlefield did not advance black freedom. Instead, war furthered racial inequality and poverty. Black neighborhoods withered as billions of dollars bought bombs and tanks. Whether they enlisted or were drafted, they argued, African Americans in the military helped maintain U.S. neo-colonialism. African Americans from all backgrounds and organizations as diverse as FOR, CORE, SNCC, the Mississippi Freedom Democratic Party (MFDP), and the Black Panther Party insisted that their destiny, as well as the nation's, rested on justice born from the end of violence against all oppressed peoples.[30]

This diverse activism did not simply emerge from the struggle for civil rights in the South or blacks' attention to anticolonial struggles. Rather, this activism emerged from a people who had repeatedly served—or sent their children to serve—on segregated battlefields at home and abroad. Nikhil Pal Singh argues that "the specific importance of black intellectuals to the constitution of a black counter-public cannot be underestimated. Intellectuals can be understood to be among the primary producers of public discourse—theoretical and practical knowledge of the social world—knowledge that becomes a key stake in social and political struggles to conserve or transform the world."[31] Jones, Patterson, Rustin, and other black intellectuals helped shape an antiwar activism as they traveled the world and witnessed African and Asian independence movements, but their perspectives were deeply influenced by blacks' growing participation in war as combat troops.[32]

African Americans who fought in America's wars understood how these conflicts fueled racial violence at home and derailed their struggles for freedom. "Just carve on my tombstone," one soldier told Horace Cayton in 1942, "here lies a black man who died fighting a yellow man for the protection of the white man."[33] After World War II, black soldiers noted the hypocrisy of segregated American troops policing democracy in Germany and Japan. Assigned to the occupation forces in Okinawa just after World War II, James Forman, who later participated in the nonviolent civil rights movement, had "become an occupier." He watched black soldiers brandish guns and claim the power of the U.S. military against other "brown people" even as they served in segregated units.[34] During the Korean War, this question of how African Americans might achieve equality and freedom by killing others took on a new valence. In a segregated and poorly equipped unit, Curtis Morrow assessed the battlefield and wondered, "Whatever had these people done to me?"[35] Increasing numbers of African American soldiers insisted that "ordinary people, both colored and white," did not "make these wars." Resisting the rhetoric that wars made democracy, black soldiers correlated "the homeless victims of war" in Korea with the assaults on and murders of African Americans in Mississippi and Florida. "These people," one soldier observed on behalf of his unit, "are like us, the victims of hate and deceit."[36]

African Americans in the military were politicized by its systematic violence used against civilians that also reaffirmed its acceptance and use of racial violence against them and other American citizens. In every war of the twentieth century, the military sanctioned and tolerated racial violence, including rape (and other forms of gendered violence), mutilation, lynching, and genocide, against nonwhite soldiers and civilians. During World War I and World War II, military officials allowed white troops to provoke, harass, and attack black troops for entertainment. The military encouraged or did not halt racial violence, including assaults, harassment, and lynching, in areas around its bases. During World War II and Korea, it displayed a remarkable willingness to relegate dangerous labor to nonwhite civilians and black troops when it did not assign white troops to do the same. Until the early 1960s, the military refused to protect blacks in uniform when they traveled on buses and trains or in cars, and instead, it ignored and tolerated the repeated harassment, assaults, murders, and disappearances of black soldiers, sailors, and Marines.[37]

This expansive and sanctioned violence used in wars against civilians and by the military against its own troops became part of the hidden violence used in racial terrorism outside the military, including violence used by white supremacists and law enforcement officers—many of whom were veterans—to stop civil rights activism. The Citizens' Council was organized by veterans and became the largest post–Korean War white nationalist organization.[38] The military's official use of chemical warfare against combatants and civilians in Korea and Vietnam had its counterpart in the use of teargas during urban, labor, and student uprisings. These associated violences did not cease as the numbers of black and Latino soldiers rose in the volunteer military established after 1973. The violence against Iraqi prisoners and civilians in the nation's most recent wars originated in tactics used against African American and Latino prisoners and police tactics practiced in their urban neighborhoods.[39]

Whether African Americans were drafted or enlisted, most found little compensation as veterans. In the aftermath of World War II, politicians tacitly or explicitly accepted racial violence and political suppression against black veterans who demanded that their military service should give them the right to vote. When blacks left the military, many returned to segregation and lived on the margins of full citizenship. Even as black veterans became the "foot soldiers" of the long civil rights movement, much of what they struggled for in their own communities, including equal access to employment, the right to vote, equal education, and an end to racial violence, was subverted by a rhetoric that tolerated incremental change in blacks' civil rights and compelled them into military service.[40] The majority in the generation that fought for democracy in World War II and lived in segregation afterward sent their children off to war in Vietnam in a period when their communities remained excluded from or on the margins of civic and economic equality.

If the "revitalizing powers" of the integrated battlefield proved doubtful to the increasing numbers of black men in the military, their communities continued to feel the immediate impact of the integrated draft, since it ensured that increasing numbers of men prepared for or found themselves facing nonwhite troops and civilians across Asia, the Middle East, and the Caribbean. The Selective Service Act that was passed in 1948 and amended during and after the Korean War encoded myriad class and racial inequalities. The exclusion of blacks from draft boards across the South and their minimal appointment to boards in other regions meant that their communities had higher draft rates overall. With limited access to employment because of discrimination and deindustrialization, many considered the military as work, and they enlisted at twice the rates of whites. Over the next decade, the nation's need for war labor, blacks' constricted access to labor markets, and the class and racial inequalities of draft policies pulled and impressed poor black men into the military in disproportionate percentages and rates.[41]

By the 1960s, the idea of combat as a "right" and a declaration of black citizenship and the military as "equal opportunity" no longer retained its rhetorical and organizing power for civil rights struggles as it had in the previous two decades. On the contrary, many African Americans considered their high presence in the military and combat as evidence of their political and economic inequality in American society, and the majority believed their participation in war thwarted their struggles for freedom and racial justice. By 1967 a considerable percentage of African Americans were questioning the logic that made militarism and war integral to their concepts of citizenship, equality, and freedom, a perspective the majority have held into the twenty-first century. That many African Americans have considered the military as the most integrated institution in America, where they found more "opportunity" than in any other American institution, while they have also argued that the nation's wars have distorted and suppressed their freedom struggles remains one of the paradoxes of U.S. history.

Demands by blacks for freedom as they also denounced war gathered a mass political force as young men were disproportionately compelled into the military and as they experienced violence, terror, and a marginalized citizenship at home. Their particular experiences with these multiple violences between 1940 and 1973 created a grassroots antidraft movement whereby men and their communities actively avoided the draft. During the Vietnam War, black troops became the foundation for antiwar struggles within the military. Together, these strands of an antiwar effort generated a black critical and political consciousness about the relationship between these wars abroad and the racial violence at home. By 1966, for the majority of African Americans, this activism had fundamentally destroyed the conception that their civil rights were tied to their participation in America's wars. After decades of fighting on every continent, often in segregated conditions, blacks from the Delta of the Deep South to the streets of Chicago and Harlem crafted a racial justice movement that forcefully and simultaneously challenged America's racial practices and its practices of war.[42] Many black veterans, such as Walter Hayes, who endured the segregated Marine Corps during World War II, joined the CORE chapter in St. Louis. He became a "dedicated member of CORE, channeling" his "anger and resentment of segregation and the war" into nonviolent direct action. Many black veterans and pacifists had the same organizational impulse, and they became key architects of the nonviolent civil rights and antidraft movements.[43]

War! addresses the political and social impact of combat on African Americans' understanding of racial violence as a global phenomenon. As numerous scholars have documented, African Americans measured their struggles for full citizenship against the larger global struggles of oppressed peoples, but more than any other phenomenon, their experiences in the overlapping wars at home and abroad informed this collective critical consciousness. Decades before the Reverend Martin Luther King Jr. denounced the Vietnam War "as gangrene in the soul of America" and then tied the war's escalating costs to blacks' poverty and oppression, ordinary African Americans claimed that their participation in war narrowed their civil rights struggles and pitted them against the struggles of colonized people seeking freedom. While deeply troubled by the war in Vietnam, King was compelled to speak out against the inequities of the draft because young black men, many of whom were veterans and draftees, pressed him to do so.[44]

Attention to this critical consciousness that emerged from the entwined history of African Americans' participation in military service and the attendant racial violence they experienced at home that then influenced their antiwar and antiviolence activism challenges a narrative that they assented to the Cold War rhetoric of militarism and war. And it challenges the conception that critics of war and militarism were largely intellectuals and prominent progressive (and male) journalists. Blacks' critical consciousness informed by war and militarism fueled grassroots antidraft and antiwar movements that included women in prominent roles. This diverse antiwar movement had a long history, and we must rethink a narrative of the civil rights movement that has viewed the military's integration as a decisive victory yet ignored ordinary African Americans' resistances to the racial and class inequalities that pulled them into the draft at high rates and compelled them to enlist.

This study suggests how the nation's organized and systematic violence in war cannot be considered simply as a backdrop to our narration of black freedom struggles or as a moment that provided African Americans an opportunity to advance appeals for their own legal and civil rights. In its attention to African Americans' participation in and resistance to America's successive wars alongside their civil rights struggles, *War!* documents and narrates how the U.S. military continually reorganized race, class, and gender inequalities. It considers how the appeals and resources used for war simultaneously invalidated full equality for the nation's own citizens and tolerated the use of systematic violence against them.

This book is arranged in three parts, each with two chapters that probe the dynamic between blacks' experiences with and in the military and their struggles for freedom in the larger society. The first two chapters focus on World War II and its aftermath as African Americans opposed a segregated draft and military that compelled them to serve and as they resisted the racial rhetoric that endorsed their exclusion from combat units because they "were unfit for the fight." Chapter 1 considers how the "V for Victory" campaign, intended to garner Americans' support for the war by depicting white soldiers as brave and sacrificing citizens, was part of a broader effort to reconcile segregation with the rhetoric of "saving democracy" by excluding African Americans from the wartime narrative. Tasked with managing the campaign, the Office of War Information (OWI) relegated news about the "Negro soldier" to the black press and excised most information, especially news about blacks in combat, from white audiences. African Americans responded to the segregated military and the OWI policies by launching the Double Victory campaign to battle against "fascism abroad and Jim Crow at home." As the War Department sent thousands of blacks into battle as laborers and soldiers but hid their efforts from the majority of Americans, African Americans intended the Double V campaign not only to expose the contradictions of the Jim Crow military but to make visible their competency as soldiers. African Americans' challenge to segregation on the "second front" continued after the war as African American soldiers, veterans, and their communities demanded the rights of full citizens as recompense for wartime service, but they faced an organized and violent resistance, especially from white southerners, many of whom were veterans. As military occupation in Europe and Asia and the threat of a confrontation with the Soviet Union required Americans to create a permanent draft military, African Americans refused to serve in a segregated military and insisted that "first-class citizenship" included equal access to the draft and the battlefield.

The second part of this book considers how after a half-century of struggle for "the right to fight," black men had "equal opportunity" to serve in the military, but their "obligations and privileges to serve" meant they went to war for a society that resisted their full citizenship. Chapter 3 examines how a presidential order established "equality of opportunity" in the military but did not explicitly call for its desegregation. The army, which had the largest population of black troops, clung to its "Negro Policy" as the United States went to war in Korea.[45] Even as the need for combat troops forced the military to integrate, racial and class inequalities inside and outside the military shaped the postwar draft and pulled blacks into the army in disproportionate numbers. Chapter 4 examines how the mass nonviolent civil rights movement that emerged during and after the Korean War had its origins in this generation of black Americans who experienced racial violence at home, labored in the military in record numbers as the rest of American society remained segregated, and participated in the violence of wars abroad. The inequities of the draft and the racial politics of the Cold War battlefields compelled a growing population of black soldiers, veterans, pacifists, and rights activists to correlate the violent rhetoric and practices of anticommunism to the violence against integration. This critical consciousness and nonviolent mass activism that emerged between 1950 and 1960 challenged a civil rights activism that associated full citizenship with an integrated battlefield.

The final section documents how African Americans' struggle for freedom at home and their disproportionate presence in the military moved their antiwar sensibilities from the margins of civil rights activism to its core. African American soldiers shaped and were shaped by their overlapping struggles for civil rights and their experiences in Vietnam. As many black troops considered themselves part of a larger colonial endeavor at odds with their own freedom struggles, they questioned their complicity in the war and became a vanguard of resistance to it. Chapter 6 considers how African Americans' rebellions against U.S. draft policies challenged mainstream civil rights organizations that had long silenced antiwar dissent. As activists organized communities for the vote and against poverty, they were galvanized by African Americans who linked their everyday inequities and their significant presence in the military to a vision of racial justice that challenged war and violence. Through community-based agitation and the ballot, these communities demanded that civil rights leaders and organizations make critiques of the war integral to the movement for racial justice and black freedom.[46]

One key feature in this story about African Americans' struggles to reconcile integration of the military and the battlefield with an expansive politics of racial justice predicated on peace is how ordinary people demanded the right to question U.S. foreign policy and how their efforts became integral to the concepts and practices of racial justice. Bob Moses, who was a

CO and a civil rights activist in SNCC, argued that "one of the most basic rights" African Americans sought was "the right to participate fully in the life of this country." He argued that he had the right to speak out against the war in Vietnam. And doing so should not jeopardize his struggles for freedom and justice, "otherwise we have to begin to wonder whether the right is real." Fannie Lou Hamer and others in the MFDP claimed this right when their organization became the first organization to call for blacks to protest the draft.[47] This demand for racial justice and peace for themselves and others informed how the majority of African Americans came to insist "there had to be a better way." They then pushed the civil rights movement and leaders to think beyond the courts and state legislatures and consider mass activism in the global arena for racial justice *and* peace.

After Vietnam, America staffed its wars and military interventions with volunteers, and African Americans have enlisted in high percentages even as the majority in their own communities have not supported these wars. Since 1973, many African Americans have voluntarily enlisted in the military as a step toward adulthood and economic independence at a time when jobs, particularly union jobs with adequate wages, have vanished. In the twenty-first century, black men *and* women walk point in the bloody streets of Fallujah and Kabul. Others, including black veterans, demand an end to these wars. Policymakers and the intellectual political classes may debate a muscular American foreign policy that should take "pre-emptive action," as George W. Bush chose in 2001, but the policy of war, torture, and counterinsurgency has been borne unevenly and with catastrophic consequences by young men and women in the military, many of them African American and Latino, the overwhelming majority from working-class families. Black citizenship in the twenty-first century remains remarkably fragile, and these young men and women consider themselves the foot soldiers in unwarranted wars. Still, they do a "soldier's duty" with pride, and they wear their uniforms with dignity.[48]

Since the early twentieth century, African Americans have argued that "there's got to be a better way" besides war. They have consistently and in such high percentages—frequently more so than any other group—made such a claim. And no other group has so consistently and disproportionately served in the American military. "Listen to me," Starr pleaded in the closing lines of his 1970 "War!" Here he repeated the demands of communities mourning their dead from wars near and afar: "War can't give life / It can only take it away." The grandchildren, nieces, and nephews from the

Vietnam War epoch now walk point in the streets of Baghdad and Kabul, chanting,

I've been around the block
I've seen what's happening
This is just a game to some of you
But the rest of us are not laughin'.[49]

While many African Americans participate in these wars as proud and reluctant soldiers, others serve as the architects of peace and war. The juxtaposition of blacks' disproportionate presence in the military with their long pursuit of freedom and their collective and organized critique of war is a paradox that remains unresolved. This study attempts to document how African American soldiers and their communities have struggled with the question, "War, what is it good for?"

1

Where Are the Negro Soldiers?

The Double V Campaign and the Segregated Military

After the United States entered World War II in early December 1941, editors of the black weeklies urged readers to embrace the V for Victory campaign. In the weeks following the bombing of Pearl Harbor, the national effort to solicit support for the war gained momentum. African Americans who looked through the flurry of advertisements, photo-essays, posters, comics, and newsreels produced by the new Office of War Information (OWI) wondered, "Where were the images of the navy messman, the 'Negro hero'" who reportedly manned a machine gun during the attack? Black editors pressed the navy to release images of the black messman, but the agency refused and claimed "national security" required silence.[1] After the organization of the segregated Tuskegee Airmen in July 1941, photographs of blacks training to be support pilots circulated in the black press, but they did not appear in the white dailies or magazines.[2] Acknowledging black readers' frustrations, editors of the *Pittsburgh Courier* noted how the army "has given out much information of great importance to the white public at home whose menfolk are defending the nation." As thousands of black men enlisted in or were drafted into the segregated army and as thousands enlisted in the segregated navy, African Americans demanded to know "where are our Negro soldiers? We have heard or read nothing."[3]

Over the next months federal agencies organized an aggressive campaign to gain Americans' support for the war, including support from

Newsboy selling the Chicago Defender *in Chicago, Ill., November 1942.*
Reports of riots and discrimination from black troops under General Douglas
MacArthur's command in Australia filled the black newspapers. Photo by Jack Delano;
Library of Congress, Prints & Photographs Division, FSA/OWI Collection.

African Americans, yet officials deliberately avoided publicizing blacks' participation to a national audience.[4] In contrast to the publication of a variety of images that displayed white Americans as heroic and sacrificing citizens in war industries and the military, federal agencies used segregated wartime news and propaganda "to improve Negro morale without incurring too much criticism from whites." Bowing to the demands of southern congressional representatives, the War Department did not release images of black men training for combat to white viewers, and the OWI did not push white dailies to report blacks' military participation. At the same time, the OWI pressed black weeklies to support the segregated military and diminish attention to the daily attacks, lynchings, and other deadly assaults on black soldiers.[5] Reports about violence against black soldiers and rumors that they would remain confined to labor units added to their critiques of and resistances to the segregated military and draft.

The military unofficially established its new "Negro Policy" when Congress passed the Selective Service and Training Act of 1940, which created the first peacetime draft in U.S. history and compelled blacks and some other nonwhite groups to accept a segregated and unequal system. Since the early twentieth century, some military officials preferred only white troops, but each service also needed considerable labor, including on the battlefield. Despite the rhetoric of patriotic manhood that surrounded each war, many men did not go willingly to war, and those who did often balked at menial labor, especially tasks that resembled the work of servants and women. As a group, African Americans had been forced into or confined to such labor in every war since the War for Independence, and officials intended to continue this policy in the 1940 draft. Though the military did not create an official directive that enunciated its policies about African Americans, each service nonetheless had an unwritten but official "Negro Policy" that limited the number of blacks and relegated them to labor units. This policy differed from practices used during World War I, when blacks were drafted or volunteered at a rate higher than that of whites and other nonwhite troops. Despite being only one-tenth of the population, blacks were one-eighth of the troops and close to one-half of the 213 labor battalions. When Congress approved the 1940 peacetime draft, the army relied on a quota of 9 percent, a threshold established in the late 1930s.[6]

African Americans had long resisted these policies, and they protested them in 1940. Persistent pressure from Walter White, executive secretary of the NAACP; A. Philip Randolph, president of the Brotherhood of Sleeping Car Porters; and T. Arnold Hill, assistant to the director of the National Youth Administration, pushed President Franklin D. Roosevelt to overturn the quota system and end segregation in the military. Instead, a month after the creation of the new Selective Service System, the president affirmed in October 1940 that he supported blacks' participation in the army but only in segregated labor battalions. Pressed further by mainstream civil rights organizations, Roosevelt acceded to blacks' enlistment in other services but as no more than 10 percent overall and in segregated units. The army needed many more troops than the other services, but it agreed to enlist blacks in segregated units only "when and where manpower shortages and public pressures" made their presence a necessity. These troops were to be trained in labor units and largely in the South. All of the services made segregation an explicit policy. All of the services mandated that whites—typically southern whites—command these troops. The army agreed to have a limited number of black officers serve as chaplains and doctors. After significant pressure, it established a training school at Tuskegee Institute to train black pilots to fly service planes. In the United States, regardless of skin color, African Americans were assigned to units based on race, not qualification.[7]

When Walter White agitated for information about how the nation's full participation in the war might change the role of blacks in the military, the army reaffirmed that few black soldiers would serve as officers and few, if any, would command troops. When pressed further, War Department officials refused to reveal whether or not they planned to train blacks for combat or send them overseas.[8]

News about threats against and harassment of black soldiers as they traveled to posts in the South further raised blacks' ire. "Whether traveling on duty or on furlough the colored soldier experiences the indignity of segregation," Thurgood Marshall noted.[9] Why, some readers asked, should they enlist in the Jim Crow military and participate in their own segregation? Why should they participate in the war "to save democracy" when they were relegated to the fringes in Jim Crow America? Nashville resident Walter Hadley captured the collective ill-temper when he suggested to folklorist Alan Lomax that the U.S. government might "declare war on that nation in Dixieland to help us all have one common cause to fight for: liberty, equality, and justice for all."[10]

The contradiction between the exhortations for African Americans to support the war through their subjugation to the military's segregation launched a public debate. Anticipating a draft notice, John Hope Franklin, who had nearly completed his dissertation in history at Harvard University, became "painfully aware [as a historian] that, going back to the American Revolution, black participation in America's wars had never brought African Americans any meaningful change in their status." Blacks had served in every one of America's wars, and they were still "second-class citizens. Nothing," he observed, "suggested this war would be any different."[11] Rather than seeing "the Negro's stake in the war," journalist Roi Ottley observed, readers sent bitter letters to the editors and demanded the nation "extend democracy to the American Negro."[12] Others refused to fight "the white man's war." As this torrent of criticism against the "Negro Policy" formed into a protracted storm, blacks debated whether or not to subordinate their struggles against segregation and support the defeat of Germany and Japan. Surveys, rumors, and investigations documented blacks' plummeting morale and escalating rebelliousness that formed into collective dissent.[13]

African Americans did not diminish their resistance to a draft that compelled them into a segregated army and to their invisibility in the V for Victory campaign. In a letter to the *Pittsburgh Courier*, Anne Martin asked why black soldiers had to fight "on two fronts," one abroad and one at home.[14] Newly drafted James G. Thompson questioned why he should "serve his country" in its "victory over the forces of evil" while the army inducted him as "half-American" in a Jim Crow military. How could he sacrifice for a country that planned to continue racial segregation after the war ended? "Would it be too much," he asked,

> to demand full citizenship rights in exchange for the sacrificing of my life? The V for Victory sign is being displayed prominently in all so-called democratic countries fighting for victory over aggression, slavery, and tyranny. If this V sign means [all] that to those now engaged in this great conflict, then let we colored Americans adopt the double VV for a double victory over our enemies within. For surely those who perpetuate these ugly prejudices here are seeking to destroy our democratic form of government just as surely as the axis forces.[15]

Thompson's call to recast the national campaign into a "two front war" against fascism abroad and Jim Crow in America fueled blacks' rebellion to their invisibility as soldiers in the V for Victory campaign and the nation's refusal to abolish its own racial subjugation and violence.[16]

The *Courier* editors hoped the campaign might provide African Americans with an incentive to support the war, and it seized Thompson's call for a "double victory," but readers did not yield. Over the next months, they demanded to see images of blacks in "the fight."[17] As the OWI campaign continued to display images of white soldiers and war workers, readers sent the black newspapers snapshots of African Americans in uniform and denounced the "Negro Policy." When the Navy Department refused to identify the "unnamed Negro hero" who participated in the attack on Pearl Harbor, black artists drew illustrations of him. Under pressure, the navy revealed that the messman who took over the guns at Pearl Harbor was Dorie Miller, but officials declined to release his photograph. His proud and defiant mother, Henriette Miller, provided the *Courier* with photographs of her son pulled from her family picture albums.[18]

Excised from the national victory campaign launched by the OWI and relegated to segregated labor units, African Americans used the Double V campaign to challenge a national visual narrative that refused acknowledgment of their participation in the war campaigns, compelled them to accommodate to segregation, and denied the violence of American segregation, especially in the military. They balked at editors' claims that images of black men training for combat or black women tending wounded white soldiers alarmed white readers. They protested when major newsreel companies removed footage of black troops and inserted racial stereotypes that entertained or humored whites.[19] They questioned why the white dailies rarely published images of or information about black troops.[20]

In defiance of their public excision from the unfolding visual narrative about the war, African Americans used the Double V campaign to create their own, one that included photographs, illustrations, comics, cartoons, and sketches. The images they produced appeared alongside the personal photographs and snapshots they submitted to the weeklies as evidence of their wartime efforts. Newspapers, especially, provided the forum where African Americans displayed these images that challenged the wartime visual campaign pushing for the defeat of Nazism while it ignored American practices of racial violence and segregation.[21] These photographs and other vernacular images, such as comics and editorial cartoons, also represented and documented the skill, courage, and everyday experiences of blacks in the military. As the War Department sent thousands of blacks into combat and used their absent images in the dominant press as evidence that they "were unfit for the fight," African Americans intended the Double V to counter these claims and expose the humiliations and violence of the Jim Crow military.

Beginning with the Civil War, photographs amplified the collective and popular war narratives about national identity, purpose, and memory, but the plethora of mass-produced images in American wartime cultural life and politics made the World War II epoch distinctive.[22] By World War II, the federal government's efforts to use popular images to win support for the war had significantly expanded to include photographs, illustrations, comics, advertisements, and films.[23] Federal agencies implemented new forms of public persuasion in posters for military recruitment, advertisements for war bonds, and appeals to conserve food and other resources. Officials used the national and local presses "to sell and manage the war" through "management of the news," especially through strategically placed images.[24] New film and sound technology aided these endeavors, but photographs and illustrations in the mass press predominated. Images of the extraordinary and the ordinary, the spontaneous and the posed, were printed faster and circulated over wider geographies as never before. The variety and volume of images included the symbolic, such as Roosevelt's four freedoms—freedom of speech and religion, freedom from want and fear. Positive symbols portrayed "why we fight" and negative images "vilified" the enemy. Official and popular images documented the "daily story of the war" and helped spectators living thousands of miles from the front lines understand the war effort. Newsreels presented the military's progress, especially on the battlefield, in every American theater. These photographs, films, and other images used and disseminated a visual rhetoric of individual and communal sacrificing citizens that was as powerful as, if not more powerful than, the textual and aural.[25]

While drawing on the latest technologies, these wartime editorial policies also reinforced long-held racial caricatures and stereotypes. Popular print images continued to portray blacks—and other nonwhites more generally—as sinister, degenerate, and disease-ridden. Images of Japanese Americans confined to internment camps and African Americans protesting racial discrimination reinforced popular ideas that they were dangerous and should be denied rights of citizens.[26] But these visual racial stereotypes also ignored segregation and its impact on African Americans. Few U.S. officials admitted how America's racial policies undermined the nation's appeals for democracy, the morale of soldiers, or the military's efficiency as it moved millions of men and women into combat. Instead, War Department officials insisted that the war was not the moment when America's racial policies could be abolished. Secretary of War Henry Stimson insisted black men could not master the "weapons of modern war" and "lacked the moral and mental qualifications" for combat. Instead, throughout the war, the United States waged an aggressive effort to impose segregation wherever it sent American troops, frequently with grave consequences.[27]

Yet federal agencies needed African Americans' participation in the war effort, and civil rights organizations hoped to exploit that need as a way to challenge segregation, especially in the military. The National Urban League and the NAACP pressed for positions in the new war departments. William H. Hastie, a judge in the federal district court of the Virgin Islands and longtime advisor to the Roosevelt administration, served as civilian aid to Stimson. Lester Granger, a World War I veteran and assistant executive secretary of the National Urban League, became an advisor to James V. Forrestal, undersecretary of the navy. He served, too, as the president's chief mobilizer of industrial war production. Finessed by Roy Stryker, who directed the photographic division of the Farm Security Administration (FSA) in the 1930s, African American writers, photographers, and illustrators worked in the controversial OWI.[28]

The Roosevelt administration created the OWI to explain the aims of the war to a skeptical public. Considered part of the administration's propaganda campaign, the agency's efforts remained underfunded and inconsistent. Few in the agency agreed about its goals, messages, and audiences; all too frequently, the agency presented competing claims. In turn, Congress and the president contested the agency's intent and purpose. More generally, anti-integrationists in Congress and the public railed against the OWI as an extension of New Deal agencies perceived as eager to eradicate segregation.[29] Even those within the OWI who personally advocated a positive presentation of all in the war effort, regardless of race, did not openly advocate policies that might change the "racial status quo." Whatever private thoughts some individuals held, they collectively yielded to the consensus that war agencies could not instigate social change beyond support for the war effort. In this atmosphere, the OWI deflected repeated criticism whenever it portrayed African Americans in positive ways. Few in the OWI wanted to spar with those in the military and Congress who claimed the black press "unduly emphasize[d]" the role of black combat units, and agency officials pressed this point to the weeklies.[30]

Still, the OWI hoped its carefully circulated images might simultaneously boost the morale of blacks and minimize the concerns of whites. "Unwilling to press for structural change," Lauren Sklaroff notes, the OWI and the War Department advocated the use of "black cultural symbols," such as boxer Joe Louis, to "represent heroism, patriotic values, and black military significance" and "advocate an ethos of racial liberalism."[31] Through its repeated displays of Louis as a willing participant in the status quo in film and photographs, the OWI downplayed the politically charged aspects of race discrimination, especially the segregated military.

Yet, the image of Joe Louis thrusting a gun invited multiple readings, depending on the audience. For blacks, the photograph might suggest the possibility of their participation in combat; for whites, Louis was a boxer posing with, and not using, a gun. He wore an outdated military uniform, and his image was removed from the context of combat. More typically, the agency designed a few films—such as newsreels about the Tuskegee pilots—and war publications specifically addressed to black audiences. Few of the hundreds of OWI posters depicted blacks in uniform or in interracial groups in wartime industrial jobs. Pamphlets created for troops in the allied nations made no mention of African Americans or racial segregation. Throughout the war, the War Department campaigned to convince allies that African American troops were dangerous and racial segregation was needed to protect white women.[32]

Black photographers and writers rarely found permanent positions on the major magazines and newspapers to challenge these practices, but at the start of the war a few found positions in the OWI. Photographer Robert McNeill worked for the Federal Writers' Project, and Steve Wright joined the Federal Works Agency after preparing and taking photographs for the Public Works Administration.[33] A recipient of a Rosenwald fellowship in 1941, photographer Gordon Parks went to work for the FSA in 1942. He admired the work of FSA photographers and received support from Jack Delano, who worked for the agency. Initially, Roy Stryker did not want to have Parks in the FSA, as Stryker feared others in the agency and city might object to a black photographer. Will Alexander, former head of the FSA and then vice president of the Rosenwald fund, pressed Stryker to hire Parks. During his time with the FSA, Parks honed his skills in arrangement and lighting. He abandoned his initial plans to "document intolerance" and instead "showed the people who suffered" and struggled to make a life in a system of "discrimination and bigotry." For Parks, the camera was a "weapon" for social change.[34]

Along with a handful of photographers, Gordon Parks followed FSA photographic director Roy Stryker to the OWI soon after its creation. One of Parks's first assignments was to photograph the training of the 332nd Fighter Group commanded by Colonel Benjamin O. Davis Jr., the highest-ranking black officer in the military. Once trained, the pilots had orders to go overseas, and Parks made plans to accompany them; but army officials claimed he did not have the proper travel orders. He later learned he had the correct travel credentials, but by then the Pentagon had mysteriously canceled his orders. Ted Poston, one of the few black writers in the OWI press section, told Parks that southern politicians objected to any "international publicity for black airmen."[35] Parks never acquired the official paperwork to follow the 332nd Fighter Group overseas. By 1944, the OWI's efforts to portray black soldiers and black war workers more favorably were further thwarted by southern congressional representatives who objected to any money spent on blacks photographing blacks' contributions to the war. Seeking alternatives, the OWI assigned white photographers late in the war to take photographs of blacks troops and war workers. Toni Frissell, who apprenticed to Cecil Beaton and worked for *Vogue* in the 1930s, photographed the 332nd Fighter Group when it went overseas.[36]

Ted Poston and photographer Roger Smith had considerable editorial and photographic input in the agency, but as the OWI fielded criticism about "undue" attention to African Americans and charges of black radicalism, agency officials expected them to dampen any militant rhetoric in the black press. When Poston read *New York Amsterdam News* writer Ellen Tarry's accounts of discrimination by naval officers against blacks in their command, he asked her to soften her articles. After Tarry told Poston he could not "muzzle" her, he instructed her editor to pressure her to rewrite the articles. Poston or others in the OWI pressed Carl Murphy, editor of the *Baltimore Afro-American*, to either "tone down" stories they considered inflammatory or not print them at all.[37]

As the OWI deliberately minimized or removed blacks' presence in publications for white audiences, it also produced publications it deemed "appropriate" for black audiences. The "typical OWI black images," Nicholas Natanson observes, "accent[ed] minority contributions in 'safe' contexts ranging from civilian defense meetings and scrap drives in Washington, D.C., to shipyards in Oakland, from classrooms at Bethune-Cookman College to defense assembly lines in New Britain, Connecticut." After the bombing of Pearl Harbor, a limited number of interracial images appeared in the popular press. Photographer Howard Liberman's "Americans All" was noteworthy in this effort. Acknowledging blacks' presence in American life, the OWI composed "non-threatening" images and texts of blacks in the armed services.[38]

Through these "safe" images, the OWI hoped to assuage the skepticism of blacks and persuade them that their participation in the segregated military would advance racial progress. Once considered radical because of his antiwar and antisegregation critiques during World War I, a far more conservative Chandler Owen wrote *What Will Happen to the Negro if Hitler Wins!*, a booklet designed to quell rumors that some blacks might enjoy a war between the "white races." Misapprehending *why* African Americans balked at defending one racist nation against another, Owen posited that blacks might see little difference "in their lot" if Hitler won the war. "The intelligent Negro who weighs the situation with poise and an even temper is a meliorist." He concluded that lynching and disfranchisement "are bad, but they could be worse if Hitler prevailed."[39] However terrible the Jim Crow conditions in the Deep South or the military might be, Owen stressed, blacks would fare far worse under Nazi domination. Owen then emphasized blacks' successes in education, entertainment, and federal policy, implying that even under their dire conditions in the United States, blacks fared better than they would in Nazi Germany. In weighing the outcome of a war, Owen urged "Negroes to choose the lesser wrong."[40]

Mainstream civil rights activists characterized Owen's arguments in favor of the war as those produced by an apologist of segregation. Reviewing the text before its publication, William Hastie feared readers would perceive the pamphlet as "an unconvincing apology for the shortcomings of our nation rather than a critical study of Hitlerism." Owen, he argued, minimized segregation and violence. "In brief," Hastie concluded, "the basic thesis of the 'meliorist,' which you state on page 6 that 'conditions are bad but they could be worse' is not a thesis, however true, which can win any enthusiasm." Propaganda, Hastie concluded, should be directed "at indifferent or prejudiced whites, not at resentful Negroes."[41]

Ignoring blacks' objections to Owen's argument, the OWI arranged to expand the text into a photo-essay. Milton MacKaye, a former reporter for the *New York Evening Post* who followed Roy Stryker from the FSA to the OWI, provided the editorial layout for the new pamphlet, re-titled *Negroes and the War*. MacKaye arranged FSA and OWI photographs, including file photographs taken by Gordon Parks. Despite the agency's plan to add photographs from private sources, the majority of which would be portraits of prominent African Americans, the NAACP launched a protest. Walter White asked the OWI to halt the publication, but Stryker refused. Cincinnati attorney and longtime NAACP activist Theodore Berry, who had been hired by the OWI to address black morale, raised strong reservations about the textual and visual tone of the pamphlet. Describing the booklet as a "'scare' document for Negroes," Berry warned White that it "should not be given government endorsement." He considered the agency's plans to add pictures to "tell Negroes how well off they were and artificially stimulate their patriotic fervor [through] the use of Negro artists and heroes, etc." offensive, "since the Nazi race pattern also prevailed here in so many instances." The project continued, and when Berry realized that the agency ignored his criticisms, he resigned.[42]

With the addition of photographs and testimonies, *Negroes and the War* became a seventy-one-page pictorial essay that emphasized the progress of blacks despite racial discrimination.[43] Images of black professionals, skilled workers, and soldiers — typically in formation and not in combat — crowded each page, suggesting a people on the ascent. The OWI's strategy to merge text and image as evidence of blacks' progress within segregation was not unusual to many black readers. Similar close-cropped portraits of familiar success stories had circulated in the black press for years, but the accompanying text reminded readers of the context. In contrast, the OWI arranged photographs of ordinary African Americans working in wartime industries, including images of blacks making parachutes in a factory owned by radio star Eddie Rochester, to suggest that the segregated war aided black progress. Neither the photographs nor the text explicitly addressed the segregation, lynching, disfranchisement, and poverty that the majority of African Americans experienced. Since only one image in the booklet presented an integrated workplace, the group portraits of segregated congregations, classrooms, and workplaces implicitly stressed the barriers blacks faced in America. Similarly, the eighteen photographs of African Americans in the armed forces depicted blacks training for combat, but many readers might have wondered for what end, since the War Department emphatically insisted that black troops would serve in labor units. The pamphlet's final image was the already ubiquitous image of Joe Louis thrusting a bayonet.[44]

The OWI released *Negroes and the War* to the public early in 1943. After review of the publication, Walter White did not find it as "objectionable as it was in its original form." The pamphlet "doubtless will do some good," he mused. Still, he found it problematic that the publication included much of Owen's text from *What Will Happen to the Negro if Hitler Wins!* White stressed, again, to Milton MacKaye that the OWI need not lecture blacks about how their lives would be "worse under Hitler." Instead, he suggested, the government might gain blacks' support if it "had taken effective and uncompromising action against some of the evils from which Negroes suffer."[45] The OWI remained impervious to blacks' criticisms and suggestions. Instead, MacKaye informed White that the agency had already distributed 1.75 million copies of *Negroes and the War*.

Over the following two weeks, the Urban League, the CIO (Congress of Industrial Organizations), and the military services dispensed another 2 million copies. In addition, excerpts of the publication appeared in some white newspapers. Describing the publication "as one of the most ambitious projects to boost morale on the home front," reporter Frank Kelley noted in the *New York Herald Tribune* that "leading newspapers in the country, which had never published a picture of a Negro except on the sports page, came out with several column layouts of pictures and text devoted to *Negroes and the War*."[46] By 1943, the number of black troops had reached nearly 1 million, but few images of them training for combat or their transport to European or the Pacific Theaters appeared in white publications.

While black newspapers duly noted in editorials and front page stories that their readers supported the war, these dailies also nearly burst with news of the beatings, killings, and abuses black troops suffered. A flurry of news detailed how at Camp Van Dorn "small fights grew into big fights that mushroomed into a full-scale riot" involving nearly 2,000 black troops. Rumors circulated in black newspapers that the skirmishes in the camp had resulted in the execution of hundreds, if not more than a thousand black troops. Added to this tumult, in black neighborhoods across the United States, civilian police—frequently aided by military police and white soldiers and sailors—prowled the streets looking for black soldiers on furlough. Insulted and attacked, black soldiers and sailors resisted and fought back. Their arrests and detainment followed. For African Americans, the assaulted black soldier symbolized the struggle of the Double V campaign. Though some of the 500,000 Hispanic soldiers in uniform were occasionally classified as another ethnic group and served in integrated units, others, including Puerto Rican soldiers, fared little better than black troops. In the 1943 riot in Los Angeles that became known as the "zoot suit riot," whites attacked both blacks and Mexican Americans—many of whom were soldiers—with equal ferocity.[47]

In 1943 James Baldwin worked near Newark and visited Harlem, both sites for riots. The steady news of abuses against black soldiers and sailors "had repercussions, naturally, in every Negro ghetto." Everybody in Harlem, he noted, had someone in the army. "The churchly women and the matter-of-fact, no-nonsense men had children in the army. The sleazy girls had lovers there, the sharpies and the 'race' men had friends and brothers there." He felt a palpable rage as he walked Harlem's streets. "It would have demanded an unquestioning patriotism, happily as uncommon in this country as it is undesirable, for these people not to have been disturbed by the bitter letters they received, by the newspaper stories they read, not to have been enraged by the posters, then to be found all over New York, which described the Japanese as 'yellow-bellied Japs.'" No one, he concluded, except the radical "race men" had any idea how to avenge the "bitter indignities suffered by Negro boys in uniform."[48]

By late May 1943, African America stood poised to roil. Over the next weeks, rumors of a soldier's abuse or death ignited rebellions in black Los Angeles, Newark, Harlem, and Detroit. During the summer months, more than 200 riots erupted, including scores in the South. Hundreds suffered wounds and dozens were killed. In Detroit, twenty-five African Americans died, most killed by police. Many African Americans understood, as did one Harlemite, "that the outbreak in our midst was not a single isolated incident, not merely a local affair." He observed "grim, certain identical conditions; a certain sinister sameness of pattern."[49]

Many African Americans simply refused to enlist or they resisted their draft notices. Early in the war, John Hope Franklin embraced the Double V effort and decided to volunteer for the navy, which had pleaded for men with skills in typing, shorthand, and accounting. Franklin had these skills, but "the recruiter looked [at Franklin] with what appeared to be a combination of incredulity and distress." Nearly "speechless," the recruiter told Franklin that he had skills the navy desperately needed, but he "lack[ed] one important qualification, and that was color." His younger brother, Buck Franklin, received a draft notice that forced him out of his position as a principal and into a labor battalion where he faced repeated verbal harassment and physical assault from whites because of his education. Shaken by his brother's experiences, Franklin came "reluctantly to one irrevocable conclusion, that the United States, however much it was devoted to protecting the freedoms and rights of Europeans, had no respect for me, little interest in my well being, and not even a desire to use my professional services." When he received his draft notice in 1943, he argued with the draft board official that he was only one of two black historians with a Ph.D. in North Carolina, and he successfully persuaded the Selective Service to grant him a deferment.[50]

Black men used a variety of ways to avoid the draft. Some men ignored their draft notices, including jazz musician Lester Young. Others pursued more elaborate means to register their outrage and defiance. After Malcolm Little, who later renamed himself Malcolm X and became one of the most prominent leaders in the Nation of Islam, received his induction notice in early 1943, he was determined to avoid the army. He arrived for his physical examination on June 1, 1943, "costumed like an actor in a wild zoot suit, yellow knob-toe shoes, his hair frizzed into a reddish bush of a conk." As he greeted the army clerk, he used a jive patter certain to suggest a drug-induced hipster: "Crazy-o, daddy-o get me moving. I can't wait to get in that brown." By then he had caught the attention of a nurse, and she ushered him into the psychiatrist's office. There he claimed he looked forward to organizing other black soldiers into a rebellion and stealing "some guns to kill us crackers!" As he intended, his erratic behavior and inflammatory talk induced alarm among the army officials. He was declared mentally unfit for service and given a 4-F card.[51]

Black men already in the military resisted, too. Black soldiers' and sailors' resistances and strikes continued, some with deadly results. After an explosion killed hundreds of sailors at Port Chicago, as many black men refused to load explosives onto the ships. The navy charged and convicted fifty of the men with mutiny. Reviewing the images from the trial, Langston Hughes noted,

> I remember a few weeks ago seeing in the newspapers a photograph released by the navy of the court-martial of these fifty Negro sailors. There, on the front page of the paper were pictured a mass of Negro sailors on trial and, in front of them at the judicial tables, the judges and accusers ALL were white. What do white folks think we are— imbeciles, morons, dolts, complete fools—that we do not notice these things? For so long in this country it has been the same old story—judge and jury ALL white. At this stage of the crisis on the war fronts, it seemed to me most unwise to release on the front pages of our papers a visual version of such justice.[52]

BEGINNING WITH THEIR ENSLAVEMENT, African Americans considered how images could provide competing representations and disturb racial stereotypes. As the mass circulation of images in the United States included derogatory depictions and gross caricatures of them, African Americans countered with mass-produced images of their own. For W. E. B. Du Bois, Shawn Michelle Smith argues, "the color line represented not only the systematic inequity of racialized labor, but also a visual field in which racial identities are inscribed and experienced through the lens" of white supremacy. Du Bois understood how these "lurid" and "distorted images of blackness" were "projected through the eyes" of whites and precipitated the experience of "two-ness, two souls, two thoughts, two unreconciled strivings, two warring ideals." African Americans' "negotiation of disparate gazes and competing visions," Smith concludes, "imposes the 'two-ness' of double consciousness." The double consciousness that Du Bois so eloquently described in the early twentieth century had at its heart a visual component.[53]

African Americans mounted a vigorous and collective effort to reject the image of them as the menacing, reviled, and mutilated "other." They created and displayed positive and dignified images of themselves for community and mass audiences. From visits to private studios for individual and family portraits to the large photographic exhibits at the world's fairs, black Americans put themselves on display. While the Jim Crow color line narrowed material considered appropriate for this display— respectable men and women should have visible wedding rings and carefully coiffed hair—the efforts nonetheless sought to show the individuality and complexity of African Americans as well as represent their dignity and humanity. "Their central task in the face of their negative or diminished depictions in art and literature," Henry Louis Gates Jr. notes, "was to transform themselves from objects to subjects, a process that was essential to effect before they could assume the prerogatives of full American citizenship." African Americans shared common notions of themselves as self-respecting historical subjects and actors. They hoped the images they produced about and for themselves could bring about profound historical change.[54]

African Americans' positive reconstruction and re-representation of their communities through text and image acquired a new urgency in the World War I epoch. With the permanent movement of tens of thousands of African Americans from the South to cities in the Midwest and Northeast, African Americans' uses of images to document their progress and assail racial violence became ubiquitous. The increased affordability and accessibility of photography also made it available as a business and profession for African Americans. Many African Americans posed for, produced, and acquired photographs and illustrations, but many more viewed such images in newspapers and magazines published for their benefit. These mass-produced images provided a record of black life as well as examples of black art.

As rates of urban residency for African Americans soared after the war, many read widely from local, national, and international publications.[55] The dramatic migration of blacks into southern and northern urban centers expanded urban communities and the population of readers; the turn-of-the-century perambulations of black workers and elites into Africa, Europe, and Asia reshaped the news of the black Diaspora and political struggles in the Americas to become a global struggle against colonialism. Black readers played critical roles in both the demand for and the dissemination of news. Complex networks of Pullman porters distributed the *Chicago Defender* as they stopped in towns and cities where small black populations did not have newspapers of their own. As a result, newspapers became commonplace in African Americans' everyday lives, even in rural areas. By 1940, more than 150 black weeklies were published with an estimated 2 million subscribers, and millions more individuals read these publications each week. In addition, mass-produced magazines such as the *Crisis, Opportunity, Negro Digest,* and *Negro Story* added to the diversity of publications available to black readers.[56]

With this mass migration into cities where the mainstream presses ignored or demeaned blacks, black newspapers and magazines occupied a prominent place in black popular and national culture. Described as sensationalist by some and integral to community formation by others, newspapers and magazines provided blacks with a key site to acquire information about their experiences and concerns that were ignored in the mainstream press. As a forum for news and entertainment specifically created for black readers, these newspapers were also highly communal, even in the context of national and international news. As George Lipsitz notes, "Mass communications also embody some of our deepest hopes and engage some of our most profound sympathies. People ingeniously enter these discourses to which they have access; the saxophone or the guitar, the stage or the camera can offer precious and unique opportunities for expression."[57] The weekly newspaper in black communities and cities presented such opportunities to readers for both textual and visual participation.

For black readers, these newspapers and magazines served as a constant and visible reminder that the dominant national newspapers, magazines, and journals largely excluded important and positive information about their lives. They knew that businesses welcomed them as customers but refused to advertise in black newspapers. When World War I began, they questioned why the War Department refused black editors' requests to allow black correspondents to accompany troops overseas. Instead, Carl Murphy noted, the *Afro-American* "depended altogether on letters from service men abroad, on occasional interviews with returned soldiers, and on War Department handouts."[58] Editors and columnists encouraged black readers to become active participants in gathering information, such as news and photographs, and supplying it to the newspapers. As well as being consumers, readers assumed a new role as contributors. Thus newspapers produced in Chicago and Pittsburgh became national publications, with readers providing news about local events in Baltimore, Omaha, and Seattle. Papers with larger circulations, such as the *Defender*, *Courier*, and *Afro-American*, had a growing network of reporters and photographers outside the newspaper's city of publication. By 1941, only the *Defender*, *Courier*, and *Afro-American* had reporters in cities throughout the northeastern and mid-Atlantic states. For the majority of black newspapers, however, readers sent reports and photographs, providing news that otherwise would not get reported.

During the first years of World War II, black weeklies relied on their readers to help them cover the war, since only the four largest newspapers had the ability to include extensive visuals. Black newspapers worked with the army through the special Division of Negro Affairs in the Bureau of Public Relations to receive a variety of stories and photographs for publication in the black press. Still, the War Department did not grant credentials to African American correspondents and photographers to go to the war front until 1944, and only a few newspapers had the resources for such travel. The *Afro-American* posted six reporters overseas to cover the war, including Ollie Stewart in North Africa and Art Carter in Italy.[59] Because so few of these newspapers were allowed to assign photographers overseas until late in the war, and the majority were unable to do so at all, readers played critical roles in the newspapers' visual production.

Black newspapers provided their readers with a variety of opportunities to respond to the dilemma their wartime participation posed. As the *Courier*, *Defender*, and other black weeklies composed variations of the Double V campaign to advertise their newspapers, readers expanded the campaign beyond the papers' rhetoric of assent to their participation despite segregation and agitated for a wide assault against racial discrimination in American life. Earl Patterson suggested that readers produce "banners to hang in our windows and buttons to pin on our coats. These should be distributed to Negroes all over the world. Only a few white people read race papers but if they see the banners and buttons they will start asking questions." Beyden A. Steele did not wait for buttons to arrive in St. Louis: "We have cut the emblem out of the *Courier* and glued them to our house windows."[60]

African Americans rapidly spread the campaign into daily life. Women wore Double V pins on their hats, coats, and dresses; soldiers requested Double V tattoos. Popular with soldiers, bandleader Lucky Millinder painted a Double V on his swing band's tour bus. Bassist Duke Morgan composed "We Want a Double-V in Our Victory" for the forty-third annual convention of the Grand Lodge IBPOE. After a concert at the University of Southern California's Royce Hall, singer Marian Anderson endorsed the campaign and posed with her own V underneath the V-crested curtain. Black people performed the campaign's symbol by forming the Double V with fingers, arms, and legs, creating a kinesthetic response of protest. In Los Angeles, attorney Loren Miller recalled how while whites "would go around giving the V sign for victory, the Negroes were giving the Double V sign."[61] Through images and other displays of the Double V, African Americans intended to turn their battle for democracy into a battle against segregation in the military. Dozens of men in the 364th Infantry Regiment reportedly formed a Double V club to challenge the military's segregation. First stationed in Arizona at Fort Huachuca, the unit rioted in 1942, and the army moved the men to the South. A core of men in the unit adhered to the Double V campaign, and when they arrived at Camp Van Dorn near Centerville, Mississippi, the men reportedly vowed to rid the area of white supremacy.[62]

Ordinary African Americans launched their challenge to the military's segregation after the navy declined to reveal the identity of Dorie Miller. In the weeks after Pearl Harbor, African Americans circulated rumors and reports that a black mess attendant had abandoned the galley and rescued the wounded; he then manned a machine gun and shot down several planes. Despite the NAACP's repeated inquiries to the War Department, the navy refused to release the mess attendant's name. The *Courier* used its own resources, and Henrietta Miller, his mother, readily provided the paper with photographs. The mess attendant turned machine gunner had a name: Dorie Miller. His mother emphasized that she had two sons in the military, one in the navy and the other in the army. Readers learned she had raised Dorie on a tenant farm outside Waco, Texas, where he became an excellent marksman. Tall and athletic, he and his three brothers survived the local Klan but found little work in rural Texas. Dorie Miller enlisted in 1939, but despite his skills and aptitude, the navy's segregation and scorn for black men confined him to the rank of mess attendant and prevented him from training in battleship positions.[63]

Once his identity became more widely known, only the black press reported that Miller had excelled as a marksman and that he had temporarily served aboard the USS *Nevada* (BB-36), which housed the Secondary Battery Gunnery School. He had not trained on the navy gun he used during the attack, but he knew about weapons and watched and listened as the white sailors trained. Other rumors indicated that Miller's watchfulness was not unusual. The *Courier* described Miller as belonging to a "phantom brigade of fighting black men." When Henrietta Miller revealed to the nation her son's name and photograph, she noted her fears about the safety of her son in "the war" and in the navy's segregation. And she challenged a military that refused to acknowledge her son's participation in combat and only did so when black Americans protested and provided their own images. With her son's photograph and statements about his marksmanship, she demonstrated the radical role images played in the Double V campaign.[64]

Federal agencies considered these activities and agitations by ordinary readers in the black press with alarm. The Federal Bureau of Investigation (FBI) surveilled black communities when reports and rumors circulated about their disloyalty and interest in a Japanese victory. After months of investigation, the FBI found little to support their initial suspicions: "Conclusion which may be drawn from the foregoing with reference to the causes for Negro unrest or dissatisfaction reflect that although many complaints, reports, and rumors have been received to the effect that un-American sentiments and activities exist among the Negroes, the apparent forces responsible for this situation are entirely national in scope."[65] Unable to find evidence of pro-Japanese activity, FBI sources identified the "Negro press" as "a strong provocator [*sic*] of discontent among Negroes." Investigators described the *Chicago Defender* as "militant." The Double V campaign, the FBI insisted, demonstrated evidence of the *Pittsburgh Courier*'s "inflammatory tendencies." Ignoring the violence and harassment against blacks in uniform, federal officials determined that the black press, and not American racial practices, produced widespread discontent. In turn, this unrest and dissatisfaction—displayed in newspapers, rumors, daily utterances, and other displays of blacks' anger—revealed "un-American" activity.[66] "Negroes," Roi Ottley noted, "declared war on America." In response, the OWI pressed newspaper editors to quiet the restiveness. With articles under special scrutiny, images became blacks' "weapon" of choice.[67]

Photographs and illustrations in black newspapers, especially by 1941, were far more diverse and reflected the expansion of black production by professional photographers beyond studios and into the everyday life of the community. By 1930, the U.S. Census listed more than 500 black photographers. Cameras and the personal photograph were especially important. By the next decade, buying, owning, and using the camera became part of everyday life as a way for blacks to gain control over how they represented themselves. As bell hooks notes, "Cameras gave to black folks irrespective of class, a means by which they could participate fully in the production of images." With greater access to the camera than ever before, "an oppositional black aesthetic emerged. In the world before racial integration, there was a constant struggle on the part of black folks to create a counter-hegemonic world of images that would stand as visual resistance, challenging racist images." Everyday snapshots were especially important in this endeavor. "Photographs taken in everyday life, snapshots in particular," hooks notes, "rebelled against all of those photographic practices that re-inscribed colonial ways of looking and capturing the images of the black 'other.' Shot spontaneously, without any notion of remaking black bodies in the image of whiteness, snapshots posed a challenge to black viewers."[68]

African Americans used images to document and scrutinize the nation's racial practices. While this examination and interrogation had origins in blacks' resistance to late nineteenth-century scientific racism, Susan V. Donaldson notes that racial ideologies and practices came under intense inspection at the turn of the twentieth century and again after World War I. Donaldson notes that as writers, painters, and photographers of the Harlem Renaissance began "dismantling old racial stereotypes in the process of constructing the New Negro," the social and cultural construction of whiteness suddenly became visible. The white gaze had been about "reducing the black subject to the status of an object," but white Americans now found themselves "under a counter-gaze, that of African American writers, painters, and photographers who implicitly define their alliance with the 'New Negro' and with destabilizing inherited categories of whiteness and blackness." The wartime rhetoric and practices of Nazism provided new opportunities to destabilize ideas about whiteness and blackness. As Jesse Owens in the 1936 Olympics in Berlin and Joe Louis in his 1938 boxing match with Max Schmeling represented battles between American democracy and Nazi supremacy abroad, African Americans questioned white supremacy at home.[69] In this context, African Americans not only considered images integral to their examination of racial inequalities, but they intended these images to challenge the official record that ignored segregation. During the 1930s and 1940s, for example, African Americans sent photographs to document segregation in Shenandoah National Park when government officials claimed otherwise.[70]

Surveilled and pressured to contain their textual agitation for the war, black newspapers used images to protest the contradictions of the war. Like blues music that critiqued racial inequalities and violence, such as Billie Holiday's "Strange Fruit," these wartime images highlighted the inequities and danger in everyday black life made more dangerous in a segregated society at war. Whereas the OWI hoped to minimize depictions of segregation, the images African Americans produced portrayed the violence in and the humiliation of the segregated military. Black newspapers became the repository of photographs, illustrations, and editorial cartoons that exposed the danger of the Jim Crow military and reconfigured it as the front line in war. Editorial illustrations in the *People's Voice*, for example, compared lynching of soldiers and other African Americans in the South with hangings in Nazi Germany. Advertisements denounced the Red Cross plan to segregate blood. These images insisted that U.S. segregation, especially the military's segregation, included violence as horrific as the practices of the Nazis. The double war put African Americans in constant danger.[71] With their emphasis on exposure and accountability, such images provided visual testimony that played a role akin to that of testimony in black oral practices.

As the United States entered World War II, artist William H. Johnson responded to an appeal made by the U.S. Office of Emergency Management for art that could "inform the public about war and defense activities." As Johnson joined hundreds of other painters, illustrators, cartoonists, and graphic artists in this effort, his paintings thrust Jim Crow into view for public scrutiny. In *K.P.* (ca. 1942), Johnson arranged twelve men standing or sitting in groups of five, four, and three in a tent held up with poles off kilter, its flaps billowing and revealing a distant background of sky, trees, and a field. Eleven of the men wear breeches, khaki shirts, and spats. The men cluster in the foreground, their eyes downcast, closed, or with a fixed gaze into the distance. While the men appear to perform chores frequently reserved for black soldiers, only one man holds food or a kitchen utensil in his hand.[72] The object he grasps could be a potato or a stone. From its wash of purple, green, and cobalt blue to the men's clasped hands, *K.P.* creates a somber, uneasy tone. The men bow over the basins, pots, and bowls, their hands poised as if in prayer.

Johnson's later paintings present a far more militant tone, with stronger colors and repetition of the Double V. The 1942 *Station Stop, Red Cross* captures the everyday work of black Red Cross workers in the wartime South.[73] In this painting, black women occupy center stage as caretakers of African American dignity. Throughout the war, the American Red Cross refused to recruit black women, yet hundreds joined self-organized and segregated units to meet the health care needs of black soldiers. Despite rejection of this policy by civil rights organizations, black women responded to the immediate needs of soldiers in their self-organized units.[74]

The painting suggests that black women's volunteerism in segregated Red Cross units also provided black soldiers protection from violence. The four blue-suited workers, all of them women, stand near three soldiers arrayed on stretchers, two with their right arms arranged in V formations. The soldiers' pants, boots, guns, and ammunition cases have been strewn beside them, as if hastily removed. Perhaps the clatter of dropped guns and other sounds of men diving for safety registered and resonated to black viewers familiar with the experiences of black troops in the South. From newspaper and personal reports of the daily insults and violence, including lynchings, against blacks in uniform, they knew that the arrival of uniformed and armed black men, as in previous wars, provoked whites' vigilantism. In this larger context, which occurred outside the painting and is documented in newspapers or NAACP reports, the women serve as more than tenders of wounded soldiers; rather, they become sentinels against the violence that awaited black troops in the South.[75] Johnson's visual reportage of the multiple dangers faced by African Americans during World War II were echoed in the weekly reports published in the black press.

Other African Americans participated in creating illustrations of the dangers and struggles of wartime segregation that remained undocumented in the mainstream press but were policed in the black press. Black artists Charles Alston and Romare Bearden trained in the fine arts, and others trained as illustrators and cartoonists; all provided rich and varied images for mainstream popular magazines aimed at a more liberal readership. Henry Luce's *Fortune* magazine reached a more elite and educated audience than *Life*, which Luce also owned. Known for its cover art and illustrated articles, *Fortune* introduced new artists to readers each month. *Fortune*'s unattributed article "The Negro at War" appeared in June 1942 with illustrations attributed to two acclaimed artists from the Works Progress Administration (WPA), Charles Alston and Romare Bearden, both of whom had a history of inserting strong political statements into their work. Alston had produced controversial images of lynch victims in the 1930s. For the 1942 article, Alston provided the majority of the illustrations, and Bearden, who had illustrated other articles for the magazine, provided the large frontispiece.

Alston's black-and-white drawings, like the text, provided another form of visual reportage about "one tenth of the U.S. population" that did not have "a full share in America's greatest undertaking."[76] Whereas the infrequent photo-essays in *Life* magazine depicted African Americans in the military as properly supervised and contained, Alston, who later served in the army, rendered the segregated military as a "liability" with his illustration of idle soldiers clustered and with downcast eyes. This drawing was not linked directly with a text emphasizing the "total" segregation in the army. Confronted first with a somber drawing of soldiers, readers then read about the complete segregation policies practiced by the military. If the readers of the article in *Life* were reassured by photographs of dancing soldiers—a stereotyped image that implied accommodation to the military's racial order—the readers of *Fortune*'s sparingly illustrated article viewed more ominous images. Alston's illustrations included strongly worded captions about blacks' frustrations with segregation and low morale, especially in the military. These images created a visual unease, and along with the text, they raised questions about the nation's racial policies and practices.[77]

Nurtured first in the dynamic milieu of 1920s Harlem and then among radical artists of the WPA, Bearden and Alston honed an aesthetic that combined the formal qualities of art with a historical narrative meant to challenge established racial and class hierarchies. Alston and other black artists in the 1930s were interested in "art, new movements, new attitudes, new ways of seeing, completely on an aesthetic level." Black artists, Alston concluded, "cannot but be concerned about what's going on." He committed to rendering the struggle around him and capturing the diversity of black life he witnessed. He benefited, too, from the "new impulses, the new ideas" of jazz and the 1930s Popular Front. In this period, he and other artists "experimented and explored."[78] All the while, Alston created and contributed to shows that addressed the violence blacks faced in everyday life. In 1935 he submitted a painting to a gallery exhibition of art on lynching, but it was rejected because its image of a castrated man was considered too graphic.[79]

In the early 1930s Alston worked as an illustrator and directed the College Art Association's Harlem Art Workshop in the 135th Street public library. While there, he mentored Jacob Lawrence and became steeped in Alain Locke's and Aaron Douglas's debates about and depictions of African influences in black art. He also spent time with muralists Diego Rivera and José Clemente Orozco as they worked in New York City.[80] Alston created drawings for Langston Hughes's poems, and he provided the cover for Countee Cullen's 1932 novel, *One Way to Heaven*. Like many black artists in the 1930s, Alston struggled to find work as an artist, but between 1934 and 1938 he worked variously as an illustrator for *Crisis*, *Opportunity*, *Collier's*, and the *New Yorker*. Along with Augusta Savage, Gwendolyn Bennett, and Aaron Douglas, Alston helped organize the Harlem Artists' Guild. This organization pressured the WPA to open opportunities to black artists, and Alston supervised the WPA mural project for Harlem Hospital, which became the first federal project awarded to African American artists. Though not a segregated hospital, the Harlem Hospital provided care to a largely black population, and Alston's mural depicted the history of blacks in medicine. The hospital considered this depiction incendiary, however, and demanded its removal. Alston's determination to maintain the mural, along with the intervention of Stuart Davis and Aaron Douglas, heads of the Artists' Union, favorably settled the debate.[81]

Beginning in late 1940 and continuing through 1942, Alston became an artist for the OWI and the Bureau of Public Relations. Throughout the war, his illustrations appeared in black newspapers, frequently alongside his own syndicated drawings. "Lest We Forget," Alston's tribute to Dorie Miller and the anniversary of Pearl Harbor in the *New York Amsterdam News*, followed reports of Miller's death on the USS *Liscome Bay*, which sank in late November 1943. His illustrations did not take subjects dictated by the OWI; rather, he created images that mattered to African Americans, and they typically contested the nation's racial policies. One appeal for the war bond, which showed a black soldier dressed in full combat gear, ready to throw a grenade, notes, "If you can't stand beside him, stand behind him!!" Photographs of black men participating in combat had yet to appear, even in the black weeklies; further, the War Department refused to acknowledge that blacks were trained for combat. These images, however, resonated with a population anxious for evidence of blacks' presence in combat. One OWI image of a crashed plane bore the caption "All he needed was a little more gas!!" Such an appeal might have elicited support from black audiences when considered alongside reports of the Tuskegee Airmen ferrying planes. The one OWI poster that depicted an African American showed Tuskegee pilot Robert W. Diez, whose photograph regularly appeared in the weeklies.[82]

Many of Alston's images reminded readers of the war's broad impact on black life. Several images depicted Ethiopia's struggle against Mussolini. In another, Alston appealed directly to African Americans when he reported Nazi roundups of "Negroes in German occupied territory." His images of civilians, including the illustration *Labor Day 1942*, were typically of interracial groups. Decidedly pro-labor, this image also favorably depicted the benefits of interracial labor organizing and implicitly critiqued the hate strikes that plagued many plants. *Democracy's Forge* suggested that the new democracy would be forged on the shop floor as much as on the battlefield. In Alston's images, black and white workers did not simply wield tools like weapons but instead crafted them, presumably for the "double victory." Other images portrayed—even honored—African Americans engaged in the least glamorous work, including cannery workers and black soldiers engaged in military labor.[83]

Other artists had similar sensibilities about the role of illustration for and about African Americans during the war. Beginning in World War I and continuing through World War II, these men and women created editorial cartoons, single-panel cartoons, and comic strips for black newspapers and magazines. Most received art training in New York City, Chicago, and Paris. They used familiar patriotic symbols, such as Liberty or the Statue of Liberty, to critique America's racial violence. Walton Holloway drew lavish editorial cartoons for the *Pittsburgh Courier*, and Sammy Milai's complex drawings accompanied J. A. Rogers's pan-Africanist columns on black history. Albert Alex Smith, Cornelius Johnson, and Laura Wheeler Waring regularly created illustrations for the *Crisis*, the *Messenger*, and *Opportunity*. E. Simms Campbell won a prize for an editorial cartoon he drew for the *Crisis* during World War I. After studying first in Chicago and then with George Grosz at the Art Students League, Campbell began drawing editorial cartoons and comic strips for the *Courier*. Ollie Harrington first drew for the *Crisis* and then for Adam Clayton Powell's *People's Voice*, a short-lived paper that began publication in 1942. On the eve of the war, many of these artists had their illustrations in syndication through the Continental Features Syndicate. These comics reached national audiences, and along with single-panel cartoons, they proliferated and flourished in the war years.

These illustrations, comic strips, and editorial cartoons provided black readers, including blacks in the military, with information and entertainment not found in the white dailies. In a context where black stereotypes continued to humor and soothe racial anxieties in the dominant culture, officials did little to encourage a dissemination of illustrations that depicted African American soldiers' dignity or labor to a wide audience. Confined to the black weeklies, comic strips and editorial cartoons for black audiences provided pleasure and relieved stress without the typical derogatory racial stereotypes. Ranging from the respectable to the ribald, these images entertained black audiences, but they also informed and politicized them about their wartime experiences. The complex displays of black experiences through simple line drawings were most evident in the representations of black women.

The single-panel cartoons depicting black women's sexuality echoed the portrayals of white women during wartime. They also challenged the exclusion of women from patriotic work and included a new emphasis on patriotic femininity. On one hand, World War II propaganda, as in World War I images, linked the protection of the nation with the protection of white women from rape and molestation by "the other," typically represented as nonwhite men with grotesque and animalistic features. On the other hand, women, regardless of race, were also portrayed in highly sexual ways. To encourage men's participation in battle, movie studios, advertisers, and the OWI deployed images emphasizing white women's sexuality. The confluence of danger and desire in comics demonstrated the fluidity in gender roles during the war as women moved from traditional caretakers of the home to participants in industrial and military jobs considered typically male.[84] While representations of women's sexuality were unstable symbols, the broad circulation of these images significantly shaped and reshaped how ordinary women viewed and presented themselves. This self-representation included what Sherri Tucker calls "sexual patriotism" that referenced the "titillatingly posed movie stars sanctioned by the U.S. government because of their ability to 'boost morale.'" These "young women, under the obligation of making themselves worth fighting for, came to believe that 'entertaining young servicemen on leave' was their patriotic duty."[85]

Black officials encouraged pinups of black women to motivate men's commitment to the war and as a substitute for black soldiers' limited access to recreation, films, and USO shows. Black soldiers repeatedly asked for studio photographs of Lena Horne, Hazel Scott, and Maxine Sullivan. Dick Campbell, head of the Negro Division, USO Camp Shows, reported "the boys overseas are virtually begging for some of the pin-up girls."[86] Black men's arrests, assaults, imprisonments, and lynchings based on charges of associating with or looking at white women stressed that images of white women were to be consumed only by white men. As the rules and dangers of segregation limited black troops' access to USO shows and recreation off base, black men expressed no desire to "look" at white women and instead pleaded for more pictures of Horne and Scott. One soldier implored in the pages of the *Pittsburgh Courier* for "colored pin-up girls. We have enough of the Grables, Lamours, etc."[87] On behalf of an entire company stationed in New Guinea, one soldier requested the *New York Amsterdam News* to send pictures of young women. Their list of autographed pinup photos included Count Basie singer Thelma Carpenter, Horne, Scott, Sullivan, Ella Fitzgerald, and the International Sweet Hearts of Rhythm. Campbell assured the newspaper that the photos would "embellish the now cheerless walls of the Company day room."[88]

Along with their pleas for photographs of black celebrities, men requested photographs of ordinary black women. The *Pittsburgh Courier* displayed the "Race Patriot Girl of the Week" as part of its Double V campaign. The *Chicago Defender* and the *New York Amsterdam News* featured photographs of young black women especially for soldiers. The *Courier* and the *Defender* included young women's mailing addresses and encouraged the young men to write. And they did. In a letter to the editor of the *New York Amsterdam News*, Corporal Pennick boldly begged: "Chicks, send us GIs pinups. What could be a better morale-builder than to receive a few pin-ups of the 'brown-body beautiful' as one guy terms them. Please add my name to your list for pin-ups."[89]

Images of impeccably dressed black women posed in demure ways contrasted sharply with the provocative displays of Betty Grable's legs. Neither the images the studios distributed of a glamorous Lena Horne nor the photographs and snapshots that black women sent to newspapers ever depicted more than their discreetly poised upper torsos and elegantly crossed legs. Photographs of wives published in the black newspapers stressed the marital status of the women through captions, such as the one for "Mrs. Evelyn B. Knighten, who is a pin-up any day for her husband, Cpl. William Knighten."[90] While her photo was meant for her husband, Evelyn Knighten, who worked as a schoolteacher, struck a respectable pose in a tailored suit. Such decorous positions emphasized black women's sexual propriety, and while intended as entertainment for black soldiers, these photographs also sought to train their gaze on respectable black women, not highly sexualized white women.[91] Photographs of black women in newspapers, then, took on new roles. They were meant to boost morale and provide visual entertainment, but they served, too, as substitutes for the limited recreation provided to black soldiers and as bulwarks against the surveillance and violence levied against them.

The visual roles black women were to play in boosting the morale of black soldiers were a response to, but were also complicated by, debates about the containment of black male sexuality more generally. Since there were more than 1.2 million black men in uniform, the military's efforts to prevent miscegenation escalated. Throughout the war, justifications for a Jim Crow military rested equally on claims of African Americans' cowardice in combat and their hypersexuality. According to widely held beliefs, black men had an innate desire to rape white women. Considered criminal and deviant, this sexual behavior not only breached racial categories; it also exemplified black men's savagery that, officials argued, threatened the war effort. As the military transported black soldiers through every region of the United States and into Europe, North Africa, Asia, and Australia, officials warned U.S. allies of "abnormal" black male sexual tendencies for venereal diseases, rape, and desire for white women. The military used a variety of methods to control the movement and behavior of black troops, especially in the South.[92]

The majority of black troops still stateside were based in the South; thus impetus to maintain segregation, not concerns about black soldiers' morale, shaped the policing of their access to recreation on bases and in nearby communities. Officials admonished blacks to abide by local segregation laws and generally confined blacks to the post.[93] Black troops, many of them from the North, chafed under these elaborate rules. The strict curfews, base confinements, and restricted access to facilities such as clubs, theaters, and pools also stoked their anger. With few opportunities for leisure or recreation, black troops frequently rioted and engaged in various forms of resistance. While wartime popular culture endorsed white soldiers' aggressive, even assaultive, access to white women, it also endorsed violent punishment for any perceived transgressions of the racial and sexual codes. White troops accused of assault or suspect behavior were turned over to base commanders for reprimand; for this and other infractions, even minor ones, black troops faced courts-martial that carried serious penalties such as execution or extended jail sentences. Frequently, the military left black men to the local police or, worse, local mobs that meted out their own forms of "justice." In the Jim Crow South, civilian policing of segregation subjected blacks in the military to daily humiliations and assaults.[94]

As the military bolstered and legitimized the racial politics of violence during the war, black communities strove to provide entertainment and recreation to black troops. Black leaders encouraged wives and sweethearts to visit soldiers and sailors, but in this charged scenario, black women became the most vulnerable, on and off base. Visiting wives and sweethearts of black troops regularly experienced attacks, assaults, and insults from white civilian and military police. Segregated travel made visits especially horrific and demeaning. Soldiers wrote Langston Hughes about the humiliation black women faced when they traveled south. "A colored soldier is walking down the streets of Savannah with his wife who came from a Northern city to visit him. Officers stop him and demand of the woman a health card, usually demanded of prostitutes. The soldier explains that she is his wife. He is accused of lying. One word brings another. Both are arrested."[95] Away from these camps, the sexual assaults against black women escalated.[96]

These shifting cartographies of discrimination and racial violence in the heightened sexual and racial politics of war meant black women's bodies came under increased sexualized display, but only in comics and illustrations. In contrast to the circumspect poses of black movie stars and singers in photographs, newspaper cartoons displayed black women in far more provocative poses. The majority of these cartoons and illustrations depicted black women and uniformed men in private settings, portraying a sexual intimacy most frequently confined to black secular music. Other images presented black men and women in public settings, such as buses, allowing black men to gaze fully on female sexuality (here we have the double gaze of black male viewers watching black men look) not allowed in white-controlled settings of the South. Buses were configured as sites for pleasure, not as settings for assaults and humiliation. In these public associations, black women acted with either restraint or naiveté; they neither presented nor encountered sexual danger. Instead, they were implored to provide their sexuality for the protection of the race and the pleasure of black men.

Ted Shearer, a longtime illustrator and newly enlisted soldier, provided humorous visual puns on black military experiences. His single-panel cartoon "Next Door," which appeared in the *Pittsburgh Courier*, and "Around Harlem," in the *Amsterdam News*, showed black women either in ribald poses for soldiers or engaged in everyday home front experiences with black soldiers. Generally, these images presented sharp swipes at the racial inequalities the appeals to black home front citizenship demanded. His drawings in early 1943 poked at black soldiers' and sailors' restriction to manual labor. Surrounded by piles of dishes, a soldier murmurs, "Darling I would have written much sooner, but there are certain jobs that needed my personal attention." In another cartoon, a soldier holds a letter and a new washboard. The caption quotes his sweetheart's letter: "Darling, I know you can use this in the Army, so practice up for when you come home on furlough." Responding to the repeated requests for blacks to buy war bonds, Shearer drew a panel of an older white man speaking to a black man similarly aged. The first leans close and comments to the other, "I understand they've whipped Italy, and all they need now is for you to buy a war bond and they'll take Germany."[97] Shearer's sly critique of wartime advertising that insisted black Americans' sacrifices and thrift would ensure victory abroad included a dig at the War Department's refusal to acknowledge the contributions of the 99th Pursuit Squadron. African Americans bought war bonds and sent men and women into uniform, but to what end? This cartoon functioned far more like an editorial than as a humorous comment on black life.

Shearer's raunchy single-panel cartoons also highlighted the particular racial barriers black soldiers faced. In one image, an army private and a woman wearing a very short dress jitterbugged cheek-to-cheek. "Y'know honey," he said, "this makes a guy realize what he's fightin' for." The jitterbug was considered a sexually charged "Negro dance," and the USO banned it from white and mixed-raced USO clubs. Segregated and dancing in a style considered too black and sexual but nonetheless pleasurable, the soldier "finds" personal meaning for a war that claimed to end fascism abroad but not racial inequalities in the United States. Shearer's depiction of black women was far more ambivalent. In this particular panel, the woman's sexuality—and sexual availability—was implied by her short dress. In other panels of this sort, Shearer drew voluptuous young women, in sharp contrast to the newspaper photographs of modestly posed and demurely dressed women in the weeklies.

"Around Harlem," Shearer's single-panel cartoon for the *New York Amsterdam News*, portrayed intimate relationships between young black men and women. These images were highly suggestive in both visual and tex-

tual presentation, as Shearer captured black men's and women's inter-
actions and values away from the view of whites. At once intimate and
circumspect, black men openly displayed their desire and appreciation
for black women, but their uniform instilled restraint. Still, black women
were to be, at the very least, visually available to black men. In one panel
a young black woman stands in a bus, and a sailor stands behind her. She
ignores him, and he pleads for her attention: "But, Baby, you're betrayin'
the whole naval morale program." Shearer added a boxed plea of his own
in the upper right corner of the panel: "Girls, morale means a lot!—So do
your part."[98] Such appeals for women to display their bodies for men's
morale, pleasure, and protection became the dominant representation of
black women's sexuality.

Most often depicted in racially segregated or private settings, such as
homes and clubs, Shearer's imagined women only suggest physical intimacy with particular men. While the cartoons rarely provide clues to
whether or not these couples are married, engaged, or just dating, the
women appear to relish being kissed and fondled, and the men seem reluctant to leave. Through gestures and words, the men barely contain their
desire. As frequently, women express an eager physical attraction, though
presented naively and within respectable bounds of feminine deference
and decorum. These women react and respond to men's advances, but
only to men in uniform. Countering the stereotype of the sexual danger
black soldiers posed, Shearer implied that military service allowed for
both women's challenge to sexual decorum *and* men's restrained behavior.

Many of the illustrations in the weeklies focused on black women
in uniform. In one panel, a couple, both in uniform, walks arm in arm;
the young woman leans toward the young man and says, "A WACs Basic
Training—Saying 'Yes ma'am' all day—and 'No sir' at night!"[99] At first
this woman's remark seems funny and innocuous. Placed in the context
of reports of sexual assault of black women in uniform, however, her remark appears disingenuous at best. Yet these cartoon portrayals of black
women in highly sexualized poses were created by black men and contrasted sharply with how black women in uniform presented themselves
in public and private. While white women who volunteered for service did
not want to be seen as camp followers and prostitutes, many also nego-
tiated the demands for sexualized display in private, not public, ways, as
part of the equation for a gendered citizenship.[100] Outside black print culture, music, film, and stage, black women rarely factored into the public
or private constructions of "patriotic femininity." Moreover, black commu-

nities were not in agreement on just what women's public roles would be during the war, especially in the segregated military.

WHEN JESSIE ADA RICHARDSON enlisted in the WAVES in mid-October 1944, she faced a wall of cameras. Over the next weeks, photographers from the black and white presses followed her every move, beginning when she boarded the train in Chicago for the trip to New York City, where she was sworn in and received her assignment. Cameras captured her fittings for her uniform at Saks Fifth Avenue and her departure for her assignment. Richardson found the interest from the white press astonishing. "When I left Chicago [and] when I got to New York," Richardson said, "there was a great deal of press there and I was told I was the first Negro WAVE." She later learned that two other black women volunteered the day she enlisted. Over the next months the three women became celebrities as photographs of their uniforms, travel, and work continued to appear on the front pages of the black weeklies and in the newsreels shown in black theaters. Richardson described her work experiences in the WAVES as ordinary, but she concluded that the attention she received from the press made her enlistment different.[101]

The documentation about and display of Richardson and the other black women in the military who challenged dominant stereotypes of race and gender launched an unusual period of reportage about the participation of African American women in the World War II military.[102] Until early 1943, black women had limited access to the WACs (Women's Army Corps), and they were barred from the WAVES (Women Accepted for Volunteer Emergency Service) until late 1944. The first black women who volunteered for the WAVES were roundly rejected. Pressing labor needs, especially in the nursing corps, prompted both services to open access to black women, in late 1944 for the army and in early 1945 for the navy. All the services barred black nurses with college degrees from working in white wards, whereas black women with little or no nursing training replaced white nurses in non-nursing jobs who were needed in combat hospitals. In white hospitals, black women cleaned wards, washed linens, and performed other unskilled domestic tasks.[103]

While recruitment efforts in black newspapers presented black women's volunteerism on behalf of black troops as necessary and heroic, many readers believed that women who enlisted were limited to menial labor and subjected to segregation that placed them in sexual danger. The differences between the popular representation of women as heroic and the perceptions of women as duped or endangered by racism instigated considerable debate in the black press. Women who enlisted and then protested Jim Crow policies, such as the six black nurses at Fort Devens who refused to do menial labor and insisted on equal treatment with white nurses, were viewed as strong "race women." Newspapers, Leisa D. Meyer notes, provided a space for black servicewomen to refute "official" military versions that discounted discrimination and accused women of insubordination. Though the nurses received some criticism because they went on strike, many African Americans saw their response as a victory for female competency and civil rights.[104]

As these debates erupted over women who were "lured" into the services to learn or perform skilled work and then were assigned menial work, women used the newspapers to explain why they volunteered for segregated military service. Lieutenant Ermayne Faulk told her story on the front page of the *Amsterdam News*. Using rhetoric not unlike the statements found in the material officials produced to recruit white women, Faulk claimed her skills relieved a man for combat. In the context of black men's efforts to participate in combat, Faulk's self-sacrifice—framed in language of gender and nation—included a reason that stressed addressing black men's particular needs and experiences: She believed her enlistment allowed her to share men's struggle to end segregation at home and fascism abroad.[105]

Black men, too, encouraged black women to join the WACs, but not necessarily to join in the struggle against the military's segregation. Writing in late August 1944, a private thanked the *New York Amsterdam News* for its articles on women's enlistments. He included a plea for more black women to come overseas. "I speak on behalf of my regiment and the Negro personnel of the ETO (European Theater of Operations) in the armed forces of the United States when I say the boys would enjoy the treatment and the companionship that only the girls of his own race and birthplace can give him."[106] This appeal appeared alongside reports that the U.S. military urged Great Britain to adopt and enforce policies of segregation against black Americans, claiming that black men raped women and had tails like monkeys.[107]

Other men expressed concern and caution about black women's enlistment. A black sailor urged full disclosure to women before they volunteered. "I have seen many a good boy mistreated in the navy. Now they want to increase this treatment by getting our Negro girls, also. It may turn out to be OK in boot training, but it will come after some of them are sent down South and even in the East. Then they will protest about it. They will be sent out of the service with a mark against them going back into Civilian life." He declared himself "a sailor and a Negro citizen"—a claim freighted with textual (and visual) tension and contradiction—and he intended to "hold my people responsible for sending our girls into service without first giving them the knowledge of what they are about to take part in."[108]

By 1944, African Americans' awareness of their exclusion from the war narrative reached its peak. The *New York Amsterdam News* concluded that in the white press "the role of the Negro soldier, sailor, and Marine on foreign soil is cloaked in mystery. Most of America will never know we were in the war."[109] The OWI's goal and efforts to increase black morale had been hampered from the start by southerners in Congress, and these representatives further curtailed the agency's efforts in 1944. These critics specifically wanted the agency to cease efforts to document blacks' training for combat. The exclusion of blacks from the dominant and official press did not escape notice by some whites. After analyzing Hollywood films released between late 1942 and early 1943, the OWI confirmed the fears of some officials: Blacks appeared in less than a quarter of the films, and in the majority of these films they played stereotyped roles. With few exceptions, the absence of blacks in the visual narrative of national identity and purpose extended beyond U.S. borders and portended a further entrenchment of racial hierarchies.[110] "[In] general," the OWI concluded, "Negroes are presented as basically different from other people, as taking no relevant part in the life of the nation, as offering nothing, contributing nothing, expecting nothing."[111]

Alarmed at the sinking morale of black troops precisely when the military needed more black men in combat units, the War Department sought help from the OWI. General George C. Marshall, chief of staff of the army, asked filmmaker Frank Capra to include *The Negro Soldier* in his series of military orientation films. Many in the War Department and the OWI believed that film, more than any other media, would teach troops a range of shared ideals and values. Marshall hoped *The Negro Soldier* would build racial tolerance and instill a sense of common purpose. They also hoped the film could be an effective instrument to change minds inside and outside the military about the ability of African Americans to serve in combat.[112]

Desperate for combat troops to prepare for the invasion of France, the War Department planned to include black soldiers, but it found that the racial ideologies and policies that had subordinated these men and relegated them to labor units hampered preparations. Extensive studies by the department demonstrated that its policies of segregation, along with white officers' racial attitudes, had made many of the soldiers restive and "non-cooperative." The numerous race riots across the United States, the South Pacific, and Australia added additional evidence of the stresses segregation imposed on black men.

As early as 1940, the military had set an overall quota for blacks at 9 percent and then confined the majority of the men to labor. The army had the majority of blacks in uniform, and it assigned them to every branch, where they were trained for combat positions. The army reassigned them, regardless of ability or education, to the branches of the Service Forces. This pattern of training black men for combat and then reassigning them to labor units intensified over the course of the war. By the eve of the Normandy invasion, the army had assigned three-quarters of black soldiers to the Service Force branches, which now claimed 39 percent of the army's strength. Two-thirds of the black men in these units served in three branches: the Quartermaster Corps, the Corps of Engineers, and the Transportation Corps. These men accompanied combat units everywhere the army went. As laborers, black soldiers were the first to arrive on the front lines, where they built roads and handled chemicals and explosives; they loaded and carried equipment and material. They were the last troops to leave as they gathered and loaded the wounded and dead. In the last two years of the war, a higher percentage of these troops served overseas than did white troops. Trained for combat and service, black troops, especially, provided a range of options on the battlefield.[113]

If the military had any initial plans to use blacks in combat, the machinations of southern politicians, generals, and white soldiers soon thwarted them. For months, the military evaded questions from civil rights leaders, the black press, and congressional leaders who pressed for blacks to serve in combat units and as officers.[114] Initially, the War Department insisted that black troops would be trained for combat, but when southern congressional representatives expressed outrage over these reports, the War Department claimed that America's "Colored troops," like the "Colored troops" of its allies, served in labor battalions. Impervious to the criticism from civil rights activists and William Hastie's resignation in protest to his policies, Secretary of State Henry Stimson argued throughout 1943 that black troops were "unreliable" and not ready for combat.[115]

Despite such public claims that black troops were labor troops, the military sent black antitank, antiaircraft, and combat units into the North African campaign and into Australia as early as late 1942. And the Army Air Corps had black pilots trained at Tuskegee ready for bombing campaigns. Black army nurses went to care for the wounded. Just how many black combat and combat support units were sent into North Africa remains largely unknown, but these campaigns and their impact on North Africans in Libya, Chad, and Morocco deserve a complete study. The Germans and Italians surrendered by May 1943, and black MPs stayed on to police more than 200,000 prisoners. Suffering defeat with white combat units elsewhere in Europe and the Pacific, the military told various groups different accounts about black combat troops, partly because the use of these troops initiated anticolonial efforts in the Congo. Even images of black combat officers in the Congo appeared to instigate Africans' defiance to European colonialism. Alarmed, the War Department removed black troops and ceased to circulate images of them. When faced with claims and evidence about the success of black troops, Stimson offered a revealing clue to the military's policy on its use of black combat troops: "Units are sent to theaters of operation when they have demonstrated their readiness for combat." Most Americans, including African Americans, believed that black troops could not and would not fight in combat, but the military did use blacks in combat when needed.[116]

While doing research for a script he was commissioned to write, playwright Arthur Miller heard the same claim from white officers as he observed white tank men and black cadre men at a camp in the South. He quickly surmised that "at this fort, Negro cadre men have been the means by which many hundreds, perhaps thousands of tank men have learned their weapon." He learned, too, that "white trainees objected to being instructed by Negroes. I heard an officer say that the Negro cadre men were to be eased out as a consequence; the outfit did not want any trouble." The trainees were often rescued by black soldiers. Miller watched as one of the black cadre men hauled yet another white trainee and his tank out of a ditch. One white soldier told Miller how "the dumb fools run the tank into a deep cut they had no business falling into." He could see the tank upended and feared it would flip onto its back. "That's the best way to start an engine fire," he said. Fortunately, he remarked to Miller, "the colored fella told them not to move and he got a cable and tied the tank to a big tree and held her that way till those kids could get out." Miller wondered if the men were "thankful." The soldier replied, "I guess they are, but I know they'd rather it'd been a white man did it for them."[117]

Miller found similar attitudes on other bases. Everywhere he went, the army officials denied his requests to see the black men train. Maybe, Miller concluded, "they simply didn't take my request seriously—watching the Negroes didn't seem important to them." The racial attitudes of the white army officers distracted and troubled him. "At the infantry replacement center [at Fort Benning] there were several Negro companies. Without exception, every officer I asked said they were the best soldiers in the camp, and that's coming from southern officers. None of them was sure, however, of how the Negroes would act in combat. They fell back on the old stories of the Negro shaking in the traditional burlesque manner in the presence of death or danger." Black soldiers and officers understood the implications of these stereotypes in strikingly different ways. Miller asked the black private driving him what he and other black soldiers thought about the army. "He didn't know anyone who wanted to be in the Army." A black lawyer training in the Officer Candidate School thought "that despite the outrages against us, deep down inside is the instinctive knowledge they must show themselves as good soldiers, first, last, and all the time. That is one thing they will not let anyone deprive them of. They have an intense burning wish to be regarded as good troops." More than anything, the man continued, "the uniform itself says [they belong to America] and that's why they feel hope when they wear it. At the same time, though, the uniform highlights all the irony of our position; we are asked to die for a country that literally doesn't let us live." Miller wanted to include what he saw and heard from these black men in his script, but "it wouldn't do at this time to aggravate their justifiable grievance by portraying it naturalistically, it seemed, and yet it simply could not be ignored. I just couldn't see anything hopeful in the situation and I couldn't lie about it."[118] Others revised Miller's script, and what he originally wrote appeared unrecognizable when *The Story of G.I. Joe* was released in 1945. The film did not include the experiences of black troops.

Miller imagined a script that included the scene of the lawyer affirming blacks' support for the war despite the inequalities they faced, but Donald Young, the War Department's expert on race relations, and Samuel Stouffer, who headed the professional staff of the military's Research Branch, found significant evidence that the majority of black troops expressed deep ambivalence about fighting to save segregation. The War Department had to do more than stem black dissent through a movie. Prolonged combat broke down soldiers' morale and unit cohesion, but segregation added another form of combat trauma. "There is no evidence that Negroes, in overt behavior, were less loyal than whites, that they were draft evaders, or political conscientious objectors or allies of enemy agents more than were whites," Stouffer noted. But more than half of the black troops questioned why they had to fight, and nearly three-quarters of black Americans wondered if the war was "worth fighting for." Many believed that they did more for the war effort than they should, since segregation meant they could not reap its benefits. The majority—57 percent—of soldiers believed that the war would have little, if any, impact on their rights, and equal numbers believed black people overall would not be much better off after the war.[119]

By 1943, nearly one-third of blacks in the army came from the North, and the overall majority of these men had close to, or more than, a high school education. Black southerners were better educated than white southerners. These men, generally, expressed a greater politicization than the army realized. What happened to black Americans outside the military mattered intensely to these soldiers. Black troops trained, lived, and fought under intense circumstances made worse by their constant subjugation to military segregation. On and off the bases these men and women faced scorn, threats, intimidation, and even harm because of their race and status. Required to wear uniforms off base, blacks encountered danger and harassment. At the same time, they witnessed and heard about similar experiences from their families and their communities. These men and women bombarded Stouffer and the other interviewers with prepared questions: "Did they fight to maintain Jim Crow, or end it?" "Why doesn't the President stop the lynching?" "If it's not going to benefit our race, why should we be called to shed our blood?" "After the Negro men go and fight their best, would they have equal rights?"[120]

At the same time, white troops revealed a tremendous lack of knowledge of or interest in what black troops thought or faced. The overwhelming majority thought African Americans "were satisfied" with their status. Sixty-four percent of white troops surveyed believed blacks would not, and should not, gain anything from the war. When Stouffer and the other researchers probed deeper, they discovered that whites' resistance to black civil rights, more than any knowledge about the ability of blacks to fight, shaped the military's combat assignments and racial ideas. "Society," Stouffer noted, "set certain standards of behavior," including attitudes about the relationship between combat and rights. "White soldiers could expect rewards from their society for acquitting themselves well." They expected and heard that society would reward them for sacrifice to the nation. In contrast, the majority of white Americans, including the majority of white soldiers, believed that blacks should not accrue any reward for participation in battle. The perceived idea that blacks might expect and receive expanded and new rights, including equal access to jobs and the ballot, fueled the demand by politicians and civilians to keep them out of combat. That many senior officers were southern enabled this policy within the War Department.[121]

Unwilling or unable to show images of blacks in combat to white audiences, the army intended to use the film *The Negro Soldier* to motivate black troops to go to the battlefield in spite of the military's segregation and America's racial terrorism. Now under the direction of black filmmaker Carlton Moss, the film presented a montage of illustrations, created scenes, and other artwork that suggested a long history of the roles of blacks in American wars for their own liberation. From Crispus Attucks, the first casualty during the War for Independence, to Peter Salem, who fought in the battle at Bunker Hill, the film "documented" a history of blacks' participation in efforts to save an expansive idea of their own liberty and not simply conserve the nation for white property holders. During the War for Independence, blacks defined liberty as the end of slavery and an expansion of their political participation. The film used archival illustrations and paintings, such as Emanuel Gottlieb Leutze's 1851 painting *George Washington Crossing the Delaware*, which prominently features Prince Whipple rowing the boat, as proof of this history. The film, then, sutures African Americans into the visual and martial narrative of the nation. These insertions continue with the accounts of Thomas Wilson's soldiering in the War of 1812, of the Massachusetts 54th during the Civil War, and of the bravery of the 371st in a battle in France on April 21, 1918. This history, the narrator insists, while ignored, contested, or reviled by white America, "remains written in the hearts of Negro soldiers." The film's dynamic and authoritative documentation of blacks' sacrifice had few antecedents in America. For black viewers, these inserted images recalled illustrations by Sammy Milai that accompanied J. A. Rogers's history columns and Charles Alston's syndicated drawings of blacks in combat.[122] The film, then, included a graphic history typically used in the black press and ignored by the dominant press.

With nearly half of black Americans and as many black soldiers questioning why they should participate in combat, the film's recuperation of a heroic black combat history linked to blacks' aspirations for full citizenship challenged the OWI's excision of blacks from newsreels. Moss concluded the film with a montage of images that reached a visual climax with black bodies marching in a V that doubled and formed a Double V, all set to a medley of black martial music, including "Onward Christian Soldiers" and "Joshua Fought the Battle of Jericho." This blend of image and sound recalled key moments in African Americans' fight for liberation—particularly from slavery—that also challenged U.S. racial domination.

These martial sensibilities drawn from a history of black struggles to end bondage and for civil rights appeared to offer alternative meanings to the film. Writing for the New York *PM* magazine, John T. McManus reported his surprise at black soldiers' responses to the film.

> At one camp an audience of all Negro soldiers was collected for it, and they weren't too pleased at the prospect. Maybe their morale was dragging, maybe something else. Anyway, they were described to me (umpteenth-hand, of course) as an unfriendly audience, expecting more of the same old Army game.
>
> They sat through the film pretty much in silence. But as it came to a close with its swelling orchestraization of fighting men and Jericho music and the lights in the theater flashed on, a lone soldier in the front row, rose, snapped to attention and stood at salute before the empty screen.
>
> One by one, then groups, and finally in unison to the last man, the whole audience rose, came to attention, and joined in the mass salute to a soldier's job well done.[123]

Reviewers in northern mainstream newspapers and journals noted the omission of anything controversial. The careful excisions of scenes of black troops fighting in World War I and World War II and black officers commanding black troops elicited the most criticism. In a review of the film for the *New York Post*, Archer Winstein observed, "The only omission, an expected one, is the avoidance of anything touching controversy. This will limit its appeal for people who are aware of the full extent of discrimination and segregation many Negroes have bitterly resented in his war for the various freedoms. But that is a story which will be told neither by the War Department nor apologists for things as they are." Still, Winstein concluded, "'The Negro Soldier' should be seen for what it demonstrates positively, pride, ability, courage, and dignity."[124] Bosley Crowther's review in the *New York Times* described the film as "inspirational" and "aimed to convey to Negro soldiers a realization of their stake in democracy—and, more particularly, an enthusiasm for their part in the war." But, he concluded, "it is to be noted that it very discreetly avoids the more realistic race problems which are generally recognized today. For this reason, it is questionable whether the purpose which it is intended now to serve publicly may not be defeated by the film's own."[125]

Other reviewers offered more critical responses to the film and its purposes. After he saw the film, critic Michael Carter dryly noted, "Flashbacks of old newsreel clips show Nazi soldiers in training. They are contrasted against what the army probably calls 'The American Way'—jim-crow regiments in training." Nonetheless, critics found the film wanting, not because of its use of black stereotypes and its refusal to comment about the segregated military, but because of fabrications of a different sort. "Still other shots," Carter observed, "show scenes that our enemies have yet to witness: colored tankists, howitzer crews, and other specialized units of colored soldiers."[126] Unknown to most Americans, including many African Americans, all-black tank, artillery, and howitzer units had arrived for the invasion of France.

While black men in combat units in Europe expressed confidence in their abilities, some troops in the South Pacific expressed greater frustration as they fought under conditions made worse by segregation. As Robert Jefferson notes, commanders' reports were replete with distortions of black soldiers' capabilities and with racial ideas about how to use black troops to goad white troops. As frequently, the soldiers in the 93rd resented fighting in a segregated military that made everyday life a misery and that did not adequately convey what it meant to go into battle under segregated conditions. As one soldier told *Defender* correspondent Enoch Waters, he had enough of black leaders pushing for his unit to go into combat. "You folks are sitting back at home and too old or too beat up to be drafted. It's easy to say let them fight and die." Waters insisted that black men on the battlefield represented equal opportunity. The soldier responded with the collective anger of his unit. "Why should we volunteer to sacrifice our lives for a Jim Crow country?"[127]

While many black troops went into combat with little knowledge about the extent of blacks' participation in combat, these men soon witnessed thousands of troops serving in a range of positions on the battlefield. For these troops, the sight of black men with guns or driving jeeps and tanks confirmed their suspicions that the claims they were cowards were false.

More disturbing, these men performed well and with discipline in spite of the efforts by their own government to thwart and malign them. Having endured battles from Utah Beach to Belgium, Emiel W. Owens, an artilleryman in the 777th Field Artillery, arrived in Germany in late 1944. Believing himself well-trained, Owens discovered that nothing had prepared him for the "spectacular violence" the armies levied on each other and on the towns and villages of the western section of Germany near Hurtgen Forest.[128] Beginning in early November 1944 and continuing for weeks, Owens managed and fired four guns in his battery. African American quartermaster troops laid down chemicals and provided smoke screens for trucks, tanks, and artillery to pass; others in the quartermaster units classified and buried thousands of the dead. "The soldier pallbearers were very efficient. They stacked the dead soldiers like cords of wood. They had been trained to collect the dead, just as I had been trained to kill."[129] The men then classified the corpses and hauled the dead away. Black medics tended to the wounded, sorting the dead from the dying. They formed an efficient assembly line of death "in the killing fields" of Germany.

Unable to draft and train combat troops fast enough after the move into Germany, General Dwight Eisenhower called for black volunteers from the service branches. The thousands who immediately volunteered overwhelmed army commanders and threatened to deplete the labor units. In France and Germany, the army reclassified support personnel to combat positions and moved black men from building roads to firing weapons. Most of the images African Americans produced or the articles they wrote about these men never appeared in the American press. And the OWI censored photographs of wounded African Americans at the request of the army.[130]

The meaning of blacks' combat participation remained unsettled into the final months of the war. In a *Chicago Defender* article that accompanied a photograph of 332nd pilot Lieutenant Felix Kirkpatrick, correspondent Richard Durham noted that black pilots "hoped that Europe's skies would prove Jim Crow's graveyard," as "one of the Dixie-born pilots hugged" Kirkpatrick "for bringing him back alive." Race prejudice seemed to vanish. "At 27,000 feet, Nazi flak and fighter pilots are deadly accurate in knocking down Jim Crow." But such pronouncements made from the battlefield had little meaning on the home front. Within weeks, the *Defender* reported that returning black soldiers learned quickly that "Dixie prefers Nazis to Negroes."[131]

The mass of black soldiers would not have disagreed with the latter assessment, a perspective Sterling Brown, the noted poet and Howard University professor, observed firsthand sometime in late 1944. Brown heard how black soldiers marched by a large photograph in a northern train station, a "picture, 'blown up' by marvelous photographic technique." The picture, a soldier recounted to Brown, "showed what Americans were fighting for: a sea of American faces looking out anxiously, proudly. All white." The observer noted how the men "gave the eye-catching picture a swift glance, snapped their heads away," and continued their march. Brown wondered what thoughts the men had as they made their disciplined pass by the poster. As Brown traveled through the South in 1944 and spoke to African Americans, he discovered a sense of "protest, sometimes not loud but always deeply felt." These black soldiers, schoolteachers, and sharecroppers noted "with bitter desperation and daring" that the Jim Crow buses and diners "ain't no way to win the war."[132] As the governors of Alabama, Mississippi, and Louisiana assailed black soldiers for "having their minds poisoned" by "seeing the war period as a time to initiate full equality," Roy Wilkins warned that "certain it is that the Negro soldiers are not fighting and dying to maintain the status quo for their race. Nor will they take kindly, to put it in its mildest form, to surly suggestions as to their 'place.' Their place now is in front of the bullets of the enemy, and below the bombs in enemy planes." And, he added, "bullets, or threats of bullets, are not likely to cause them to bow and scrape once they are home. No, the threats of civil war will not turn the trick."[133] African Americans determined to change the "status quo"; but wartime surveys suggested that many whites believed the war had made blacks "unruly and unmanageable," and already they believed challenges "to their place" were "undertaken too swiftly." Sounding the bellicose language that soon shaped the anti-integrationist ethos after the war, Mississippi senator Theodore Bilbo exhorted whites to "draw the color line tighter and tighter."[134] Black soldiers who returned home did not see their demands for the right to vote as too fast or too incendiary. Already familiar with the war to sustain Jim Crow in the military, African Americans turned from their battle for democracy in Africa, Europe, and the South Pacific and focused on the second front from Mississippi to New York. These former soldiers joined civil rights activists and pondered what role, if any, their struggles against the segregated military might play in the long civil rights movement.

2

Jim Crow Shock
and the Second Front,
1945–1950

"Yes, 'a wind is rising and the rivers flow,'" Private First Class James P. Stanley informed NAACP executive secretary Walter White. Instead of a "democratic spirit" that White predicted the war against fascism would produce within white soldiers, Stanley discovered that "the rising wind" carried "racial hatred and wanton murder." Already, he warned, "a river of blood is flowing freely." As they left the European front and waited for ships bound for U.S. ports, troops choked the streets of Le Havre, France. Adding to the congestion, soldiers assigned to guard German prisoners prowled the streets with loaded weapons and taunted black troops. At night, white soldiers kept their loaded pistols, but the military police confiscated blacks' guns and knives. "It has been dangerous for us," Stanley wrote. "Their mission finished with the Germans, they now return to attack and murder their long hated enemy, the Negro." As the violence surged, black soldiers concealed their weapons. "Many soldiers of both races are being killed."[1]

The violence that Stanley and other black soldiers encountered in the weeks after the war continued, and African Americans argued that the United States had won the war against fascism in Europe; but the vast U.S. military sustained policies of racial segregation and violence that spread

Pallbearers with casket during the NAACP "Parade for Victory" held during the annual NAACP national meeting, July 1944. Courtesy of California Newsreel.

across America and through Europe and Asia. As the military settled into a long demobilization and occupations in Europe and Japan, blacks who did not yield to the military's racial subordination faced harsh punishments and courts-martial. The military allowed and encouraged white soldiers and local populations to participate in this violence and subjugation. German and Italian prisoners of war helped white troops enforce segregation. Military officials did not protect blacks as they mobilized out of the services, and neither the War Department nor the Justice Department punished those who intimidated, assaulted, or murdered these soldiers. The efforts of African Americans to withstand the violence *within* the military were as significant as their efforts to endure the horrors of combat.[2]

News of these deadly skirmishes, assaults, and murders leaked into the black press. From everywhere, Langston Hughes wrote in his popular *Chicago Defender* column, came reports from the clashes between black and white soldiers. "White-Negro relations are a national problem affecting both civilian and military life. It illustrates how the army has helped to worsen these relations." He noted something else in these reports about

African Americans: their willingness to take up weapons to "fight and die on American soil for their democratic rights." Their response, Hughes observed, "shows that often to achieve even the simplest things, Negroes must make an abnormal effort, even put up a fight, or show of a fight that other citizens do not have to be bothered with."[3] After numerous soldiers and veterans were assaulted, shot, and lynched in the first months of 1946, *Chicago Defender* columnist Earl Conrad agreed. "The Negro press still reads like war," he observed. "Now we are confronted with a wave of Negro GIs beaten and killed for standing up for their rights."[4]

As black troops and veterans defended themselves from harassment and terror in and out of the military, they also demanded full citizenship for themselves and their communities. When Leon Mosley entered the segregated army, he concluded that his rights did not mean much in America. After months in battle, he "knew those Germans wanted to kill [him] as much as they wanted to kill every other foreign soldier." Those attacks made him realize he "really was an American." And as an American, "in danger and under fire in war," Mosley returned to the United States determined to vote, own a home, and earn equal wages.[5] He and other veterans who faced similar experiences demanded that their sacrifices for the nation should ensure their having full rights as citizens. Earl Conrad concluded that African Americans' push for immediate integration in all aspects of American society, from its military, politics, and education to its unions, buses, and movie theaters, had become a revolutionary demand. Postwar surveys revealed that the overwhelming majority of white Americans—and not just whites in the South—perceived their own demands for affordable housing, steady wages, and better schools as appropriate recompense for their service, but many also considered blacks' similar expectations to be unwarranted. The protracted and ultimately unsuccessful efforts to create a permanent Fair Employment Practices Commission (FEPC) that would have challenged employment discrimination based on race demonstrated this resistance to equal access to jobs. Over the next decades, white America fought back with ferocity and viciousness against equal access to schools and housing for blacks. Returning Mexican American veterans faced similar resistance to their appeals for equal access to employment, housing, and schools.[6]

African American soldiers and veterans did not fight alone for the vote, the integration of education, and the end to segregation on transportation, but in the years after the war they were frequently at the epicenter of these struggles that erupted between 1945 and 1950.[7] Empowered by the contradiction of having served in a segregated military sent to battle fascism, African American soldiers and veterans articulated concepts of freedom that linked their sacrifices on the battlefield to their demands for full and immediate citizenship. But as they pressed for the right to vote, for access to jobs, and for the right to travel free from terror and segregation, these men and women encountered unprecedented violence, from assaults and beatings to mutilations and murder. As the press reported the gruesome news, African Americans asked why the nation, which had claimed victory over Nazism, now allowed violence against and subjugation of its black citizens, including soldiers and veterans. As black soldiers' and veterans' demands for civil and political rights engendered violence and repression, their assaulted bodies represented the egregious failure of American democracy at home and abroad. Civil rights activists called for national attention to, and international scrutiny of, America's racial segregation and violence.

These activists expanded their exposure of the horrific violence targeting black soldiers and veterans to include a challenge of the segregated military, the most visible representation of American power abroad. After the War Department demobilized millions of troops in the months after the war's end, the Truman administration faced severe shortages in all of the armed services. Desperate for military labor, the new Department of Defense considered how it might adapt its "Negro Policy"—a policy that openly advocated racial segregation of blacks—to the demands of occupation and the burgeoning Cold War. For many in the civil rights movement, the military's insistence on a segregated "manpower" presented a conundrum to President Truman. How could the segregated military now occupying Europe and Asia represent an expansive American democracy? Civil rights activists believed the need for a large Cold War military provided an unprecedented opportunity to end segregation not just in the armed services but in the entire society as well. As Americans were debating how to create a permanent draft military, one prepared to go to war at a moment's notice, and as many in Congress and the military insisted on retaining segregation of the armed forces, African Americans emphatically announced they would not serve in a Jim Crow military.

Jim Crow Fatigue

Two days before the United States declared victory over Japan, Second Sergeant James F. Scott sent a letter to the NAACP. Like many other letters addressed to the NAACP in the months before and after the war's end, Scott's letter reported blacks' resistance to the widespread discrimination and violence they faced on and near camps and bases. Newly returned from combat in Europe and bound for battle in the South Pacific, Scott expressed black men's collective frustration with "obeying Jim Crow." "I've tried to be a good soldier and perform every duty before us," he wrote. "We [helped] destroy our enemy, the 'Master Race of Germany.'" He was prepared to fight on the beaches in the South Pacific, but he and the other soldiers in infantry battalions stationed at Camp Bowie, Texas, feared "facing the dreadful laws" of the state more. Local residents terrorized the soldiers and forced them to remain on base. The conditions on the post were no better. When the men attempted to see a movie at the base's theater, attendants forcefully refused to admit them and told them they had "a theater of our own." For Scott, the refusal to seat the men did not "make the Constitution, the words, 'Give me liberty or Give me death,' or any other right which America stands [for] look very good."[8] Scott's questions about the diminution of his civil rights after he helped fight a war were not unusual.[9]

Military officials stressed that their use of quotas for blacks and aggressive efforts to ensure their segregation, practices they called the "Negro Policy," did not depart from America's racial order, especially in the South. By the war's end, the military sustained its recruitment quota of blacks in each service at 10 percent, and most military bases remained rigidly segregated. Base commanders set aside separate barracks, mess, and recreation areas for black troops, and few posts created equal facilities. Overwhelmingly assigned to labor units, black soldiers and sailors lived on bases in every region of the United States, but the majority of troops were concentrated on posts in the South. When black troops went to northern posts or posts overseas, the military's segregation policies followed. These military policies frequently mandated or expanded segregation in the surrounding communities. As the war ended, the military continued these regulations and practices.

Throughout the war, African Americans soldiers, sailors, and Marines used riots and melees to protest these racial policies. At Camp Claiborne in central Louisiana, soldiers rioted after local civilians in nearby Forest Hills in Rapides Parish shot several soldiers. During the riots, state and local officials patrolled the nearby woods and attacked soldiers; on base, military police and officers punched and kicked soldiers. When a mob later lynched a soldier accused of raping a white woman, black troops rioted again. Many soldiers believed the woman's claim needed a fair investigation, not "southern justice," and they rioted. At Fort Lawton, Washington, black soldiers objected to the heavily policed segregation they faced while hundreds of Italian POWs moved freely about the base and town. Provoked by the military police, the soldiers reportedly attacked the barracks of the prisoners. Dozens were charged with killing two prisoners.[10]

While the NAACP viewed these confrontations as consequences of local tensions, the association also considered these riots as responses to the abuse white officers and troops perpetrated against black and other nonwhite troops. The military's "Negro Policy" was not simply an effort to maintain American segregation but a far more elaborate part of the institution's establishment of racial hierarchies to maintain order and discipline of all troops, a tactic used since the nineteenth century. The military's "Negro Policy" was the most enduring.[11] During his tour of the South Pacific in late 1944, Walter White learned about the incessant punishment meted out to black Marines and soldiers. On Guam, he discovered many white officers and enlisted men alike took pleasure in provoking blacks. Racial taunting and terrorizing were part of the charged discourse used to prepare troops for combat against the Japanese military. White confirmed what he had long argued to War Department officials: Racial abuse against blacks in the military was an organized and "deliberate campaign to defame" them and prove their unfitness for service. But White observed more as he defended sixty-nine navy seamen charged with mutiny in Guam. After weeks of attacks, the men "rebelled against being made the target of constant abuse, including the throwing of live hand grenades at them." The sailors claimed commanders allowed the white Marines to stalk them. Troops had little recreation and monotonous rations, and this sanctioned behavior provided white men with entertainment, much like the lynching and torment of blacks in the segregated South provided whites with "fun."[12]

Fearing black troops' morale would plummet just as tens of thousands readied to go into combat in the European and Pacific Theaters, the War Department banned segregation in army post exchanges (PXs), theaters, and buses.[13] The majority of base commanders did not inform troops and commanders about the directive, and most troops learned about the order when news appeared on the front pages of black weeklies. Out of frustration, soldiers wrote the NAACP and asked for clarification, and the association affirmed the army's circular. Roy Wilkins suggested to one soldier "that in view of this sweeping order, you and other American soldiers of your race take full advantage of these War Department facilities, knowing that your rights are protected in so doing."[14] Some base commanders ignored the order or refused to post the memorandum; others announced the policy in derisive ways, giving what one soldier at Fort Benning, Georgia, described as a "southern interpretation." Letters from black soldiers, some with multiple signatures, testified to commanders' refusal to implement the order. Because the order allowed broad interpretation to fit "local conditions," the War Department determined soldiers had no grounds for complaint.[15]

Galvanized by the order, black soldiers pressed for admittance to all base facilities, but most found their access to theaters and clubs limited or denied. Leland Jones was refused a ticket at the Amarillo Army Air Field theater because "the colored section was sold out." He insisted he had a right to a seat and was finally admitted. As soon as he walked through the doors of the theater, military police arrested him and held him for an hour before he was released without charges.[16] Jesse O. Dedmon, the new NAACP secretary of veterans' affairs, sent a letter of inquiry to the executive commander of field operations for the Army Air Corps at Amarillo. The base commander, Colonel S. V. Satterfield, informed Dedmon that segregation did not exist in the theaters "since blocks of seats were reserved at two of the theaters for the use of particular squadrons." So numerous were soldiers' complaints that Leslie Perry, assistant to NAACP secretary Walter White, advised White to consider "placing a copy [of the order] in the hands of every person who will investigate these posts."[17]

Many camp commanders used a variety of methods to circumvent the policy. Some responded to the integration order by closing the camp and post theaters and then relocated entertainment to other halls where segregation still existed. At Eglin Field near Fort Walton Beach, Florida, commanders sent black soldiers to additional training during their free time; others barred black troops from areas of the camp where white soldiers had recreation facilities. On bases with several theaters, base commanders assigned the segregated units to a particular theater, typically the least desirable. On a base with only one theater, the commander restricted black troops to a makeshift outdoor theater. Many posts established pass systems, which restricted blacks to "the colored area."[18]

White soldiers occasionally joined blacks in the protests against these restrictions. Herman Recht witnessed a brawl at Camp Peary, Virginia, when hundreds of sailors attended a movie, including "3 or 400 Negroes." Military police "had instructions to segregate—whites to one side, Negroes at [the] other side of the theater (apparently no Negroes in center section)."

The police lost control of the process when blacks and whites sat where they pleased. When the police attempted to segregate the men, first approaching a black sailor, the man refused and fought back. He began "a general uproar, whites and Negroes started to get up. The Officer of the Day removed his pistol from its holster and started brandishing it." The start of the movie quieted the men; all remained in the seats of their own choosing.[19]

In addition to joining black men in their resistance to segregation, some white soldiers expressed their incredulity at these policies in the military press. Writing to *Yank*, one soldier commented how white and black soldiers held "a jam session." The next day, he "read an order which prohibits us to associate with the colored troops, 'except on business.'" He wondered why. "A colored tank outfit fought side by side with this regiment clear to Stayr, Austria, and we were never ordered not to fight alongside of American troops of the colored race." If black and white soldiers could fight and die together, was it right to order them to no longer play together?[20]

The military's insistence on spreading its segregation from bases into local communities especially angered black troops. Private Bert Barbero described to Langston Hughes how the military camp spread segregation in Pennsylvania where none had previously existed.[21] "Are my fellow men fighting and dying in vain?" he asked. Leonard Jackson, too, wrote Hughes for advice about protesting segregation on and off a naval base in California. Over the next weeks Jackson documented the spread of segregation in areas around the base. In late July 1945, he informed Hughes that signs soon appeared warning blacks not to patronize particular stores.[22] Even as many members in communities near bases strongly endorsed military segregation, some individuals and organizations embraced the desegregation orders for the bases as an opportunity to extend integration into soldiers' activities off base. In Fayetteville, North Carolina, W. P. Ryan, a Catholic priest and a longtime member of the NAACP, held integrated church services but was then ordered to stop. He persisted, claiming the autonomy of his church over military policy, which drew the ire of the base commander.[23]

Black enlisted personnel were not alone in their protests against the violence and segregation. When white commanders at Freeman Field, Indiana, ordered the men in the 477th Bombardment Group, the first all-black bomber unit, to use the separate club for black officers, a policy that violated the army's ban on segregation, the men sought counsel from the NAACP. In a letter to the Dayton, Ohio, NAACP, the men detailed the variety of restrictions Colonel Robert R. Seleway imposed on the base and in the town. Seleway purposely ignored the army's ban on post segregation and, instead, removed club facilities set aside for enlisted men and reassigned them as the "negro officers club." Stripped of their club, the black enlisted men had to use a separate USO club in nearby Seymour, Indiana, which had been a stable, and the odor of horses lingered. Because Seleway reportedly instructed local businesses to refuse service to the men, they remained confined to the segregated club.

In April 1945, sixty black officers defied the ban on their use of the officers' club. Military police immediately arrested the men. As these men were arrested, another group entered the club, and their arrests immediately followed. Over the next days, groups of officers entered the banned club and faced arrest. These mass arrests captured national attention. Many of the men had served overseas and received the Distinguished Flying Cross. The officers mounted a disciplined protest throughout the month as squads of men continued to enter the banned club after others had been arrested. That month alone, the military made 162 arrests, and some men had multiple arrests. The majority of the men faced a court-martial, though the NAACP managed to secure the release of all but two. Faced with heavy scrutiny from the black press and civil rights organizations, the Army Air Corps removed Seleway and assigned Colonel Benjamin O. Davis Jr., then the highest-ranking black officer in the military, as the unit's commander.[24]

At the war's end, all troops generally demanded more access to recreation, and with more black troops returned to U.S. bases, commanders' policies of segregation expanded and hardened despite the army's policies or local practices. NAACP branch secretary R. H. Hines reported from Amarillo, Texas, that before the arrival of troops, whites and blacks sat wherever they pleased in the town's new theater. Then the military arrived and forced its policies of segregation onto the town. "Recently," Hines wrote, "a small section [of the theater] has been cut off for Negro soldiers [from Amarillo Field], and when this is filled, no more Negro soldiers are admitted," even when there were vacant seats. With no access to recreation on or off base, the restrictions in the movie theater created what Private Bernard Perry described as a "grave situation." Some confrontations over segregation became violent. At a camp in Tennessee, MPs reportedly brandished submachine guns and ordered black officers, including high-ranking officers, out of a post theater because they sat in the section for officers instead of in the segregated section.[25]

Camp Investigations

The NAACP hoped that the end of the war and the mass demobilization of troops would diminish the number of black troops on bases overall and liberalize military policies of segregation, but the flood of letters from soldiers indicated conditions continued to deteriorate. Fearing more race riots, the association considered how to prevent these deadly confrontations, like those that had erupted at Camp Clairborne and Fort Lawton. Walter White decided to investigate the camps, but a visit to each of the thousands of camps, bases, and facilities appeared beyond the association's resources. Further, the War Department restricted access to most of these camps, and many were not open to the public. Still, the association hoped that the military might allow local branches to investigate some of the camps. Leslie Perry expressed confidence that "word will be passed down from the War Department to the post commander requesting that courtesies be extended."[26] He drafted an elaborate questionnaire for investigators to use and included what to look for, what buildings to investigate, and whom to interview. He especially pressed the investigators to ask, "Is Order No. 97 prohibiting segregation in recreational facilities posted and complied with?"[27]

The number of camps and their wide geographic dispersal prompted the NAACP to confine its investigation to a dozen camps and only those on a list decided by Walter White. Leslie Perry planned to visit these camps, and the national office sent letters asking branches near other army posts to send someone to investigate. Late in December, White mailed a final questionnaire and a letter to twenty-one branches near military bases. The national association asked branches located in an area with many bases, such as Baltimore, Maryland, which had five, to make multiple visits. By April, only the Baltimore branch had investigated and sent information about three camps. Gregory Hawkins, an attorney in Baltimore, found gaining access to the bases difficult or impossible; he resorted to interviewing "soldiers on the streets" about the local camp conditions. He discovered, too, that his escort on one post easily evaded questions about soldiers' access to, and the conditions of, recreation. A "personable young officer" showed Hawkins a "fine looking theater," but not the one black soldiers used. He was told "there was a PX and movies over in their own area." Hawkins saw nothing objectionable about the clean grounds and airy buildings white soldiers used, but the black camp was off limits for his inspection.[28]

Soldiers' reports about the dangerous and segregated camp conditions continued to arrive. Startled that only two branches had investigated camps, Walter White compiled a list of camps with "a chief concentration of Negro troops" and asked Jesse O. Dedmon to conduct "an immediate investigation" of thirteen camps and one hospital. A lawyer from Tulsa, Oklahoma, Dedmon had served in the army as an officer, reaching the rank of captain before he was discharged. He planned to return to a law practice, but the NAACP immediately appointed him to organize the association's program for veterans. With more than 1 million black men and women in the military, Dedmon faced a monumental task, and he had no office staff. He immediately left to tour Fort Dix and Fort Monmouth in New Jersey.[29] He received a warm welcome on most bases, even effusive greetings on some. Acquiring accurate information from the personable young officers proved far more difficult. He observed firsthand the ingenious methods army commanders used to evade scrutiny of racial practices and compliance with the service's Memorandum 97.

Dedmon found uniformity in commanders' use of rigid racial policies on the largest camps, posts, and bases, particularly those in the South. Fort Bragg, North Carolina, and Fort Benning, Georgia, drew men from the Deep South and Tennessee. Both camps processed and trained close to 50,000 troops in 1943 and nearly double that number in 1944. At the time of Dedmon's investigation, the number of troops at each camp had dropped to half of the wartime high. Not surprisingly, these two bases presented the most egregious displays of racial restrictions. While the number of troops at Fort Bragg had dropped from 90,000 to 32,000, 4,000 of whom were African American, the practices of segregation had strengthened, not relaxed as White had hoped. There were few black officers, especially in the WACs. With the base no longer congested, white troops had access to more recreational and club facilities, whereas black troops were confined in more restrictive ways. No longer preparing soldiers for battle against the Nazis, commanders now argued for the "separation of the races." At Fort Benning, which was the largest of the training bases, commanders maintained separate facilities, including swimming pools, service clubs, and bus stations. In every instance, black troops used smaller, poorly equipped and maintained facilities. As the primary location for training black troops before they shipped out to Europe, the base still had a great deal of activity. Black troops in the parachute school were not allowed to complete the full training, as they were prevented from jumping fully equipped into a swimming pool used by the white soldiers. Before troops were shipped out, commanders placed black soldiers in the stockades, reportedly "to keep them from going AWOL, though policy is not followed for white soldiers," despite this group's high rate of disappearance before departure.[30]

Other camps in the South practiced similar restrictions. Camp Dale Mabry near Tallahassee, Florida, maintained full segregation, including in its hospital. Black wives of soldiers were put on the wards with male troops. Reports about the environment off base alarmed Dedmon. Civilian police regularly attacked soldiers, and the MPs ignored, even encouraged, these attacks. Camp MacDill, which was near Tampa, Florida, also had policies of strict segregation, and the commanders used a pass system to keep blacks out of areas considered "white," including training and living areas. German POWs policed the segregated mess halls. Black troops resisted these practices. In April 1945, hundreds of black troops from Camp Dale Mabry and Camp Gordon Johnson rioted as a protest against base and local segregation.[31]

On every base Dedmon investigated, he found few black officers. Those he interviewed described a sense of isolation and hostility from white officers. As a former officer, Dedmon displayed in his reports a visceral response to the spatial restrictions intended to humiliate African Americans. Only a handful of these bases had complete facilities for black officers; most required that the officers share facilities with black enlisted men, a policy white officers did not follow. At Camp Gordon Johnson, the black officers were not housed or messed and, instead, had to find their own facilities off base in nearby Carabelle, Florida. Tuskegee Airbase was fully integrated, but integration occurred only after commanders insisted that white personnel follow this policy. At Camp Planche near New Orleans, the white commander supported the policy of integrated base facilities, but it required him to police white behavior and take immediate action when he found violations. White officers were the most resistant, so he closed the officers' club to African Americans.[32]

Everywhere the harsh tactics used by MPs and their civilian allies tended to escalate difficulties. Melees and riots erupted with frequency near posts, camps, and bases. Black soldiers received frequent attacks from military and civilian police, often at the same time. That military police arrested greater numbers of black troops while leaving whites alone added to already explosive environments. As Dedmon completed his investigation, reports of attacks, provocations, and undue punishments against black soldiers continued. Soldiers stationed at Aberdeen Proving Ground, Maryland, reported that MPs aimed submachine guns at them "for psychological reasons."[33] The repeated occurrence of police attacks against soldiers near Fort Benning and other bases in Georgia prompted Marcus Ray, the civilian aide to the secretary of the War Department, to note that police brutality had become one of the "burrs of Georgia Army life." More generally, Ray observed, it was "difficult for the Army to change attitudes of local communities." This pessimistic assessment included, apparently, white soldiers' attacks on bases. Unwilling to enforce policy or mount a campaign to change attitudes, army commanders ordered black soldiers to obey local and base Jim Crow policies or face a court-martial.[34]

Jim Crow Shock

The frustration, anger, and humiliation felt by black soldiers, Marines, and sailors manifested in individual and collective acts of resistance, some violent. Individual soldiers struck, punched, and kicked officers, military police, and white soldiers; others disobeyed orders and went AWOL. They organized work stoppages, brawls, riots, and protests. As frequently, blacks harmed themselves, in acts ranging from self-injury to suicide. Along with the violence and humiliation particularly reserved for blacks, other systems of racial control, from the distribution of labor to the differences in punishment, shaped blacks' resistances to the wartime and postwar military. Many harbored a deep resentment when they did not see opportunity, mobility, and dignity for their discipline and efforts. As many faced violence and discrimination on and off base, their resentment and resistance escalated.[35]

Whether belligerent or despondent, Langston Hughes noted, soldiers suffered from "Jim Crow Shock." Many black soldiers found facing Jim Crow in the South worse than the encounter with the enemy in the South Pacific or Germany. "Here in our own Dixieland," Hughes wrote in his weekly *Chicago Defender* column, the military subjected black soldiers to segregation, and "some go off the beam." Hughes understood why many blacks resisted discrimination in the military by striking white officers and enlisted men or refusing to ride in segregated transportation. The soldier who "struck a white officer, . . . might have been merely a case of Jim Crow shock, too much discrimination—segregation fatigue, which to a sensitive Negro can be just as damaging as days of heavy bombardment or a continuous barrage of artillery fire." Ordered "to fight for one's country for months on some dangerous and vital front" and then to "be subjected to the irritations and humiliations of Jim Crow" drove "sensitive, patriotic colored American[s] NUTS." Hughes suggested the army should specifically treat black soldiers for segregation fatigue to prevent "a Jim Crow breakdown." In turn, Hughes urged that black troops feeling such fatigue "coming on" should "rush to the post hospital right away for expert advice from a psychiatrist."[36] Hughes's appropriation of psychiatric language and diagnoses to describe blacks' "sensitivity" to segregation as similar to battle shock arose from black soldiers' repeated claim that their struggle against Jim Crow in the military was really a war. The American South was the second front, where withstanding segregation was no different from withstanding the enemy's bombardment in the South Pacific.

Many black soldiers, sailors, and Marines described their encounter with segregation as one of horror and dislocation. Private Archie Gittens noted that his posting to Dale Mabry Field in Tallahassee, Florida, made him feel as if he had arrived "in another world, no longer in the United States." In addition to the stark signs of Jim Crow, Gittens witnessed brutal beatings of black soldiers. Born and reared in New York, Gittens found these almost daily occurrences particularly horrific. Near a mental collapse and no longer able "to take it anymore," Gittens "ran away" and returned home. How he managed this long journey is not clear. Shortly after he arrived, his mother and others, including Doxey Wilkerson, editor of the *People's Voice*, urged him to return to his base. "They have made me understand that this is no way to fight against discrimination in the Army, that I should return to camp and be a good soldier, and let the people in civilian life carry on the fight for democratic equality in the armed forces, and everyplace else." The army declared Gittens AWOL.[37]

Viewing segregation as not just unequal and unpatriotic, but physically and psychologically injurious as well, became a widespread charge by civil rights advocates. During his furlough in April 1944, Private Norman Spaulding slashed his wrists in his Washington, D.C., home. Rushed to the hospital, Spaulding reported that he decided to commit suicide as a way to call attention to the segregated army. Two years earlier, Spaulding had made a "pact" with two friends "to commit suicide on the steps of the capitol as a way to arouse public opinion." Refused admittance to training for the Army Air Corps because it had reached its racial quota, Spaulding first went on a hunger strike and then slashed his wrists.[38] How many black soldiers described suffering under the military's segregation as an impetus to commit suicide is not known, but many did report that segregation deeply affected their morale. Soldiers expressed the despair they felt in their work done under demeaning conditions that seemed to be reserved for black troops, including the poor camp facilities, limited recreation, and daily humiliation. Sergeant Thurman Dillard wrote Langston Hughes that he neared a psychic collapse. "Physically I feel okay. But mentally, I am very miserable. The accumulated strain of doing two-and-a-half year's work that I detest is exerting an almost intolerable pressure." He stressed he could not allow himself the "luxury of going to pieces." Other soldiers, he noted, "may 'go over the hill,' kill somebody, commit suicide, or live irresponsibly from minute to minute, or simply do their work carelessly if it bores them."[39]

The national NAACP and local branches collected data on the military's mistreatment of soldiers and detailed the impact on their morale and psychological well-being. The repeated incidents of racial violence and segregation practiced and ignored by the U.S. Army, one Mississippi branch argued, created not just low morale but also fear, "affecting their effectiveness as soldiers." The local branch noted in its letter to the War Department that it "owes a duty to men in the armed forces to protect them from abuse and violence when it sends them into camps and strange surroundings. An attack on a soldier is an attack on the United States, whether perpetrated by a foreign or domestic enemy." The black GI was at war with, and a prisoner to, American segregation.[40]

As these patterns of military segregation and blacks' resistance to it continued after the war, some army psychiatrists did not disagree. Speaking at the American Psychiatric Association meeting in 1946, Major Rutherford Stevens Jr. described the army's segregation as a "constantly annoying emotional cancer" caused by discrimination. The inadequate facilities for black troops' recreation, "racial bigotry practiced in the nearby communities," and "fascist attitudes" by some white commanders needed more than treatment, these doctors concluded. The tumor of race discrimination needed to be excised.[41]

While some soldiers experienced psychological collapse in the face of such abuse, many more became radicalized. At Camp Crowder, Robert F. Williams lived in segregated and "dilapidated, tar-papered sheds," called "Shanty-town" by the soldiers. Williams's experiences in the segregated army at first made him introspective. Friends and his brother had served in combat in similar segregated conditions. "I wondered how a so-called civilized nation could do what America had done to us, and then force us to go to the other side of the world in a supposed conflict to save 'democracy.'" Williams decided that he "just wasn't going to let any white man have that much authority over me." Like some other black soldiers who resisted the military's racial practices, Williams repeatedly went AWOL and refused to obey orders. These defiances earned him status among black soldiers, but his commander charged him with insubordination and put him in the stockade for three months.[42] News from other soldiers with views similar to Williams's streamed into the NAACP. Evidence of blacks' resistance, documented in the increased incidences of melees and courts-martial, alarmed Walter White and Thurgood Marshall. The two men braced themselves for news of riots. Such occurrences posed difficulties for the association, as it had few resources to defend the soldiers.[43]

Before the war, blacks' struggles against the segregated military had acquired an organized form, and it continued throughout the war. This prewar agitation included the national mass effort of A. Philip Randolph and other civil rights activists, the March on Washington Movement (MOWM), which unsuccessfully pressured the federal government to allow equal enlistment of blacks and integration of the military. This effort and pressure from the NAACP resulted in the placement of black advisors in the War Department, including Truman Gibson and William H. Hastie, who eventually resigned in protest. After the war began, black civil rights organizations pressed the War Department to train blacks for combat units and include black women in the newly organized Women's Auxiliary Army Corps, which later became the WACs.

While these efforts yielded some gains, the military remained segregated. The navy and army relegated blacks to the lowest ranks and confined all but a few men and women to labor units. The Tuskegee Airmen were to fly as support units and as support to combat pilots. Only when the army and Marines needed more combat troops in the fall 1944 campaigns in Europe and the various campaigns in the Pacific did the War Department assign some black troops to combat units. Some white units in Europe temporarily integrated or fought alongside all-black units in a pattern that the army called "side-by-side" combat. Black pilots assumed the role of combat pilots as they flew over Europe. Black tank crews and gunnery units ably fought, sometimes in integrated units or in segregated units. While officials privately pronounced these "experiments" successful, black combat troops were returned to segregated units and labor assignments.

Despite postwar shortages of military personnel, many in the War Department remained resolute in sustaining its "Negro Policy," including its quota system. The army reduced the number of black troops in Europe from half a million to hundreds and assigned the overwhelming majority of these troops to labor and transportation battalions.[44] In response, northern senators and representatives, judges, and labor leaders joined civil rights organizations, including the NAACP, the National Negro Congress, and the National Council of Negro Women, to petition the president and the secretary of the War Department to consider "mixed" combat units and "full equality" for black troops.[45] Despite these appeals from civil rights organizations and ordinary citizens, the War Department refused to abandon its policy of segregation.[46]

As the coalition for a desegregated military grew, James O. Eastland, the staunch segregationist Mississippi senator, asserted on the Senate floor that blacks troops were "an utter and abysmal failure." Irate over blacks' demands in the South for the vote and the national effort to ensure their equal access to employment, Eastland meant his charges to bolster southern politicians' filibuster of the FEPC. Infuriated by the growing sentiment that black soldiers had made sacrifices during the war and now deserved "equal opportunity" and the "right to work," he challenged any effort to "give unfair preference against the white soldier." His harangues about blacks' innate inferiority turned to a denunciation of black combat units. "A high-ranking general informed me," he claimed, "that Negro troops would neither work nor fight." His arms flailed and his voice grew louder as he spoke to the few senators on the floor and the visitors in the gallery. Fellow Mississippi senator Theodore G. Bilbo joined Eastland. The FEPC, Bilbo thundered, was "a gigantic plot to Sovietize the United States." He, too, claimed to know that black troops deserted at high rates in combat, especially the 92nd Division. "The whole division, without cause, rhyme, or reason," he insisted, "quit fighting."[47]

While no senator on the floor that night rebutted the Mississippi senators' charges, in the days that followed the challenges erupted. Other senators noted that Eastland failed to consult with War Department officials, and his "facts were faulty." New York senator Robert F. Wagner quoted several generals, including Dwight D. Eisenhower, who said the soldiers had done well. General Ira Eaker, deputy commander of the Army Air Corps, praised black pilots.[48] War Department officials did not issue a statement, but some commanders of black combat units defended their troops. Major General M. S. Eddy, commander of one of the army corps units with the 761st Tank Battalion, told black correspondents that the men in the units "entered combat with such conscious courage and success." Others argued that use of black troops in combat had "increased manpower" and had been a "boon to the morale of our fighting men."[49]

Blacks' participation in combat had been largely invisible to most white Americans, and Eastland's remarks created a storm in the black press. Editors informed readers that Eastland embellished his remarks based on statements attributed to Truman Gibson, civilian aide to the secretary of war. Earlier, Gibson had claimed the 92nd Division "had failed in combat." Gibson made these allegations during a March press conference in Rome about the division "melting away," which prompted a roar of admonishment from the NAACP and the black press. In early June, the NAACP "censored" Gibson, who later claimed he quoted from reports he described as biased. Interviews with War Department officials led Gibson to conclude that commanders in the division believed "the Negro is panicky and his environment hasn't conditioned him to accept responsibilities." German and Italian soldiers' descriptions of the 92nd as "tough soldiers" and "gentleman liberators" were omitted from the reports, a point revealed in later testimony from military officials.[50]

The senators' claims and the many refutations sparked debate in the white dailies. Columnists in New York and California described Eastland's comments as fiction. Some white southerners denounced him for "race-baiting." Hodding Carter, editor of the *Greenville-Delta Times*, characterized the comments as "ill-timed and ill-advised."[51] Seventy-five percent of 251 white editors of papers in thirteen southern states "condemned the remarks."[52] Congressional representative Helen Gahagan Douglas offered the most extended response to Eastland and Bilbo. With half of voters in her district in Los Angeles African American—and many veterans—Douglas felt compelled to honor these men and challenge the allegations. While many of her Democratic and Republican colleagues considered the statements part of the history of racist vitriol expressed by Eastland and Bilbo, Douglas believed the men tapped into widely held racial stereotypes that limited blacks' participation in combat and stalled support for the FEPC. Curious about the extent of "the Negro record in war" largely ignored by the national press, Douglas requested information from the War Department. Over the next several weeks, the arrival of so many boxes of reports, much ignored by the white press and unknown by the majority of Americans, overwhelmed her. She wrote a sixty-page report about the courage and perseverance of men relegated to segregated units. She then delivered much of it on the House floor in early 1946. She prefaced her remarks with an explanation: "It is about the Negro soldier I wish to speak—to pay him respect and to expose the gratitude of the American people for his contribution to the greatest battle of all time. We should be especially mindful of the Negro soldier, remembering he shed his blood for a freedom he has not as yet been permitted to fully share."[53]

African Americans applauded Douglas's efforts and amended her remarks to emphasize the special burdens blacks experienced as they trained and fought in segregated units. Veteran John Robert Badger described her speech as "a roster of heroes, [b]ut the historian of the future will need to juxtapose these bright pates against many cloudy ones. He [sic] will have to represent the Negro's contribution to victory as a process of struggle, in which the contribution was made against numerous obstacles and efforts to prevent its being made." As Robert Jefferson has shown in his study of the 93rd Infantry Division during its station in the South Pacific, black soldiers resented the white press for ignoring their combat roles and the black press for overstating their roles: Neither group adequately addressed the struggles the men had as they were compelled to fight for and in segregation. Some black combat troops revealed how they went into combat poorly trained and badly equipped.[54]

Fearing the debate about blacks' roles in combat would unleash more fury from white segregationists and stall his postwar legislation, President Truman ordered the army to review its "Negro Policy." Lieutenant General Alvan C. Gillem Jr., former commanding general of the armed forces and commander of the 13th Corps in Europe, convened a board, named the Gillem Board, to determine the army's future use of black troops. The War Department directed the board to determine how to utilize black officers in the postwar period. As the army's labor shortages continued, this narrow focus widened to include consideration of how the army might adapt its "Negro Policy" to the demands of the postwar military. The War Department wanted "a broad policy for utilization of Negro manpower in the military establishment, including the development of means required in the event of a national emergency." Board members included Brigadier General Benjamin O. Davis and Major General E. M. Almond, commander of the 92nd Division. Over the next weeks, the board called in experts, ordered senior officers from overseas, and collected data from numerous sources, including educational, industrial, and social policy experts. In addition, it utilized reports about the mixed-race combat units that fought during the invasion and later in Germany. Walter White, Will Alexander, A. A. (Sandy) Liveright from the American Council on Race Relations, and Charles Houston, who directed the NAACP Legal Defense, gave testimonies. Jesse O. Dedmon and Leslie S. Perry, assistant to White, also attended these meetings.[55]

When Walter White spoke before the board in late October, he pressed for immediate and full integration. The military's present policy of segregation, he insisted, endorsed whites' superiority and created black "resentment." Informed by discussions with officers, troops, and military officials, White knew many believed segregation hampered the military's efficiency; he knew some State Department officials considered American segregation a burden to diplomatic efforts. White reported what puzzled Europeans most when he toured Europe in 1944: "If the United States is really fighting for democracy why does it send two armies, one white and one black?" Segregation, he argued, was not "equal opportunity." Third-rate white officers, "many of whom failed in other units," commanded black units. Many commanders, including senior officers who commanded the 92nd Division, despised blacks and believed them racially inferior, no matter their education and skills. These attitudes and policies, he argued, deprived black officers of the "highest caliber [of] the chance to lead."[56] He revealed that some in the War Department, including its secretary, Robert B. Patterson, expressed qualified support to end segregation in key areas, including the Veterans' Administration hospitals, aviation training, and the assignment of black officers in the army to lead black or mixed units.[57]

Shortly after their appearances before the board, White, Perry, and William H. Hastie debated whether or not its members seriously considered integration of the army. Did the board intend to influence American social policy or make an empty gesture? Hastie expressed little confidence that the Gillem Board would challenge the racial status quo. From experience, he expected the board to insist it had "interest only in the use of Negro personnel in the Army and, therefore, could very properly say that matters involving the relations between the races in the [S]outh" fall outside "the scope of the Committee." Perry suggested the association pressure the board and "issue a statement saying in effect that it will oppose peace time military training and urge the Army be limited to its pre-war size, unless the Armed Services takes these, and the other forward steps we suggested during the conference." He predicted "the drive for post-war military training" would "gather momentum" and aid their pressure.[58]

In the weeks before the board issued its report, the black weeklies interpreted the hearings as the start of the military's integration. "Army to End Jim Crow!" the *Defender* proclaimed on its front page in late 1945. Veteran war reporter Venice T. Spraggs, now the weekly's Washington, D.C., correspondent, reported that the board's four generals were "expected to recommend an end to the army's policy of segregation." Spraggs conceded that he based his claim on "conjecture from several premises," including Truman Gibson's statement to the Capital Press Club that the board seemed poised to abandon its prewar and wartime policies of segregation. General Dwight D. Eisenhower's appointment as army chief of staff suggested the service now had someone who had closely observed black and white troops' "side-by-side" combat. Eisenhower's favorable public statements about black troops' performance in integrated combat units added to rumors that the Gillem Board might recommend an end to the army's "Negro Policy."[59]

Despite the absence of such a recommendation when the War Department released the board's recommendations in early March, the committee acknowledged that African Americans had to have a role in the military. The black weeklies and the northern major dailies initially characterized the overall tone of the recommendations as providing "wider" and "fuller" opportunities for black troops. The *Chicago Daily Tribune* hoped the army might offer "Negro troops a larger role." The *New York Times* described the report as "advancement" and a "trend toward eliminating segregation." The black weeklies went further and initially considered the report a signal advance for blacks' full citizenship. The *Chicago Defender* published the entire text of the report on its front page.[60]

Despite applause from the black press, the committee's report moved little beyond the army's wartime policies, and the service renewed its commitment to segregated units.[61] Perhaps the initial enthusiasm from the press was a response to the board's acknowledgment that military policy had to address the presence of black troops. But the board's report recited long-held racial stereotypes, insisting blacks had "underdeveloped" skills and "poor" leadership qualities, which limited their opportunities for officer training. The board lauded the quota system and claimed it prevented the army's ranks from being inundated with "inferior" enlistees and draftees. The War Department policies, then, "should point towards a long-range objective which visualizes over a period of time, a still greater utilization of this manpower potential in the military machine of the nation." The report did not explicitly acknowledge army segregation, and it did not recommend the War Department abandon its "Negro Policy." As he had feared, William H. Hastie noted to White that the army managed to avoid the implications of its own policies and maintain the status quo. Despite its "promise" to use all Americans in the nation's defense, Hastie concluded, the army never intended to challenge the military's segregation or the restrictions on black citizenship generally.[62]

Although it expressed no interest in ending segregation of blacks and Puerto Ricans in the army, the board urged "comprehensive study" of black labor available to the military. As 10 percent of the population, the committee noted, African Americans provided "the manpower reservoir available for use in time of peace or in the event of a National Emergency." Admitting publicly what others had claimed to the press, the board acknowledged that black troops proved capable in combat. Most important, reports from the field demonstrated that black troops, when well trained, performed with "distinction" in combat. The board recommended a wider use of black combat units based on models of equal preparation and side-by-side combat.[63] Even here the board avoided the word "integration."

Ignoring that the majority of black Americans lived and worked under segregation, board members insisted they had an obligation to participate in the military. "The Negro is a bona fide citizen enjoying the privileges conferred by citizenship under the Constitution. By the same token, he must defend his country in time of national peril. The Negro is ready and eager to accept his full responsibility as a citizen." The report then concluded that because blacks should "accept legal and moral responsibility charged by the Constitution," they should prepare for military service. In turn, the military must provide "all steps necessary to prepare the qualified manpower of the nation so it will function efficiently" during a war. Rather than change the army's "Negro Policy," the board recommended that African Americans must "morally and legally" participate in a segregated military.[64]

For the NAACP and other mainstream civil rights organizations, the report reaffirmed a segregated military. William H. Hastie characterized the recommendations of the Gillem Board as less than a half step. "The discussion of the basic difficulties involved in the efficient utilization of Negro soldiers is summarized by the statement 'Environment and lack of administrative and educational advantages in prewar days greatly handicap the Negro in performance of his war time duties.'" Jesse Dedmon noted that the report did not call for integration and instead endorsed continued segregation and segregated facilities. To the NAACP, the board's recommendation to use side-by-side units really meant segregated and separate. Most troubling, the board did not recommend the training and integration of black officers "into staff and field commands." Both Dedmon and Leslie Perry viewed the army's insistence on retaining the quota system to be another significant flaw. All of the men objected to the board's silence on the violence against black soldiers on and off bases. "It gives the Army a clean bill of health," Perry noted. He nonetheless welcomed the recommendation to use black troops in combat. "It's a desirable departure from labor battalions. Moreover, it gives Negro troops greater feeling of manhood."[65]

White and others in the national association's office amended their initial enthusiasm for the army's investigation. The totality of the recommendations and the board's emphasis on national preparedness and utilization of "Negro Manpower" under terms similar to its wartime policies led White, Hastie, and others to conclude the army now had official language that would prevent integration and allow them to better manage segregation. Even as it applauded the use of blacks in combat units, the NAACP could not insist on making the army's segregation more manageable. If African Americans were to remain part of the military, then the association had to agitate for its integration. During the months the Gilliam Board met, violence against black veterans and men and women in uniform escalated. If the newly formed Department of Defense did not intend to protect these men and women, the association was determined to make the nation aware of the military's segregation and the violence against African Americans that these policies engendered.

Bus Battles

Until late 1944, the military did not manage its own bus and train services, requiring its personnel to travel on buses and trains owned and operated by private companies that mandated rules of segregated travel, whether on or off base. Even after the army issued its 1944 order to integrate buses on bases, commanders in the South maintained segregation. Many soldiers, especially those unfamiliar with the rules and practices of segregation, found travel on Jim Crow trains and buses to be dangerous and humiliating. One soldier, born and raised outside the South, described a Jim Crow train to his family. "The train ride was long and tiresome. Jim Crow coaches are probably the dirtiest, stuffiest trains in existence. They are always over-crowded and under-aired. It is a marvel that people can travel any distance in them and survive."[66] Military train travel was little better. Jesse Johnson, an officer, noted that as blacks "traveled around the country and overseas, the maze of laws and customs was always confusing, bewildering, and morale shattering." When Robert F. Williams was transferred with his unit from Fort Bragg to Camp Crowder in late July 1945, he traveled on a segregated military train. The military reserved two rear cars for black troops. The white soldiers received hot meals, while the black soldiers ate cold sandwiches. When the train stopped, the white soldiers received hot coffee and doughnuts from the Red Cross. Train officials joined the white officers in insisting that the black men stay on the train. "You think you're going to have a white woman serve you doughnuts and coffee?" the conductor asked. "Not here, you're not."[67]

During and after the war, buses and trains became the epicenter in the second front as black soldiers, sailors, and Marines resisted the arbitrary and humiliating rules of Jim Crow. Birmingham's buses during the war, as Robin Kelley has documented, became "theaters" of conflict, even "war zones."[68] The spectacle of combat became a daily occurrence elsewhere in the South where concentrations of black soldiers moved between military and civilian buses. Black soldiers, officers and enlisted men alike, chafed against the military's segregation orders. Jesse Johnson, a newly commissioned officer, shared the rules and humiliations of segregation with other African Americans. Ordered to the rear of buses on bases, he overheard men bitterly banter about the Jim Crow transportation. Jokes and plans to resist were part of the travel dialogue, but the men stood or sat coiled and ready to take action.[69] Soldiers' struggles on these buses were part of a larger pattern of resistance against segregation taking place on or around bases. The murder of Private Edward Green, killed March 14, 1944, by a bus driver in Alexandria, Louisiana, occurred in a period when there were numerous struggles over repressive policies at nearby Camp Claiborne. Green's death was followed by the lynching of a soldier accused of rape; riots and mutiny erupted soon after in August.[70]

After commanders ignored Memorandum 97, which ordered the end of segregated buses, soldiers rebelled. At Fort Hood, Texas, Lieutenant Jackie Robinson, who would go on to become the first African American player in major league baseball, was aware of the memorandum when he refused the bus driver's order to move "to the back of the bus." Robinson insisted on his right to stay seated. His commander charged Robinson with insubordination, disturbing the peace, drunkenness, conduct unbecoming an officer, and refusing to obey the lawful orders of a superior officer. He was also accused of "insulting" a white woman. Robinson sat next to Elizabeth Poitevint, the wife of another black officer. She "looked white" to the bus driver, who instigated the arrest. With the local NAACP inundated with requests for counsel, Robinson relied on three army lawyers eager to defend him. Robinson, they argued, faced unwarranted harassment and arrest because the bus driver found him "uppity." Robinson, they insisted, claimed his rights determined by the War Department. Acquitted, Lt. Robinson was successful in his case, but the majority of soldiers who "determined their rights" rarely prevailed.[71]

Protests by individual blacks on base buses sometimes grew to include others. Herbert Gross recalled that when a black Marine boarded the base bus at Camp Lejeune in North Carolina, he took a seat in the front. "He was dressed beautifully, starched and everything. I think this Marine was from up north" and did not know the "rules of Jim Crow." The bus driver ordered him to the rear, but two white Marines sitting in the front near the man moved to the back of the bus in protest. The bus driver ordered them to the front, and they refused. The men looked ready to resist, and the black Marine left the bus, afraid for his own safety and afraid the white soldiers might riot.[72]

After the war, resistance by black soldiers continued on civilian buses where drivers retained the power to determine the rules of segregation and make arrests. Many drivers carried weapons, including pistols, billy clubs, and knives. The demarcation between seats on buses designated "colored" and "white" was fluid and often arbitrary. Drivers typically moved signs back to favor white passengers. As whites boarded buses, drivers ordered black passengers to stand or leave the bus, even when seats were available in the area marked "colored." Buses typically left black passengers stranded, even when they had paid for their tickets. African Americans disagreed with these practices, and many verbally skirmished with drivers and white passengers.[73] Soldiers or soldiers on leave traveled in uniform, and they frequently instigated or sustained these struggles.

African Americans newly discharged from the military were especially vulnerable to the vagaries of the Jim Crow system. Whites perceived the pride displayed by blacks in uniform and the respect they received from other blacks as acts of arrogance and defiance. Sometimes blacks and whites in uniform expressed camaraderie. When blacks traveled in uniform—many simply did not have other clothes—they faced accusations of misconduct and disorderly behavior. Bus drivers and passengers attacked and assaulted them. Police arbitrarily arrested them. On February 12, 1946, Isaac Woodard returned from combat in New Guinea and the Philippines, where he had served with the 429th Port Battalion. He received his discharge at Camp Gordon in Georgia. Still in uniform, Woodard bought a bus ticket to return home to New York. The bus stopped just past the border of Georgia and South Carolina, and Woodard asked the driver to wait while he used the restroom. The bus driver grumbled that he "didn't have time to wait." Woodard demanded that the driver "talk to me like I am talking to you. I am a man just like you." Though the driver waited and then continued on, when the bus arrived in Batesburg, South Carolina, the driver instructed local police to arrest Woodard "for disturbing the bus." As the discharged soldier began to dispute the driver's claim, one of the policemen struck Woodard across the face with his billy club and twisted his arm. When Woodard attempted to defend himself from the blows by grabbing the club, other police officers joined in knocking the soldier unconscious. When Woodard later "came to," the police continued to hit him. One of the officers used "the end of his billy," repeatedly "driving it into" Woodard's eyes. By the next morning, Woodard's eyes were swollen and he could no longer see. The repeated jabbing of the club into his eyes severely ruptured both corneas and caused irreparable damage. Woodard lost his eyesight permanently and was declared legally blind.[74]

Military and civilian police showed no restraint in beating or accosting women in uniform for violating Jim Crow on trains and buses. Many black women in the military refused to yield to segregation, and authorities considered their uniforms and insignia added provocation. When Marguritta Nicholson, a WAC stationed at Fort Jackson, South Carolina, was beaten on a train, her offense was that she had failed to observe the arbitrary lines of Jim Crow. The car she boarded in Pennsylvania became a whites-only car sometime after the train passed the Mason Dixon line. By then she had fallen asleep. She was awakened, arrested in Hamlet, North Carolina, and taken to jail, where the chief of police slapped and kicked her.[75]

Black women continued to assert their rights after their arrests. Helen Smith, Tommie D. Smith, and Georgia Doson, all of them WACs, sat in the "whites only" waiting room in the Elizabethtown, Kentucky, bus station after they found the "colored waiting room" overcrowded. Two white civilian policemen ordered the women to move, but all refused. The men clubbed the women with nightsticks and then arrested them. When the women returned to Godman Field and reported the incident to their commander, Colonel Throckmorton, he reprimanded them for disobeying local segregation laws and then charged them with disorderly conduct. Two officers on the court-martial board disqualified themselves and defended the women. The officers investigated and discovered the state had no specific laws stipulating segregation in waiting rooms and terminals, but the women were charged with disorderly conduct anyway. The NAACP branch president, H. J. McKinney, noted that whites in the town regularly intimidated blacks, especially soldiers. The Louisville NAACP and the local International Labor Defense group joined in the support for the women, and they were finally acquitted.[76]

Throughout the war and in the months after its end, local branches and the national NAACP received inquiries from soldiers and families reporting mysterious circumstances surrounding the deaths of husbands and sons in the United States and Europe. Initially, reports of the disappearances and murders of blacks in the South garnered attention only in the black press and received little in the national media. Thurgood Marshall lobbied the Department of Justice and the War Department for investigations into these beatings, murders, and disappearances. Even with evidence, both agencies failed to bring charges against anyone. The Justice Department endorsed legislation that made it a crime to kill or harm men and women in uniform, but neither the War Department nor the Department of Defense considered policy to protect black men and women in uniform from racial assaults.[77]

As dozens of black soldiers and veterans were assaulted and killed during fracases on buses, the NAACP pressed for a national investigation. All of the victims were men. Bus drivers shot most of the men; others were killed by police officers called to arrest the soldiers for violating Jim Crow policies. Policemen and bus drivers accused the soldiers and Marines of some form of "loud talking" or cursing, a charge particular to African Americans that dated to the post–Civil War South and resulted in their arrests or deadly assaults. When soldiers engaged in such behavior on base and against superiors, it led to courts-martial for insubordination and disobeying orders. While soldiers commented that whites "deliberately" provoked them into anger, which then led to punishments and arrests, they also used cursing—individually and collectively—as a form of verbal skirmish to intimidate and claim their rights. These verbal skirmishes erupted off base. Booker Spicely, stationed at Camp Butner, was killed by a bus driver on July 8, 1944, in Durham, North Carolina. The numerous witnesses to the assault included black and white passengers and two black and two white soldiers. All of the soldiers helped Spicely harangue the driver. In another deadly encounter the next year in late November, W. Parrot, a town officer in Johnsonville, South Carolina, murdered veteran St. Clair Pressley. Timothy Hood was shot and killed by Brighton chief of police G. B. Fant in early February 1946 in Bessemer, Alabama. Hood grew angry when bus driver W. R. Weeks moved a sign; Hood then hit Weeks and attracted the attention of Fant, who shot him.[78]

As the number of assaults against and murders of black veterans rose sharply, much of the NAACP's attention turned to the murders of blacks in uniform and veterans. Twelve murders occurred between late July and late August 1946, and the majority of the victims were veterans or their relatives. Added to these deaths were floggings, whippings, beatings, and other assaults against blacks, particularly in the South. The *Chicago Defender* reported that the "suppression of crime, when the victim is a Negro gave rise to the belief that many more unknown black bodies may be lying in the swamps, bayous, and open fields of a seething southland."[79] What was considered a "southern problem" soon proved to have no specific geography. Between November 1946 and late February the following year, at least four black veterans were murdered outside the South.

The murder of two brothers in Long Island, New York, garnered national attention. Early on February 5, 1946, Freeport, Long Island, patrolman Joseph Romeika stopped Charles and Alfonso Ferguson. He then shot and killed them. Charles, twenty-seven, a World War II veteran and the father of three young children, had newly reenlisted; his brother, Alfonso, twenty-five, was a veteran. The bullet that killed Charles Ferguson ricocheted and wounded Joseph, a third brother and a navy seaman. Romeika claimed the shootings were in self-defense, that Charles threatened he had a gun in his pocket and gestured for it. All the men, he claimed, cursed and shouted at him.[80]

Though charged with disorderly conduct, a fourth brother, Richard Ferguson, and other witnesses told a different story. The men went out to a bar to celebrate before Charles departed for Europe. As they walked to the bus station, they stopped for coffee at a small shop owned by a man known to refuse service to blacks.[81] The owner served coffee to others, but he refused the men's request. Charles grew angry, and his brothers hurried him out of the shop. They then headed toward the bus terminal for their return to nearby Roosevelt. Along the way, Charles cursed and spoke loudly, but to no one in particular. As the men entered the station, Joseph Romeika pulled his gun and ordered the men to put their hands up and stand against the wall. Charles and Alfonso cursed and "loud talked," but all of the men complied immediately. Romeika kicked Charles in the groin and then shot him in the head; he then shot Alfonso, who later died. Romeika kicked Joseph, too, who was wounded by the same bullet that had instantly killed Charles.[82]

The Freeport police feared a race riot, cordoned off the area, and quickly removed the men. Transported to a nearby hospital, the gravely wounded

Alfonso died. Police placed the wounded Joseph in the Freeport jail and questioned him for several hours. Pained, pressured, and without counsel, Joseph claimed that Charles said he "might have a .45." Only then did police take Joseph to the hospital. Again without counsel, he signed a statement that he witnessed Charles threaten Romeika. The police charged Richard with disorderly conduct; within hours after his arrest, he stood trial without a lawyer, a jury, or defense witnesses. The judge declared him guilty and sentenced him to pay a $100 fine or spend 100 days in jail. He insisted his older brother Charles did not have a gun and did not threaten Romeika; his cursing had been "just talk," not a specific threat.[83] Other witnesses corroborated Richard's statement, but despite the inconsistencies, the district attorney determined Romeika shot Charles in self-defense.

As details of the case became known in and around Long Island and New York City, labor, veterans, and civil rights organizations organized protests and demanded a full investigation. The New York City Veterans Committee against Discrimination and the United Veterans for Equality organized a citywide conference to plan a campaign to "bring [the case] before the people." The New York City chapter of the Metropolitan Interfaith and Interracial Coordinating Council (MIICC) and the American Youth for Democracy, an interracial group, described the shootings as a lynching.[84]

American Youth for Democracy linked the investigation of the shootings with the struggles against racial and class discrimination more generally, and black soldiers and veterans more specifically. "The boys who fought in the foxholes of Okinawa and stormed Hitler's ramparts in Europe, who saw the death camps of Maideneck, Buchenwald, and Dachau, have returned determined that the fascist practices and doctrines against which they fought and for which their buddies died shall not triumph in America. They have taken their place in a new battle against the same foe."[85] The MIICC pressed for investigation of the shootings and called for the investigation of numerous anti-Semitic attacks and vandalism in Greenwich Village and Queens.

These events fueled support that spread across the state and beyond. At first the people in Freeport simply wanted an investigation, but as eyewitnesses came forward, more questions about Romeika's actions and the city's responses arose. Many pointed to "the unusual speed" of the town's police department to take Richard Ferguson to court and to force a statement from Joseph, both of whom "had no counsel" or witnesses. They questioned why the Freeport district attorney could assert that Romeika's actions were justified. Romeika admitted he kicked the men in the groin and then shot them. Many wondered how the men, doubled over and in pain, posed a threat to Romeika. If Charles threatened Romeika, why did the officer also kill Alfonso and then wound Joseph? By month's end, activists believed that Romeika murdered the men, not out of fear, but because he considered them disorderly black soldiers and veterans.[86] These local and national organizations, which included representatives from eighty-seven labor organizations, called for an investigation and indictment. By early March, the coalition had created the Committee for Justice in Freeport and funded newspaper appeals, describing the case as "a fight of the workers, black and white alike, against race hatred, Jim Crow, and Anti-Semitism, and for the unity of the labor movement."[87]

As this broad coalition of labor and veterans' activists focused on the murders in New York, a black veteran's demand that a store owner in Columbia, Tennessee, show respect to his mother launched a two-day assault on the black community. On February 24, 1946, James Stephenson, a nineteen-year-old navy veteran, put on his uniform and accompanied his mother, Gladys Stephenson, to a repair shop where she told the clerk she did not like how he fixed her radio. Twenty-two-year-old Billy Fleming disagreed, then slapped her and pushed her out the door. James Stephenson punched Fleming through the store's front window. A crowd gathered, and some whites hit and kicked the Stephensons. Although Billy Fleming had assaulted Gladys Stephenson, he remained free, and the police arrested the woman and her son. Rumors about the confrontation spread through Columbia's white and black neighborhoods. Whites from the town and nearby areas congregated in the street near the store; many arrived with guns, and some threatened to lynch James Stephenson. As news about the mob reached African Americans, they readied to defend themselves and their homes. Memories of two lynchings in 1933, including that of Cordie Cheek, prompted some of the black business owners to have James Stephenson and his mother immediately transported out of town. The sheriff obliged them.[88]

As they heard of the assault and arrests, black veterans pulled out their guns to defend their neighborhood, which was known as Mud Slide. When other men asked to participate in the community's defense, the veterans showed them how to use weapons and build barricades. When an unmarked patrol car sped through the neighborhood, some men fired warning shots. Two officers were wounded. With their efforts to grab James

Stephenson thwarted, the crowd had became a mob, and it moved to the hill above Mud Slide. Some in the crowd began to shoot into the homes below. Hearing news that two police officers had been wounded, 500 troops from the Tennessee National Guard joined 100 state police and the mob of armed whites, many now drunk. Reportedly led by highway patrolmen, the army of state troops and local whites entered Mud Slide, vandalized homes and businesses, and assaulted African Americans. Some in the crowd stole money and other belongings from blacks' homes and shops. The mob left the white-owned businesses in the area undamaged.[89]

Early the next morning, the police and soldiers reentered Mud Slide, dragged African Americans from their homes, and arrested them. They then paraded 100 men, women, and children through the streets to the jail. Twenty-five men were detained and charged with attempted murder. As the local hospital was white-only, physicians left the wounded untreated. The sheriff charged undertaker James Morton and barbershop owners Saul and Julius Blair with attempted murder because they failed to "control all the Negroes." The next day, two men accused of firing on the police cars, William Gordon and James Johnson, were shot and killed in a jail cell reportedly because they "attempted to escape."[90]

The NAACP pressed the Justice Department to have federal charges brought against the mob and against the men who killed Gordon and Johnson. Not one of the nearly 400 white witnesses interviewed identified anyone who destroyed Mud Slide or assaulted people in their homes. Thurgood Marshall, along with Nashville attorney Z. Alexander Looby and Chattanooga labor lawyer Maurice Weaver, went to Lawrenceburg to defend the twenty-five men accused of attempted murder. Gravely ill from pneumonia, Marshall went to New York, where he was hospitalized, and Howard law professor Leon Ransom joined Looby and Weaver. Harassed and threatened throughout the trial—the jury considered Weaver "a white traitor"—Ransom, Looby, and Weaver pressed the limited evidence and got twenty-three of the men acquitted. Marshall returned to Tennessee and defended William Pillow and Lloyd Kennedy, both charged with firing shots at the Tennessee highway patrol. The jury acquitted Pillow and convicted Kennedy. After the trial, Marshall drove Weaver, Looby, and *Daily Worker* reporter Harry Raymond from Nashville to Columbia, Tennessee. The police stopped the car and accused Marshall of drunk driving; they placed him in the police car and drove him into the woods. Looby followed the car down to the river, where a crowd of men waited. Now aware of witnesses, the police released Marshall.[91]

As the targeted assaults and murders against African Americans who demanded their rights continued, Weaver and Looby believed they had saved Marshall from either a brutal beating or a lynching. *Ebony* described the mob in Columbia "as stalking Negro prey" and wondered if the number of murders and lynchings in 1946 "would match 1919." *Ebony* did not hesitate to compare the attacks in Tennessee to the horrific 1919 attacks in Longview, Texas, and Phillips County, Arkansas.[92] Thousands in New York City protested "the lynch murders of the Negro GIs in Freeport and the terror against an entire community in Columbia, Tennessee."[93] W. E. B. Du Bois reminded black America that riots like those in Columbia appeared "in patterns" and as part of larger upheavals, usually economic and demographic.[94] As always, Du Bois's remarks proved prescient.

Across the South, black veterans resisted the violence, political barriers, and economic exclusions through collective action that ranged from armed self-defense to mass protests. Black veterans insisted on the right to vote, often en masse and frequently wearing their military uniforms. One hundred black veterans marched in double file through the main streets of Birmingham, Alabama, to the Jefferson County courthouse, presented their discharge papers, and asked for applications to register for voting. Dressed in uniform, former army chaplain Captain H. C. Terrell led the contingent. City police asked the MPs from a nearby base to arrest him "for wearing his uniform for political purposes." No arrest took place, and the men were rejected en masse. The visible presence of veterans during elections in Georgia precipitated a wave of violence intended to quash their participation. Macio Snipes of Butler, Georgia, who voted in the Taylor County primary in Georgia, was fatally shot on his front porch.[95] Along with the influence of the efforts of black voters throughout the South, resistance by black veterans in Columbia lingered in Tennessee. In Athens, black and white veterans mobilized in the GI Nonpartisan League and objected to the voting fraud practiced by county officials.[96]

The National Urban League became concerned that veterans organized the resistance. Lester Granger linked inattention from the new Veterans' Administration to the men's high unemployment and the subsequent rise of "race conflicts." He concluded that organized groups of black veterans "cropped up in areas where the local leadership was weak." Granger "attributed much community conflict to 'excitable elements, which seek to lead without knowing what to work toward.'" He stressed, "If we want to keep Communists from leading these people, we must teach them to lead themselves." Communists did help the Southern Negro Youth Congress, which was headquartered in Birmingham, register black voters there and elsewhere in the South. Granger urged "'less talk' and 'more grass roots' work directed toward reducing race conflicts."[97]

Veterans did engage in grassroots efforts, which elicited violent responses. Black veterans returned to Jackson, Mississippi, and organized the local efforts to vote into a vibrant political action committee. Senator Theodore Bilbo threatened black voters and harangued "red-blooded white people" to terrorize blacks, especially veterans who dared to register to vote. After black and white voters filed a complaint, a Senate committee held hearings to assess the impact of Bilbo's "reign of terror" on the election, and black veterans figured prominently. Etoy Fletcher and Richard Daniel described how whites seized and flogged them. Others testified how local police and election officials wanted to prevent the soldiers from voting. The mayor of Greenwood gave J. D. Collins, a business owner, and A. C. Montgomery a list of black veterans and told them to warn them not to vote. Despite the vivid testimony from numerous witnesses, the largely southern-born committee denied any evidence that Bilbo intimidated black voters.[98]

Black veterans did not limit their organizing to their right to vote. The murders of two veterans and their wives in Monroe, Georgia, demonstrated that the "reign of terror" extended to blacks who claimed control over their own labor and defense of their families. Roger Malcolm reportedly objected to the terms of his sharecropping arrangement with Barney Hester. He also objected to the sexual advances Hester made toward Dorothy Malcolm, his wife. Roger Malcolm pulled a penknife and slashed Hester's face. He was immediately arrested. J. Loy Harrison, another white farmer, made bond for Malcolm and then drove the couple home, along with another veteran, George Dorsey, and his wife, Mae Murray Dorsey, Dorothy Malcolm's sister. Several men stopped the car, dragged the two couples into the woods and then repeatedly shot them. The women did not go quietly, and they reportedly knew the white men by name. Dorothy Malcolm was seven months pregnant. Harrison was not harmed and claimed he did not recognize any of the men. Unlike the earlier murders, news of these slayings immediately appeared on the front pages of white and international dailies. Moderates and civil rights organizations decried the deaths as a massacre and lynching. Despite the national attention and promises of investigations, the family members continued to receive threats, and they were so frightened no one attended the burials.[99]

Many observers tied the murders of the Malcolms and the Dorseys to the inflammatory speeches delivered by the state's new governor, Eugene Talmadge. Weeks before the murders, Talmadge remonstrated whites "to keep the Negroes in their place." Whether the murders were caused by Talmadge's racial tirades or were merely coincident with them is difficult to discern. Over the next months, the state Ku Klux Klan claimed responsibility for assaulting black veterans. In Atlanta, another vigilante group known as the Kavalier Klub repeatedly struck Hugh Johnson, a twenty-one-year-old navy veteran. Though one of his attackers wore a mask, he boasted to Johnson that he was a veteran.[100] Reportedly, many whites "feared that 'those niggers' were coming back [from the war] with the idea that since they fought for their country it owed them the same rights as white soldiers and that, being accustomed to violence, they would use it."[101] Local observers blamed the rise in beatings and shootings of blacks on the historic animosity from poor whites, but others insisted more affluent whites and local police organized to stop black political assertiveness.[102]

Other paramilitary groups modeled their dress and practices on Nazi organizations. They reportedly emerged to stop the "new Negro" emboldened by military service. Some of the members in the newly formed Columbians, Inc., and the Gentile Army were war veterans or worked for local police departments; others aspired to join military or police services. These organizations used military drills and organization to attract young white men, perhaps to "train them" before they either enlisted or were drafted into the military. Members of the Columbians, Inc., who wore khaki shirts and black ties like Nazi groups in the 1930s, patrolled Atlanta's white neighborhoods. They bombed blacks' homes, stockpiled dynamite and ammunition, and began organizing in other states. During the postwar elections, members intimidated black voters at the polls and attacked Jews, union members, and antiracist organizers. By 1947 the organization had spawned other like-minded organizations and sponsored a broad pattern of intimidation and violence that swept through the South between 1947 and 1952.[103]

Despite the violence and intimidation, black veterans did not end their agitation for full political and economic participation. Corporal John C. Jones was one of those soldiers who returned and asserted his rights. Jones claimed he had been swindled out of his land, which had oil on it, in Minden, Louisiana. He wanted his land back, and he filed a complaint. An anonymous caller to the police alleged Jones and his seventeen-year-old cousin were loitering in a white woman's yard, and the police arrested them. The woman objected to the claim and refused to press charges. The local police eventually released the men. Relatives later found Jones's body in an isolated bayou about seven miles from town. The murderers used a cleaver, blowtorch, and ice pick to mutilate his body. His hands were missing. Benjamin Geary Gantt, the local chief of police, was charged with the murder but later exonerated by an all-white jury.[104]

The murders in Georgia and Louisiana precipitated a wave of protests across the United States. Americans sent a "flood" of telegrams to the White House, the Justice Department, and the governor's office in Georgia. Thousands took to the streets. In San Francisco, the local branch of the NAACP led a silent march where muffled drums accompanied the interracial crowd. Over 12,000 attended an interracial mass protest in Detroit, and veterans in uniform led the crowd, which gathered in Cadillac Square at the foot of a statue of Sojourner Truth. A crowd of 1,500 attended a protest in Chicago where Herb Marsh of the packinghouse workers and Deton J. Brooks, national editor of the *Chicago Defender*, spoke. A much larger interracial gathering of 15,000 met at the Negro Soldier Memorial. Madison Square Garden hosted a rally of 15,000. Max Yergan, who worked with Paul Robeson, spoke and then led a march of 1,500 to a rally in Washington, D.C. Black Philadelphians closed their businesses and held protest meetings.[105]

The protests continued. Labor unions from New York to San Francisco denounced the murders. New York congressional representative Adam Clayton Powell Jr. vowed to renew "agitation for an anti-lynching bill." City council representative Ben Davis linked the killings in Georgia with the attacks against minorities and Jews in New York City, which had escalated as well. African Methodist Episcopal churches in St. Louis passed resolutions and raised money for the victims' families.[106] The violent crimes inspired international condemnation. *London Pictorial Today* carried a double-page spread on the murders in Monroe. European observers tartly noted that "America has nerve" for criticizing British action in India and Palestine. Swedish, Russian, and French newspapers carried front-page articles about the killings in Monroe.[107]

The harassment of and violence against black veterans and soldiers continued unabated. In late August, two veterans were murdered in Marshall, Texas. Officials refused to call the murders lynchings, but both men died under horrible circumstances. Richard F. Gordon's throat had been slashed, and his body bore the marks of having been dragged through the streets tied to the rear of an automobile. Alonza Brooks had blows to his neck and died from strangulation. Both men had been involved in labor disputes with their employers. Aided by civilian and military police, local populations continued to provoke and intimidate blacks in the military. When hundreds of black soldiers traveled to southern bases to be demobilized, train officials accused them of drunken and disorderly behavior; they telegraphed military police at Camp Croft near Florence, South Carolina, who met the train. The MPs arrived and clubbed men the railroad police identified as drunk and disorderly. More than 200 black troops were on the train, and many began to defend the soldiers. All were unarmed. The MPs arrested 135 men and paraded them through town. Two weeks earlier, train officials had accused hundreds of white soldiers of disorderly behavior, but at no time did officials call on military police to subdue or arrest the men.[108]

The lynchings and violence prompted prominent Americans to organize. Albert Einstein, Eleanor Roosevelt, and Pearl Buck spoke out against the mobs. Paul Robeson and John Sengstacke, publisher of the *Chicago Defender*, chaired the American Crusade to End Lynching. Members held a mass meeting at the Lincoln Memorial where eyewitnesses gathered to give accounts of the assaults. A delegation from the committee met with President Truman and delivered a letter from Albert Einstein, who stated "that security against lynching is one of the most urgent tasks of our generation." Robeson reportedly told Truman that if the government did not "curb lynching, the Negroes will." He also rebuked the president, saying it "seemed inept for the United States to take the lead in the Nuremberg trials and fall so far behind in respect to justice to Negroes in this country." Hundreds of delegates attending the fiftieth anniversary of the founding of the National Council of Negro Women stopped the meeting and picketed the White House. These organizations continued to pressure the Truman administration to take action. At year's end, the national press reported that forty-one lynchings had been documented since the war and no court had secured a conviction of the perpetrators. Seventeen attempted lynchings were prevented.[109]

To Secure These Rights

Walter White channeled the national momentum against racial violence and pressed the president for a federal response. Nearly 600,000 black voters had registered in the South, and untold numbers of blacks in the North registered and voted. The large migration of blacks out of the South meant this number would only grow. Moderate and liberal candidates were elected from California to Virginia, some of them Republicans. Backed by the successes at the polls and the national call for the end to racial violence, White organized a meeting with the president and took along Leslie Perry, Channing Tobias, James Carey of the CIO, and Charles E. Wilson, former director of the War Production Board and president of General Electric. As Kenneth Janken describes, White "insisted that the president use his 'bully pulpit' to protect the lives of African Americans." From an international perspective, the violence against black soldiers and veterans, the segregated military in Europe and Asia, and the violence against and the suppression of black voters made civil rights the Achilles' heel of Truman's international agenda. At home, Truman feared more blacks in the North would abandon the Democratic Party and vote for Republicans. On December 5, 1946, the president issued Executive Order 9808 and announced the formation of the Presidential Committee on Civil Rights. Wilson became the head of the fifteen-member committee, which included two white southerners known for their racial liberalism, University of North Carolina president Frank Porter Graham and Southern Regional Council member Dorothy R. Tilly—who signed her name as Mrs. M. E. Tilly. Sadie T. Alexander, a Philadelphia attorney, and Channing Tobias, a member of the NAACP executive board and director of interracial services for the YMCA, were also on the committee.[110]

After months examining the nation's civil rights record, the committee issued its report in late 1947. Committee members considered a range of civil rights but concentrated on four: the personal right to safety, the right to citizenship and its privileges, the right to freedom of conscience and expression, and the right to equality of opportunity. In each area, the committee found the national record wanting. The committee claimed the United States had made progress in protecting human liberty and focused, instead, on the experiences of racial minorities in general and black southerners in particular. Two members of the committee, Tilly and Franklin D. Roosevelt Jr., had participated in organizations concerned about the treatment of black veterans: Tilly belonged to the Southern Regional Council, and Roosevelt was one of the founding members of the American Veteran's Committee, an interracial and pro-labor veterans' organization. Using data collected from a variety of sources, including evidence compiled by the NAACP, the report gave concentrated attention to the experiences of black soldiers and veterans.

The presidential committee convened as Congress considered a policy for compulsory military service for young men that would also retain the

"Negro Policy," so the committee also addressed the impact of the segregated military on civil rights. Noting that the services practiced discrimination on the basis of race yet drafted black men for war, the committee delivered its harshest indictment: "Prejudice in any area is an ugly, undemocratic phenomenon; in the armed services, where all men run the risk of death, it is particularly repugnant." Each service needed immediate and "remedial action." The army had a quota system for African Americans, and the Marine Corps confined them to the steward's branch. The failure of each service to implement its own policies at every level of training, particularly at the officers' ranks, "negated many of the benefits of the proposed universal training program."[111]

The committee found the threats against black men and women in the services particularly egregious.

> Some of our servicemen are all too often treated with rudeness and discourtesy by civil authorities and the public. There are numerous instances in which they have been forced to move to segregated cars on public carriers. They have been denied access to places of public accommodation and recreation. When they attempt to assert their rights, they are sometimes met with threats and even outright attack. Federal officials find they have no present authority to intervene directly to protect men [*sic*] in uniform against such abuses.[112]

The horrific racial violence in 1946 hovered over these observations.

The report stressed moral, economic, and international reasons for the nation to redress its abysmal history of civil rights. This braiding of ethical, diplomatic, and "manpower" concerns took a particular tack as arguments for and against the military's desegregation threatened to stall the legislation for universal military training (UMT).

> Perhaps most important of all, we are not making use of one of the most effective techniques for educating the public to the practicability of American ideals as a way of life. During the last war we and our allies, with varying but undeniable success, found that the military services can be used to educate citizens on a broad range of social and political problems. The war experience brought to our attention a laboratory in which we may prove that the majority and minorities of our population can train and work and fight side by side in cooperation and harmony. We should not hesitate to take full advantage of this opportunity.[113]

The committee suggested that the military become the nation's "laboratory" for democracy.[114] By the time the committee issued its report, Congress had refused to consider key features of President Truman's civil rights agenda, which included antilynching legislation, a permanent civil rights commission, and protections for voting. Yet in its clarion call and moral stance, *To Secure These Rights* became a blueprint for civil rights organizations. As the new Department of Defense ignored the report, the NAACP continued to press for desegregation of the armed services. The chances for an immediate change in the military's racial policies looked bleak as Congress ignored other parts of the president's civil rights agenda.

THROUGHOUT BOTH WORLD WARS, the NAACP challenged the military's policies of segregation. During World War II, Walter White in the national office, Roy Wilkins in Washington, D.C., and Thurgood Marshall, head of the legal office in New York, insisted on the pursuit of legal justice for men and women in uniform. This battle claimed a significant portion of the association's attention and strained its limited resources. At the same time, the thousands of women and men in the branches became the eyes and ears of the association and agitated for African Americans stationed in the camps and bases. As he battled on behalf of the "Negro Soldier," White increased the association's membership, found new audiences, and displayed a new facet of his leadership skills. Informed by his tours of bases and camps in the United States and on the warfront and by the thousands of letters he received from soldiers, sailors, and Marines, White used his speeches, newspaper columns, and radio broadcasts to air the grievances of black America. Wherever and whenever possible, White made the case for the nation's failure to live up to democracy. He argued that the desegregation of the military and the battlefield were critical to African Americans' struggle for equal rights. White was not alone in his intense focus on the military's desegregation or in his belief that its change might precipitate integration elsewhere.

Many in the national and branch offices had some affiliation with the military, either through their own service or because family members were in uniform. In late 1944, White hired Jesse O. Dedmon, an attorney and a captain in the army, as the association's secretary of veterans' affairs. Franklin H. Williams, who worked with Thurgood Marshall, had served in the 93rd Infantry Division for eighteen months and then attended Fordham Law School before he joined the legal office.[115] Walter White's son,

Walter Carl Darrow, enlisted in the military. Marshall's nephew, Buddy Marshall, was in the Air Corps. At the branch level, new members and branch workers had similar associations. The segregated military, then, was part of the everyday experiences of the NAACP, and the military's segregation policies were personal.

Robert L. Carter, another veteran, joined Marshall's office in late 1944. Carter received a Master of Law degree at Columbia University and his law degree from Howard Law School, but he was drafted in 1941 before he could begin practice. Initially he welcomed military service, although he possessed no "great patriotic fervor" for the segregated military. He was placed in the Army Air Corps and based in Augusta, Georgia, where his white captain made it clear that education made "niggers uppity." Carter recalled that he received virtually no training for combat. Instead, black men were assigned to hard manual labor. After Pearl Harbor, Carter became one of the small cadre of black men allowed to enter officers' training. After his commission, he was assigned to a base in Louisiana, where he served as the only black officer. His experiences thereafter were fairly typical: isolated, denied access to most facilities available to officers, and ridiculed by white troops, Carter had to stand his ground and fend for himself. Superior officers expected him to snitch on black soldiers and ferret out those who complained of discrimination. Instead, Carter successfully defended a soldier from a rape charge. Unwilling to capitulate to his superior officers, Carter faced his own administrative discharge and reduction to enlisted status. William Hastie intervened and successfully defended him. Released from the military, Carter studied for the New York bar exam and joined the NAACP legal office. He was one of the tens of thousands of African Americans who came to a new racial consciousness because of the military. He also became one of the many politicized by its segregation and violence.[116]

A. Philip Randolph remained the most visible, and at times controversial, critic of the segregated military. His efforts in 1940 and 1941 to have the army integrated were undermined by President Roosevelt's executive order that allowed segregation and the quota system. Randolph continued to pressure the president to issue an executive order that would end segregation in the military. While civil rights organizations, including the NAACP, and the black press called for desegregation of the military, Randolph threatened mass protest. Throughout the war, Randolph galvanized other organizations, including labor unions, to sustain pressure on the government to address the inequities and violence of the segregated military. Randolph's efforts acquired a singularity because of his ability to articulate a collective outrage and organize it into mass action.

In early January 1945, Randolph again concentrated on organizing a movement to end segregation and discrimination in the military. An outgrowth of his earlier MOWM, this renewed effort responded to the War Department's failure to enforce its own policies that mandated integration of buses, clubs, recreation, and PXs. Still called the MOWM, the new committee drew in labor activists and interracial civil rights organizations. Willard Townsend of the United Transport Service Employees Union, CIO, and Morris Milgrim of the Workers Defense League were the first of many in labor to join the committee. William Kerr, co-chair of the Winfred Lynn Committee (Lynn initiated the only legal challenge to the army's "Negro Policy"), also became an organizer. A small group of labor and civil rights activists met in New Jersey in late April to form the National Committee to Abolish Segregation in the Armed Forces. As veterans returned to unions and workplaces, Randolph viewed these activists, many allies from the 1930s labor struggles, key to bringing veterans and soldiers into the movement. The MOWM was largely ad hoc in its new formation, but Randolph nonetheless intended to combine the tactics of a mass movement with a political action committee.[117]

Those who received Randolph's letter calling for a new movement immediately objected to its timing and tactics. Roger Baldwin, director of the American Civil Liberties Union (ACLU), chastised Randolph for organizing an effort so late. "I question whether it is timely now in what is presumably the last year of the war when changes would be administratively difficult." Baldwin suggested that Randolph take a "step-by-step" approach rather than calling for immediate desegregation. Like many others, Baldwin accepted reports that the military had completely and successfully ended segregation in "certain services." He also expressed concern that Randolph had not received support from "the major agencies, which carry political weight. A small movement would do more harm than good because its failure might set back the whole campaign."[118]

Through the summer of 1945, Randolph and others on the planning committee debated Baldwin's question about the timing of the campaign. Why begin a national campaign at the end of the war? If prominent African Americans and the most powerful civil rights organizations, including the NAACP, had not persuaded the president to issue an executive order ending segregation in the military during the war, how would it be possible to push for such an order during peacetime? Moreover, widespread unemployment for veterans, particularly black veterans, claimed the attention and limited resources of organizations Randolph hoped would join his effort. When William Kerr called a meeting in June 1945, only A. J. Mustie from the Congress of Racial Equality attended. By late October, Louis Greenberg from the American Jewish Committee, along with Ezra Parrot of the United Transport Service Employees Union, Conrad J. Lynn, a prominent civil rights lawyer and Winfred Lynn's brother, and Kerr, informed Randolph that too many considered the issue no longer important and the campaign all but impossible, as the military appeared to shrink rapidly. They voted to end the committee's efforts.[119]

Randolph soon revived his efforts as the possibility of a prolonged military standoff in Europe and war in Asia gave new urgency to congressional approval of a permanent and segregated draft. By 1947, the demands of occupation and the Cold War precipitated the President's Commission on Universal Training to recommend a segregated peacetime conscription. Randolph and Reynolds responded with a press release that rebuked an American democracy that ignored violations of civil rights. Rather than the progress that President Truman had promised in his speech to the NAACP that June at the Lincoln Memorial (White's version of the MOWM), the president's proposed bill for UMT "fasten[s] jimcrow on American youth at their most impressionable age." Truman's approach—one that he would follow throughout his campaign—was simultaneously to appease southern white Democrats and to appeal to black voters. Grant Reynolds challenged the commission's claim that a segregated military would "contribute to the development of national unity [by] bringing together young men from all parts of the country to share a common experience." How, Reynolds asked, "can national unity be promoted by subjecting a million young men each year to federally sponsored jimcrow? So long as the American government attempts to sponsor any program of jimcrow, its aspiration to moral leadership in the world will be seriously impaired."[120]

Randolph's committee began a new organizational effort. It was renamed the Committee against Jimcrow in Military Service and Training, and veteran Grant Reynolds served as its chair and A. Philip Randolph as its treasurer. Now fortified by a national committee with hundreds of members, Randolph's electric public statements energized African Americans' widespread indignation. When Truman spoke to Congress on civil rights in February 1948 and asked it to act on a ten-point program that included a request to the secretary of defense "to take steps to have the remaining instances of discrimination in the Armed Forces eliminated,"

Randolph delivered an instant response. African Americans, Randolph argued, "would see through the hypocrisy of the Eightieth Congress if it passes even a model Fair Employment Practices Bill and then herded 18-year old youths into jimcrow garrisons commanded by bigoted generals." He called for a "crack down on this new-style lynch party which would surrender Negro boys to Mississippi Army officers without legislative safeguards."[121]

Over the next months Reynolds and Randolph challenged other civil rights organizations and leaders to support their efforts to pressure Congress and the president to end segregation in the military. After receiving an appeal for support, Walter White asked Thurgood Marshall for advice. In the intervening weeks, the matter went to the NAACP board of directors. Though White did not press the NAACP to mount an aggressive response to the proposed draft policy, he informed Randolph that the NAACP planned its own efforts. Unaware of White's claims to Randolph, Marshall sent a testy reply to the director, chiding him for the association's inaction. "It seems to me," Marshall wrote, "that this is the type of job that should be done by the NAACP and we should be working on it."[122] White maintained his distance, gauging the various responses to Randolph's efforts. When the labor leader's charged statements about the legislation precipitated a hearing with the Senate, White saw the opportunity to insert a more moderate tone.

In his testimony before the Senate Committee on Armed Services that March, Randolph did not temper his assessment of African Americans' response to a postwar segregated military. "Negroes," he said, "are in no mood to shoulder a gun for democracy abroad so long as they are denied democracy here at home." Randolph noted how news of the segregated draft law had been leaked. He claimed that he did not intend to suggest that blacks' refusal to serve in a "Jim Crow military" was a "threat" but that it was meant "rather as a frank, factual survey of Negro opinion." But, he warned, "I would like to make clear to the Senate Armed Services Committee and through you, to Congress and the American people that passage now of a Jim Crow draft may only result in a mass civil disobedience movement along the lines of the magnificent struggles of the people of India against British imperialism." In African Americans' quest for civil rights, the demand for an integrated military was a "resolute" call "for full manhood." It also had meaning for the larger black public's "demand [for] full, unqualified, first-class citizenship." Randolph offered "a frank factual survey" and suggested black men intended to go on strike if the legislation passed.[123]

Randolph knew African Americans' experiences of the segregated military during World War II provided the strongest appeal for mass action. When asked, young black men stressed they had no intention of being subjected to "compulsory military segregation." Over the next months, Randolph amplified this statement. African Americans, Randolph insisted, had a "moral obligation not to lend themselves as worldwide carriers of an evil and hellish doctrine" abroad. He had no strong certainty how effective a mass movement against the legislation might be, but he "would advise Negroes to refuse to fight as slaves for a democracy they cannot possess and cannot enjoy." He admitted that his radical appeal had limited, if little, support from the mainstream civil rights leaders. He nonetheless asserted that black leaders "would be derelict in their duty if they did not support such a justified civil disobedience movement."[124]

Walter White and Roy Wilkins monitored the Senate's reaction to Randolph's statement, and when Oregon senator Wayne Morse charged Randolph with treason for his remarks before Congress, White moved into action. Morse was a member of the NAACP's national board, and White viewed his rebuke of Randolph as an opportunity to offer a moderate tone and broker a compromise through his contacts with the Truman administration. White sent letters to every NAACP branch and asked them to telegraph their state congressional representatives and senators. White sent a telegram to Morse that simultaneously set the NAACP apart from Randolph's call for civil disobedience yet warned Morse about the depth of black support for Randolph's appeal. "You have been a good friend of minority groups," he reminded Morse, "but it apparently is not possible for you to realize how bitterly Negro Americans feel about Jim Crow in the armed forces." If Morse and other senators had "darkened their faces and donned a uniform for six weeks," White wrote, they would have been "valiant supporters" of the NAACP's fight against the military's discrimination. "Our Association is not advising Negroes to refuse to defend their country if there is danger," but the "bitter green" memories of treatment in the "last war," combined with outrage against the lynching and terrorizing of blacks, many of whom were veterans, made black Americans sympathetic to "Randolph's point of view." White recommended Morse and others "not threaten treason trials, but to give these loyal citizens the democracy they are expected and asked to die to defend."[125]

The debate continued when Morse sent a stern letter to White insisting that the NAACP's refusal to rebuke Randolph "gave comfort to [his] approach to this problem." He warned White that such encouragement "will set back several years in our fight for civil rights program."[126] White sent an unequivocal reply attesting to Randolph's integrity. If Morse thought Randolph did not accurately capture African Americans' collective temper, White said, he should think again. Randolph "articulated what has been going on in the minds of a great many Negroes." White realized the depth of the anger, and he and Leslie Perry had discussed the possibility of calling for blacks to refuse to heed the draft when the Gillem Board met in 1945. By 1948 the dissent had not waned, and White considered it of no importance whether the association encouraged Randolph. "He derives his encouragement from the righteous resentment of Negroes against the national hypocrisy which preaches democracy while practicing vile forms of racism." White challenged Morse's assertion that Randolph's statement damaged support for civil rights legislation. White noted that Republicans backed off from civil rights legislation weeks before Randolph's testimony. "Those who now say that they are handicapped in working for civil rights legislation" because of Randolph's testimony "are quite shamelessly using that as an excuse for non-action."[127]

Branches sent letters to Congress and replied to White. Some worried that Randolph's statements "damaged your cause more than any democratic abuse." Others expressed concern that "Randolph went too far and we feel he should be censured by the National Board." While some, like members in the Decatur, Illinois, branch, balked at Randolph's presumption to "speak for millions" of African Americans, others registered concern about his use of rhetoric that might harm the association's civil rights agenda. These members preferred White's style, and they urged him to balance African Americans' critiques of discrimination with the language of martial fidelity, the latter now part of the burgeoning Cold War rhetoric. White's way of describing "how the Negroes feel" without also "giv[ing] us cause to fear reaction to what you have said" struck a comforting tone.[128]

As White anticipated, support poured in for Randolph's testimony and for White's measured support. Poet and civil rights activist Lenore G. Marshall informed White that she "applauded" Randolph. "Many people feel as I do," she wrote. "He made a sound and stirring statement and should be supported by as many groups as possible." She added what White repeatedly heard: "We oppose the draft and the plan to militarize this country; the discrimination against colored people, which the Army and Navy

have always fostered, is one of the dangerous, undemocratic, and negative angles of a draft." She urged White to join with Randolph "to press
for complete racial equality in all armed services bills. Many white groups
and individuals are giving Mr. Randolph their admiration and support. He
has taken a magnificent stand." White may have found the trickle of letters
that denounced Randolph troubling, but those like Marshall's anticipated
the public support that flowed into black and liberal white newspapers.
A. A. Heist, Methodist minister and director of the Southern California
branch of the ACLU, urged White to stand firm against Morse's charges.
The politics of gradualism were over, he wrote. "It is high time for the
Negro to stand up and resist—and that not by the destructive road of violence, but by the only sure and constructive means of non-violence."[129]

The support for Randolph's outspokenness remained strong, and some
branches pressured the national office to sponsor its own demonstration
against the UMT bill. Wilkins stressed to White and the board that its effort
need not be affiliated with Randolph, adding, "It would be in line with our
policy on segregation in the armed services and would give some punch
to our protest—a punch that was lacking in the testimony of Jesse O. Dedmon, which was smothered by Randolph's dramatic declaration." Wilkins
began to organize such a demonstration.[130]

White's measured response hid a general outrage in the national office.
If some branches praised White for his tone, privately Morse's response
ignited a firestorm in White, and he sought advice on how best to craft a
tempered response. Equally incensed by the call for the association to accept the status quo—and divide African Americans—White retorted in a
memorandum to Wilkins that it "would be 40,000 words in length if I were
to attempt to set down a mere illustrated outline of what Negro soldiers
and sailors suffered in World War II under the Jim Crow system." Wilkins
spoke for many in the organization when he suggested that White remind
Morse of the great admiration that Randolph enjoyed across racial lines.
"He is regarded as a man of integrity and he enjoys the respect and esteem
of millions." Wilkins added, "The NAACP does not believe in civil disobedience as an effective technique for solving our problem here in America.
We have not counseled Negroes to refuse to serve their country. But we
would be less than honest with Senator Morse if we led him to believe that
there is not the ripest discontent among them over both Jim Crow in the
armed services, and the lagging civil rights program." In these private exchanges between two veterans of the civil rights struggles, Wilkins turned
introspective and acknowledged the deep river of dissent: "As an organi-

zation we have not encouraged Randolph. Negro citizens in every walk of life have done that. He and we have a people's mandate to express in the strongest terms their resentment of Jim Crow, if not one to pledge civil disobedience."[131]

White used portions of Wilkins's memo—at Wilkins's urging—in his long reply to Morse, a reply that again affirmed the association's support for Randolph. White did not offer the NAACP's explicit endorsement for civil disobedience. Instead, he advocated that the federal government could make civil disobedience "unnecessary by wiping out segregation forthwith."[132] He followed with his habit of agitating in the black press. White made public Morse's letters and his replies. Henry Lee Moon, the NAACP director of public relations, had the correspondence between White and Morse printed in the newspapers, including the *New York Times*. As telegrams and letters flew between Washington, D.C., and New York City, the black and white presses excerpted the heated debate between the senator and the director of the largest and most influential civil rights organization. White had the association poll black college students and interview members about their support for the UMT legislation. The results startled everyone. The majority of those polled remarked that they would not fight in a war with a Jim Crow military. Even the 37 percent who said they would register also noted they would not go to war if the military remained segregated. The survey revealed what White suspected and Randolph had assessed: Seventy-six percent of draft-age black men noted they would refuse to serve in a segregated military. A. Philip Randolph tapped into a deep reservoir of black grievance ready to be used for civil disobedience.[133]

While White publicly supported Randolph's statements, the activist's call for civil disobedience alarmed him. Randolph defined civil disobedience as "non-resistance, non-cooperation, and non-participation, but no overt acts." To White and others in the association, Randolph acknowledged that blacks' civil disobedience would, no doubt, instigate "overt acts" of violent retaliation. Randolph conceded, "That's a price we have to pay to get our democratic rights." The ACLU agreed and added, "American Negroes are pretty well accustomed to terror."[134] Along with debate about the military bill, the call for civil disobedience commanded black Americans' attention over the next months. Despite the debate and criticism of the legislation, Congress passed it with the segregation and quotas intact.[135]

Pushed by blacks' protests about the segregated military, his unease about a southern white backlash in the upcoming elections, his concern about the criticism of America's civil rights image abroad, and his awareness of a too-small military for a possible war in Asia, Truman responded to the new segregated Selective Service Act with Executive Order 9981, which mandated "equality of opportunity" in the armed services. But the order avoided language that explicitly mandated desegregation. The army had used similar language in the Gillem Board report that ultimately affirmed the service's segregation practices. But the order also included the creation of a committee, chosen by the president, to oversee the mandate. In a deft political move that he hoped would appease African Americans and the military, Truman's order merged the moral tone and urgency of *To Secure These Rights* with the military's language meant to manage segregation. Would his gambit to satisfy disparate groups be successful?

The order did not explicitly call for integration, and officials in the army and the navy immediately insisted their segregation policies complied with the president's order on "equal treatment and opportunity." Only the new air force considered segregation "inefficient," and some high-ranking officers and civilians had already explored ways to end such policies. As some outside the military viewed the implications of the order as a call for the military's integration, General Omar Bradley announced the army did not intend to change its policies. When Truman's chances for reelection appeared in doubt to some, the Defense Department saw no reason to consider the order "an integration plan."

While some groups insisted President Truman's call for "equality of opportunity" did not immediately end segregation in the military, and especially the army, mainstream civil rights leaders and many ordinary African Americans read the order as a critical gesture toward integration. During World War II, the military justified its policies based on segregation in American society. After decades of fighting for the "right to fight," many African Americans hailed Truman's executive order, however limited and tentative, as a significant victory. Many African Americans hoped, too, that their expanded participation in the military would force Truman to end segregation in the larger society. Just as Truman hoped, African American voters provided the critical push that gave him a victory in the November election.

3

Glory on the Battlefield

*The Korean War, Cold War Civil Rights, and the
Paradox of Black Military Service*

In 1948, eighteen-year-old Ivory Perry accepted whatever job he found in
and around Pine Bluff, Arkansas. After his mother died and his father mi-
grated, he turned to an older sister and her husband for help. Frustrated
that he earned so little to contribute to the household and his own care,
he left high school and looked for full-time work. Besides picking cotton,
Perry and a cousin found only low-wage jobs. Discouraged, the two young
men went to the local recruiting office and enlisted in the army; they then
immediately traveled to Fort Knox, Kentucky, for basic training. There they
joined hundreds of other black enlistees, including many unemployed veterans of World War II. The military provided steady income and "room and
board," Perry reasoned.[1]

Many young black men made similar choices as they assessed their
limited economic and social prospects in postwar America. In Indiana,
seventeen-year-old Arthur Rucker boasted to his friends that the army "got
better schools, offers travel, and career training that will make your country head swim." He reserved special praise for his new uniform: "The U.S.
Army provides these sharp threads to its men—dig me!" Fourteen-year-
old Willie Ruff listened with rapt attention. Born in northwest Alabama,
Ruff followed his father to Indiana as he searched for work. Hungry, Ruff

Front page of the Chicago Defender, *July 31, 1948, announcing President Harry Truman's Executive Order 9981. While the order did not specifically abolish segregation in the U.S. armed forces, African American newspapers presented it as the "President's desegregation order." Courtesy of the* Chicago Defender.

forged his father's signature and joined the army in late 1945. Tutored by older black men aware of his age, Ruff finished high school and became a master French horn player. He used his military benefits to support his younger siblings and pay for their medical care. With the new GI Bill, Ruff applied to Yale College and received a scholarship.[2] Poverty pushed Willie Ruff into the military, and the benefits it provided helped him become a professional musician after he left.

After Truman's Executive Order 9981, the economic incentives offered by the military increased its appeal among working-class African Americans. Nineteen-year-old Stephen Hopkins enlisted in the spring of 1950 because he "thought it would be a way to bring more money into the house." After his demobilization, World War II veteran Ransom Wayman went to Detroit, where he found work at the Briggs plant. The terrible working conditions and the wave of wildcat strikes that rolled through his plant in 1946 pushed him back into the army. Again he went to war, this time to Korea. Shot six times, captured by the Chinese army, and nearly executed, Wayman weighed the army against the options he found in Detroit. He did not particularly like the army, but he considered it a better job than any other he had held.[3]

Black men who enlisted in late 1948 and early 1949 expected to join an integrated military. They heard about President Truman's executive order and they read about the military's opportunities in the black weeklies, but they found a rigidly segregated army. Perry, Hopkins, and Wayman were trained and assigned to all-black units commanded by white officers. One thing differed from the previous war, however: This time the army immediately assigned men to combat units. Despite the army's continued adherence to its "Negro Policy," poor and working-class black men like Perry, Hopkins, and Wayman viewed the military as a step above the underemployment and unemployment they faced in the late 1940s and into the 1950s. But they discovered that racial equality did not begin in the barracks or on the battlefield. In July 1950, almost two years since the president had issued Executive Order 9981, these three men and thousands of other black men who enlisted in the army trained and served in segregated units.

Since Executive Order 9981 did not explicitly call for the military's desegregation, the army did not consider "equality of opportunity" a mandate to abandon its "Negro Policy." While the navy and the new air force announced plans for gradual integration, the army assented only to lift the quota on the number of black men allowed into its ranks. Recruiters and local draft boards enlisted and inducted them in record numbers. While some in the army insisted black men were unsuited for combat and more "naturally fit" for labor, commanders minimally trained and outfitted them for diverse positions on the battlefield, including artillery and tank positions. Many continued to serve in segregated labor units. In July 1950, the U.S. Army had the majority of blacks in uniform, and it went to war in Korea nearly as segregated as it had been at the end of World War II.[4] After a half-century of struggle for the "the right to fight," black men now had the "obligations and privileges to serve," but they went to war under horrible conditions made worse by segregation. Even as the military reluctantly integrated during the Korean War, racial and class inequalities shaped the Korean War draft and pulled blacks into the military in disproportionate numbers. Black men labored in the military in record numbers not because the military promised integration but because the rest of American society remained segregated.

In every region of the United States, African Americans faced narrowed job opportunities in labor markets that excluded them or relegated them to the margins. In the Deep South, black veterans with technical training rarely found better employment as discrimination shaped the unequal administration of the GI Bill. White veterans received training and then worked in the new industries dotting the South; in contrast, employment agencies directed black veterans to service work and denied them access to training courses.[5] During and after World War II, southern landowners responded to workers' emigration by mechanizing agricultural work, simultaneously preventing veterans from returning to the land and fueling a postwar out-migration. As sociologist Charles S. Johnson documented these trends, he noted how the "shadow of the automatic cotton picker loom[ed] over the remaining workers of both races."[6]

In areas with significant wartime industries, reconversion was slow, and black workers felt the impact as industrial employers fired them first and rehired them last, if at all. In the period between 1945 and 1950, strikes erupted with frequency, and shop floor clashes over blacks' hire or presence precipitated waves of unrest that spilled into communities. At the same time, thousands of black and white migrants arrived in northern, midwestern, and southern cities in numbers that exceeded the migration of the World War I period. Excluded from many jobs and prevented from purchasing homes in the new suburbs, black migrants had difficulty finding work and homes. Competition among these workers and veterans for the constricted industrial employment and overtaxed urban infrastructure, especially in housing and schools, had a detrimental impact on the fragile cross-racial alliances in unions and veterans' organizations.[7]

The start of the new decade did not provide much relief. Between 1950 and 1960, deindustrialization in the major industrial cities, especially Detroit, Chicago, and Cleveland, coincided with the disappearance of skilled and semiskilled wage work. Black men, especially younger men, were particularly vulnerable to the vagaries of the interwar economy. In southern industries where black men had previously labored, such as in the lumber industries, they found fewer jobs. Overall, black men faced higher rates of unemployment, part-time work, and underemployment than did other groups of male wage earners. Black men had higher rates of withdrawal from the workforce. They were the group least likely to have access to technical training or two-year and four-year colleges. The constriction in black women's job opportunities also exacerbated household economies.[8]

These workers were part of a new black working class whose employment options in every region of the United States underwent episodic expansion and contraction in the decades between 1940 and 1960. As James Gregory has noted, "skin color mattered" in the postwar labor market. Black migrants laboring in northern cities earned much less than white workers. While poorly educated black men fared the worst, black men with more education faced even greater wage gaps when compared with their white counterparts of similar age and education. "College experience earned a black male migrant on average only 63 percent of his white counterpart's income in 1949," Gregory observes. A decade later, this gap had decreased only slightly, to 60 percent.[9] Black migrants, especially black male migrants, faced numerous obstacles to employment in small and large cities alike. After blacks enjoyed unprecedented access to industrial and public sector jobs during the war, some of it precipitated by labor shortages and federal intervention through the FEPC, the racialized labor market became more pronounced in the decade after World War II. While some blacks had access to white-collar work, the majority of workers received the least desirable jobs. As restricted as the labor markets appeared to southern migrants, northern-born blacks found increased restrictions between 1950 and 1970. As Manning Marable has concluded, black labor "became less essential than at any previous stage of its development." The industrial black working class that formed between 1915 and 1945 began a slow contraction in the two decades that followed.[10] Overall, many fathers fared better than their sons. Faced with fewer employment options, young black men turned to alternative opportunities for work, including the military. As Perry and Wayman faced job restrictions, the military seemed more attractive.

Black men found an army averse to racial integration but desperate for their presence as combat laborers, a dramatic shift in its "Negro Policy." The demands of occupation in Europe and Asia forced the military to agitate for a continued draft and a large standing military, yet the creation of a large peacetime force that was also prepared for war proved politically and economically daunting.[11] As the military shrank rapidly from its high of 16 million in 1944 to 500,000 by 1947, black men continued to enlist in the army. Between August and December of 1945, more than 140,000 African Americans enlisted, comprising two-thirds of the army's estimated needed troops. The high black enlistments, along with those black troops still in the service, significantly increased African Americans' overall participation in the army from 10.4 to 16 percent. Alarmed, the army halted both the draft and voluntary enlistment of black men. The concentration of black units in Europe and Asia drew increasing public scrutiny of the segregated military. In response, military officials used films, advertising, and military envoys to educate local populations in the practices of American Jim Crow.[12] Between 1946 and 1948, the army quickly reduced the number of black troops through dishonorable discharges—"unfitness for the military"—and many of these men became ineligible for benefits.[13]

Both the pressure of the president's executive order and the incessant demands of occupation and a possible war in Korea forced the army to drop its quota system and advertise its need for recruits in the black weeklies. The 1948 Selective Service Act required all young men between the ages of eighteen and twenty-six to register for the draft, regardless of race. Despite rumors of war, most men who went into the military between 1948 and 1950 volunteered, and few communities had to enact the draft to meet a quota. But black men who enlisted in the army in this period were assigned to all-black units. Using policies similar to those established during World War II, the army provided the majority of these men with minimal preparation for combat and planned to use them in a variety of labor positions.

Black communities considered the integrated draft without racial quotas a major civil rights victory, and newspapers stressed that the military promised young black men opportunity and training. The military appeared to launch men into unusual careers, and it promised a secure—even ordinary—life afterward. The new *Ebony* made such narratives a regular feature in its articles about World War II veterans. Former Tuskegee Airman James O. Plinton started an airline in Haiti; Dunbar Simms McLaurin rehabilitated junk military vehicles in Manila; war veterans and brothers Howard, Clifford, and Robert Wilson fulfilled their dream to open a chicken farm in California through the GI Bill.[14] Although riddled with practices that discriminated against poor veterans of all races—the preponderance of men in the military after 1945—the GI Bill promised some men a "leg-up." Black colleges reported that scores of black veterans filled their classes and strained the infrastructure of many of the colleges. Ironically, because African Americans had no access to white-only state colleges and universities in the South, black colleges experienced some benefits from the establishment of Reserve Officers' Training Corps (ROTC) programs.[15]

James L. Hicks, who wrote the "Veterans Whirl" column for the *Baltimore Afro-American*, provided a steady flow of information about the "new opportunities" in the army. Just after enactment of the president's executive order, Hicks observed that the Selective Service planned to pursue men of draft age, and he urged black men to enlist. The "best soldier," he argued, arranged his destiny and did not wait for the local draft to call him. Over the next months, he repeated this claim. "Army Offers New Course to Train Newspapermen," the newspaper announced in late October. Enlisted men accepted into the program would receive "the very best of training." After they were trained, the army planned to place participants at designated newspapers and radio and television stations. Hicks added, "Here is an excellent opportunity, especially since/if you are draft-age you must join the Army anyway."[16]

Mindful about the possibilities of war, Hicks reported that the military considered combat positions the most important. Hicks admonished, "Momma, the aim and purpose of the United States Army as expressed in its training and field manuals, is to close with the enemy in mortal combat and destroy him." With this skill came honor. "If war comes and Junior kills a few men he will be highly respected by the men of his unit. If he kills quite a few men he will be honored by his commanding officers. If he becomes a great killer of men, he will be taken to the White House and decorated by the President." Hicks reasoned that the "highest paid and most respected killers" were officers, so he urged black mothers to encourage their sons to attend ROTC programs to ensure better pay and more respect for the work of killing. Having served in the army during World War II, Hicks insisted his advice came from someone "who was highly paid and well respected for killing" and who did not regret the role he played in war.[17]

The press framed its encouragement to enlist in the armed services or enroll in ROTC as a civil rights imperative. One *Afro-American* editorial announced the navy wanted to enroll black men in the Naval ROTC. Unlike the army, the navy did not want black men in the NROTC confined to the black colleges.[18] In the navy, Hicks noted, "an alert person can pursue an exciting profitable career with a minimum of segregation." Photographs in *Afro-American Magazine* presented the navy as dramatically altered by Truman's order. No longer confined to serve as stewards and messmen, young men worked as radiomen, electronic technicians, and aerial photographers. *Ebony* assured readers that black enlistees did not get shunted off to the steward's branch. No longer "experimental," black men served on submarines in a "democratic" fashion in "completely mixed, family-like crews." These highly skilled technicians symbolized "the Navy's new era in race relations."[19] Few readers knew that the navy had dramatically reduced the number of black sailors and officers. The new air force, *Ebony* announced, relied on the famed Tuskegee Airmen and produced the first and most far-reaching plans for full integration. Its "swift and amazing upset of racial policy" had turned the air force "topsy-turvy" as it re-assigned blacks, including black pilots, to every base around the world. At the same time, it announced efforts to recruit more African Americans for its technical programs. Even before Executive Order 9981, the air force planned to integrate its elite Air War College in Montgomery, Alabama. Training at Maxwell Air Force Base was "democratic but rugged." Here black cadets displayed how they "flew," just like the other pilots.[20]

As the committee monitoring Executive Order 9981 claimed some success in negotiating "equal opportunity," black magazines touted the desegregation of the military as important and "quiet progress" for African Americans.[21] In its many articles on blacks' experiences in the services, *Ebony* emphasized the skill, commitment, and opportunity African Americans acquired on "the job." One submariner announced he planned to "never leave the submarine service. Every man on a sub has a dependable job." He stressed, too, that he felt "important."[22] Similar articles and photo essays charted the military's progress through vivid pictures of integrated mess halls and training. The occasional image of a white soldier saluting a black officer provided visual testimony of the military's acceptance of Truman's executive order. In the context of blacks' struggle for civil rights, enlistment in the military acquired an additional characteristic of racial activism.

Most black soldiers, sailors, or airmen did not describe their experiences so expansively and glowingly. Most blacks, instead, emphasized how the military offered work when finding other employment proved difficult. Thus, enlisted men's experiences rarely figured in *Ebony*'s narratives of success. Nor did the articles reveal that the army assigned the men to all-black units. Lured by the claims they read about in the articles, young black men like Charles Rangel discovered that this new army in late 1948 and early 1949 looked very much like the old army they had heard about from men in their communities. The rigid segregation startled Rangel, as did the low expectations the army had for black soldiers. Stationed at Fort Lewis, Washington, Rangel received little training that prepared him for combat. With the increased bellicose rhetoric between the United States and the Soviet Union, Rangel grew anxious about war. Still, as a high school dropout, Rangel considered the army better than what he might find in Harlem.

Despite its continued segregation, the army received a steady stream of black enlistments and reenlistments. In the first years of the reformed Selective Service, draft boards did not use the draft to meet quotas. On the eve of the Korean War, the *Baltimore Afro-American* described how "the colored soldier is America's best 'Good Neighbor' salesman. He is a mobile public relations delegate usually creating goodwill and understanding wherever he goes." Stationed around the world, the black GI "is an international public relationist."[23] Yet, the army still considered black troops a problem and segregation the answer to its management.

As mainstream civil rights leaders registered Truman's executive order as a significant victory in black civil rights, they also wondered how the president planned to push the military to integrate without an explicit demand and timetable. The order established a committee to put the policy "into effect as rapidly as possible, having due regard to the time required to effectuate any necessary changes without impairing efficiency or morale." After signing the order one day and mentioning it to Congress the next day, the president spoke no more about it or civil rights more generally.[24] The president may have gone quiet, but the army did not. Immediate comments about the order from the army and the white press in the South sounded an ominous tone. General Omar Bradley, the army chief of staff, announced that the army did not expect to change until America changed first, thereby dispensing with both the order and the earlier civil rights document, *To Secure These Rights*. If the general had any influence, the army did not plan to serve as a laboratory for democracy. The southern press reviled the order. The *Montgomery Advertiser* described it as one of a "raw and repugnant character." Other newspapers in the South characterized Truman's efforts as "grandstanding" for "the Negro vote which seems to be swinging to the Wallace-Communist progressive banner in some areas."[25] In one sentence, the newspaper linked racial integration of the military with the specter of communism and the black vote.

Though the president maintained a public silence about civil rights after he issued his order, he moved with some haste to establish the committee his executive order mandated. The White House announced Charles Fahy as director of the committee, which planned to convene at the start of 1949 after Fahy returned from Europe. The other members included Dwight R. G. Palmer, president of General Cable Corporation; William E. Stevenson, president of Oberlin College; Lester Granger, executive secretary of the National Urban League (and former assistant to Secretary of Defense James Forrestal during World War II); and John H. Sengstacke, publisher of the *Chicago Defender*. Truman appointed a formidable committee with considerable experience in public policy. All had made public commitments to civil rights.

Truman's appointment of Charles H. Fahy as director of the committee charged with crafting policy for the military's integration indicated how he viewed the committee's formidable, if not impossible, charge. At the time of his appointment, Fahy served on the U.S. Court of Appeals in Washington, D.C. A Georgia-born lawyer and New Deal liberal, Fahy had served as general counsel for the National Labor Relations Board from 1935 to 1940 and then litigated cases brought by workers against the federal government and unions. In 1944 he argued as a "friend of the court" on a case brought by two black firemen against the racial barriers established by the Brotherhood of Locomotive Firemen and Engineers. During Fahy's time on the labor relations board, observers noted that he absorbed the intellectual, legal, and moral reasons against racial discrimination and segregation until these issues became his own.[26] David Niles, administrative assistant to Truman, described Fahy as "totally reconstructed on the subject of race."[27] As committee director, Fahy hoped to have the president's authority to desegregate the military. When President Truman met with the committee and the three secretaries of the services, Fahy was pleased. Using his typical "plain language," the president said he wanted "concrete results—that's what I'm after—not publicity on it." If he did not see progress, he "intended to knock somebody's ears down."[28] Without any power except the president's order and his private promise, Fahy planned to persuade, negotiate, and goad the civilian and military leadership into accepting desegregation. For him, integration was ethical, moral, and efficient.[29] Despite his resolve, Fahy encountered the greatest resistance from another southerner, Secretary of the Army Kenneth Royall.

The army immediately objected to the appointment of Lester Granger to Fahy's new committee. Before Truman's order, Royall met with Granger and fifteen other African Americans, a group that included lawyer Sadie T. Alexander, Truman Gibson, Howard University president Mordecai Johnson, Walter White's assistant Roy Wilkins, NAACP lawyer Charles H. Houston, and Phelps-Stokes Fund director Channing Tobias. Hoping to stanch A. Phillip Randolph's criticism of the proposed Universal Training Act, Royall wanted the group to endorse the segregated army. "Any improvement must be made within the framework of segregation," he argued. Members of the committee objected and told him no such plan would be possible and that he had to integrate the army. Undaunted, Royall insisted the army's policies of Jim Crow worked better than either the policies or the practices of the navy or the new air force.[30]

From the start of the new committee's efforts, the majority of civilians and the senior staff in the new Department of Defense equivocated over the order's implied intent to integrate the services. All of the services, including the new air force, feared integration would disrupt the efficiency of the military, demoralize whites and inhibit their enlistment, and lead to a rapid enlistment of blacks. Experienced with recalcitrant employers who refused to negotiate with unions, Fahy encouraged each of the services to create plans for integration. The proposals the services later presented arose out of the very different responses each had to the use and presence of black labor during and after World War II. As the newest service with a small but visible cadre of black officers trained in the Army Air Corps, the air force planned for its rapid integration within the year. Fahy and the others on the committee were heartened and pleased. Beginning with the all-black 332nd Fighter unit, the air force proceeded. Over the next months, it integrated with little incident, and the majority of blacks in the segregated Army Air Corps units found positions in integrated units. By early 1950, the air force announced it neared full integration.[31]

Encouraged by the air force's positive response, the committee pressed the navy and the army to present their plans. The secretary of the navy, too, expressed enthusiasm for the president's order, but in the months after the directive, the navy deliberately reduced the number of black officers to two and enlisted personnel to less than 2 percent. The service's dismal treatment of black sailors during World War II, along with their over-all diminished presence, sent a signal far different from one of support for integration. Forced to recall black officers it had dismissed, the navy erected other barriers to diminish blacks' presence. Continued obfuscation by senior officers and equivocation within the Department of the Navy slowed the pace of change. By mid-1950, the navy reported incremental growth in the number of black officers from two to seventeen.[32]

However cautiously and crablike the air force and the navy moved, by any measure the army's defiance bordered on revolt as it refused to respond to the committee's directives. Kenneth C. Royall, who ended his tenure as the secretary of the War Department and became the new secretary of the army, simply ignored the directive to present a plan for integration. Southern-born and a Harvard-educated lawyer, Royall barely concealed his animosity toward blacks and Mexican Americans. He laced his testimony to the Fahy Committee with comments about his personal abhorrence of "race mixing." He frequently used racial stereotypes and defended segregation as efficient management of black men's personal and cultural deficiencies. The army, he stressed, was "not an instrument for social evolution. It is not the Army's job either to favor or to impede social doctrines, no matter how progressive they may be. It is not for us to lead or to lag behind the civilian procession except to the extent that the national defense is affected." He argued that the army provided as much equal treatment and opportunity for blacks as their habits allowed. He claimed that, according to his experience, blacks did not qualify for combat and instead were "exceptionally and peculiarly qualified" for labor.[33] Ignoring years of black troops' riots and strikes against segregation, Royall characterized their high volunteer rates as evidence that they did not mind segregation. "Negroes," he concluded, "liked the Army a little better than the white man" and "were well satisfied with the Army." Royall argued that because most whites in the military came from the South and found "close personal associations with Negroes distasteful," the army endorsed segregation.[34]

Royall remained adamant that the innate racial characteristics and low intelligence of black men made them "unfit for the fight." He insisted from personal experience that black men were "fearful, unreliable, and lacked the manly virtues of the warrior."[35] More troubling, he insisted, their race disrupted the brotherhood of the foxhole and on the battlefield. Combat was white men's work and honor. Since black men lacked the capacity for combat, their presence diminished whites' "natural aptitude" for courage.

He cobbled together his argument from popular ideas about racial inferiority and racialist sociology, concepts that sociologists inside and outside the military had questioned since the late nineteenth century.[36] Conceding segregation may have made the army inefficient, Royall argued its social and psychological benefits for white troops outweighed such concerns. For him, segregation in combat provided the heroic and moral benefits of whiteness on the battlefield.[37] It was unwise to require white men, northerners and southerners alike, he argued, to serve under black officers or NCOs (noncommissioned officers).[38] When properly policed, he insisted, segregation did not subject blacks to discrimination.[39]

Lester Granger, like Fahy, had faced employers resistant to hiring African Americans, and he questioned Royall with a palpable disbelief. He demanded to know how Royall determined blacks' satisfaction with segregation. Drawing on years of experience with blacks' barriers to employment, Granger reminded Royall that black men enlisted and reenlisted in the army because of the difficulties they faced finding work. "They choose a lesser of two evils, a good deal of inequality in certain parts of the country in civilian life and less inequality in the Army." These men, Granger continued, followed the advice of their leaders, and it was "the faith in this leadership [and] in the sincerity of the [Truman] Administration and its intention to get rid of these things" that compelled African Americans to enlist.[40] Quiet throughout Royall's testimony, *Chicago Defender* editor and committee member John Sengstacke asked, "Is it your thinking that you can have equality of opportunity within a segregated setup?" "Yes," Royall replied, "I do think so."[41]

The army remained entrenched and resisted the committee's efforts to enforce the directive. Gordon Gray, who replaced Royall as secretary of the army, joined Omar Bradley, the new army chief of staff, and remained adamant that the army had no plans to desegregate in the immediate future. Instead, the army insisted on a timetable of "gradual integration" that suited its perspectives about blacks' inferiority. Frustrated and exasperated, the committee sought a compromise. Before Fahy could broker another plan, the new secretary of defense, Louis Johnson, accepted the army's promise to end its quota system in exchange for retaining all-black units. Anxious to establish a unified military, Johnson traded integration for the army's support. The president agreed and allowed the army wide discretion to reinstate the quota system if it saw a need. Except for lifting the quota, the army remained segregated.[42]

Though frustrated and alarmed by the president's concessions to the army, neither members of the Fahy Committee nor the black press publicly characterized the impasse as a failure. *Defender* editor and committee member John Sengstacke expressed cautious optimism that the army might integrate "in time," and he greeted the army's abandonment of its quota system as a sign of progress.[43] Publicly, the black press remained supportive, as it had promised the president in late 1948. Yet when the first troops landed in Korea, Lester Granger and other African Americans privately expressed alarm at the army's continued segregation, and many African Americans saw the start of the war in Korea as a test of American democracy on the battlefield. As some African Americans questioned or denounced the war, others saw the battlefield as a place to advance black civil rights.[44]

The U.S. occupation of Korea began in September 1945 as American troops intended to invade Japan from the south and the Soviets planned to invade Manchuria from Korea's north. Afterward, the former allies divided Korea at the 38th parallel. Occupied by the Japanese for half a century and now partitioned by the United States and the Soviet Union, the two Koreas escalated their threats and counterthreats. Korea emerged as the epicenter of the Cold War. A variety of nationalist groups, some procommunist and others anticommunist, sought Korea's unification, but the United States relied on conservative elements—many of whom were former collaborators with the Japanese occupation—to represent its interests. As the occupation became more turbulent, the Americans turned to the United Nations Temporary Commission on Korea, which supported majority-backed elections in the south. Syngman Ree, who led South Korea's conservative party, gained the majority of the seats and quickly organized a dictatorship. A wary President Truman ordered U.S. troops to withdraw, and they left the Republic of Korea with little military support. At the same time, the Soviet Union trained and supplied the North Korean military. After North Korean troops moved across the 38th parallel in late June 1950, President Truman declared the action as "lawless aggression." Asserting its agreement to honor the demarcation with the Soviet Union, the United States pressed the newly constituted United Nations to act. Within days, the United States agreed to defend South Korea, and the American military began its "police action," providing the bulk of the troops and assigning General Douglas MacArthur to be the supreme commander.[45]

Simultaneously alarmed at the Soviets' move across the 38th parallel and concerned that World War III loomed, most Americans expressed little, if any, desire for mobilization. With fewer than 700,000 personnel in the armed services scattered across five continents, the United States did not have much troop strength to mount an immediate large-scale response. That so few of these troops were anywhere close to Korea or combat-ready added to the military's woes. Still, the Department of Defense mobilized part of the Eighth Army, including the all-black 24th Infantry Regiment, which had served as occupation troops with the 25th Infantry Division in Japan. Other all-black units received orders to prepare for combat in Korea.

In Japan since early 1947, the 24th Infantry Regiment, 3rd Battalion, served as part of the U.S. occupation force in the 25th Infantry Division based in Okinawa. The remaining two battalions of the 24th followed later that spring, bringing the number of black troops to 5,000.[46] Established and commissioned by the U.S. Congress in 1866, the 24th had its origins in the Civil War all-black regiments. The regiment served in the Pacific during World War II, and it remained an all-black unit overwhelmingly commanded by white officers. It was the largest black unit in the army, and new black enlistees and draftees were typically sent to the regiment in Okinawa. Assigned garrison, blacks also prepared for combat in early 1950, but under adverse conditions. All of the regiments in the four Eighth Army divisions stationed in Japan lacked heavy artillery; not one had an authorized heavy tank company. The artillery units were especially ill-equipped and under strength.[47]

Added to the systemic problems of equipment and combat preparation in the division, the majority of the white senior commanders in the 24th Regiment ascribed to the army's belief that blacks were racially inferior and not suited for combat. Assigned to MacArthur's general headquarters in Tokyo, General Edward "Ned" Almond, the former commander of the 92nd Infantry Division during World War II, was considered an "expert" on black troop behavior. He managed the segregation of the unit and designed the blueprint for its training. He claimed black troops more often failed than succeeded in combat, and his initial training regimen lacked rigor and consistency. As in World War II, he characterized black troops as cowardly and lazy, prone to panic and hysteria. In Japan, he "wanted the blacks out of sight and in one place."[48] MacArthur and Almond adamantly refused to initiate the president's executive order. Between 1948 and 1950, Almond removed black officers from the regiment; he confined the remaining officers to the lowest levels of command. Few received promotions at the pace of white officers. Many white officers resented assignment to the 24th, and black officers and troops resented the segregation and limited opportunities.

Almond and his commanders cleaved to earlier practices of segregation even as other units loosened these policies on some bases in the United States. Commanders in Japan vigilantly policed segregation. Clubs for both enlisted men and officers remained segregated; black soldiers could not enter recreation areas assigned to white troops, and swimming pools, theaters, and other recreation facilities remained segregated. Adhering to dominant ideas about the former enemy as inferior and in need of rehabilitation, U.S. military commanders used segregation of U.S. troops to establish authority over the Japanese. Vigilant policing of black troops' public and private behavior helped in this process. The military ordered the Japanese authorities to create separate districts for prostitution, one for white troops and the other for black troops. During the war, the Japanese military forced more than 70,000 women, many Korean, into prostitution. Immediately after the war, the U.S. military ordered Japanese officials to reorganize this system into segregated districts or "comfort stations"— some for black troops and some for white troops. MacArthur ordered these districts closed in 1946, but private "comfort facilities" replaced the earlier brothels and maintained the racial designations.[49]

The participation of black soldiers and airmen in the occupation created contradictory experiences for many. The military occupation organized prostitution that reaffirmed racial hierarchy, but it also allowed black men to participate in the domination of Japanese and Korean women. Red Cross worker Ethel Payne observed that the organized prostitution meant many black soldiers "never had it so good," even with the military's racial restrictions. Yet some men found the combination of women's sexual exploitation and racial segregation debilitating. Sent to Okinawa in late 1947 in a segregated unit, James Forman also acquired a sense of empowerment over Japanese civilians, especially Japanese women. As black, Native American, and Chinese American soldiers visited bars and brothels, he realized he had "become an occupier. Here lived brown people, and the white soldiers called them gooks just like they called me nigger. The Okinawans had to take it because the Americans had guns, just as we had to take it during slavery time. They had captured Okinawa; they had captured us, too. But now I was with them. I was an occupier, too." Some black soldiers, he observed, "also called the Okinawans gooks. They adopted the superior attitude of the American white man and they, too, thought they were better than the Okinawans." Some of the men harmed Okinawan women, "as if they were things, instead of human beings."[50]

In this arrangement of multiple gender and racial hierarchies under military occupation, few Japanese found it possible to critique the American regime. When Wilbert Walker, a lieutenant assigned to the Chemical, Biological, and Radiological Warfare School in Gifu, passed through Nagasaki in 1951, he saw how "the warped, twisted and burned structures of some buildings" that stood alongside new buildings and rebuilt streets "gave silent testimony of the devastation." His contact with some Japanese led him to believe that "they were fiercely proud, that they loathed this occupation of their country."[51] Yet Japan had a long history of dispersion against darker people, especially the Chinese, Koreans, and Filipinos. In Japanese literature, black Americans appeared as the most savage and animalistic characters; their dark skin marked them as different and inferior. When Japanese and Korean women associated with black troops, through force or by choice, many Japanese came to see them as beyond acceptance. As occupation forces used spatial and militaristic practices to affirm American superiority, they imposed racial segregation and the concomitant demand that the Japanese abide by these practices. Indigenous ideas about the racial inferiority of Korean women also supported U.S. conquest.[52]

THE ALL-BLACK 503RD FIELD ARTILLERY landed in Korea in early August 1950 and moved north to aid another all-black unit. What Private Charles Rangel and others in his unit saw next startled them. "Three truckloads of GIs—dead GIs—stacked up just like wood, in their uniforms. And they were black." Minimally prepared for the combat conditions in Korea and low on ammunition, Rangel and the other men in his artillery company barely withstood the relentless combat. Along with other artillery units in the Eighth Army, the 503rd spent the next months struggling to gain ground against the much larger North Korean army. Rangel soon realized that the entire division lacked proper equipment for the extreme weather and mountainous terrain, and they seemed poorly prepared to counter the tactics of the North Korean military. For his all-black unit, the circumstances proved deadly, and their situation did not improve. By the fall his unit finally had enough ammunition, but in the severe cold, their outdated automatic rifles froze.[53]

Conflicting reports about the conditions of troops and equipment appeared in the national news. Some observers noted the dire conditions and contradicted the military's claims that troops had sufficient supplies. One correspondent described "American GI's scrounging for food for their mess."[54] Another reported the inadequate equipment: "An anti-tank battery was forced to retreat before an onslaught of forty North Korean tanks." While "a thunderous" air force gave the 24th Infantry cover, the troops had little additional support. Many accounts gave no indication that American troops lacked equipment, including clothing, food, and weapons. Most articles in the newspapers reassured readers that full-strength divisions arrived in Korea with artillery, armor, and support divisions.[55] Correspondents adopted the army's habit of describing the enemy in racialist and animal terms. The North Korean troops moved like "swarms" of insects; they sounded and moved "like a herd of cattle" and "screamed" like Japanese soldiers during World War II.[56]

Some early newspaper reports from Korea questioned U.S. combat strength and superiority. One *Times* correspondent conceded that troops faced "the best trained advance guards of the North Korean Army," no longer dismissed as a horde of animals or as bees waiting to be swatted. Correspondents now claimed that the North Korean troops fought as well in small groups as they did in large assaults.[57] Veteran correspondent Marguerite Higgins captured the army's distress as it faced larger and better-trained troops. Americans, she described, moved in a "long retreat." Everywhere she saw "raw, young" recruits shocked by what they found in battle. Their commanders described them as "scared." Many units suffered from "bugout fever," Higgins reported. "I saw young Americans turn in battle, or throw down their arms, cursing their government for what they thought was embroilment in a hopeless cause." Armed with tanks and bazookas that lacked adequate ammunition, the troops pulled back and retreated. Again and again, she wrote, "the pattern of retreat was all too painfully familiar."[58]

The American army went to war with too few troops and inadequately equipped, and it was outmatched in every way by the North Korean military. These developments contradicted assessments made in late 1949. Then, many in the new Defense Department believed the American navy, air force, and artillery units superior to the North Korean troops. These perceptions quickly evaporated in late 1950. Army commanders reported that the ground artillery did not "penetrate Soviet T-34 tank armor." All of the regiments in the four Eighth Army divisions stationed in Japan lacked heavy artillery; not one had an armor company with heavy equipment. The artillery units, especially, were ill-prepared and under strength. The troops' frequent and rapid retreats exacerbated the army's equipment shortages. As the men "dropped arms, equipment, sometimes even helmets, boots, and personal weapons," cohesion quickly vanished. The debris of retreat lay strewn behind them as they went.[59]

These repeated retreats throughout the divisions suggested the widespread and inadequate preparation of American troops. These men quickly became "disoriented." Many were ill from the water or suffered from dysentery. Others were "savaged by mosquitoes." Inexperienced and "confused" junior officers and experienced senior officers alike fared no better. All buckled under the high heat and humidity. The troops, commanders conceded, "looked like a bunch of Boy Scouts [and] faced tried combat soldiers." Sergeant Chester Van Arman, a veteran of the Battle of the Bulge, found the action around the Kum River "far tougher than anything he saw in Europe." One American commander explained to a reporter that he no longer had 183 men (the equivalent of several companies). No mention was made of how the men came to be "lost." Were the men killed, captured, or gone AWOL? Secretary of State Dean Acheson remained "circumspect about the course of fighting." In public statements, General MacArthur expressed confidence in the military's ability to finish the war quickly.[60]

Four weeks into the "police action," Truman went before Congress and asked for a partial mobilization of troops and equipment. In a radio address, the president warned Americans that Korea was part of a larger war on the "Communist challenge" and he needed a larger "military program to strengthen the United States and its allies." The war "caught the anti-Communist countries dangerously under-armed." While the United States had stockpiled atomic weapons and had a better navy and air force, he needed more troops and tanks to counter the Soviet military, which appeared to be three times larger than the Western European and U.S. military combined. Faced with this imbalance, yet determined to defend the world from Communism in Korea, President Truman called for "the mobilization of manpower" through the draft, the reserves, and the National Guard. He added a call for more troops at a moment when unemployment had fallen.[61]

Part of the Eighth Army division assigned to occupation duties in Japan, the all-black 24th Infantry Regiment arrived two weeks after other units in the division. Assigned to the 25th Division, the regiment had three battalions for a total of 3,000 troops and was part of the 25th's complement of 18,000 troops. Although designated as an "all-Negro unit," the 24th also included Puerto Ricans assigned to the 24th because of their darker skin color. Overall, black and Puerto Rican soldiers made up less than 10 percent of this first contingent of troops to arrive.[62]

As the largest and oldest of the all-black units, the 24th Infantry Regiment acquired significant visibility in the black press. By early July, the front pages of black newspapers announced that the regiment, stationed in Gifu, Japan, "had already been moved up [to] face the Korean reds."[63] Bradford T. Laws, the *Baltimore Afro-American* Far East correspondent, reported that many men in the 24th were "old hands in Asiatic campaigns." As one of the first accredited black war correspondents approved by the Department of Defense, James Hicks joined Laws. In contrast to World War II, when the OWI did not permit black correspondents and photographers to report from the war zone until late in the war, Hicks and six other correspondents for the black weeklies received immediate approval to write from the front lines. Within days, Hicks, Laws, and Albert L. Hinton, associate editor of the *Norfolk Journal and Guide*, traveled to Korea. Ralph Matthews from the *Baltimore Afro-American* and L. Alex Wilson from the *Chicago Defender* joined Hicks, Laws, and Hinton. Assigned as pool correspondents, Laws and Hinton planned to have their articles appear in a half-dozen black papers; Hicks wrote exclusively for the *Afro-American*. An army veteran, Hicks had served in New Guinea and Australia for three years. He received a field promotion and became a second lieutenant in 1943. He began his career as a journalist in 1945, working first in the War Department Bureau of Public Relations and then for the National Negro Press Association, which he joined in 1947. A year later he began reporting for the *Afro-American*, where he wrote a variety of columns, including the "Veterans Whirl."[64] Having served in combat, Hicks was ideally suited as a war correspondent.

The first reports from correspondents shocked readers. *Afro-American* reporter Albert Hinton was missing and then confirmed dead in an airplane crash. Hicks reported, too, that the "situation" had become "grave in Korea" and that the 24th faced repeated and heavy attacks over fourteen days of continuous fighting. The regiment held its positions, but the all-white First Cavalry gave way on its left flank in a fierce conflict and seriously weakened its position. "If Kumshon [sic] falls," he wrote, "the 24th may be completely cut off. The situation is grave." Three of the battalions bore "the brunt of the attack."[65]

However grim, Hicks's descriptions of black men's "glory" on the battlefield also thrilled readers. The military had barred black reporters from the front lines, and black correspondents had been unable to follow black combat units so closely. Wearing a uniform without insignia, the tall and lanky Hicks moved among the men. He reported their names and home addresses. He described what they wore, what they ate, and what they thought. Throughout days of heavy fighting, Hicks became a witness "to the fight" as he "watched men of the 24th stand off two heavy enemy attacks in which they suffered losses but held ground without yielding an inch." Hicks described in vivid detail how Sergeant Joe Simmons from Detroit held "his machine gun fire until the enemy patrol was trapped and then cut loose. He has been credited unofficially with killing 30 of the enemy." Whatever their assignment, all men on the battlefield were "pressed into service," Hicks noted, including "medical aid men." Chaplains, too, were in the thick of the fire "to give battling troops and wounded spiritual support."[66]

No longer optimistic about immediate victory, Hicks and the other reporters questioned the army's tactics. Why did the army not hold against the troops they considered inferior in every way? "The homefolks assumed that in this area of possible trouble we had placed our toughest combat units right on the threshold of communism," Ralph Matthews reported; "but when hostilities broke out, our forces turned out to be a bunch of green kids." Hicks's daily cables to the *Afro-American* described the mismatched armies. American troops "were outnumbered 3 to 1 in some places and from 10 to 1 in others." American divisions lacked full strength and had inadequate preparation for mountainous terrain. Despite reinforcements, the Americans "have been compelled to retreat."[67]

Hicks's articles praised the largest of the all-black units, the 24th Infantry Regiment, but he soon expressed caution. The regiment was "hit hard," he reported, by the "staggering" casualties, and "this crack regiment is continually being sent into the line without vital equipment necessary for combat." These problems, he charged, were present months before the men went to war. He discovered that "the enlisted men from a headquarters company chipped in their own money to have [some equipment] fixed." Hicks investigated and discovered that many, possibly all, of the black units lacked parts for jeeps and had too few weapons. As soon as the supplies were available, he was told, the men would have what they needed. "This made sense to me, a former Quartermaster officer trained in the ways of supply, but these facts are recorded now because the 24th Regiment is currently being judged on its performance, the lack of vital equipment notwithstanding." Already the 24th, he noted, was accused of leaving equipment to the enemy. Company commanders were later told that no new equipment was to come, since the regiment "had carelessly used it and allowed it to get away." But from Hicks's view, the 24th had been in combat longer than the other units, and all of the units "had been run off," leaving equipment behind.[68]

Even as they fought in segregated units, black soldiers understood that their participation in combat signaled progress to many readers. But these men also considered the conditions they faced on the battlefield as consequences of their segregation. Unlike white units, the men did not rotate out of combat, and the entire regiment fought without relief for 126 days, beginning in late July and continuing through the start of the bitter winter.[69] They were poorly supplied. Their shoes disintegrated, and they bound their feet with rags and ropes until new ones arrived weeks later. When the temperatures dropped, the men fought without jackets and gloves. Charles Armstrong and his unit "lived like bandits. [We] didn't get much sleep. Sometimes we had rations, other times we had to eat what we could find." At one point, the men caught and barbecued a pig stolen from a Korean farmer.[70]

In spite of these conditions, black soldiers persisted. An assistant platoon sergeant in the 24th, Robert Yancy faced his work with precision and diligence. He had fifty-three men to command. They laid minefields and set up perimeters. The men moved quickly after he ordered them to "dig in" and locate the enemy. He intended to stay alive and keep his men alive. He taught them how to control their fears and stay down. Some men wanted to look, "and so they'd get hit right through the head." He realized a battle exacted casualties. "A soldier is a warrior," Yancy said, "and to be a warrior you kill, or be killed." Yet he found many things unequal for the segregated regiment. The men were always sent first into combat, and they went with the worst equipment.[71] The men felt other inequities, too, although they hesitated to mention them. Black troops carried all their own gear, equipment, and weapons up and down the mountainous terrain. One rifle typically weighed twenty-three to twenty-five pounds. In contrast, South Korean civilians carried the equipment and supplies for the white troops.[72] Yancy was not alone in making his assessment. Eighteen-year-old Curtis Morrow experienced waves of exaltation, relief, and regret as he survived the frequent ambushes. Discouraged by the limited food and outdated equipment, Morrow and the other men took pride in how they conducted their patrols and ambushes. They scattered when necessary, found cover, then regrouped and faced the North Korean troops. The men knew that their commanders scrutinized them more and considered them "unfit for the fight" because of their race. While their successes went unnoticed outside the black press, they praised one another. "Yes, we were damn good combat soldiers and knew it."[73]

Moving among the few black officers, correspondent L. Alex Wilson learned segregation exacted a heavy toll in the regiment's first three months of combat. "The list of wounded, missing in action, and the number of dead officers stood at more than 90 percent." Casualty rates for the enlisted men were little better. One battalion lost more than 50 percent of its troops. Some commanders conceded that segregation had led to poor staffing and equipping of the regiment. Many interpreted these high combat death rates as indications of black men's unfitness for command and combat roles. Morale sank when the new commander of the regiment, Colonel Arthur Champeny, described the men as the "24th Frightened Regiment." Champeny did not remain in command very long. "Against the advice of the men," Wilson reported, he stood "upright" and was hit by a sniper.[74]

Confined to the battlefield for weeks, the men learned quickly how to advance and stay alive. Curtis Morrow found the enemy and reported its positions. "We lost quite a few men like that, but I was always lucky. I never got hit." His sense of luck elicited in him "a certain feeling of jubilation that only a combat infantryman experiences." This "state of mind" made him feel "invincible," a feeling he knew put him in greater danger. Mostly, he charged into gunfire. He did not look back, and he prayed that he would not get hit or killed or run out of ammunition. For him, combat was like "putting a loaded revolver in your mouth, with one bullet in the chamber, then pulling the trigger five or six times, while praying the firing pin lands on an empty chamber each time."[75]

The segregated work of killing created an individual and collective critical consciousness, and the men's responses to combat shifted from "exaltation" to disbelief. Whole black companies were killed, and many had repeated injuries.[76] Experienced soldiers complained about the inadequate and outdated equipment and uniforms; they detested the inexperienced white officers who expressed contempt for the black men.[77] They despised the segregation and the racist language used to describe them and the enemy. Ivory Perry questioned the shooting and killing of "somebody I don't know nothing about, never had any conflict toward." His constant fear for his own life under horrific conditions of sleep deprivation, cold, and dysentery eroded how he understood himself and others as human beings.[78] James Milton Harp, a gunner in the 231st Field Artillery, took pride in his ability to handle the guns. He and others in his unit "blew up anything," comforted that "he did not see the face of the enemy." When he did, he "didn't want any more part of it." For Curtis Morrow and other men in the 24th, the experience of their segregated conditions—mixed with fear, repulsion, and glory on the battlefield—generated a deep resistance to the work of combat. He wondered if the young Korean and Chinese men he killed were really his enemy. "What the hell had we black people ever done to them that merited such inhumane treatment?"[79]

Despite their poor equipment and their doubts about the work, the men maintained combat discipline. After observing the men in combat, one division officer noted, "They just kept that mail going out."[80] Despite the intense and relentless fighting, overall the Eighth Army made little progress. The men had "too much real estate" to cover "and not enough men," James Hicks reported. The men complained to him that the North Korean troops "just keep coming no matter how many we kill." A week later, Hicks was with the 24th along the Yongdong and Sangju front. "Each night there is an attack," he wrote, "and each night it is beaten off. And each night an attack is beaten off, there are casualties, wounded, missing, and dead." When ordered, they also retreated. At times, the division commanders ordered the regiment to stop its advance so as to avoid moving too far forward and separating from other divisions.[81]

By late August, Hicks's reports about the 24th acquired an ominous tone as he noted the various "judgments" about the regiment's record in combat. "The reputation and integrity of the colored people as fighting Americans is on the wings of every bullet, every bazooka shell, every mortar shell, and every artillery barrage which the men of the 24th send in the direction of the enemy." They knew, he observed, that "the entire race" was being judged "by one war effort of one regiment." Within weeks, the praise for the regiment's prowess evaporated, and the tone shifted from admiration to condemnation.[82]

Lieutenant Leon Gilbert, one of the regiment's few black junior officers, led his unit under particularly terrible circumstances. The men fought in trenches and foxholes without bayonets, machine guns, or automatic weapons. For days the men stayed on alert and went without sleep. Gilbert had acute dysentery. Colonel Horton V. White, Gilbert's commander, ordered the men to return to their positions. Assessing the unit's severe equipment shortages, his own debilitating illness, and high losses of men,

Gilbert ordered his unit to pull back. By then, additional North Korean troops occupied Bloody Ridge at Yechon. Ordered forward, Gilbert refused again and then described to his commander the impossibility of completing the mission with too few men and inadequate weapons. A major argued with Gilbert and accused him of being afraid to fight—a charge typically used to belittle black troops. The colonel and major placed Gilbert under arrest and charged him with violating the Seventy-fifth Article of War, which included "misbehaving himself before the enemy by refusing to advance his command when ordered to do so." Gilbert, the charge declared, was a coward.[83]

By the late fall, the NAACP began to receive reports from dozens of black soldiers who were charged with cowardice. The overwhelming majority of these reports and complaints came from soldiers in the army assigned to segregated units in Korea. News rumbled through the black and white presses that the army had charged a high number of black troops with cowardice in the early months of the war. The reports from black soldiers described the poor conditions on the field, including shortages of food and warm clothing. Along with his articles, James Hicks sent separate reports to the NAACP describing the black prisoners pulled out of the foxholes and then "shackled, being brought into the railroad station in Tokyo." The men then received hastily conducted courts-martial. After weeks watching white and black troops retreat, Hicks suspected army commanders were embarrassed by the disarray of their troops in Korea, but only black troops faced excessive charges, inadequate counsel, and lengthy prison terms. Several received life sentences, and the army court sentenced Gilbert to death.[84]

As the soldiers, including Lieutenant Leon Gilbert, asked the NAACP for help, Thurgood Marshall agreed to travel to Japan and investigate. As he arranged for his trip, his office also prepared to serve as counsel to the black soldiers facing courts-martial. Though Lieutenant Gilbert had been charged, tried, and convicted in Korea, Marshall served as his legal counsel for the appeal held in Washington, D.C. Marshall had Gilbert's sentence reduced from death to twenty years upon the review board's recommendation to President Truman. Eventually Gilbert was released in 1955.[85]

General MacArthur took steps to prevent Marshall's clearance and asked the FBI for any information that might let him deny Marshall's request to travel. After FBI agents claimed Marshall belonged to "two groups cited as Communist fronts" by the House Un-American Activities Committee (HUAC), MacArthur denied Marshall's request. Walter White and

Roy Wilkins pressed the White House, and an angry Truman provided the clearance. "Who's running this damned show?" he reportedly asked when he heard about MacArthur's obstructions. Once Marshall was in Korea, his encounters with MacArthur hardly reassured the lawyer. He noticed the general did not have black officers on his staff or assigned to his head-quarters. Marshall suspected these exclusions were deliberate. Before he began his investigation, he "thought there was a good probability that the men had been victims of racial bias and unfair trials based on conditions inherent in the army's segregation policies."[86]

Marshall began a careful series of interviews with military officials and prisoners. During his review of the courts-martial records in Washing-ton, D.C., Marshall had interviewed Lieutenant Gilbert. Once in Korea, he made daily visits to the men in the stockades and interviewed each man. He created a chart for each man and then compared them, looking for "patterns in how the trials were handled." He spoke to others, includ-ing witnesses and members of the men's units. Once Marshall completed these interviews and assessed the reports, he met with MacArthur. One of the general's aides encouraged Marshall to visit the 24th on the front lines in Korea.[87] Marshall agreed, but the trip proved harrowing. He traveled by jeep as bullets whizzed and shells exploded over his head. At one point, he and his escort, Colonel D. D. Martin, ended up in a ditch.[88]

Marshall found the reports he heard from black soldiers still in combat as disturbing as the reports from the convicted men. First, he interviewed several men from each company of the 24th and from every battery of the 159th. In Pusan, he went through 118 complaints filed in the 25th Divi-sion "from all types of offenses." From the interviews and review of the records, he determined commanders disproportionately charged black soldiers with cowardice and disobeying orders. "Twice as many Negroes were tried, although there were four times as many whites in the Division!" Thirty-two black soldiers were charged; thirty received sentences of ten or more years, including one with a death sentence. Only two white soldiers received sentences of five years or less.[89]

The accused and convicted men reported how white soldiers and their units repeatedly retreated. Earlier Hicks had described how he and others witnessed whites' flight, concluding that "white men have actually done more running." Only black soldiers were arrested out of the foxhole, courts-martialed in less than fifty minutes, and sentenced to life in prison. In con-trast, Hicks reported, John P. Kean, the son of General William Kean, one of the senior commanders of the Eighth Army, was accused of cowardice in late November 1950 but returned to command the next day. Others corroborated the claim that the younger Kean and his company "stampeded and ran away." Hicks "steadfastly claimed that the entire U.S. Army in Korea was running in face of enemy fire."[90] What looked like a terrified stampede and cowardice in August appeared orderly and prudent in November once the military conceded it was unprepared for the war.

Marshall focused on the courts-martial procedures of the thirty-six accused and sentenced men. If he heard the swirl of news about troops and their "orderly withdrawals," he did not include it in his report. He concentrated on the protocol of military justice and concluded that the courts-martial of the black men occurred in haste; some trials lasted no more than fifty minutes. Experienced with the time and process needed to prepare such cases, Marshall insisted that "counsel did not have time to prepare defense for the men who were rushed from the fox holes to trial." Many of the men did not testify at their own hearings or have time to give vital information to their lawyers. He was equally disturbed by the repeated use of "nigger" by some white officers and the aspersions cast against black troops more generally. These patterns of daily condemnation, along with Lieutenant Gilbert's death sentence, made the men expect no less than life sentences for themselves. The men told Marshall, "They are not paying any attention to anything we say." Returning to U.S. headquarters in Tokyo, Marshall managed to have sentences dramatically reduced for twenty-one soldiers. Four men with lengthy sentences had all charges dropped; the soldier with a life sentence had it reduced to five years.[91]

Marshall completed his investigation, returned to the United States by ship, and began a tour of branches, where he recounted his trip to the warfront. Members organized gatherings to raise money for the NAACP and to hear Marshall speak about his investigations. The courts-martial, the behavior of senior officers, and the rigid segregation he blamed on MacArthur. Sidestepping the contentious months during the Fahy meetings that had failed to bring about the army's integration, Marshall argued that "the responsibility for maintaining the color line in the army in the Far East rests with General MacArthur, who has failed to implement the President's order for the elimination of segregation from the armed services." He set the tone for the entire command, Marshall concluded. The president's executive order had failed to compel the army to end segregation, and Marshall's investigations exposed its impact on black combat troops. Back in his New York office, Marshall crafted a thorough report that aired the soldiers' grievances and the racial bias of military justice. Disturbed by the reason for his trip to Korea, Marshall was nonetheless satisfied with the outcome of his investigations and counsel.[92]

As Marshall detailed the continued segregation in the army and the inequalities in its use of punishment, he pondered the repeated pattern of claims about black soldiers' cowardice. The charges "little varied from war to war. First come reports from the front of some heroic deed done by Negro soldiers, . . . and then suddenly the reports change. As if in a concerted effort to discredit the record of Negro fighting men, the tales we begin to hear are of incompetency, failure, and cowardice—accounts which would make it appear that Negroes are not capable of combat duty and should be restricted to labor battalions." Even the battlefield song "Bugout Fever," which white soldiers created to describe their own re-treats, was now believed to be about black troops' cowardice. Marshall found it difficult "to believe that these men could change over from heroes to cowards, all within days, even under the violent pressures of warfare." He observed, too, that not one soldier in an integrated unit was charged with cowardice.[93]

In the wake of Marshall's investigations, General Matthew Ridgway, the new commander of the beleaguered Eighth Army, wondered, too, about the charges against the 24th Regiment.[94] Ridgway's divisions faced an enormous disadvantage in their overall troop strength after nearly 350,000 Chinese troops joined the North Korean troops and broke the right flank of the Eighth Army. Again the divisions were pushed down the peninsula, and North Korea reclaimed Seoul. The depleted American and United Nations troops began a slow ascent up the peninsula. With every division desperate for replacements, Ridgway considered the official integration of the army "high priority."[95]

As Ridgway and the other commanders in the division debated whether to integrate combat units, the popular press continued to depict black men as "cowardly" soldiers. Harold Martin wrote in the *Saturday Evening Post* that the men in the 24th "fought hard when [they were] in the mood to fight." Again Martin repeated the popular claims of blacks' innate cow-ardice in combat: Black soldiers feared the night and refused to fight; they dropped their weapons; they fell asleep in the foxholes; and even the North Koreans knew the men took flight. Martin admitted that black soldiers integrated into white units fought adequately, and some all-black units had strong combat records. Martin conceded, too, that the problems the 24th displayed "affected [some] white soldiers, too," but these men, he insisted, were exceptions. Black soldiers in the 24th displayed characteristics common to all blacks in combat: They grinned and sang religious songs in the daylight, but they took flight at night.[96] Martin wrote the article in 1951 about charges filed against troops in August 1950. Why the particular and continued criticism of the 24th when many war correspondents during the first months of the war described the American army as an army on the run?

The stereotype of the cowardly black soldier, which had been a common depiction since the War of 1898 as a means to explain segregation in the military "fighting for democracy," was challenged after World War II. But popular and military rhetoric infused this idea with new power as the North Koreans and Chinese were depicted in racial and animalistic terms. The press described these troops as "savages" who indiscriminately killed troops and treated prisoners of war with brutality. Korea, the military charged, smelled of human excrement; the mountains made the landscape a deathtrap for tanks. All the Koreans "looked alike," and it was difficult to tell the difference between allies and enemies. As the United States floundered on the battlefield, these descriptions of Korea and North Korean troops became more horrific.[97]

Many in the army subscribed to the idea that race was biological and immutable, especially under combat conditions. Based on long-held racial stereotypes and ideas of blacks' biological inferiority, some commanders believed African Americans occupied the lowest strata in the hierarchy of races. Wartime and postwar studies by the biological, psychological, and social sciences challenged these pervasive ideas, but racialist sensibilities prevailed and informed the army's convictions about the need for segregation in the foxhole.[98] White commanders committed to racialist ideas and practices argued from "their experiences" that the 24th Regiment's cowardice on the battlefield irrefutably proved these beliefs: Black men refused to fight and they took flight. Troops who did not run would soon "bug out" when given the chance, just as black troops had run in previous wars. It was "common knowledge," white troops and commanders repeated again and again, that black men fought only when pressed to do so and only when properly supervised. Recounting an example that appeared reminiscent of a scene in Theodore Roosevelt's account of black troops at San Juan Hill, one commander explained how he stopped the men in Korea, took them by the hand, and returned them to their positions. He claimed he threatened them with a gun. Left unattended (and always at night), he insisted, they fled and left their guns, jeeps, and tanks behind.

From his perspective, the men's race and history ensured disaster on the battlefield. With such a history, black troops always dissolved into disorder and chaos.[99]

White officers' repeated characterization of black troops as "unreliable" and unstable pervaded the enlisted ranks, too. "A good black soldier in combat," one soldier insisted, "was exceptional." They were only reliable, one man remarked, when white men retained command. "The Koreans, Puerto Ricans and the Negroes are all the same in that respect." Some white soldiers were most vehement in their assessments of black troops. "They're no damn good. They're piss poor. They run into chinks; they drop their packs and all their equipment."[100]

Ridgway considered the charges against the 24th as he investigated the overall weaknesses and failures of the Eighth Army. Black troops could not fight, some commanders repeatedly claimed. Yet the field reports, known as "after-action reports," that Ridgway read about the 24th at Pusan and Yechon, along with the praise he heard from commanders of black troops in other units, contradicted these arguments and assessments. Moreover, he knew black paratroopers in the 82nd Airborne performed well in combat, and some of those men now commanded all-black units in Korea. He pressed the white commanders in the 24th Regiment about the high death rates of the troops and the inadequate equipment. Ridgway concluded that many white commanders, in particular General Ned Almond, who commanded all-black units during World War II, demonstrated a palpable racial intolerance that hindered the 24th.[101]

Faced with constant shortages, especially of combat troops, yet fearful about white troops' reactions, the army ordered another battlefield survey that elicited considerable debate among white commanders.[102] While some insisted that all-black units were structurally and ideologically designed to fail, others reported black troops performed well in combat, regardless of segregation. One commander insisted that in all his "traveling around at night I have not found a sleeping guard or an unmanned weapon." Other commanders watched black men fight as well as white men, and that was all the evidence they needed. Overall, one officer noted, in battle black troops were "credible" and "equal to and comparable in every respect to any other unit he had commanded." If the 24th failed, some commanders concluded, it was due to poor leadership from white commanders and the low morale segregated units engendered.[103]

Little empirical evidence supported whether blacks fought better or worse in combat than whites, but the military knew that segregation hin-

dered the use of black troops on the battlefield and in the military generally. Because of the dominant racial beliefs, the army had actively discounted this evidence, and it suppressed data that demonstrated black
men had prevailed in combat during World War II despite segregation,
limited training, and poor equipment. During World War II, some commanders argued that segregation limited the availability of black troops
for use in combat. In Korea, commanders repeated these claims. "It's a
problem," one officer reported, "because if we're going into a war with Russia, we'll need to make use of all our manpower." One commander bluntly
calculated the possibility of combat casualties. "Everybody knows you've
got to be able to use all available manpower, and we have some 13 million
Negroes. That's a vast pool." One commander bristled at such quotas of
death to justify integration. "I've heard it said that they're 10 percent of
the population and they ought to do 10 percent of the dying. I don't send
men into battle to die, I send them out to do a job. I want them to do it efficiently. I don't send them out to die."[104]

Many commanders, including General Ridgway, knew that black troops
resented segregation and the condemnation of their ability. Army surveys
revealed that black troops especially balked at characterizations of their
actions in combat as a cowardice born from racial inferiority. The resentment in Korea was especially high. "If we get surrounded and have to pull
out and lose a lot of things, we get a bad name," one soldier noted. White
troops retreated, too, he said. A white company "lost a whole battery and
ten tanks; never heard anything about it. Happens to us, it's all over Korea
that we bugged out." Another soldier agreed. "I'll tell you all this here shit
about the Negro soldier will bug out is just baloney. They'll all drop them
hats when that stuff gets hot. I've seen them tanks turn around and get out
when that shit got too much." They resented, especially, the poor leadership from white commanders. "The men know he don't know what he's
doing, how the hell can they have any confidence in him. I tell you, the
leadership stinks."[105]

After Ridgway replaced MacArthur as overall U.N. commander and
pressed for full integration, he encountered widely different responses
that suggested both personal and tactical considerations. While a few
commanders, most notably General Ned Almond, called for the removal
of black troops from combat, others did not resist. General Kean sent
Ridgway "an earnest and thoughtful recommendation for the integration
of white and Negro troops." Kean commanded black troops after the war
while stationed at Fort Benning, and again in Korea, which included as-

sociation with the 24th Infantry Regiment. Kean, Ridgway learned, "felt from a human and a military point of view, it was wholly inefficient, not to say improper, to segregate troops this way. This coincided precisely with my own views." Other senior officers agreed, including General Maxwell Taylor, then the army's assistant chief of staff. Ridgway considered integration as a morale and moral issue. "It was my conviction, as it was General Kean's" that integration would "assure the sort of *esprit* a fighting army needs, where each soldier stands proudly on his own feet, knowing himself to be as good as the next fellow. Besides, it had always seemed to me both un-American and un-Christian for free citizens to be taught to downgrade themselves this way, as if they were unfit to associate with their fellows or to accept leadership themselves."[106] Ridgway concluded that whites' attitudes, not black troops' aptitude, shaped the segregated battlefield.

Months before Ridgway made integration the official army policy, some commanders abandoned the army's segregation in response to the shortages of combat troops. One division had such high casualty and desertion rates that the commander was relieved of duty, and the new commander called for any replacements, including black troops. Just weeks into the war, the high troop loss compelled commanders to place black soldiers into units in the 9th Regiment, 2nd Infantry. By October, black officers commanded integrated units in the regiment. With the numbers of men in the companies so depleted throughout the Eighth Army, troops expressed anxiety when black junior commanders received assignments elsewhere; some white troops reportedly resisted the removal of black officers they considered "leaders" and "fair." When L. Alex Wilson interviewed white troops for the *Chicago Defender*, they claimed senior officers, not junior officers or the enlisted men, had resisted integration.[107] The all-volunteer 89th Medium Tank Battalion in the 25th Infantry Division arrived in Korea already integrated. Cadres of five, which included black tankmen, crowded into a "rolling hunk of iron." Before the army's shift in policy, war correspondents laced their columns with whites' testimonies of support for integration. Wounded and carried down a winding road, one white southerner announced to the correspondents on the crowded road, "Everything is going o.k. up there and if any SOB tells me here or back home that Negroes can't fight I am going to use my gun on him."[108]

L. Alex Wilson returned to Chicago in December 1950 and told radio audiences how he witnessed integration on the battlefield. "The Korean War has done more to wipe out Jim Crow in the army than any other campaign," Wilson reported. "Negro and white GIs during the grave crisis in Korea—the first armed showdown between American democracy and communism—have made liars out of bigoted politicians." "War," he declared, provided "the purgative [for] race hate among comrades on the front lines." Readers lauded men who died in integrated units for "a life given in the cause of freedom."[109]

As reports like Wilson's appeared in the black press, General Matthew Ridgway assessed commanders' differing responses to troop shortages and integration. He found common ground regarding making black troops available and limiting their presence in each unit. He agreed to limit black troops to 12 percent under his command and no more than 10 percent of the total. For those opposed to integration, the dispersion of troops across units appeared to make black troops "inconspicuous."[110] From his perspective, these quotas might assuage reluctant commanders, and blacks' limited presence need not disrupt combat. Now placed in integrated units, black troops would receive training and equipment with white troops, and all units would be more efficient on the battlefield.

Will (Wilbert) Walker was among a group of demobilized black officers ordered to return and command integrated units in the Korean War. Walker received his notice in the spring of 1951 and was assigned to train troops with the 5th Infantry Division at Indiantown Gap, Pennsylvania. One of two African Americans assigned to the unit, Walker was the only officer. "I was a Second Lieutenant, I had no difficulty with the cadre in my company." Over the next weeks, several white officers joined him, and together they trained integrated units, about 225 in each group, one-fourth African American. A veteran of World War II, Walker had been in the navy. In the army he witnessed no unrest among the men, most of whom were eighteen- to twenty-two-year-olds from mid-Atlantic states. Other groups had more southern-born troops, with half of each unit black. "Their assignment to platoons and bunks were done in alphabetical order. Black and white youth slept side by side here. I knew how different this was for them, for in their home towns the races were separated." These troops, too, he observed, were well-organized and cohesive.[111]

By the time Walker arrived in Korea to command an artillery company, his regiment's main task was reconnaissance and to prepare "a cease fire line" for the United Nations truce. His platoon manned long-range weapons, so they sought higher ground and built bunkers. Walker and his units endured cold temperatures as they traversed steep, nearly impassable hills. Moving and positioning the heavy equipment exhausted the platoons. Digging bunkers, cutting logs, and clearing snow, Walker noted, was much like work in a labor battalion, and it made the men low. Having served in an all-black labor battalion during World War II, Walker knew the mostly white unit did not do the heavy work like black troops had done in the previous war. "There is one significant difference in what we are doing from a labor battalion," he observed. "We are assigned men from the Korean Service Corp to do the hard labor. Every day the groups assigned log and trail cutting duties place requisitions for laborers. The Koreans do the real labor."[112]

The army's process of integration unfolded in uneven and contested patterns. Some white units suddenly became integrated, and a few black officers at the junior ranks arrived to command them. As commander of one of the first integrated companies, Charles Armstrong recalled that "one of the [white soldiers] said to me, 'Nigger give me a light,' and I said, 'What did you say?' and [he] said 'A light nigger.' And I said, 'I don't play that.'" Later, "some of the white guys in my troops told him I was an officer and not to do that to me." Isolated and without mentorship, Armstrong felt forced out in 1956. "I knew it was a losing battle, but I wanted to serve my country. So few of us were commissioned officers, people were looking to me to be successful. I felt it was my obligation to fight. I thought I would benefit, but I didn't."[113]

In contrast to the army, the new air force appeared to move faster to "provide equality of opportunity" to African Americans. Despite having high scores when tested in 1947, James Forman and the other men in his all-black unit were assigned to a labor unit. Once the air force integrated, Forman's assignment changed. Now the only African American in an engineer aviation unit, Forman "found no trouble." Instead, his new unit gave him access to abundant and fresh food, better accommodations, and a better job. Every morning, he now ate fresh, not powdered, eggs. And he stopped building roads and worked in a technical position. "The damn segregated Air Force touched a man not only in his head and his dignity, but even in his stomach."[114]

Integration of the army happened slowly outside combat conditions. Robert Yancy, who earlier served in a segregated army unit, experienced desegregation on a U.S. base in ways that he found slow and disheartening. Without clear oversight or criteria, senior officers either prevented or haphazardly implemented integration. A senior NCO, Yancy was ordered by a major to work like a corporal. "An infantry colonel came back there, saw me, and said, 'Sarge, you are a disgrace to the NCO Corps down there on your knees like a private.'" Yancy told him a major had ordered him "to paint pedestrian lines on the street." The colonel took Yancy to see the major and "chewed the major out. He told him the army's changing and if he didn't change, he should get out." For months, Yancy had to replay the same scenario and then watch colonels command majors to accept integration.[115]

Despite the uneven integration that followed the Korean War, the black press pronounced the rapid desegregation of the army and the military a civil rights victory. Article after article described the emerging cadre of black pilots and officers integrated into army, air force, and navy units as the vanguard of integration elsewhere in American life. The NAACP moved quickly to leverage this desegregation into other aspects of American life, including the stalled efforts to establish the FEPC. As the Cold War military rapidly reshaped American lives, the nation's landscapes, and built spaces, including the creation of bases the size of small towns, many African Americans hoped its desegregation might accelerate the desegregation of American life more generally.[116]

As the drama of integration unfolded in Korea, few noticed the disproportionately high enlistments, reenlistments, and draft rates of black men that coincided with blacks' particular economic and political subordination. In the decade after the Korean War, many observers misunderstood the high enlistment rates of black men as a sign that they favored the military. But this pattern masked blacks' struggles to find work more generally, the protracted efforts to desegregate the armed services, and the establishment of an unequal draft system to meet the needs of the Cold War military. After 1952, the Selective Service defined conscription as an obligation for some men, particularly men of the poor and working classes. And at the same time, opportunities for black men to participate in the civilian labor market decreased. With so few alternatives outside the military, many African Americans enlisted. Yet inside the military, many of these men faced harsh labor and living conditions; a disproportionate number were punished under the code of military justice, and for them the benefits of military service were diminished.[117] The large and combat-ready military emerged and benefited from the racial, gender, and class inequalities of the larger society.

While the military struggled to achieve full integration, the Selective Service System immediately abolished the racial quota system. The 1948 Selective Service Act required that all men between the ages of eighteen and twenty-five register for the draft. These men were subject to "call-up" unless specifically exempted or deferred. Subsequent revisions and amendments exempted most married men and allowed deferments for men in college. Black newspapers dutifully reported these revisions. These deferments were neither automatic nor guaranteed. Men had to take the Selective Service Qualification Test, and only if they achieved a particular score could they expect deferments for time in college. This testing system was established in 1951 and in place until 1967, and more than 200,000 men were deferred through it. Many colleges offered young men other opportunities to avoid induction. The list included membership in advance reserve units, which was compulsory at some colleges and unavailable at others. When surveyed, white college students consistently expressed that the draft was a negative and personal intrusion, but they did not object to it as an obligation for others. Most favored the system of deferment, and increasing numbers considered it their right to be deferred. During and following the Korean War, few college students, most of them white, felt vulnerable to the draft.[118]

Between late 1948 and early 1950, enlistments increased and few men received draft notices. The high volunteerism of the period was especially pronounced for African Americans. During the Korean War, 1.5 million men were inducted; nearly one-quarter of these new troops were African American (13.5 percent inducted; 13.4 percent enlisted). After the Korean War, black draftees in the army remained at more than 13.5 percent (blacks constituted 11 percent of the population as a whole). Voluntary enlistment of blacks remained close to or more than 10 percent until 1965, when the percentage of black enlistments rose to 14. It climbed steadily to well over 20 percent by the 1970s.[119]

Despite the national mandate requiring all men between the ages of eighteen and twenty-five to register for the draft regardless of race, members of the local draft boards were overwhelmingly homogeneous. A professional and managerial white elite staffed these boards, and nonwhites as well as working-class and poor staff members were excluded. Advisors to registrants, appeal agents, and members of the state appeal boards and the president's appeal board were also racially and economically homogeneous. Even in the North, few blacks were appointed to the draft boards. Southern states denied black representation on boards. Moreover, the appeals process required considerable personal and economic resources. The "friends and neighbors" who made up the local boards also retained jurisdiction over which men received draft notices and which men served. In the initial stages, college students and other individuals deemed vital to the national interest (determined by local draft boards) received deferments. The structure and administration of the postwar draft favored selective conscription, which did not follow strict guidelines.[120]

As the military did not need so many men inducted through the draft, the elaborate system of deferments accelerated between 1954 and 1962. The Selective Service raised its physical and mental standards and added a new standard: "qualified for service only in emergency." Few of these interwar deferment policies favored African Americans.[121] Few African Americans had access to student and occupational deferments. Whites had a high rate of failure for "physical" reasons. Between 1950 and 1966, 21 percent of whites failed the physical examination, while only 14.5 percent of blacks failed.[122] Most blacks were rejected because of low scores on the Armed Forces Qualification Test. More than half of African Americans—54.1 percent of black draftees compared with 18.6 percent of whites—failed the test. Even with this higher rejection rate, draft boards inducted more blacks than whites proportionately. The class and race dimensions of the Selective Service were very apparent in the 1950s, even when fewer whites went to colleges and universities. Even then, local, state, and national pressures, along with segregation in the South, created distortions in the selection of who was deferred and who was drafted. Finally, local employers imposed influence on some boards. Very young men arrested for petty crimes were impressed into the military as civilian courts were used to help yield "enlistees."[123]

Black men used myriad ways to stay out or get out of the military. When the FBI visited Malcolm X in 1952 to compel him to register for the draft, he did not resort to another performance of insanity and radicalism like the one he used when he received his induction notice in 1943. The FBI agent inquired as to why the twenty-eight-year-old ex-convict had not registered for the draft. Since the upper age limit for the 1951 draft was 26½, perhaps the agent merely meant to harass Malcolm. While in prison, Malcolm had spoken out against the Korean War and professed an interest in, if not a commitment to, the Nation of Islam. More likely, the agent intended to stop him from making similar statements in Detroit's black neighborhoods, by then a leading source of inductees. Malcolm stayed cool and told the agent he had just gotten "out of prison." He told the agent that he did not "know [the government] took anybody with prison records." He did not say he knew the army drafted black men with prison records to meet its quota. He did say that he had no "intention to put on the white man's uniform." When the agent told Malcolm he needed to register, Malcolm quietly and firmly stated that he was a Muslim and a conscientious objector. The agent asked if he knew what "'conscientious objector' meant." Malcolm replied "that when the white man asked [him] to go off somewhere to fight and maybe die to preserve the way the white man treated the black man in America, then [his] conscience made [him] object."[124]

Black men readily shared with one another ways to avoid the draft by failing either the mental or the physical exam. Their informal practices circulated through men's networks. Many men simply ignored their draft notices. Others gave wrong or old addresses. Family members and neighbors helped in this subterfuge, denying any knowledge of current "whereabouts." Along with playing crazy, playing dumb became a typical response to the state's use of the draft system to force poorly educated and underemployed black men into the army. If white men were rejected because of "poor health," certainly black men may have used to their advantage the stereotype that as a group they had "limited intelligence."[125]

BECAUSE OF THE CONSTRICTION of their access to better jobs, some African Americans made calculated decisions about enlistment, viewing the military as steady work. Future boxing champion Rubin "Hurricane" Carter was one of these men. After he escaped from a New Jersey juvenile detention home in 1953, Carter joined 150 other African American men in the Philadelphia/New York City area and "boarded the Army Special," a segregated train bound for basic training in Columbia, South Carolina. Not one of the black men had been to the Deep South. While white recruits "relaxe[d] in comparative luxury," the black men crowded into "a decrepit old cattle car . . . like sardines." After their arrival, the men were "taken to two trucks and prodded in like cattle." At Fort Jackson, South Carolina, Carter discovered a military in flux. Integrated units trained together, and he found himself calling cadence, infusing the parade of male bodies with pride and dignity in a "bebop style." He described his ability to order white men around as nothing less than a miracle: "I'm saying that my pride, my individual pride was all that I ever had in life. Stronger than dirt, mightier than the sword, more satisfying than sex, than life, is pride!" Despite his enthusiasm for calling cadence, Carter could not fully reconcile the humiliation of segregation off base with the military's seeming integration.[126] Nor could James Forman, who suffered a psychic weariness as he fought racism "every time, all of the time" outside the military. For him, such a fight meant he might "commit a kind of suicide." The virulent segregation he encountered in the South after he left the military made him feel "duped for volunteering." Unable to fight segregation on his own, Forman decided he "would not commit suicide" and, instead, should save his energy for "an organized struggle."[127]

Barely seventeen, Walter Dean Myers by his own admission was "adrift." Raised in Bedford-Stuyvesant and uncertain about how to pursue his desire to write, "he hoped for a miracle." And he read about war. "The violence of war attracted me. Wars, I believed, were fought for noble causes, and it was easy to imagine myself lying in the trenches, weighing my words against the pain of dying, thinking that death could be a satisfactory answer to failed promise."[128] Many white and black young men had similar dreams about war, about glory in battle. Hollywood movies and exposés on General Ike Eisenhower's victories against the Nazis figured prominently in the masculinist narrative of the mid-1950s. Everyday life was saturated with praise of war.

Myers measured these images of warriors against his father's struggle to house and feed his family. Myers loved his father, but he feared the limited options he found in the urban North. "Did he simply become a Negro, sweating and straining through the streets of the garment center with all the other Negroes?" His skirmishes with gangs in Harlem fueled his dreams of dying in battle and propelled him into the army recruiting office on 125th Street. There he met a black sergeant anxious to help the teenager. Myers took a physical exam, passed the entrance test with a high score, and filled out an application for enlistment. "Do you really want to be in the army?" the recruiter asked. His parents' refusal to sign the form bothered the recruiter. The man filled out a new form for Meyers. Now he had "dead parents." Defiantly, Meyers told his parents about his enlistment, but they surprised him as they expressed a mixture of relief and concern. "My dad said that it was a good thing that I had entered the army, that I would be all right there. I heard him say to Mama that it would make a man out of me."[129]

Myers and the other African Americans who enlisted in the military after 1955 entered a newly desegregated army, but many Americans openly supported segregation. For many African Americans, the military came to represent an escape from segregation, a chance for opportunity, and steady work. Myers was also part of the first generation of young black men specifically prepared for Cold War combat.[130] As African Americans read about how black men used their machine guns well and made glory on the battlefield, they also wondered how war might "kill Jim Crow."

In the decade after the Korean War, African American men who volunteered or were enlisted at disproportionate rates for military service calculated their decisions based on their struggles to find work or acquire some economic and social mobility. This overwhelmingly young, male, and frequently underemployed population viewed the military as a means to have regular wages, better their education, and acquire new job training and skills. Thousands of black men turned to the military for its promise of citizenship and steady work. As these black men became incorporated into America's overlapping and frequently covert wars, they also witnessed massive, violent, and organized resistance to black aspirations of integration and full citizenship. Like James Forman, many African Americans at first quietly, then more forcefully, questioned how war advanced their freedom struggles.[131]

4

Did the Battlefield Kill Jim Crow?

*Black Freedom Struggles, the Korean War,
and the Cold War Military*

"The Korean War," *Ebony* observed in late 1954, "is given real credit for hastening complete integration in the Army." While conceding many white southerners vehemently resisted *Brown v. Board of Education*, the recent Supreme Court decision that mandated the integration of schools, the article also insisted "integration in the Army is having a big impact on the South's racial patterns." Some white-only restaurants near bases reportedly served blacks in uniform, and white and black soldiers socialized together in private homes. These changes apparently spilled beyond the military's gates: "In Columbus, Georgia, soon after Negro and white MPs began to patrol the streets, Negroes were added to the city's civilian police force."[1] Walter White echoed *Ebony*'s positive assessment and linked the military's integration to black America's historic quest for full citizenship. "Once again, as has been true throughout American history, armed conflict and national danger brought the Negro advancement toward his goal of full citizenship." If black Americans lived on the outskirts of democracy, as Roi Ottley claimed in 1951, White argued that "the [integrated] armed forces of the United States of America demonstrate to the world that the di-

Louise Sneed leads her third grade class in the Pledge of Allegiance at the Fort Myer Elementary School, September 7, 1954. Although the public schools of surrounding Maryland and Virginia were segregated, this school at Fort Myer, Va., and another school on the military post were integrated by order of the Department of Defense. © Corbis.

rection of democracy's movement is forward." He expected the military's integration would be "like snowballs" rolling "far beyond its boundaries."[2]

To many observers, the apparent absence of "bloodshed" in the military's integration seemed a startling change from a decade earlier, when deadly race riots roiled bases and posts, and it contrasted with the war white supremacists organized to prevent integration of schools and in American society more generally.[3] Walter White and other leaders in the mainstream civil rights movement interpreted the combat role of African Americans on the Korean War battlefield as a critical step toward full citizenship for blacks, and they applauded the military's transformation, including the desegregation of base schools a year after *Brown*. As hundreds of thousands of U.S. troops occupied nations in Europe and Asia, went to wars in Korea and Indochina, and participated in the numerous military interventions after 1953, many African Americans hoped the integrated military would have far-reaching consequences for their civil rights struggles in the United States. By 1955, White imagined that as blacks and whites bled together in foxholes, and as their children attended school and played together on military bases, they would "carry the attitude of respect" into American life. Observers such as White insisted a new American democracy had emerged on the Korean battlefield and would flourish in the Cold War integrated military.[4]

As some claimed the Korean War "killed Jim Crow in the military," others insisted that "democracy on the battlefield" did not launch a cascade of changes elsewhere in American life. Civil rights activist Virginia Durr contrasted the integration on Maxwell Air Force Base with whites' violent opposition to blacks' nonviolent protest against Montgomery's segregated buses. "With the rise of the White Citizens Council the whole situation is explosive—but the curious thing is that integration goes on at the [Air Force base]—no segregation of any kind, and no trouble of any kind."[5] When African Americans stepped through the base gates and into the city, such calm evaporated. Over the next half-decade, Durr observed the city police regularly arrest or harass blacks in uniform "as a measure of intimidation for anything they can think of."[6]

Other observers questioned the motivation behind the changes within the military. For more than half a century, African Americans had challenged the segregated military and fought "for the right to fight for democracy," but shortages of soldiers during the Korean War, not the president's 1948 executive order, accelerated integration of combat troops. The army may have integrated the battlefield, but it did so out of need for critical combat labor, not any clear commitment to bring about equality in American life or within its ranks. Throughout the 1950s, many black soldiers remained in segregated labor units in the United States, and they traveled on segregated trains. Blacks wearing a uniform in the South faced as much danger in the late 1950s as they had in the half-decade after World War II. "Why," one soldier asked on behalf of fifty-four men who served in the all-black 857th Quartermaster Laundry Company, "are we in the Army? Why is this country fighting in Korea? What have we got to fight for? Can the United States possibly bring freedom to colored people in other countries if we are not free at home?"[7]

William Worthy, who wrote for the *Baltimore Afro-American* and the *Crisis*, measured the experiences of black soldiers against civil rights leaders' capitulation to Cold War militarism. After observing a generation of African Americans who experienced waves of violence at home and participated in wars against "colored peoples" abroad, Worthy concluded these "GIs have died in vain, utterly in vain." He argued that White's acquiescence to wars in Asia made blacks' struggles for freedom "narrowly defined and internationally myopic." U.S. policy "backed every broken down reactionary and all the discredited puppets that have no future. Our Asian policies are wrong A to Z."[8] Black people "entertain illusions about their growing stake of 'equality' in an economic and [a military] social order that is not only doomed but a menace to mankind." Instead of achieving "equality," Worthy insisted, the participation of blacks in wars made them "collaborators" in the new colonialism.[9]

As African Americans questioned the implication of U.S. policies that compelled them to fight wars in Asia but refused to protect their rights as citizens, they correlated the rising antiblack violence in the United States to the violence of the Korean War. The racialized language used to describe Koreans and the anticommunist rhetoric of combating the "Red Menace" not only incited widespread resistance to civil rights laws; it also justified horrific violence toward nonwhites generally. Pettis Perry, William Patterson, Paul Robeson, and others in the Civil Rights Congress noted in their 1951 petition to the United Nations that U.S. wars against the "Communist scourge" masked a systematic assault on "colored peoples" seeking self-determination that then fueled "domestic genocide" against African Americans claiming their rights as citizens. Perry drafted another pamphlet that explained how black intellectuals who denounced wars and U.S. militarism could also support the integration of the military. He downplayed the contradiction between the struggle against the Jim Crow military and the peace movement, arguing that the fight for an integrated military would lead to "rallying the Negro people for the peace movement" and sensitizing whites to the violence against blacks.[10]

Worthy's indictment of civil rights leaders as collaborators with American imperialism and the CRC's correlation of racial violence with wars in Asia found their genesis in the inequalities of the Cold War draft and economic policies that compelled disproportionate numbers of African Americans into successive wars while the nation condoned violence against them. As the Korean War launched America's new incursions into Asia, many African Americans questioned how their pursuit of an integrated military and their participation in these wars and occupations hastened their demands for full citizenship. Between 1945 and 1960, increasing numbers of African Americans considered the implications of a civil rights agenda that included participation in these wars as they also mounted mass and direct action against segregation and violence. They questioned how the rhetoric of anticommunism fueled resistance to integration. Equally important, as they observed anticolonial and democratic struggles in Asia and Africa, black antiwar activists strengthened their arguments that the Cold War not only fueled and justified the terror blacks experienced at home, but that the wars it engendered were inimical to their pursuit of a racial justice based on human dignity and freedom.[11]

The mass nonviolent civil rights movement that emerged during and after the Korean War had its origins in a generation of black Americans familiar with their participation in the violence of wars abroad and the violence they experienced at home. Nearly two decades before the Reverend Martin Luther King Jr. associated America's racial and class inequalities with its wars, black pacifists, rights activists, soldiers, and veterans correlated the violent rhetoric and practices of anticommunism to the violence against integration and anticolonialism. Their critical consciousness drew on pacifist, anticolonial, and racial justice struggles that predated World War II, but it acquired momentum in the late 1940s and 1950s as the inequities of the draft compelled a growing population of young black men into military occupations and wars against other people of color while they experienced violence, terror, and resistance to their calls for full citizenship. Their experiences in the overlapping wars between 1948 and 1960 shaped the nonviolent philosophy that became integral to the civil rights movement, and they challenged ideas that associated full citizenship with blacks' participation in an integrated battlefield.

"Not a Race War"

As U.S. troops landed in Korea, editorials in black newspapers considered the appeals for blacks' assent to the war against its implications as they pressed for full citizenship. Despite the eagerness to draft and enlist blacks for war labor, America appeared reluctant to abandon its agenda of Jim Crow. *Defender* columnist Willard Townsend argued the war put black Americans—"the loyal American Negro"—in a "difficult position." Should they back segregated America's stance or Communist Russia's? The answer, he concluded, depended on whether or not white Americans planned to abandon segregation. The Communists had long denounced it, and "the Dixiecrats and their fellow travelers must give up the luxury of racial bigotry or find the darker races of the world united under the banner" of communism. Black Americans, Townsend argued, should take their cues from the responses of native peoples to colonial oppression in Asia, where a "seething resentment" grew against racial, economic, and political exploitation. In India, British colonialism included practices of racial hierarchy. Subjugated African Americans, like segregated Asians, understood "the superior attitude manifested in a thousand humiliating ways." In turn, Indians and other Asians found "repulsive" the "treatment of the American Negro by white Americans."[12]

Unlike World War II, to which many prominent African Americans gave their assent, a substantial list of prominent African Americans opposed the Korean War. W. E. B. Du Bois and *California Eagle* editor Charlotta Bass immediately and unequivocally denounced the war. African American luminaries from academia to the arts aligned themselves with international peace movements. Paul Robeson held a series of peace rallies, which precipitated an intense backlash from the Truman administration and mainstream civil rights organizations. Ralph Matthews described these peace rallies as the voice "for a world revolution challenging the status quo." Undaunted, Robeson and many other African Americans, including jazz player Charlie Parker, singer Marian Anderson, and sociologist E. Franklin Frazier, signed the World Peace Appeal of 1950.[13]

Other African Americans countered this rising dissent and insisted that the war was against the Red Menace and was not a "race war." While some "tr[y] to paint the Korean War as a racial conflict," one editor of a West Coast black weekly insisted, "the Korean conflict is a clash between two widely differing political ideologies." And "colored peoples were similarly divided." Democratic and communist nations suffered under the weight of racial discrimination, but the former offered greater opportunities for dignity. African Americans, the editor stressed, were again in a "two front" battle for democracy and against Jim Crow.[14] If some African Americans were attracted to communism, Walter White and other mainstream civil rights leaders argued, it was because of racism in the United States. In the attempts to disentangle the nation's history of race discrimination from Cold War ideology, many African Americans depicted North Korean and Chinese troops as "ruthless" communists. As some African Americans described the Korean War as a war of ideologies, not a race war, White and others in mainstream civil rights organizations represented themselves as "loyal" Americans. In this context, African Americans made distinctions between themselves and other "colored peoples" who allied with communism. African Americans who bound themselves to anticommunism also argued that democratic nations needed to end racial segregation. These black Cold War warriors evinced a commitment to a democracy based on racial equality, and they stressed that full citizenship at home would diminish, if not extinguish, the Red Menace.[15]

The popular depiction of communism as the Red Menace originally described the Soviet Union's actions in Eastern Europe. It became synonymous with the Korean War and nonaligned people seeking independence and self-determination, including antiwar African American civil rights activists. This Korean War discourse about communism typically rested on official and popular constructions of racial differences and racial anxieties. As Bill Mullen has noted, such discourse merged rhetoric from World War II about the "Yellow Peril" with the new "Red Scare" in Asia, creating a new "color curtain." Even African Americans who bound themselves to the anticommunist agenda while they supported anticolonial struggles found themselves targets.[16] Despite civil rights activists' careful attempts to disassociate their struggles from communism, anti-integrationists successfully associated African Americans who insisted on their rights and agitated for integration with communism and political perversion.[17]

In the two years between Truman's Executive Order 9981 and the start of the war, White and the NAACP quietly pressed Truman to accelerate the army's integration, but they also suppressed open criticism of his foreign policies. Eager to make advances at home, White narrowed the association's pre–World War II global civil rights agenda that comported with the administration's anticommunist foreign policy. W. E. B. Du Bois, who had returned to the association, disagreed and linked domestic discrimination with anticolonialism and a global struggle for human rights. "The NAACP," he argued, "is called upon to take a stand concerning Africa, Asia, Indonesia, and Israel."[18] When White agreed to serve as a consultant to the American United Nation's delegation for the Truman administration in 1948, Du Bois accused him of harnessing the association to "the reactionary, war-mongering colonial imperialism of the present administration." When Du Bois's remarks generated controversy with U.S. foreign policy, the NAACP's board used the furor to dismiss him from the association.[19]

Undeterred, Du Bois helped organize the international Peace Information Center, which became a platform for him to speak and write about anticolonial and peace struggles. After World War II, he wrote, he had hoped for an "era of peace." Instead, the era "transformed into plans for universal world war: a theory of progress by war and more war, each more savage and destructive than the last." As he launched a seemingly improbable senate campaign in New York, he described civil rights as the pursuit of peace.[20] For Du Bois, the problem of the twentieth century remained the injustice of the color line, but it now included the grievous imbalance between the poor and the wealthy. The call for racial and economic justice, he insisted, was made all the more urgent as nations armed for more war. He stressed that the struggle for economic justice, not the struggle against communism, deserved attention. In order to prove China and Russia wrong, he noted, the "democratic nations" embarked on "continuous war." War was big business, he argued. It made more profit than education.[21]

The FBI arrested Du Bois after he wrote "An Appeal" to ban nuclear weapons in 1950. Photographs of the handcuffed eighty-three-year-old intellectual appeared in newspapers across the United States. Federal officials then seized his passport and closed his peace office. The U.S. government barred him and other activists from attending the numerous peace congresses held over the next half-decade. The octogenarian successfully fought the federal government's efforts to jail him as an "unregistered foreign agent." Accompanied by Shirley Graham Du Bois, he began a cross-country speaking tour. In Chicago he addressed an audience of 7,000 gathered for the People's Congress of the American Peace Crusade. The crowds he addressed in other cities were equally large. Du Bois considered civil rights, peace, and economic justice as vital to "vast social change in the United States."[22] In his keynote address to the Progressive Party convention in early July 1952, he described the United States as "the greatest warmonger of all history." American citizens, in contrast, "demand the end and end now of this senseless war in Korea. The American Negroes are declaring that war destroys civil rights, lowers wages, and stops housing."[23]

Other prominent African Americans who openly opposed the Korean War and America's militarism were hounded and silenced. The government confiscated Paul Robeson's passport in 1950.[24] Claudia Jones became one of many antiwar leftist black activists targeted by the U.S. government, but as a Trinidadian, she became the only black woman to be tried, incarcerated, and deported. Like Robeson, Jones openly criticized U.S. imperialism and the Korean War. Her advocacy of peace, as much as her ties to the Left and communism, made her suspect. As Du Bois noted, speaking for peace made one a criminal, but because of race, blacks' participation in these activities invited charges of treason. Other black writers and intellectuals on the Left faced tremendous pressure to renounce Communism and leftist politics more generally. As scores of writers and artists faced censure or watched as their careers were derailed by these charges, others felt pressured to become vocal anti-Communists. Many simply refrained from making overt critiques of U.S. wars and foreign policy, a practice that poet Langston Hughes began in 1950 and continued for the next decade and a half.[25]

As federal officials questioned or deported black antiwar leftists, the mass movement for peace exploded outside the United States. Twenty-three million people in Japan signed a petition against nuclear warfare. This swell of peace activism appeared even in nations where governments suppressed democracy. Yet, Du Bois charged, Americans knew little about how other nations in North America, Europe, Latin America, and Asia moved "strongly, steadily, and persuasively to raise their voices for peace." After half a century of participating in the international peace movement, the United States now prepared "for [organized] murder and destruction." In the United States, Du Bois observed, "it is practically impossible to hold a mass meeting for peace or to say a word for peace." Instead, war talk reverberated through nearly every U.S. institution, including the "Christian Church." The suppression of antiwar activism resulted in peace becoming synonymous with "'Communism' and 'Communism' is attributed to every vile or evil object." Now, he concluded, "Communism is regarded as a 'cause' of Peace and US officials used the threat of peace to fulminate for a vaster army, atomic and hydrogen bombs, and universal military service."[26]

The NAACP distanced itself from the Left's sharp critique of American racism and U.S. foreign policy and, instead, presented an image of an America determined to shed its violent and racist past. White, who had left the NAACP and returned a year later as chief administrator, was convinced that America had made considerable progress in advancing blacks' civil rights since the 1947 *To Secure These Rights*. He used the progress report he wrote each year to tell "the story of America, particularly on the race issue," and refute "Soviet Propaganda," which used the nation's violence against African Americans to agitate for communism. He insisted that in 1949, black Americans had gained greater parity with whites in employment, housing, education, and voting. White's report ignored the escalation in violence against blacks and the dozens of African Americans who were murdered and assaulted after the 1947 report.[27]

For many African Americans, including William Patterson, director of the radical CRC, White's efforts to refute this gruesome evidence, especially the systematic racial violence, rang false. Patterson and others in the CRC compiled data from NAACP records, evidence used in *To Secure*

These Rights, and Fisk's and Tuskegee's yearly reports on murders of blacks by vigilantes, including lynchings, but they added much more, creating a "shocking document." The dismal facts about racial violence, poor housing, limited voting, poverty, and high unemployment appeared in other reports presented to the White House by civil rights organizations in 1946. While these organizations, including the National Negro Congress and the NAACP, had earlier charged the United States with violating blacks' human rights, the CRC documented the ferocious violence against African Americans. The assaults against, and murders of, black veterans continued, as did the unrecorded disappearances of the "many black men and women [who] leave their homes and are never seen alive again." Their mutilated bodies "appeared weeks later." Patterson and others in the CRC insisted the widespread and systematic violence against African Americans met the United Nations definition of genocide. The CRC presented its claims and charges in a report titled *We Charge Genocide* to the United Nations Convention on Genocide. Over the weeks following its publication, tens of thousands of Americans and Europeans bought and read the petition.[28]

Along with the systematic violence, the CRC report posited that systemic segregation provided additional evidence of the federal and state institutions' organized effort to deny African Americans' human rights. The report noted the legal and extralegal exclusion of blacks from many sectors of the labor market and that they faced deliberate suppression of their political participation. The CRC charged that Georgia governor Eugene Talmadge and South Carolina governor Strom Thurmond mobilized the new Dixiecrat movement by equating the assault on black political rights with civic virtue. Added to this documented terrorism, the report noted that the patterns of botched trials and the abuse of prisoners bolstered the claims about the organized and systemic violence against African Americans. Every year, Patterson argued, the United States "willfully" created the conditions for the deaths of 32,000 African Americans. Prevented from equal and adequate access to counsel, health care, jobs, housing, and education, African Americans died in droves. The conditions created by Jim Crow and racial terrorism, Patterson insisted, amounted to genocide.[29]

Presented just months after the start of the Korean War, the CRC's petition predicted that U.S. preparation for war abroad fueled this "domestic genocide," evident in the organized and widespread violence used to terrorize those who worked for integration and blacks who claimed their rights as citizens, such as the right to vote. Many anti-integrationists were also ardent anticommunists, black critics noted. "White supremacy at home," the petitioners charged, "makes for colored massacres abroad. Both reveal contempt for human life in a colored skin. The lyncher and the atom bomb are related." The petitioners concluded that the surge in murders, beatings, burnings, rapes, and false imprisonments of African Americans between 1947 and 1951 correlated "almost in direct ration to the surge towards war." They asserted that the legal and violent defense of segregation trained a generation to kill abroad.[30] Along with an indictment that racism inflicted harm on African Americans in the United States, *We Charge Genocide* boldly claimed that racist practices fueled wars abroad. The document challenged the argument advanced by the mainstream civil rights movement that blacks' participation in wars abroad advanced their freedom struggles at home.

Alarmed that the CRC report might undermine blacks' support for anti-communism and the newly desegregated military, Roy Wilkins, who became the NAACP executive secretary when White left in 1948, moved to temper the CRC's claims through a series of press releases. The association had prominent African Americans refute the CRC's claims. Boxer Sugar Ray Robinson insisted "America provides opportunity for everyone, regardless of race, creed, or color." Yet the CRC persisted with its efforts. Paul Robeson spoke and wrote about the escalating abuse against blacks at the polls, the attacks in the streets, and the murders of civil rights activists. The NAACP countered his efforts by emphasizing the ties of the CRC and the peace movement to communism. After Walter White wrote an article for *Ebony* diagnosing Robeson's ties to the Communist Party as signs of mental instability, Eslanda Robeson sent a rebuttal to the magazine, arguing that "Negro leaders go out of their way to insist that American democracy, with all its faults, is the best there is and therefore we must all fight, if need be die for it. Since most of the *faults* and few of the *benefits* of this democracy apply directly to Negroes, these Leaders find themselves in the very strange position of insisting that Negroes fight and die for the faults of our democracy." *Ebony* refused to publish her response, and instead her article appeared in the *California Eagle*.[31]

Reporting Critical

Despite White's efforts to minimize the debate, a new generation of black reporters, many of them experienced war correspondents or antiwar intellectuals, connected the violence against African Americans and the suppression of their freedom struggles to wars abroad and American imperialism. Articles by William Worthy, a CO from World War II, linked the rising American imperialism and violence in Asia with the violence against African Americans. Other journalists, including James Hicks, Ethel Payne, and L. Alex Wilson, were former Korean War correspondents who correlated black civil rights struggles with anticolonial struggles. Along with these writers, Bayard Rustin, a World War II CO and foremost authority on Gandhian nonviolence; Claudia Jones; Pettis Perry, a member of the CRC; W. E. B. Du Bois; and Eslanda and Paul Robeson published journals, pamphlets, and weeklies that provided consistent critiques of U.S. militarism that claimed to advance democracy but imposed, instead, a new imperialism abroad and accelerated antiblack violence at home.

Many of these writers had been on the front lines in World War II and the Korean War, and others faced violence and attacks as they reported the civil rights struggles in the South. Both Hicks and L. Alex Wilson had documented the detrimental impact of segregation in Korea and returned to the United States to report on civil rights. They faced attacks as they investigated Emmett Till's murder and reported the integration of Central High in Little Rock two years later. Wilson received life-threatening injuries in Little Rock. Assigned to the White House, Payne soon learned that President Eisenhower refused to answer her questions about civil rights. The Robesons, Du Bois, Jones, Rustin, and Worthy were both politically and physically courageous as they repeatedly called America to a reckoning for its racial and class injustices at home and abroad. Rustin spent time in prison for his CO status during World War II and for his participation in FOR's 1947 Freedom Rides, which the organization launched to call attention to refusals by southern bus companies to abide by the 1946 *Morgan* decision that ended segregation on interstate bus transportation. (Irene Morgan, a worker in the Baltimore shipyards who refused to yield to segregation laws on a bus in 1944, renewed blacks' open resistance to segregation on buses and trains. Rustin and others in FOR launched the Freedom Rides a year after the 1946 Supreme Court ruling.) After Worthy and the Robesons traveled abroad—Worthy went to Indochina, Korea, and China—and then spoke out against and wrote about the links between U.S. racism and imperialism, the federal government took away their passports; Paul Robeson became a prisoner in his own home, and Worthy battled several years for the return of his passport. Claudia Jones was tried for treason, convicted, and deported because she dared write about peace and against U.S. imperialism.[32]

William Worthy was especially audacious in ignoring the topical and geographic borders deemed off-limits by U.S. officials and instead produced articles that described the implications of blacks' war participation on their freedom struggles. In the mind-set of many, being black, anti-imperialist, and antiwar meant being Red, but for Worthy, these attributes provided a critical subjectivity. In the decade after the Korean War, he reported from the Soviet Union, Korea, Thailand, China, Vietnam, South Africa, and Cuba. His articles in 1953 about the horrors of combat countered the popular characterizations of the Korean War as blacks' march to full citizenship.[33] Black leaders, William Worthy argued, had learned little from black soldiers' experiences in the Korean War and wrongly considered the integrated battlefield a marker of success. After interviewing black soldiers and traveling through China and Korea, Worthy presciently concluded that the U.S. intention to salvage European military and economic imperialism would plunge the American people into protracted wars.[34]

By 1953 he was concentrating his attention on America's presence in Asia, which included military occupations or interventions across that continent. As White declared the Korean War had killed Jim Crow, Worthy insisted black Americans needed to focus on the events unfolding in Indochina. Worthy reminded readers that America now provided diplomatic support, money, equipment, and advisors to its pro-Western leaders. He warned that America's support for the seven-year-old war in Indochina "was a dirty war" and a "colonial prelude to a World War III of color." Not only did the United States suppress independence movements in Southeast Asia, but "the Washington-bank-rolled war" extended to Africa. The mainstream press, he insisted, helped persuade ordinary Americans that U.S. efforts stemmed the tide of the Red Menace. He estimated that few Vietnamese ascribed to communism and instead fought for their own liberation. Like many others struggling against colonialism, the Vietnamese wanted the Soviets and the United States to leave them alone. In a conclusion that proved prescient, Worthy predicted that officials would insist the United States could not let Indochina be lost to the communists. Already, he warned, this claim persuaded Eisenhower to increase military support. This war, he noted, would be fought between an endless supply of soldiers and guerillas, where there would be "no real battle lines." Already U.S. military advisors claimed that "the enemy is everywhere, coming through the walls, the ceilings and the floors." The peaceless peace in Korea laid the foundation for endless war in Vietnam.[35]

Worthy chided black Americans for their failure to "wake up to the color realities of today's world." Asians and Europeans, he noted, repeatedly asked, "Why don't the molders of Negro opinion seize this historic opportunity to rally support for Nehru's peace efforts, for the freedoms of colonials, for the newly independent and economically precarious countries?" President Eisenhower's foreign policy, Worthy observed, was "based on the need for America to obtain profitable foreign markets and raw materials to sustain her economy." This "mineral diplomacy," he argued, meant assenting to "policies of economic imperialism," the presence of "a million and a half soldiers, airmen, sailors, and Marines in 63 lands overseas, and American military advisory groups in 34 foreign countries."[36]

Worthy was not alone in considering the deleterious implications that blacks' participation in wars and covert operations had on their freedom struggles. Sociologist St. Clair Drake and Walter Weiskopf, a professor of economics, both scholars at Roosevelt University in Chicago, presented a similar critique as they taught veterans, labor activists, and civil rights organizers. Drake wove together these critiques with observations from his travels to Africa, where he witnessed political independence and numerous anticolonial struggles. His analysis was informed, too, by his experiences as a veteran of the integrated Merchant Marines, his long battle against fascism, and his commitment to peace. A pragmatic anticommunist, he believed red-baiting would distract critics of racism and racial violence. Communists, he argued, "manipulated racial sentiments to 'set in motion the oppressed'" for their own purposes.[37] In his articles and teaching he gave special attention to the emerging Asian, African, and Caribbean nations that had become independent from European colonialism. In these independence movements, he argued, Africans and Asians "developed counter-thought styles" that "repudiated the racist ideologies" used by Europeans and Americans to sanction their dominance.[38] Drake's community of students grew to include faculty and residents. Among themselves, the students debated and compared the NAACP's legal strategies to integrate schools with Drake's vivid accounts of the 1940s bus boycotts in South Africa and the recent nonviolent mass actions in Ghana—organized by veterans of the British army—and South Africa. Air force veteran James Forman discovered that many blacks and whites did not want to discuss the cases as they thought "the NAACP was 'pushing too hard,'" while others questioned the merits of integrating into an unequal society.[39]

Bandung

The call for nonaligned nations to meet in Bandung in April 1955 provided a larger forum for African Americans to consider a new political paradigm beyond war. The appeal of "twenty-nine free and independent nations of Asia and Africa meeting in Bandung, Indonesia, to discuss 'racialism and colonialism'" drew scores of African American journalists, including Richard Wright, *Chicago Defender* journalist Ethel Payne, and Louis Lautier. The conference occurred in the wake of the shrill anticommunist rhetoric that linked southern whites' outrage over the *Brown* decision and foment raised by the U.S. display of military force in defense of Formosa (now Taiwan) against Chinese communists.[40]

The delegates came from newly independent nations or nations that continued their struggles for independence, including South Africa. Richard Wright observed that these nations represented "something beyond Left and Right. These nations represented races and religions, vague but potent." Their shared history of living as subjugated races "under the rigors of colonial rule" brought them to Bandung. "The conditions under which these men had lived had become their tradition, their culture, their *raison d'être*."[41] For African Americans, the gathering demonstrated a new and collective black political power, awakening in some a new nationalism; in others it nurtured a radical internationalism. As Penny Von Eschen has noted, the conference "not only had world-wide ramifications," but "Bandung and nonalignment created an alternative to viewing global politics through the prism of the Cold War and helped to create a new vocabulary for critiquing American policies."[42] Equally important, African Americans assessed how some of these new nations emerged out of armed struggle, while others had mounted persistent and effective nonviolent campaigns for independence.

Bandung was Payne's first extended tour as the *Defender*'s foreign correspondent, and her articles about the two-week conference and subsequent trip through Asia and Europe dominated the pages of the newspaper. Payne began her journalistic career at the age of thirty-eight after she wrote articles critiquing the military's continuing racial strictures imposed on black soldiers in Japan during the Korean War. Born and raised in Chicago, Payne traveled to Japan in 1948 and worked for the Red Cross. Appalled by the segregation and treatment of black soldiers as the Korean War began, she gave her written observations to L. Alex Wilson, a war correspondent for the *Chicago Defender*, who then passed them on to his editor. Impressed by her forthright style and investigative techniques—Payne charmed her subjects, who then spoke frankly to her—the paper published her articles and then hired her. Though popular with readers, she struggled with barriers imposed by a white press that ignored black journalists and by editors who paid her male colleagues significantly more. She was assigned as a White House correspondent, and President Eisenhower tried to ignore her; but she prevailed nonetheless. By 1955 the confluence of the civil rights movement and the anticolonial struggles propelled her career in a new direction. Her experience abroad and her indefatigable approach to reporting and writing about the civil rights movement made her invaluable to the *Defender*. The editor, John H. Sengstacke, promoted her to foreign correspondent, and she immediately left for the Bandung Conference.

Payne's articles appeared as the conference unfolded, and she captured the excitement and daring of the 3,000 "colored" delegates who represented the majority of the world. She predicted that some in the West might find the gathering of thousands of "darker people" "alarming," she noted, because the delegates represented an ethical and a political challenge to the West. Writing for an audience increasingly restive and skeptical of U.S. policies in Asia and Africa, Payne reminded readers that these delegates representing "550 million colored people who form the balance of power between communism and democracy" had the potential to reshape the dynamics of power between the United States and the Soviet Union. Along with these vivid impressions, Payne provided readers with concise summaries of the key issues and concerns delegates discussed in the meetings. She described how these representatives claimed their nations' right for self-determination and the right to settle their own problems without interference from the West. Many of the newly independent nations defended themselves from the new wave of imperialism and racialism launched by the United States and the Soviet Union. As the dominant U.S. papers described Indian prime minister Jawaharlal Nehru and China's premier, Chou En-Lai, as either an impediment to or an enemy of Western interests, Payne's interviews with these and other leaders of Asia and Africa provided vivid images of thoughtful and powerful men.[43]

Massive Resistance: Violence Abroad, Violence at Home

The demand for self-determination, dignity, and freedom from violence articulated at Bandung resonated with African Americans as they faced the massive resistance to *Brown*. The home front vigilantism in the South, which had been present since before the Civil War, became virulent during the World War II and Korean War years as blacks demanded political rights. The violence accelerated after the Supreme Court ruling ended segregated education and challenged the legal basis for segregation generally. Robert Patterson, a former World War II paratrooper, and other extreme segregationists in the Mississippi Delta organized the Citizens' Council to halt black political activism. The council grew rapidly and attracted prominent politicians, including Senator James Eastland, business owners, and newspaper editors, many of whom were equally virulent in opposing communism. Over the next months, the Citizens' Councils spread to other states in the South and attracted moderates who now participated in the denunciation of the *Brown* decision. These organizations used economic pressure, intimidation, and threats against blacks and whites who opposed segregation. Members overtly and openly supported vigilante violence, and these councils shared members with the Ku Klux Klan and other violent anti-integrationist organizations.

The Citizens' Councils were launched in response to the *Brown* decision, but intimidation and violence had been present in Mississippi for decades. Veteran Amzie Moore returned to Mississippi in 1945 after the regimented segregation of the army and found that whites, many of whom were veterans, had organized a "home guard" to protect themselves from black veterans who demanded the right to vote. "For about six or eight months," before the 1946 election, Moore recalled, "at least one Negro each week was killed as deterrence." No white group, politician, or newspaper admitted to Moore's claim that more than thirty-two African Americans were murdered that year in the South, but many then and since agreed that the terrorism against blacks was widespread, especially in Mississippi. Rumors, assaults, and the repeated recovery of mutilated bodies had a cumulative effect. As Moore noted, "It certainly had a psychological effect."[44]

Undeterred by the violence, Moore and other African American veterans continued the push for voting rights. Moore and physician and surgeon T. R. M. Howard organized the Regional Council of Negro Leadership in 1950, creating a visible and large political organization with the explicit intention to register voters. The organization held mass meetings, and that May 13,000 blacks arrived to discuss how to vote. "We spoke about freedom, about first-class citizenship, with the associated rights of voting." The Korean War draft gave added urgency to the claims of black veterans. Poor whites, too, responded to these arguments, and their organizing spread to other counties, alarming white elites. Gus Courts, who owned a small gas station, and George Lee, a minister, organized the Belzoni branch of the NAACP. Lee pastored four churches, owned a thriving printing business, and was the first African American in the county to get his name on the voting roll. He also called for black voting rights from the pulpit. Whites threatened the men, and by April 1955, Courts was forced out of his store. Lee received death threats. Other members of the NAACP had their rents increased; some lost their jobs. Still, the charismatic Lee drew thousands to a rally later that month. The evening after the meeting, he was fatally shot while driving home; the only witness disappeared.[45]

The violence continued through the summer. Emmett Till, a teenager from Chicago visiting cousins, entered the Delta store where Caroline Bryant worked without her husband. The woman claimed Till "bragged about some white girl," "whistled," and said "bye, baby" as he walked out of the store. She threatened him with a pistol, and the teenagers left. Till's cousin, who accompanied Till into the store, remembered the teenager stuttered his goodbye to Bryant, whistling as he struggled to speak, a tactic his mother taught him to use whenever he began to stammer. Four days later, Roy Bryant and his older half-brother, J. W. Milam, arrived at Mose Wright's house and asked for the teenager "who did all that talk." They put the boy in the back of a truck and drove away. Three days later, a boy fishing in the Tallahatchie River pulled out Till's mangled and decomposed body. He was bound and had a cotton gin tied around his neck. He had been shot several times. The sheriff, when summoned, found the body half-clothed. One eye dangled from its socket, and the boy's face was so beaten and swollen that he was hardly recognizable. Mose Wright, Till's uncle, identified Till only from a ring he wore. Local officials eventually arrested Milam and Bryant and charged them with murder; they arrested another man who was later released.[46]

Emmett Till's murder in late August 1955 generated immediate and intense scrutiny from the boy's family, from the black press, and from a mobilized black America already galvanized by the murder of George Lee. With the help of the local NAACP, including Mississippi civil rights leader Dr. T. M. Howard, Mose Wright contacted his cousin Mamie Till Bradley and told her about her son's murder. With support from the Chicago NAACP, she had her son returned north and prepared a public funeral. Grief-stricken, Bradley displayed her son's beaten and bloated body to thousands of mourners because she wanted "the whole world to see what they did to my boy." Twin images, one of the smiling teenager, the other of his mutilated corpse, appeared side-by-side in *Jet*, one of most popular black magazines. Black newspapers sent former war correspondents and combat photographers to Mississippi. The *Afro-American* sent veteran and Korean War correspondent James Hicks, and the *Defender* sent L. Alex Wilson and Ernest Withers, a former army photographer and policeman from Memphis. Maybe the trial would end with the acquittal of the murderers as others had ended, but black America intended to put the violence of the Jim Crow South on display.[47]

While some of the southern newspapers portrayed fourteen-year-old Till as a predator, others described the accused murderers, J. W. Milam and Roy Bryant, as war heroes. Louis Till, Emmett's father, Mississippi senator James Eastland claimed, was charged with rape and murder while serving with a transportation company in Italy. The military executed him there in 1945.[48] In contrast, Milam and Bryant were portrayed as ordinary men defending Bryant's wife from the "aggressive talk" of a black teenager visiting from the North. These men were decorated war veterans, husbands, and fathers, not murderers. Their mother, Eula Lee Bryant, repeatedly showed reporters pictures of her two sons wearing their military uniforms. And, she added, seven of her sons had served in either World War II or the Korean War. She described how Private Milam had received a field promotion and became a lieutenant in Germany during World War II and how Roy Bryant, her youngest and Milam's half-brother, had fought as a paratrooper in Korea.[49] White veterans rallied around the men. Milam's lawyer, John Whitten, was a veteran. Veterans from twenty-one states reportedly sent money to support the two defendants. Depictions of the men as brave soldiers framed the start of the trial. Whitten described Milam as a "good soldier" who "did not leave the battlefield."[50] Fourteen days after their arrest, Milam and Bryant went to court in a trial that lasted four and a half days. The all-white and all-male jury returned a not-guilty verdict after sixty-seven minutes of deliberation.[51]

African Americans learned about these events from the articles written by *Afro-American* correspondent James Hicks, who was a veteran of World War II and an experienced frontline combat correspondent in the Korean War. As he reported, Hicks wrote how he feared for his life while in Mississippi. He and other black reporters faced similar harassment, and they were repeatedly stopped by the police, "caught in the act of reporting." Hicks described how he used reconnaissance skills he learned in the military to track down witnesses and the cotton gin used to weigh down Till in the river. None of this evidence appeared in the trial, and Hicks learned that the county sheriff, H. C. Strider, confined one witness to a jail cell in another county until the trial concluded.[52] Olive Arnold Adams, editor of the Global News Network, argued that "the true, official Emmett Till story will never come to light until the Mississippi Negro is free and when the laws that protect murderers also protect him."[53]

Months later, Milam and Bryant recounted to William Bradford Huie how they murdered Till. For Milam and Bryant, Till was not just a sexual predator but a northern purveyor and representative of a dangerous integration. "As long as he lived," Milam did not intend for blacks to vote or go to school "with his children." Milam described how he pistol-whipped the boy, just as he had pistol-whipped Germans. He was not sorry he "killed a niggah who gets out of place."[54] For Milam, killing Till appears to have been another battle in the war against integration. The men's claims about why they murdered Till, the suppression of evidence, and a trial adjudicated in a segregated courtroom and deliberated by an all-white male jury made the political exclusion and racial violence of Jim Crow visible. As Mamie Till Bradley hoped, the whole world saw what happened to her boy, and more.[55]

Anti-integrationists framed their massive resistance as a war for democracy, but African Americans did not yield. In December 1955, civil rights activists, Black Nationalists, veterans of Asian and European wars, and pacifists mounted a boycott against segregation on the Montgomery, Alabama, buses. Activists cobbled together community organizations into the new Montgomery Improvement Association (MIA). Yet the name of the new organization indicated the links between long-standing local organizations and external efforts for black dignity and freedom. Organizer E. D. Nixon had been a member of the Universal Negro Improvement Association, president of the Montgomery NAACP, and longtime head of the local Brotherhood of Sleeping Car Porters. Joanne Gibson Robinson, a professor at Alabama State College, and Rosa Parks, who launched the bus boycott after her refusal to yield to the Jim Crow laws, belonged to the influential Women's Political Council. Parks had served as the secretary of the Montgomery NAACP since 1943, and she led the branch voter registration drive and youth workshops, which she organized in the 1940s. In 1955 she became secretary of the Alabama State Conference of NAACP branches. She expanded her involvement with grassroots organizing for social justice when she attended the Highlander Folk School in 1955. In her youth workshops she taught defiance as a tactic and a philosophy. For months prior to her arrest, Parks and other women in the Women's Political Council had discussed how defiance of the bus segregation might instigate a federal case to overturn the unjust laws, a practice launched after the 1946 *Morgan* decision and used in antiapartheid struggles in South Africa in 1953. Parks's refusal to yield to a bus driver's order to give her seat to a white passenger on the evening of December 1, 1955, arose from the discussions and plans occurring across the South as blacks found common cause with the defiance campaigns in South Africa. And Parks was hardly quiet. When she refused to move, "because she did not think she had to," she demonstrated the strategies she and others had learned and taught for years.[56]

Longtime nonviolent activist Bayard Rustin assessed the integral roles Parks and other women occupied in the rapid mobilization and launch of the bus boycott. Parks's actions on the bus and afterward made visible the complex networks that sustained the boycott and literally transported thousands of black Montgomerians each day. Rufus Lewis, who had created veterans' schools to organize the voting efforts for men and women, had served in World War II and the Korean War. He then worked with former veterans to coordinate car routes for daily transportation. Church members provided funds, meeting spaces, phones, cars, and drivers. These complicated personal and organizational systems were worked out each night in the churches where working-class black men, women, and their children gathered to pray, testify, and organize. Nixon and Parks understood how the boycott reinvigorated the community, and their support for the Reverend Martin Luther King Jr., the new young pastor of Dexter Avenue Baptist Church, to lead the MIA demonstrated, again, how these community ties could create a new organization that was immediately effective.[57] But the MIA's rise out of nationalist and labor organizations also brought a pastiche of ideologies and tactics, which included self-defense, passive resistance, nonviolence, and black defiance.[58]

Watching the events unfold, James Farmer and William Worthy, both members of FOR and CORE, tracked the MIA's use of nonviolence in day-to-day actions. Farmer and Worthy argued that someone with experience in the philosophy and tactics of nonviolence should go to Montgomery. Bayard Rustin was the foremost authority on nonviolence, and they urged him to offer counsel to the MIA. Now executive director of the War Resisters League, Rustin again found an opportunity to connect his antiwar activism with the racial justice movement. He traveled to Montgomery in early January and found a community cobbling together the raiment of nonviolence with communal traditions of self-defense. As the MIA members faced bombs, threats, assaults, and terror from antiblack organizations and the local police, they responded using mass direct-action nonviolence. At the same time, Rustin learned that after King received numerous threats, the community organized armed men into shifts for around-the-clock protection. "This is like war," one guard told Rustin. Surprised by the arsenal in many blacks' homes, including King's, Rustin nonetheless discerned the community's receptiveness to the philosophy and tactics of nonviolence.[59]

Months earlier, Rustin had helped write *Speak Truth to Power*, a treatise on nonviolence for the American Friends Service Committee. Because of his earlier conviction for homosexual activity in California, Rustin was not named as a coauthor, but his articulation of nonviolent direct activism in a chapter of the publication became integral to the document's authority as a blueprint for nonviolence and as a mass response to colonialism and other forms of armed oppression. In Montgomery, Rustin witnessed thousands of black men, women, and children in daily struggle against racial violence and economic oppression. Now acting as a community in radical protest against local and national racial oppression, the MIA confronted the violence used by the local Citizens' Council and police defiance. Rustin worked with King and the MIA to calibrate indigenous practices of resistance with the ideology and tactics of nonviolence that were local, national, and international. The mass efforts of black Montgomerians, Rustin observed, "would be a nonviolent protest, not a boycott as the former put forth a philosophy and not simply an action with a finite goal. [Nonviolence] would permeate the entire community culture." Whereas previous black struggles against segregation were linked to U.S. wars abroad, this victory would be "Victory without Violence." In this struggle, African Americans eschewed the language of battle and war that had characterized their earlier struggles that occurred in the midst of wars abroad.[60]

This community-based challenge to segregation nurtured a collective critical consciousness about the efficacy of nonviolence as a local response, but one with links to nonviolence elsewhere in the world, including the recent defiance campaigns in South Africa. Through workshops they learned that how they dressed, walked, and surrendered en masse could disarm their attackers. They learned how collective and nonviolent tactics turned individual and passive resistance into direct and mass action. They created forums for consciousness-raising where art, music, and oral practices advanced and sustained the political momentum, similar to protest songs in the antiapartheid movement. When Rustin first arrived, he witnessed "a prayer meeting" where the participants "sang for the first time a song which had been adopted as the theme song for the movement. The four stanzas proclaim[ed] the essential elements of a passive struggle—protest, unity, nonviolence, and equality." As the community gathered to pray and sing, the men and women who were arrested each day arrived and testified about their experiences. These were peace warriors returned from the front lines of the freedom struggle, and they "became symbols of courage." In these meetings King and other black ministers led the congregations in five prayers: "We are not struggling merely for the rights of Negroes but for all the people of Montgomery, black and white. We are determined to make America a better place for all people. Ours is a nonviolent protest. We pray God that no man shall use arms." King and others then gave lectures about the success of nonviolent mass action used elsewhere, including in India and South Africa. These mass meetings, which began as prayer meetings, became meetings where the community collectively called for "freedom!"[61]

With these claims, the Bandung Conference echoed in Montgomery. Worthy noted that "while tyranny in the South is far less efficient and infinitely less intelligent" than colonialism, he nonetheless saw its similarities to communism and white supremacy. All three systems of oppression relied on collaborators and surveillance. Activists, including King and others in the MIA, were "shadowed" and "watched." The police used informants. The effort to discredit activists challenging white supremacy in Montgomery had a counterpart in the harassment and jailing of anticolonial activists in Jakarta.[62]

When King described the Montgomery Bus Boycott to end segregation as part of the global struggle by the oppressed against colonialism and imperialism, he displayed a critical consciousness influenced by the larger context of African Americans' analyses of nonviolent direct action as radical action used elsewhere in anticolonial struggles. King compared the enormous effort by governments to sustain these systems of oppression and the people's efforts to end them. He repeatedly called attention to the unchecked violence, threats, and intimidation that blacks in Montgomery confronted daily from whites determined to maintain their control and by local and state authorities determined to defy federal law.[63]

As the nonviolent mass action incited violent retaliations from an organized and massive resistance to integration, African Americans saw the Montgomery Bus Boycott as different from passive resistance and as an action that demonstrated a mass radicalism seen in anticolonial struggles. The boycott affirmed to activist James Forman what he considered while in the segregated air force: Mass action changed the minds and culture for those in protest. In discussions in Chicago's black barbershops, men told Forman that blacks could not possibly sustain a mass movement. When blacks in Montgomery began their bus boycott, students and faculty at Roosevelt debated the strategy, arguing for a more aggressive and "creative confrontation" akin to Gandhi's efforts in the 1930 Salt March. They "admired the cultural effects of the boycott in changing the mass psychology of black people, showing them that we could do things as a group." Forman determined people acted together "when they saw their people suffering at the hands of their oppressors." The mass action in Montgomery led Forman "to think that if nonviolent confrontation could heighten consciousness and disrupt the society," then he wanted to know more about the method. Forman considered Gandhi's methods against colonialism in India and against apartheid in South Africa as a form of "soul force." Ghana's new president, Kwame Nkrumah, he noted, argued "that the campaign he led against the English had been based on the principle of direct action, nonviolent if possible, but action nonetheless. Nkrumah was not ruling out violence against the colonial masters and neither did I."[64]

Many denounced civil rights legislation imposed by the federal courts as an invasion akin to the Civil War, and others considered the South the epicenter of the anticommunist struggle. Anti-integrationists tied black activism for civil rights of any sort to communism, and, in turn, anticommunism legitimized new forms of violence against activists. Richard M. Weaver, a conservative intellectual who wrote for the *National Review*, described integration as communism. Weaver claimed that "the Communists are skilled enough in warfare" and threatened to impose "racial collectivism" and "obliterate" "our historic constitutional structure."[65] The rhetoric and practices of anticommunism included fears of "outside agitation," a coded phrase used to vilify blacks who belonged to the NAACP or any other organization calling for integration. The charges of the menacing black rapist used to justify vigilantism in the early twentieth century morphed into charges against the menacing black radical, an image that encapsulated the black teenager "with new ideas" from the North and the black veteran claiming the right to vote. Black and white southerners who organized for integration faced intimidation and violence, but so, too, did whites who were merely sympathetic to the idea. Anticommunism, then, endorsed a new wave of violence that was far more open, widespread, and legitimized by the racialized language, tactics, and philosophy that informed wars abroad.

Bellicose voices called for an organized political resistance to the *Brown* decision and black assertiveness generally, giving new energy to the violent resistance to integration. Mississippi senator James Eastland loudly and repeatedly expressed his opposition to integration. For years he and others had used inflammatory rhetoric that stirred up violence, intimidation, and economic reprisals against African Americans and white allies who challenged segregation. The waves of violence that rolled through Mississippi, Alabama, and Georgia between 1945 and 1957 attested to the impact of their agitation. In 1956, Virginia senator Harry F. Byrd called for legal efforts to halt school integration, and within two years this rhetoric of massive resistance in the legislature and courts expanded to include a grassroots assault on civil rights activists deemed "outside agitators" who were reportedly communists. Along with vigilantes, moderates and working-class whites who viewed integration as an encroachment on their material and social well-being provided new recruits. While diplomats argued segregation undermined the nation's integrity abroad, many white Americans believed integration eroded their social and economic status at home. Across the South, governors, congressional representatives, and senators encouraged the suppression of black political and economic rights in order to save states' rights.[66]

Little Rock

After two years of delays, the school board in Little Rock, Arkansas, agreed to integration of Central High School in September 1957. By then, the state university, many public schools, and the city's public bus system had integrated. The delay in the integration of the high school had much to do with the alliance between the white working and middle classes who saw the high school as the pathway to white respectability. In a context where the majority of white southerners did not complete high school and faced limited opportunities in agriculture, the segregated Central High represented upward mobility. It also presented white elites with an opportunity to reaffirm the associations between anticommunism, white supremacy, and their political and class power. Since the *Brown* decision, ardent segregationists in the state had coordinated their opposition to school integration school by school. When the city made plans in 1955 to integrate

Central High, a largely working-class white school, and not the more affluent West Little Rock, segregationists in the city and state found their next
battle. They successfully made their appeal to the Citizens' Council and
then to Governor Orval Faubus, who saw the coalition as additional support for his next gubernatorial campaign. Claiming that blacks planned a
wave of violence, the Citizens' Council and the Mothers' League of Central
High School, an organization of white women, continued their unsuccessful press in the courts to stop school integration. At the same time, they
launched a wave of intimidation and violence against blacks who planned
to send their children to the school. They paid special attention to Daisy
Bates, who headed the state's NAACP.[67]

With a coalition of whites now united in fierce defense of segregation,
the governor ordered the Arkansas National Guard to close the school to the
nine black students who planned to attend. Augmented by city police, the
troops did not stop the crowds of whites who hooted and jeered at the students. For several weeks the confrontation continued. Many in the crowd
were mothers, but many of the men belonged to the Citizens' Council
and other new anti-integrationist organizations, many goaded into existence by local white ministers decrying integration as an assault on white
womanhood. In Nashville, Tennessee, anti-integrationists bombed an elementary school where black students were scheduled to attend. Shocked
by the violence, school officials pressed forward with the integration plan.
Tennessee governor Frank G. Clement conceded that "no one who favors
integration could do as much to bring about integration as the man who
set off the dynamite at the Hattie Cotton School."[68]

Violence continued in Little Rock. By the last week of September, a
"frenzied mob cursed, shouted, and screamed" as Elizabeth Eckford,
Ernest Green, and seven other students attempted to enter Central High
School. Unimpeded by local and state officials, the crowd attacked correspondents James Hicks, Moses J. Newson, and L. Alex Wilson and photographer Earl Davy. As Hicks and Newson sprinted away, men hurled bricks
at Wilson, who never recovered from the attack. The mob then turned
their fury onto the police, who swung billy clubs as the mob surged toward
them. Only after the Eisenhower administration cabled Faubus to order
the police and guards to control the crowds did the local police attempt
to move the enraged crowd away from the school. Faced with an uncom-
municative governor, the president determined that "enforcement of the
federal court order" required a military presence, and he ordered the integrated 101st Airborne Division to Little Rock.

The battle continued the next day when more than 400 paratroopers carrying bayonets surrounded the school and a company of the men escorted the nine Negro students up the steps and into the building. Images of these "hard looking" and armed troops flooded the black, white, and international papers. With the 101st Airborne escorting the black students, the school became a daily battleground. Although soldiers "shoved" crowds of whites "far back from the scene," skirmishes erupted as the nine black students arrived and departed. Sporadic confrontations between soldiers and participants in the crowds resulted in injuries. Unlike the state National Guard and local police, who ignored the belligerence of onlookers, troops in the 101st "barked orders for the crowds to disperse." Commanders informed students to either "go to school, or leave." After the teenagers entered the school, the crowds milled about. Paul Downs, a combat veteran of World War II and Korea, plunged toward one of the paratroopers. Ordered to move back, Downs refused, and the paratrooper raised his bayonet and struck the man. Other troops raised their rifle butts as some in the crowd refused to listen to the soldiers.[69]

The 101st Airborne, which arrived from Fort Campbell, Kentucky, demonstrated federal power that had recently supported the military's integration. "The Army is integrated and the 101st is no different," the public information officer told the press. The black weeklies made much of this announcement. These "battle-tested troops," the *Defender* reported, intended to stay "indefinitely" and "fend for the Negroes." Many of the highly selected and all-volunteer combat troops came from towns in Arkansas, though none from Little Rock. Reports of black men carrying loaded carbines instigated a fierce backlash from southern governors and congressional representatives. The commanding general, Major General Edwin A. Walker, immediately ordered black paratroopers removed to the periphery. Confined to moving and organizing the division's equipment, black troops remained a visible and impressive display of federal power. The black press contrasted the disciplined and integrated 101st with the chaos of the resistance to black students attending Central High. While black readers viewed these images of white soldiers protecting black children with professionalism—some images displayed soldiers solicitous of and watchful over the children—many others considered these images of integration as incendiary and evidence of a federal government foisting integration upon the South.[70]

While the black press applauded the images of the integrated military and while images of whites shouting at black children shocked many northerners, photographs of the 101st with bayonets at the ready emboldened southerners' fury against Eisenhower. As the daily confrontations between the troops and the crowds continued, many southern whites characterized the president's decision to send troops as an "invasion." South Carolina senator Olin Johnston requested funding "to investigate a drive by Communists and fellow travelers to force integration, discredit the South and set up a dictatorship." Aided by "the encouragement of the Justice Department," he claimed, these communist subversives funded the NAACP. Conservative columnist Holmes Alexander remarked that the troops' presence was like an occupation, but one that appeared "as a matter of foreign policy." Eisenhower, Alexander observed, "has made an enemy in the South of the constructive or conservative force. The thing that the President is up against in the American South is exactly what he finds himself confronting in the Middle East—nationalism." Alexander predicted that Eisenhower's efforts to "enforce race-mixing in the South" would not prevail through "force of arms." Rather, the use of federal troops would only incite a violent backlash.[71]

While divided over the Supreme Court's desegregation order, the southern press unanimously deplored the presence of federal troops and described the military presence as an "occupation" that resembled troops in the South after the Civil War. White southerners praised Governor Faubus for resisting integration. Ignoring years of violence against blacks who struggled for civil rights, the southern press accused Eisenhower of inciting racial warfare. After five southern legislatures immediately drafted legislation preventing the presence of federal troops, the Eisenhower administration retreated. By early October, the administration had reduced the 101st's presence by half, and by the month's end, the administration had the troops removed to the perimeter. Now protected by the federalized but indifferent Arkansas National Guard, the nine black students attended a school where order eroded. Without the 101st, the taunting attacks began anew, and the students spent the remainder of the school year enduring open hostility. The nine black students realized that the local and state officials supported the segregationists, now a diverse, disciplined, and well-organized group that included students. The black students found the younger white teachers, some of whom were veterans, "more favorable" to integration, but the orchestrated resistance in and out of the school bolstered local claims that integration was too dangerous, and the state closed the school.

Self-Defense

As the 1957 standoff in Little Rock accelerated a violent and massive resistance to integration across the South, many African Americans debated the need for armed troops to halt the flouting of civil rights laws and the organized terror used against them. Once Eisenhower removed the integrated 101st Airborne and no longer showed a willingness to use federal power to enforce judicial orders or to protect black citizens from violence, many African Americans called for self-defense. "They could have integration in one minute," Louis Armstrong said, "if they'd just give the Negroes something to protect themselves with. Just give them an even chance. Then watch them cowards haul out of there."[72] Many African Americans agreed, though few openly called for organized black resistance. Instead, many African Americans quietly organized their guns to protect their homes and families.

As the danger and reprisals continued into the late 1950s and as anti-colonial struggles in Africa became armed struggles, Charles B. Strain notes, "self-defense assumed important constitutional and political roles in black empowerment," and "under certain circumstances" the "personal and localized act of defending oneself from harm" became a "prerequisite of open political challenge."[73] Men returned from war, asserted their rights as veterans and citizens, and found only resistance. Federal power, in myriad ways, had protected the rights of white veterans, and few, if any, had died at the hands of vigilantes. Not so for black veterans. The particular and persistent violence targeted at black veterans and blacks in uniform informed the consciousness of African Americans about the inequities they faced as citizens even as they were compelled into the military by the draft.

As they faced organized violence, African Americans contemplated how to defend themselves and their communities. Individual and collective acts of self-defense had diminished some violence. After activist and veteran Robert F. Williams and others in the Monroe, North Carolina, branch of the NAACP had an armed confrontation with the Klan in 1957, they did not see any further public displays of its terror. Blacks in Monroe had guns, Williams told correspondent and veteran Julian Mayfield, and they formed a "small army, drilled and disciplined."[74] Williams insisted, as did many other African Americans in the South, that they "were fighting for their lives." Williams had helped revive the Monroe NAACP branch, and his philosophy of self-defense quickly attracted other members. Blacks in the county began to protest. In the 1957 shootout, local police had arrived with the Klan. The power structure in this and other counties refused to yield, and it remained solidly backed by officials determined to prevent, and not protect, blacks' rights. After Mayfield observed the dynamics in Monroe, he concluded that the "legalistic and passive resistance" had yet to shake the power structure. "Then to the fore [came] Robert Williams, and other young men and women like him, who have concluded that the only way to win a revolution is to be a revolutionary." But even with displays of self-defense by blacks, the continued covert terrorism by the Klan and the overt political and economic discrimination did not diminish. Williams was forced to leave the area.[75]

Robert Williams did not deny the power of mass nonviolence, but he believed self-defense was necessary. "Massive civil disobedience," he noted, "is a powerful weapon under civilized conditions." Williams argued that blacks had the right to self-defense in the face of "lawless, racist violence." Authorities in North Carolina, he insisted, did not act until blacks in the state armed themselves and "showed a willingness to use their weapons in self-defense. Black people armed themselves because of the daily violence they faced."[76] In small towns and large cities across the South, African Americans found little protection from authorities, and local police frequently joined local vigilantes. Whites attacked blacks with impunity. Many African Americans condemned the government's failure or unwillingness to protect them, especially when they sought the right to vote, and many insisted on protecting themselves. By 1960, Robert Williams advocated a black revolutionary philosophy akin to the armed anticolonial struggles in Vietnam and Algeria.

For many other African Americans, nonviolent direct action became an effective challenge to massive resistance. James Forman considered it useful "and not the ultimate weapon of liberation." Yet he noted that mass nonviolent direct action heightened consciousness about racial injustice and violence in the South. To be effective, he argued, it required a committed group of people in constant opposition to segregation and who would "help develop the mass consciousness by saying 'we are ready to lay down our lives by using nonviolence, if this will lead toward revolution.'" The activists committed to this philosophy and these tactics studied the collective nonviolent actions of people elsewhere engaged in anticolonial and freedom struggles. And they sought new forms of organizations and leadership that built and perpetuated progressive and revolutionary movements for social change.[77]

For some African Americans, the choice between nonviolence and self-defense tactics as responses to the particular violence they faced in America did not adequately address the implications of American wars against nonwhites and their own increasing involvement in those wars. Just as those who called for black self-defense measured their strategies through the prism of the anticolonial struggles in Vietnam and Africa and saw self-defense as a corrective—albeit an unfortunate corrective—to colonialism, those who pursued nonviolence considered the tactics and philosophy from anticolonial successes in India and Ghana. As Bayard Rustin noted, "Preparation of the weapons of wars" abroad and "the development of policies of intimidation" at home were related. He and others proposed nonviolent resistance, demonstrations, strikes, boycotts, non-cooperation, and civil disobedience to confront the violence in their own communities and stop invasions and end wars elsewhere. These advocates intended to use nonviolence as a social revolution against racial injustice and economic exploitation and for political rights that would also alter American society. Over time, they imagined that the nation would end international conflict and profoundly shift its relationship to the international community. Nonviolence created change, they argued, not simply because of its techniques and tactics, but because it also advocated a way of life with implications for the international, and vice versa. Mass nonviolence, these advocates argued, was as revolutionary as armed self-defense. William Worthy argued that the nonviolent efforts of African Americans for full citizenship made them "custodians of American democracy."[78]

African Americans framed their struggles for freedom and their use of nonviolence within the larger context of anticolonial struggles, but only a few African Americans in the late 1950s openly associated with antiwar organizations. As Mary Helen Washington notes, "Whether on the Left or the Right, African Americans were, by virtue of their blackness, subversive in the Cold War." By 1955, according to Jack O'Dell, "every organization in Negro life which was attacking segregation per se was put on the subversive list" by the FBI. Black writers especially faced arrest or harassment from the FBI, or they were hauled in front of HUAC. By mid-decade, numerous black musicians, artists, and writers on the left, including Elizabeth Catlett, Chester Himes, Richard Wright, William Gardner Smith, James Baldwin, and Ollie Harrington, left the United States. Many on the black Left in the United States reluctantly or willingly masked the open dissent that characterized the Popular Front and World War II years. Yet dissent did occur. The 1950s, Washington concludes, was a period of "creative black struggle." Langston Hughes, Robert Hayden, Gwendolyn Brooks, Robert Browne, and other black writers and journalists found in the language of the civil rights, anticolonial, and antiwar movements a vocabulary to question the growing martial rhetoric for war abroad.[79]

Langston Hughes watched W. E. B. Du Bois and Paul Robeson suffer "banishment and ostracism," so he kept his distance from the Left and those with a leftist past, but he did not publicly repudiate the Left, Communists, or the Communist Party. When he tried to deny his own "past or present membership in the Communist Party," he found that such claims did not help him escape Senator McCarthy's charges. Whittaker Chambers accused Hughes's literary agent, Max Lieber, of being a communist operative, and he left for Mexico. Unions and veteran organizations successfully blocked groups from organizing Hughes's talks and readings; he was increasingly banned from campuses. Hughes's ability to participate in interracial civil rights efforts atrophied after critics described these events as organized by communists. In 1953, Hughes was hauled in front of HUAC, where Roy Cohn and Senator Joseph McCarthy grilled him.[80]

Even as anticommunists accused Hughes of ties to the Left, critics and publishers characterized his work as racially chauvinistic, superficial, and politically irrelevant. *Montage of a Dream Deferred*, published in 1948, documented the failed American dream for black migrants, but it received stinging reviews. By 1950, Hughes felt supplanted and surpassed by a new generation of black writers, including Richard Wright and Gwendolyn Brooks, whose *Annie Allen* won the Pulitzer Prize that year, and by Ralph Ellison and James Baldwin, whose novels and essays received national and international acclaim. Other writers, most notably Robert Hayden and Ellison, declared Hughes's continued use of vernacular language and of black folk as subjects out of step with postwar high modernism. Hughes was lauded by college students in the 1940s as an example of a radical writer, but in the 1950s students claimed they no longer found his civil rights activism radical and his writings no longer inspired their social activism. His most successful publications of these years invited speculation that he wanted to avoid controversy.[81]

More than any other black writer at midcentury, however, Hughes interrogated the vernacular language of freedom that had animated the activism of the 1930s and early 1940s. First, he revised earlier published works from the heyday of the Popular Front. *Simple Speaks His Mind* and *Simple Takes a Wife* gathered his most scathing critiques of wartime segregation. Again, his work garnered rave reviews. *I Wonder as I Wander*, the second volume of his autobiography, which he published in 1956, received favorable reviews. Rather than focus on his assent to World War II or his confrontation with HUAC in the early 1950s, Hughes crafted a memoir that began with his 1930s travels in Cuba, the Soviet Union, China, and Japan and ended with his reportage about the war against fascism in Spain. These 1950s publications mined his earlier leftist writings and goaded his readers, and perhaps himself, to revalue a period when African Americans on the Left denounced America's racial practices in the global arena and imagined freedom as expansive. In the 1930s Hughes had engaged in the Left's debate about the efficacy of war.[82]

Hughes's critique of blacks' participation in war as the means to their freedom was especially apparent in the last third of *I Wonder as I Wander*, which chronicled the months he spent as a war correspondent during the Spanish Civil War. In the months he spent in Spain, Hughes witnessed blacks from the Diaspora gathered to fight fascism; they also hoped to launch their own independence movements elsewhere. While the efforts in Spain failed, and Hitler's armies invaded France in 1940, Hughes returned from Spain and argued for black Americans' participation in a global struggle for independence from white supremacy, beginning with the assault on fascism. *I Wonder* drew extensively on these earlier and well-received writings, but not as a form of nostalgia. In his 1956 memoir, Hughes shifted from vivid descriptions of heroic black men and women gathered to fight fascism in Spain, and he reconsidered the disproportionate burden segregated and colonized blacks bore in seeking freedom through their participation in Europeans' imperial wars.

At the same time, Hughes openly considered war's deleterious impact on black bodies and souls. In *I Wonder*, he detailed the severed limbs of soldiers and civilians scattered through Madrid's streets. These soldiers, he observed, were the poor and young impressed into war. He rewrote his articles about the 1930s Spanish war as he witnessed the sedimentation of racial violence from Mississippi to South Africa in the 1950s. After publication of his autobiography, Hughes returned to his poetry and considered how blacks' assent to their impressments into imperial wars compounded their own injustice as disfranchised citizens.

> They are quite willing
> To pauperize you—
> Or use your kids as labor boys
> For army, air force, or uranium mine.

It's the same from Cairo to Chicago,
Cape Town to the Caribbean.

His poems, William Worthy noted, provided "an amazingly accurate social and political early warning system." Hughes, Worthy noted, "sounded clear warnings" about a black people

caught in a crack
that splits the world
in two from China
to Alabama
via Lenox Avenue.[83]

Hughes was not alone in using poetry and fiction to question blacks' roles in the Cold War militaries.

And Then We Heard the Thunder

John Oliver Killens's second novel, published in 1962, also sounded an early warning to African Americans as they debated how freedom might be wrestled from imperial wars abroad and self-defense at home. Set in the segregated military of World War II when African Americans linked their resistance to segregation with their demands to fight in combat, *And Then We Heard the Thunder* considered the geography of the Cold War struggle not as a battle between East and West but as a protracted and terrible war raging in the American South and Asia.[84] As Killens revisited the World War II battlefields of the two Souths—the American South and the South Pacific—he suggested the contemporary wars of the southern civil rights struggles and America's wars in Southeast Asia. His novel, then, wove together two historical moments in which America's war abroad intersected with systematic violence against African Americans in the United States. In both the American South and Asia, the promise of war as a liberation from colonial oppression remained unrealized, both for African Americans and for Asians. In each context, one form of oppression gave way to yet another. Even as African Americans fought Japanese soldiers, they understood how their battles defended white supremacy and allowed the United States to build bases in Australia and occupy islands throughout the South Pacific. In these settings, Japanese and European colonial domination gave way to American military and economic imperialism.[85]

    Killens's novel introduced a character who ultimately rejected the civil rights blueprint to claim full citizenship through the battlefield. Set in World War II, the segregated draft pulled ambitious and well-educated Solly Saunders from a northern and integrated law school into the army. Saunders eagerly embraced the military for his own advancement, and he believed his assent to its policies and his diligence to duty might upend the military's segregation. He immediately distanced himself from the men who held no such illusions. Confined to a base in Georgia where white officers subscribed to ideas about blacks' innate inferiority, Saunders found his efforts to become an officer thwarted. Though provoked into anger by racial taunts from the MPs, Saunders refused to join the other black soldiers in their revolts against the hypocrisy of a segregated army at war with Nazism. Mortified by his own unwillingness to fight back, he watched the other men claim their dignity through their daily insurrections. Saunders considered the men's ethos and politics misguided, but after local and military police terrorized and brutalized him, he finally joined the men in rebellion. Shipped to one of the islands in the Philippines, Solly's unit helped prepare the beaches for U.S. bombing raids. He's startled by the deaths of so many civilians and wonders, "What are we doing in these people's country? The United States and the Japanese Empire didn't ask these people 'May we use your country for our little old battleground?'" Still, Saunders hoped that his participation in the war would end racial segregation and advance equality. After participating in the brutal assault against the Japanese military, Saunders's unit endured fatal attacks from white soldiers in Australia. Just as his mates long realized, Saunders finally concluded the war "was no war to save democracy." Outraged by his own complicity in the carnage, he joined other black soldiers in a protracted battle against white American soldiers in an Australian town that ultimately led to each side's near-annihilation.[86]

Published the year the Selective Service escalated the draft for Vietnam and army recruiters targeted poor black men to meet their quotas, Killens's novel challenged a civil rights agenda that supported the nation's wars abroad while the federal government countenanced white supremacy at home (the year the novel appeared, black veteran James Meredith was assaulted as he attempted to enroll at the University of Mississippi). The heated debates in the novel between elite blacks who saw their participation in war as an opportunity to advance racial equality at home and working-class blacks who rejected Jim Crow in the military and the nation paralleled blacks' contemporary debates about how best to advance struggles for their freedom. Solly Saunders believed the only way to his personal advancement was to embrace the war. Sent to the South Pacific, he found himself poised, as James Baldwin noted in 1963, to "murder, or be murdered." Forced to defend himself against soldiers in the American army, he decided to shoot back, "to beat some sense" into white men's "heads" on a bridge in Australia so that they would notice that he, too, could kill efficiently. When he surveyed the dead black soldiers around him, a new and critical consciousness emerged. He wanted to "believe that all this dying was for something," but he could not be convinced that America would "come to its senses and build something new." Anticipating Frantz Fanon, Killens asked through Solly Saunders how black men killing other "colored soldiers" or slaying white men in self-defense ensured their freedom and advanced racial justice. What happened when victims of racial oppression became killers of other colored men during war?[87] Over the next decade, tens of thousands of young black men fighting in Vietnam asked the same question.

5

Machine Gun Blues

Black America and the Vietnam War

Nearly every day Jimmy Hendrix went to a restaurant in Seattle where his friends worked and asked for food. Usually he took the bags of cold burgers home to his father and younger siblings. Sometimes the teenager stayed and gulped the food. A recent high school dropout, Hendrix could not find a job, since many businesses in Seattle refused to hire young black men. He tried to join the air force, but the recruiter rejected his application. Then the police arrested him for stealing a car, though he convinced them he "only sat in the car." Two weeks later, after he was arrested again and charged with grand theft auto, Hendrix feared he might get convicted. He went to see the local army recruiter who needed to meet a higher quota, and he readily took Hendrix's application. When the judge presiding over Hendrix's case learned about the recruiter's offer, he agreed to suspend the sentence if the teenager enlisted immediately. Hendrix left for Fort Ord in late May 1961.[1]

Hendrix's various calculations about when and how to enlist were not unusual. He may have heard about volunteering for the army as an escape from jail through the informal information networks young men had about the military.[2] During periods of higher draft calls, judges frequently ordered young men to choose between the army and a jail sentence. Hendrix may have heard that many black men volunteered for combat and airborne units because of the $55 monthly bonus.[3] At Fort Ord, Hendrix ate

Viet Cong propaganda addressed to African American soldiers,
November 6, 1967. © Corbis.

three meals a day. Besides the regular pay and hot food, Hendrix enlisted
for other reasons.[4] Adrift, yet anxious to marry, Hendrix wanted a steady
wage and the probity it signaled to the young woman's family. Hendrix's
decision to solve his problem of irregular work by enlisting in the army
typified the response of many young black men to the limited economic
and social choices they faced between 1950 and 1960.

Confined to the margins of the nation's burgeoning affluence, these
overwhelmingly poor and undereducated men had little access to well-
paid, steady work. Fewer still had the means to attend college. The barriers
to these two avenues for economic mobility, the new hallmark of post–
Korean War life in the United States, not only constricted blacks' opportunities for personal improvement; they also narrowed the overall stability
and economic mobility of black households.[5] Along with the legal imperative to register, many working-class men, including many black men, considered the military a sign of impending adulthood and a step toward eco-

nomic independence. After three years in one of the services, the GI Bill promised money for education and loans to buy a home or start a business.[6] Few other employers offered such benefits, and the military provided a special appeal to young black men as they aspired toward economic citizenship in a nation that limited this status by race. After all, the black papers intoned, the integrated military remained the most important gain of the post–Korean War civil rights struggle. And it was evidence of what Nikhil Pal Singh describes as "the Myrdallian faith that the gap between American ideals and American realities was closing."[7] In the late 1950s and early 1960s, many African Americans considered the military not just personal opportunity or economic stability but an expression of widely held values of self-reliance, personal dignity, and racial activism. Despite the unease about the nation's increasing involvement in military actions in Vietnam, many African Americans viewed their visible presence in combat as hard-won symbols of manhood, honor, and dignity.[8]

Even as the draft escalated in 1963, black men's pattern of high enlistment and reenlistment continued, but not out of choice. Alongside their personal responses to their narrow economic opportunities, black men considered their high presence in the military and combat as a result of systematic economic, political, and racial inequalities. Whether they enlisted or were drafted, they went into the army or the Marines at such high rates because they were poor and black. Reporting from Vietnam, *Chicago Defender* correspondent Ethel Payne observed that "black men who couldn't find jobs otherwise gravitated to the services, because [war] did provide employment opportunity." Pride and the extra pay pushed many to volunteer for the elite combat units, and many of the high-risk combat units had 40 to 50 percent black participation. Payne observed that "blacks have to turn to war to find occupations and find a way of living, or dying."[9] "The right to fight" had been integral to the civil rights struggles in the World War II and Korean War epochs, but when Muhammad Ali refused induction in 1966, he was not alone in thinking he had been "singled out" by his draft board. As the Lyndon B. Johnson administration tied its civil rights agenda and antipoverty programs to draft programs that forced record numbers of poor black men into the military, Ali's court appeals focused attention on the class and racial inequities of the Selective Service System. By 1967, many African Americans questioned their disproportionate participation in "America's seasonal bloodlettings."[10]

African Americans pulled from poor and restive neighborhoods in Chicago became soldiers in Bien Hoa and Marines in Chu Lai, where they became a vanguard of resistance to the war in Vietnam. Many black GIs and Marines did not consider the order "kill or be killed" liberatory. As African Americans linked their struggles in the military with the organized neglect and assaults on their own communities, they also used their experiences in and with combat to interrogate the organized violence of war. Many black troops considered themselves a "gendarme"; part of a larger colonial endeavor at odds with their own freedom struggles, they questioned their complicity in this violence. After months of combat, John McDonald described himself as a "handy man. Something good to have around to help the white man fight his dirty wars." Why, he asked, should black men help white men kill yellow men, women, and children? Why should he kill other human beings?[11] This critical consciousness crafted on the battlefields of Vietnam fueled a militancy that reverberated through the front lines and in the rear, on ships, on bases, and in military prisons. The implications of African Americans' resistance to war within the military reshaped the civil rights movement.

WHEN YOUNG BLACK WOMEN and men organized sit-ins to desegregate lunch counters in Oklahoma in 1958 and in Nashville a year later, many black Americans also wondered about finding work. "Got a Job," the 1958 hit song by William "Smokey" Robinson and the Miracles, narrated a young man's search for work, which ended with long hours in a grocery store:

Walked all day till my feet were tired
I was low, I just couldn't get hired
So I sat in a grocery store
"Help is light & I need some more."

He eventually found work, but he also found himself "workin' all day & workin' all night & workin' all day." In the economic downturn after John F. Kennedy's election, African Americans were twice as likely to be unemployed. Nationally, white workers accounted for 7 percent of the unemployed, but black workers had nearly double that rate at 13.8 percent. In the very large cities, black workers had much higher rates of unemployment. Black workers faced the "harshest consequences" in the heavily industrial cities of the Midwest, the National Urban League reported. In Detroit, 39 percent of African Americans lacked jobs. In St. Louis, black workers accounted for more than half of the 72,700 reported unemployed.

The majority of those without work had also exhausted their unemployment benefits.[12]

Young black men, especially, found few economic and social opportunities. James Baldwin described these men as "growing up in a rush," and "their heads bumped against the low ceiling of their actual possibilities."[13] In Baldwin's literary reconstructions of black neighborhoods, these young men lived in cramped cities with "killing streets" where the "housing projects jutted out like rocks in the middle of a boiling sea." Few, he noted, escaped. Instead, they came out of their homes and into "the streets for light and air and found themselves encircled by disaster."[14]

The military appeared to provide one of the few and consistent responses to the economic plight of black men. The Marines and the army actively recruited working-class black men for infantry units. The army made appeals to black women with nursing degrees. In the segregated neighborhoods of large cities, army and Marine recruiters, many of them African Americans, touted the military's success in integration. Journalists, social scientists, and congressional representatives regularly reported that 5 million Americans, including service personnel, civilians, and dependents, lived on integrated bases around the world, even in the South. Congress noted that African Americans found in the military "experiences and challenges denied them as civilians." And integration extended beyond the barracks as "our mighty defense machinery, with all of its potential for destruction, is sowing seeds of brotherly love and understanding among Americans." In the South, black and white children boarded buses and attended base schools together, all without incident.[15] Morton Puner, a member of the National Civil Liberties Union, argued that the military, perhaps the most conservative of American institutions, launched "one of the most profound changes in American racial patterns since the Emancipation."[16]

The Selective Service Act Congress passed in 1948 required young men, regardless of race, to register for the draft, but the amendments passed after the Korean War allowed for a variety of deferments that typically excluded black men. Since black men faced a greater probability of being drafted, they were more likely to enlist. Better to serve two years out of choice than three years through the draft. For Don Phillips, who lived with his mother and stepfather, Mabel and Homer Markham, in a two-bedroom ranch on the edge of tomato fields in Compton, California, the prospect of a draft notice loomed as soon as he turned eighteen. He discussed his options with other working-class young men in this new city outside Los

Angeles.[17] These young men attended high school, where they studied and played sports. Smart and ambitious, Phillips did not want to work in his stepfather's demolition and hauling business. He won awards for football, and he liked his Boy Scout troop. After he graduated in 1952, he waited anxiously for any news that he might receive a draft notice for Korea, but his concerns eased when the war ended. He used savings from his after-school and summer jobs to pay for classes at Los Angeles Community College; he bought his first car and headed for San Jose. With $500 from his savings, he registered for classes at the state university, already a large, sprawling campus with nearly 28,000 students. Along with fifty other African Americans, Phillips became a full-time college student.[18]

He and his friends paid attention to the draft calls. Before they left Compton, the young men applied for college deferments and let the draft board know their new addresses in San Jose. The pace of the draft eased for white men in college, but the numerous invasions and police actions pulled black men into the army. Phillips calculated his chances and options. He knew black men with college deferments did not always escape the draft, and it hovered like tentacles, ready to pull them from school. One friend planned to go to Canada. The black men in his family and neighborhood had served in World War II and Korea, but he did not want to be in the enlisted ranks. If the draft "got him," he wanted to be prepared. When older veterans from the Korean War suggested he could become an officer, Phillips went to the ROTC department and signed up for a class. Despite such careful calculations, Phillips did not make a unique decision.[19]

Just as many black men in Compton or Seattle believed, Colin Powell thought that a young man's chance to "peer over the horizon" came through joining the navy or the Marines. Powell's parents emigrated from Jamaica and lived in the South Bronx. The couple bought a house in Queens and viewed themselves as living the "American dream."[20] They saved enough money to send him to City College of New York, where he quickly gravitated toward the ROTC program. The money he earned from the program paid his college expenses, and the uniform gave him a strong sense of being "a member of a brotherhood." Describing himself as "an average student," Powell excelled in the program's disciplined atmosphere, at the time the largest voluntary ROTC contingent in the United States. In this program, he found that "race, color, background, income meant nothing. If this was what soldicring was all about, then maybe I wanted to be a soldier."[21]

When African Americans enlisted or were commissioned in the late

1950s and early 1960s, the NAACP considered military integration one of its most important successes. Executive Secretary Roy Wilkins cast the small but steady increase in the number of black officers and blacks' high enlistment rates as evidence that the men found the military's racial policies progressive even when their rights remained truncated elsewhere. Still, the association and other civil rights organizations quietly monitored the Department of Defense's responses to segregation in travel, schools, housing, and recreation outside military bases.[22] Soldiers and sailors continued to complain about the limitations they faced *in* the military. Each year, the Department of Defense made public its lists of "Negro personnel in key military positions" in an effort to quell criticism. Considered evidence of "the progress of integration," these reports also revealed that the military was no better in providing "opportunities."[23] Instead, African Americans felt vulnerable to the vagaries of the military's policies, and a steady stream of reports to the NAACP revealed how racial inequalities haunted the military and challenged its claims of full integration. Few African Americans held rank above the junior officer grades, and there were few black senior NCOs. The navy and the Marine Corps had percentages of blacks in the single digits. Black women found the services especially closed. Courts-martial for blacks in all of the services remained high, and many received discharges for violating local segregation laws.[24]

Despite its public self-congratulations, the military did not find itself inoculated against the racial upheavals in society more generally as Americans balked at ending segregation in national life. Scattered in barracks and ships, black GIs, Marines, and sailors felt isolated as their quest for integration accelerated and whites' resistance to it grew more violent.[25] Many whites arrived in barracks and on ships experienced in tactics and sentiments against school integration and ready to resist it in the military. Raised in North Carolina, Joe Powell was "really against the black people coming to school with us. They had their school over here and then they want to mix us up. That was really uncalled for."[26] Black soldiers complained that southern whites new to the military "organized to maintain their way of life" and the military did little, if anything, to prevent these outbreaks of harassment.[27]

Aware of the efforts of personnel and their dependents to participate in local demonstrations against off-base discrimination, many unit commanders ordered men and women to avoid them. Unable to prevent such participation, the Department of Defense decided in 1961 to provide more integrated recreation and services on bases and encourage integration off base. When violence flared near bases, the Defense Department planned to use military police to protect servicemen and -women from racial conflicts. It announced it would provide legal counsel to men and women arrested for violation of segregation. And the military determined it would no longer aid local authorities in the enforcement of "racial segregation or other forms of racial discrimination."[28] With this memo, the Department of Defense quietly abandoned decades of the military's explicit or tacit enforcement of local segregation laws and practices.

Pleased to be assigned to the 101st Airborne, Jimmy Hendrix balked at the segregation outside the base and questioned his commitment to the army. Hendrix wore his green dress uniform and the brigade's distinctive patch of the screaming eagle with pride. Within months of his assignment, he loathed the army. He found the segregation of the South oppressive, far worse than anything he experienced in Seattle. He chafed under the military's "discipline," its regimentation and harassment, often framed in racially derogatory terms. He understood how all the "fussing and fighting separated the men from the boys." Mostly, the men vomited and cried as they hurtled out of planes. Hendrix remained determined to stay in the 101st. He found the physical rush of "falling over backwards" thrilling. High in the sky, he discovered "you're there all by yourself and you can talk low, you can scream or anything. I think how crazy I was for doing this thing, but I loved it anyway." When he stepped out of the C-24, he became part of the "fearless men / who jump and die."[29]

By early 1962, Hendrix's elite airborne unit began to train for rapid battle deployments into Laos and South Vietnam.[30] This training took on a new urgency as President Kennedy described a global struggle against communism that threatened to engulf Southeast Asia.[31] Hendrix's letters home no longer expressed any enthusiasm for the army. He complained to his commanders, doctors, and a psychiatrist that he masturbated too much and that he desired one of the men in his unit. He could not sleep at night, and he fell asleep when on duty. Commanders considered him a reluctant and incompetent soldier, one who thought too much about his guitar and not enough about his gun. He feigned an injury after a jump, and the army discharged him in May 1962. Hendrix left the military still fascinated by it and glad to be rid of it.[32]

Hendrix's fears about the 101st going to war were not unfounded. Not long after President Kennedy took office, the Pentagon escalated American involvement in Vietnam and ordered six U.S. divisions, nearly 200,000 troops, to prepare for deployment. While these divisions did not arrive in

Vietnam for several years, thousands of paratroopers accompanied South Vietnamese troops between 1961 and 1963, first as advisors and then as combat units. Over the next two years, the Pentagon readied volunteer combat and Special Forces units for Vietnam, many with significant numbers of black men. By 1963, Don Phillips commanded a company in the 173rd Airborne and moved his family to Fort Benning, Georgia, where he prepared troops for "Operation Junction City," the largest airborne jump the army had ever planned.[33]

After the 1960 election, few Americans noticed the escalation in the number of military "advisors" sent to Vietnam. When the *Defender* and the *Afro-American* announced the Selective Service had increased its monthly draft calls, blacks' participation in military service appeared directed to Berlin or Cuba. Two of the most popular soul songs of 1962, the Shirelles' hit "Soldier Boy" and new Motown star Marvin Gaye's "Soldier's Plea," presented soldiering as commonplace. When "Soldier's Plea" obliquely referenced "fighting to keep us free," it might have suggested Berlin or Laos, both mentioned in the black and white presses.

> While I'm away darling I hope you'll think of me
> Remember I'm over here fighting to keep us free
> Just be my little girl and always be true
> And I'll be a faithful soldier boy to you.[34]

Perhaps Gaye meant the struggle for civil rights and not the Cold War. But the funereal timbre of the song hinted at the rising death rates of military advisors in Vietnam and Laos, including African American casualties. After 1962, vague references to military alerts in Europe and South Asia coincided with announcements from draft boards for increased "call-ups."

However imprecise the geography seemed about international conflict, the increase in the draft's pace evoked mixed reactions within African American communities. Many viewed the "step-up" as opportunity. Michigan congressional representative Charles Diggs asked Secretary of Defense Robert McNamara and the new president to end all discrimination in the armed services. "Colored military personnel must be given an honest and honorable chance to prepare and to contribute fully to the mammoth effort which will be required for the preservation of life and human liberty."[35] Deputy assistant secretary of state for public affairs and former *Minneapolis Star and Tribune* reporter Carl T. Rowan argued that civil rights struggles advanced anticommunist struggles. Black newspapers reprinted photographs of soldiers with bayonets in Little Rock, recalling an earlier association between the battles against white supremacy and anticommunism. By 1961 these images had shifted from photographs of black troops outside schools poised to support integration to images of soldiers at the new wall around East Berlin. They were, the *Afro-American* declared, "poised at the ready" to toss a grenade at the Soviets.[36]

While the mainstream black press depicted decorated black soldiers and combat units as heroes in the battle for civil rights, many African Americans considered the use of troops in undeclared wars against small nations of "colored people" indefensible. *Baltimore Afro-American* correspondent William Worthy, who toured and reported from Cuba in 1961, described an American invasion of the island nation as a debacle similar to France's war in Algeria. The Cuban people, he concluded, "would fight indefinitely." He wondered how, if at all, killing Cubans or Asians expanded the rights of black Americans. He considered America's Cold War foreign policy "immoral, and crippling to domestic and foreign affairs and in need of serious change." As he had declared a decade earlier, he insisted that war did not advance black citizenship.[37]

Scattered reports about "tensions" in Vietnam continued to appear in newspapers, but substantive articles about U.S. military operations remained scant. Typically, the black press printed obituaries of men killed in Vietnam. What news appeared was frequently misleading. Besides planting false stories in the *New York Times*, the Kennedy administration deliberately kept the American press ill-informed and underinformed. On White House orders, the rapidly increasing number of U.S. advisors gave only "routine cooperation to correspondents on coverage [of] current military situation in Vietnam."[38] By 1962, correspondents found accurate information harder to come by as the military "banned" American reporters from accompanying military advisors on U.S.-sponsored missions. Reporters suspected a widening war, but President Kennedy insisted the United States had only a limited role.[39]

Carl Rowan drafted the Kennedy administration's guidelines meant to limit and control press coverage.[40] Unable to keep reporters out of Vietnam or to censor the press, U.S. officials countered the articles opposed to Diem and Americans' efforts with upbeat reports of progress against Communists. The Kennedy administration considered the press a troublesome necessity in the Cold War struggle, and Rowan, a former journalist, drafted the administration's press policy for its undeclared war in Vietnam.[41] Cable 1006 intended to ensure "maximum discretion, minimum publicity" about Vietnam in the U.S. press. The military and the State Department refused to grant the press interviews, provide information about American and civilian casualties, or detail the size of the American "advisory" presence more generally. Rowan's memo, approved by Dean Rusk, also stipulated that reporters were to be kept away "from any but the most tightly controlled and favorably stage-managed situations." Andrew Hatcher, the associate White House press secretary, also helped Rowan "manage" the war news.[42]

Louis Martin, deputy chairman of the Democratic National Committee and a frequent advisor to President Kennedy, applauded appointments of African Americans in key areas of the State Department and the White House. Martin considered "strategic" the placement of Rowan and Hatcher in advisory positions in "non-racial areas."[43] By 1964, Rowan directed the U.S. Information Agency, and he recommended that Barry Zorthian assume control over press operations in Vietnam. The Johnson administration found it difficult to suppress the news, but Rowan argued that at least Zorthian might promote "the stories we want told."[44] Black men now served as architects of war planning in the Kennedy and Johnson administrations, and they were not limited to control of information. Dozens of black officers helped plan and execute the war's progress; increasing numbers served as military advisors. Others helped plan the arrival and buildup of combat troops.[45]

Despite the participation of African Americans in the Kennedy administration and the military, few African Americans served on local draft boards or held positions in the national office of the Selective Service System. Lewis Hershey was director of the Selective Service System, a position he had held since 1940. After 1948, he had Congress continuously amend the Selective Service policies at the national level to allow a number of deferments. By the late 1950s, these deferments typically favored white middle-class men entering colleges and universities at a record pace. Hershey considered the continued education of these young men "more valuable" to the future of the nation than time spent in the military or fighting a war.[46] Other amendments granted deferments to men in large-scale agriculture; skilled trades; the sciences, especially weapons research; and the specialized medical professions. Even with these diverse exclusions, black men who were married, attended college, and had skills or medical degrees did not enjoy such widespread deferments. Black men who hoped college might defer the draft found little comfort as local draft boards in many states scrutinized their progress. Black men with low grades, low class standing, or too few credits found their deferments suddenly revoked.[47] The college deferment test favored students in elite northeastern schools, and each year one-third to one-half of the students at black colleges in the South failed the test. The test was briefly abandoned in 1963, but Hershey revived it in 1966, a policy that elicited sharp criticism. As Harlem congressman Adam Clayton Powell Jr. observed, "First we provide an inferior education for black students. Next we give them a series of tests which many will flunk because of an inferior education. Then we will pack these academic failures off to Vietnam to be killed."[48]

By August 1962, the Selective Service announced the military's expansion by 250,000. Each month, Hershey explained, the draft call would increase from 40 men in each area to 75.[49] At the same time, Hershey encouraged the army to reduce the number of rejections made during the physical exam. Here, more white men failed than black.[50] By late 1962, registration for the draft and examinations for enlistment and induction among black men became more visible to and scrutinized by their communities. While draft boards remained overwhelmingly white, nearly every black neighborhood in the North, the Midwest, and West Coast cities had recruiting offices staffed by black sergeants. Newspapers provided periodic information about the army's particular appeals for black women to join the WACs. By 1962, young men saw recruiting advertisements in movie theaters, newspapers, and popular magazines. In Washington, D.C., the army set up recruiting stations in the lobbies of the large theaters.[51]

While their limited economic opportunities forced many to enlist, black men also sought ways to avoid the draft. Since World War II, many men in the Nation of Islam had registered as conscientious objectors. Most of these COs refused to acknowledge their draft notices or notices for alternative service. In 1958, Wallace Delaney Muhammad, a presiding minister of Temple of Islam 2 in Chicago, failed to report for his CO service. He claimed he was exempt as a minister of Islam and as a CO. Convicted in 1958 and sentenced months later, Muhammad spent several years in prison. Other men in the Nation of Islam, such as Wallace Lowery Jr. of South Bend, Indiana, found their local draft board impervious to their application for CO status.[52]

By 1961, lists of the men who did not register for the draft appeared in local papers. Typically, these men registered, moved, and then failed to send notice of their change of address to local boards. In other instances, when authorities came to the door looking for men, mothers and sisters informed them that the men no longer resided at the address. These practices, which became widespread in many black neighborhoods, vexed the

Selective Service. Some men may have re-registered elsewhere, but since draft notices were controlled and sent by local boards, black men were able to exploit the system's inability to track either their compliance with registration or their subsequent moves. As the draft calls rose, these lists lengthened, and the Selective Service advertised that it planned to investigate men who failed to report for exams.[53] Local boards in Chicago announced plans to draft men unless they submitted a change of address.[54] Such lists, with accompanying threats of jail sentences and steep fines, appeared to have an effect on some men. Others remained on these lists for months.[55] Many boards reportedly drafted "delinquents" first, even those not immediately classified as 1-A. These long notices of men who failed to report appeared so frequently that the *Chicago Defender* sternly reminded its readers, "Know Your Negro History: Early in 1950, the Army dropped quotas for Negro enlistment and the Selective Service eliminated questions on race for draft registrants."[56]

With more than 12 million young men eligible for the draft in 1962, the Selective Service concentrated on the voluntary enlistments. The navy and the Marine Corps relied on voluntary enlistments, but the army used the draft sparingly, as enlistments generally remained steady and high. Through economic necessity, communal pressure, or fear of the draft, men enlisted in high numbers. As a result of the high volunteerism, only one in forty of the eligible nineteen- to twenty-six-year-olds received a draft notice. More than half of the applicants—most of whom were black or white working-class men—failed either the physical or the mental exam. In need of troops and with half its volunteers rejected, the Selective Service instituted significantly increased draft calls for 1963 and 1964. The volunteer rate escalated, as enlistment meant a shorter commitment. In the following two years, the Selective Service used similar threats of increased draft calls, cessations of deferments, and reclassifications. During this same period, enlistments in the army, navy, and air force (the Marines were still a volunteer service) increased 70 percent.[57]

THE CASCADE OF URBAN revolts that erupted first in mid-Atlantic cities between 1963 and 1964 and expanded to the Midwest and West Coast by 1965 signaled that the civil rights legislation and antipoverty programs may have arrived too late to address the systemic economic and political barriers that the majority of African Americans faced. These rebellions against segregation, too few jobs, and poor housing continued into 1966.

Riots first erupted in Cambridge, Maryland, in 1963 and Harlem and Philadelphia in 1964. The largest riot erupted in early August 1965 in South Los Angeles, which included Watts; the next summer, riots in Chicago and Cleveland occurred.

By 1967 uprisings occurred in Newark and Detroit. These cities teemed with tens of thousands of recent black and white southern migrants who had left rural and urban areas in the South where machines had eliminated jobs and where communities continued a massive resistance to integration.[58] These migrants arrived in urban areas of the West, Midwest, and Northeast, where they found inadequate infrastructure, where unions and working-class ideologies were frayed by deindustrialization, and where white ethnic aspirations for class mobility precipitated housing and workplace covenants. Black Americans turned to the streets to resist these spatial inequalities of inadequate housing, too few jobs, and poor education. They also resisted police brutality, which had become so common that even the rumor of an altercation between a young black man and the police sparked a collective response, from protests to riots. Urban officials fought back, using every means available, including the police, the National Guard, and the U.S. military. Deaths from these encounters mounted.[59]

While the poor infrastructure of these cities could be traced to the post–World War II shift in federal resources to white suburbs, war spending by Presidents Kennedy and Johnson eviscerated domestic programs, including the new "Great Society" programs created to end or ameliorate poverty. Reports that the Johnson administration spent billions each month on the war and only a fraction on domestic programs escalated the tension, especially in northern grassroots civil rights organizations. Deindustrialization and war spending resulted in rising poverty rates, especially among younger African Americans.[60]

Assistant Secretary of Labor Daniel Patrick Moynihan's 1965 report on the black family attributed African Americans' poverty, specifically urban poverty, to black women heading "broken families" without male workers. Though the study associated these ruptures in families with "a history of oppression," the study also described black households as pathological because women now controlled them. "Such women," Annelise Orleck concludes, were perceived as "too aggressive and independent, profoundly crippling and emasculating black men." The report acquired cultural and policy authority and upended the century-long efforts by black women to challenge racist and sexist stereotypes.[61] Commentators associated poor black families with an unfettered cultural pathology rather than with a variety of personal and household responses to systemic barriers against economic and social mobility that affected black men and women in similar and different ways. Some social scientists traced the high incidence of poverty in many black communities to the dominance of poor, unmarried women on welfare, and not their confinement to inadequate housing, poorly funded schools, and unsecure jobs with inadequate wages. Very quickly, Taylor Branch notes, "a pathology model subliminally reduced civil rights forces from intrepid agents of change to quarantined patients, while reasserting full diagnostic privilege for mainstream opinion makers."[62]

Moynihan determined that, more often than poor white families, black families "rotted" under the welfare system. Welfare "made poverty more endurable," but it did not compel its recipients to "escape from it." Welfare, he concluded, "corrupted its recipients," especially black men; employment provided men with the way out. When Moynihan offered these declarations in early 1964, he did not see military service as an opportunity for poor men. Instead, he insisted, these "products of poverty," these "uneducated sons of uneducated fathers, unemployed sons of unemployed fathers" made undesirable recruits.[63] By late 1964, Moynihan had changed his perspective, and by 1966 he became emphatic that rejection from the military based on test scores was "de facto job discrimination."[64]

Moynihan's transition from critic to supporter of the military as an antidote to poverty began once another committee completed its investigation on the high failure rate of men who volunteered for enlistment. Moynihan did not participate in the President's Task Force on Manpower Conservation, which included Secretary of Defense Robert McNamara, Secretary of Health, Education, and Welfare Anthony Celebrezze, and General Lewis B. Hershey. This committee, which released its report in early 1964, determined that nearly half of the voluntary recruits—49.2 percent—failed either the health or the education exams (how many failed both exams was not revealed). Overall, one-third of young men eligible for the draft, estimated at 12 million, failed. Released just as President Johnson considered separately new antipoverty programs and higher draft needs, the report offered broad connections between young men's rejection from the military and the sharp increase in teenage unemployment. Young men between the ages of fourteen and nineteen had the highest rate of unemployment of any group of young men since World War II. More young men sought work, and more were unable to find work. And young black men had a higher rate of unemployment, nearly 25.5 percent compared with 14 percent for whites. The confluence, then, of high rejection rates for the military and high unemployment led the committee initially to characterize these men as unemployable.[65]

Fearing voters' backlash against higher draft calls and the end of draft deferrals for college students and married men, the Johnson administration proposed accepting thousands of volunteers who did not at first qualify for military service. Pentagon officials considered how unemployable or only marginally employable men could be trained for military combat positions.[66] How could previously rejected men be recalled for military service? By 1966, Moynihan recommended relieving poverty by increasing black men's presence in combat units. He argued that the military needed to provide what civil rights and poverty programs could not. "Very possibly our best hope is seriously to use the armed forces as a socializing experience for the poor until somehow their environment begins turning out equal citizens."[67]

In a speech to the Veterans of Foreign Wars on August 23, 1966, Robert McNamara announced Project 100,000. Poverty, McNamara argued, "endangered national security," and this new program intended to "salvage men who were caged and oppressed" by it.[68] Almost immediately Project 100,000 provided the administration the means to give black men economic "uplift," a perspective that gained momentum as liberals and conservatives denounced the 1966 riots. By late November, McNamara described the program as a way "to salvage the poverty scarred youth of our society at the rate of 100,000 men each year."[69] This new policy, he reassured skeptics, would take care of America's "subterranean poor" who had not had "the opportunity to earn their fair share of this nation's abundance." The armed forces, McNamara insisted, planned to "teach these youths skills, discipline, and self-confidence." Project 100,000 would provide poor men "with the opportunity to serve in their country's defense and they can be given an opportunity to return to civilian life with skills and aptitudes which for them and their families will reverse the downward spiral of decay."[70]

Between 1966 and 1971, Project 100,000 filtered more than 400,000 men, 40 percent of them African American, into army and Marine combat units sent to Vietnam. Most came from the South, and many of the men had not completed high school; half had scores far lower than the military rate generally. Nearly 80 percent read at or below the seventh-grade level, with 30 percent reading at or below the fourth-grade level.[71] With an average age of twenty—higher than the average for the services—half of the men had experienced long bouts of unemployment or underemployment.[72] Many black and white working-class southerners came to the military with deficient educations caused by massive and passive resistance to *Brown*. Between 1956 and 1964, many school districts in Virginia shuttered schools after the general assembly made the operation of public schools a local option. Across the nation, black students remained in largely segregated and inadequate schools.[73]

The military's reclassification of men previously considered "low quality" to meet combat quotas was not unique. Shortly after the Selective Service Act of 1948, the army lowered its minimum physical and mental scores so it could meet induction quotas. During the Korean War, the army continued these policies and trained poorly educated men for combat or combat support units. Whenever possible, the army found ways to remove these men from the military (most often through blanket dishonorable discharges or bad-conduct charges) when it no longer needed as many combat and labor units. Unlike in World War II, the military resisted implementing remedial education until it faced "manpower" shortages in 1964. After McNamara touted Project 100,000 as part of the War on Poverty, the Pentagon conceded it conceived the plan as a way to expand the "manpower pool."[74]

The coupling of Johnson's antipoverty policies with the military's efforts to increase available volunteer combat troops occurred at an ebb in whites' support for civil rights. White liberals seemed both "preoccupied by Vietnam" and "disturbed by Negro riots." Many politicians also feared a white "backlash" from conservative voters, and more moderate whites reportedly "cooled" on civil rights. House Minority Leader Gerald Ford intended to push "revamping and redirecting the poverty war," and he planned to push for federal action against riots. Facing this greater Republican strength in Congress, Johnson declined to put forward dramatic—and expensive—civil rights legislation to address black poverty.[75] He needed bipartisan support for an expensive and expanded war, and he needed support from Republicans who desired a "law and order" response to the riots and a limited draft. Ford and other Republicans found Johnson's diminished push for civil rights legislation a hopeful sign for the coming year.[76]

Despite Project 100,000's disproportionate recruitment of poor black men, the Johnson administration touted it as both an antipoverty program and an antiriot policy, one that removed potential rioters from the streets and then sent them to Vietnam. Hershey had long despised black civil rights activists, and Project 100,000 provided the opportunity to use the draft as "punishment" for men he considered unpatriotic malcontents. He implemented this strategy as a punishment for black civil rights activists in 1956 and again in 1964. By 1965, he considered poor black men rioting in Watts unpatriotic as well.[77] After the student protests at the University of Michigan in 1965, Hershey tried to draft antiwar students. What made Project 100,000 different from Hershey's earlier efforts to coerce poor and working-class men to volunteer while giving ample opportunities for middle-class men to avoid the military was the explicit association of military conscription with civilian social policy. Framed as a deliberate form of social uplift for men the military previously considered unsuitable, Project 100,000 quashed the criticisms lobbed simultaneously by the Left and the Right. Republicans supported the limited draft. While liberals abhorred the draft, particularly its class and racial inequalities, many also tended to see the military as a place where black men, especially less-educated men, found "a greater degree of acceptance."[78] Karl H. Purnell explained to *Nation* readers that the military provided black men from the ghetto "their first taste of integration into a white man's world." The military gave poor men something better than what they found at home, especially if they had a "commanding officer [to] enforce the rules of fair treatment."[79]

"Warriors Everywhere in Combat: 1966"

He has instilled in us a pride in the Army that I'm ashamed to say we didn't have when we first entered. He first taught each of us to be men.
— *"Armed Forces: The Integrated Society,"* Time, December 23, 1966, 22

The incessant claims about African Americans' satisfaction with the integrated military and combat saturated the national media. Observers typically characterized the growing presence of so many black troops in combat as progress in civil rights, while the nation's top general described blacks' higher combat deaths as signs of "Negro valor." Even as the percentage of black combat troops and casualty rates climbed past 23 by 1966, few reports expressed alarm. Instead, one observer described the war as "the first war in history that Americans have fought on a truly integrated basis. The numbers, far from indicating discrimination, actually add to the evidence that the Negro has found in the armed forces the fair and opportunity-full society that is still rare in most sections of civilian life."[80]

For Captain Don Phillips, whose photograph accompanied one of these articles, such pronouncements did not matter as he led his airborne company into Bien Hoa. Robin Mannock, the photographer, who worked for *Time*, requested his name, but Phillips refused to give it. He had known other black soldiers whose names had appeared in magazines and newspapers and later died in combat. He planned to stay alive and wanted one more bit of luck.[81]

The Vietnam War was being touted as "the most integrated war" by the Johnson administration at a moment when blacks' support for the war was steadily declining. The reporters and photographers who reported about the volunteer combat units paid special attention to race. They wanted to know why the men volunteered for combat and why they reenlisted in the army at a rate of 49 percent, nearly four times that of whites. Black readers already understood why, *Defender* reporter Ethel Payne noted. "The [paratroopers], they lined up, they queued up for that duty, because that was another way of proving themselves."[82] National Urban League president Whitney Young agreed. Black men volunteered, he argued, "to show the others and themselves that they were men." On bases in the United States and in units in Vietnam, by late 1966 African Americans comprised 40 to 45 percent of the volunteer combat troops.[83]

Black GIs and Marines patiently explained to the national press that they found the additional pay and the higher promotion rates important incentives. A Mississippian and an enlisted man in the army, Victor Hall added, "There's a dire need for money in most Negro cases," since many men found the military's base pay "slack." Men with children considered the extra combat pay critical, since it increased the lowest-ranked private's pay by more than half. As for the high rates of reenlistment, black men remained in or returned to the military because they found civilian employment elusive, even for veterans. Many men believed what Jerry McDonald rhetorically asked: "Can I go back to New Orleans—or anywhere else—and get a job as an aircraft mechanic? I don't think so."[84]

In the first years of the war, many of the higher-ranking soldiers in combat units had served in the military since the 1950s, and they considered themselves career and professional soldiers. Master Sergeant William B. Tapp enlisted in 1954, just after the Korean War. "A painter wants to paint, a doctor wants to heal, and I'm a professional soldier. A soldier wants to apply all that he's learned. He wants to fight." Tapp's depiction of work in the military as a profession was most pronounced in the airborne units.

"The airborne community in the 1960's was a small and very proud one," Rick St. John recalled. "Even in Vietnam, where the concept of parachuting into battle had been replaced by the helicopter, we considered ourselves to be different and members of an elite fraternity of Paratroopers."[85] Don Phillips, an airborne company commander, said the men in the 173rd considered themselves better than the regular combat units. Called "Sky Soldiers," the 173rd were "crack troops." Everyone knew, Phillips said, "that if you wanted it done right, give the job to a paratrooper." David Parks's unit arrived in early 1967 and immediately entered combat. Frightened and overwhelmed, Parks felt better when he realized the 173rd "had secured the road."[86]

Black men's sense of professionalism also had a racial consciousness shaped by a sense of an unrecognized—and frequently vilified—history of black combat troops. More than an anxious careerism drove William Tapp to volunteer for combat. Aware of the disparagement leveled at black troops during the Korean War, Tapp surmised, "Negro soldiers have a more professional attitude, at least as fighting is concerned, and if you're a professional soldier you probably want to fight—that's why a lot of Negro career men are asking to go to Vietnam." Black men volunteered for point man, Tapp continued, "to prove" themselves. "I get my jollies jumping out of airplanes," one black paratrooper remarked. "People ask lots of times, 'What has the Negro done for America?'" Tapp thought "a lot, but it's unseen. Maybe the Army and sacrifice is a way of making it seen."[87]

This refrain about black men's need or desire to assert a heroic and competent combat professionalism as a corrective to years of being represented as inept cowards in war obscured the men's more ambivalent attitudes about military service and the Vietnam War, especially among the new draftees assigned to combat units. Julius Lester described these recent arrivals as men "who had grown up in the shadow of Hiroshima," but defending the flag was not their first priority. "Indeed, it could be asked if defending the flag were a priority at all."[88] When the draft notices came, many black men complied. "Not that they particularly wanted to or because they were patriotic. The prospect of five years in jail appeared to be a worse alternative than the Army."[89] As more draft calls precipitated more enlistments, black men provided a more troubling explanation for their greater presence in combat units. The threat of the draft was particularly coercive to poor men in the ghetto, and enlistment appeared to offer some control over their fate. The choices for many poor black men ricocheted between the army and the street, between unemployment and combat pay. For two decades, poor black men had served as America's gendarme compelled to fight.[90]

The challenge to this "overintegration" of the battlefield came from the voluble and popular twenty-four-year-old world champion boxer Muhammad Ali when he refused to report for induction in early 1966. When Ali, then known as Cassius Clay, had received his notice from the Louisville draft board two years earlier, he complied and reported for his examination. He failed the mental exam, repeated it, and failed again. When Ali joined the Nation of Islam later that year, his Selective Service status got special attention from the FBI and the Department of Defense.[91] The Selective Service status of other prominent African Americans, especially those involved in civil rights activism, also came under scrutiny. Student Non-Violent Coordinating Committee (SNCC) members John Lewis and Bob Moses, both COs, were questioned and threatened. The Selective Service considered these men "too depraved for peace, but not too depraved for war."[92] Like other men, Ali must have hoped that he would not be drafted, but the particular attention to him and others considered "outspoken" must have given him pause. Over the next two years, Ali was described as lacking "intelligence" and as a "nut" because of his association with Elijah Muhammad and Malcolm X, both of whom opposed the draft and denounced the Vietnam War.

Ali's reclassification occurred as the Defense Department lowered its standards for intelligence in the army draft and Congress put pressure on the Selective Service to reconsider prominent athletes, including Joe Namath and Arthur Ashe.[93] Early in January 1966, the Selective Service announced a "manpower crisis," and its director, General Lewis Hershey, intended to reconsider every deferment.[94] At the top of the age limit and previously considered of low intelligence, the married Ali seemed an unlikely figure for Hershey's plan to defuse the simmering draft politics. On the other hand, Hershey had used the threat of the draft against other visible African American critics of U.S. policy, especially men in the Nation of Islam. Along with 2.5 million other men previously rejected by the Selective Service, Ali learned the draft board "might" find him "acceptable for military service."[95] Still, Ali appeared incredulous when he received news on February 17, 1966, that he was reclassified as 1-A and faced a March draft call. "Why me? I can't understand. How did they do this to me—the heavyweight champion of the world?"[96] With Project 100,000 in place, Ali's reclassification was routine.

The draft board's particular focus on Ali because of his public beliefs rankled him, but his stature and his personal beliefs also gave him the resources to appeal the board's decision. Sometime in 1965 Ali applied for CO status, as did his brother, Rudolph. Many contemporary observers—and some critics since—claimed Ali's refusal and his personal beliefs simply echoed the Nation of Islam's characterization of the Vietnam War as another "white man's war" where black men "were tricked or forced into fighting." After World War II, the organization attracted black men who either had served in the military or consciously avoided the draft. Many of the members, including Elijah Muhammad's son, Wallace Delaney Muhammad, had convictions for violation of Selective Service laws.

When Ali converted, the Nation of Islam generally confined its antiwar statements to its community addresses and publications, such as *Muhammad Speaks*. Before Ali rejected his draft notice, he spent months with Malcolm X, a harsh critic of the war. Sam Saxon, one of Ali's security men and a member of the Miami Mosque, regularly told Ali about "the deep hurt he suffered during the Korean War when he was 'dressed in the uniform of the United States Army and they still called me nigger.'"[97] Ali absorbed these critiques and told the press that Muslims "do not carry on and go to wars to take the lives of other humans unless we ourselves are being attacked. We are peaceful people." Ali said he had "nothing against the Viet Cong, man, I ain't got no quarrel with them Vietcong." Heckled by reporters, Ali elaborated: "All I know is that they are considered as Asiatic black people and I don't have no fight with black people."[98] Many scoffed at Ali's theology and personal principles; others considered them incendiary and "unpatriotic." Boxing opponent Ernie Terrell described Ali "as an irresponsible kid."[99] Terrell and others objected to the entirety of Ali's remarks and the implication that the boxer received particular mistreatment from the army. Many considered his remarks "a kick in the teeth to American youngsters dying in Vietnam."[100] But Ali drew on a history of African Americans' critique of the Cold War military. During the Korean War, black GIs wondered, as Curtis Morrow had asked, "Whatever had these people (Koreans) done to me?"

However shocking some Americans found Ali's statements, many also appeared stunned by Ali's draft notice. Older, married, and a father, Ali did not fit the profile of the Vietnam recruit. In 1966, 33 million men remained registered for the draft. With such large populations of eligible men between the ages of nineteen and twenty-two, and with so many men voluntarily enlisting, why Ali received a draft notice was as much about

Hershey's habit of retribution against outspoken men as his desire to pressure prominent men to enlist as a way to jump-start voluntary enlistment of blacks. Hershey intended other black men to follow Ali into the army and then to Vietnam, just like they supposedly followed Joe Louis into the segregated World War II army.[101] Yet Ali appeared to be one of the "special cases" that required Hershey's intercession. The repeated statements that Ali faced imminent induction seemed manufactured between Hershey's office and the local draft board. In late February, the chair of the Louisville draft board announced that the board did not have legal authority to include Ali in the March draft call. Hershey's interventions apparently changed this policy.[102]

The new attention to Ali's status uncovered the unusual and frequent communication between the all-white local board and Selective Service officials in Washington, D.C. Instead of the local board, the national office commented on "the pending change in status" for Ali.[103] For all of General Lewis Hershey's claims that the local, and not national, offices controlled draft boards, his pressure shaped many of the draft decisions, including the decision to draft Ali. Perhaps Hershey simply intended to shame Ali, a man many considered as arrogant as boxer Jack Johnson, whose physical prowess in the ring and defiance of segregation led to his conviction in the early twentieth century. In thinly veiled language borrowed from the proponents of a black pathology, critics denounced Ali as a "cosseted" man "nested among Black Muslims, all of whom have rejected the mainstream of American life."[104] Within days, promoters, exhibitors, and state boxing officials refused to sponsor the Ali–Terrell match originally scheduled for late March. Outrage from veterans' organizations fueled the rejections.[105]

Across the nation, many African Americans rejected the critiques against Ali, and they pointed to the inequities of the draft. When a riot erupted in Watts in mid-March 1966, observers called it a war of the poor against the indifference of the federal government to implement antipoverty programs. Floyd McKissick, new national director of CORE, remarked that other cities faced similar battles because of economic inequalities. Equally important, he added, blacks in Watts and elsewhere registered their solidarity with Ali's dissent against his reclassification to 1-A status. Along with resistance to the brutality of civilian police, African Americans resented the military police who trolled their neighborhoods and forced them to report for induction.[106]

Some African Americans joined in the critique of Ali. *Chicago Defender* columnist Harry Golden described Ali's remarks as illogical and unpatriotic.[107] Cassius Clay Sr. believed the Nation of Islam had manipulated his son, and he hoped the army "might straighten [him] out." He and Ali's mother believed that the draft was the law of the land and their son had the obligation to obey.[108] Largely respectful of Ali, the black press began to lob regular criticisms, describing his earlier remarks as "enraged." The *Defender* continued to call him Cassius Clay and snidely referred to him as someone who "talked too much."[109] After Ali refused to take the oath of induction in May 1967, older black Americans openly chastised him. Jackie Robinson, a World War II veteran, insisted he "admired" Ali as a "man who speaks his mind," but he "wondered how he can expect to make millions of dollars in this country and then refuse to fight for it."[110] Ironically, Robinson had left the army after he was acquitted of protesting its segregation policies on buses.

Now twenty-five, Ali launched his appeals. He first sought CO status and retained Hayden Covington, an attorney who handled similar cases for Jehovah's Witnesses during World War II. Ali added a deferment based on his status as a minister in the Nation of Islam. In early 1967, the Selective Service denied his appeals and upheld his 1-A status. Within months, Ali's tactics shifted and his lawyers filed a federal suit arguing that the Louisville draft board had no black members and was "illegally constituted." And of the 641 draft board members in the state of Kentucky, only 2 African Americans served. Erastus X. Williams, also from Louisville, joined Ali as a co-petitioner. For the first time, the *Defender* acknowledged Ali's changed name.[111]

As the Louisville draft board complained that Ali's new efforts "delayed" his induction, the Johnson administration responded to the charges that the largely segregated draft boards and the inequities of the draft unfavorably targeted poor black men. Johnson issued Executive Order 11289, which established the National Advisory Committee on Selective Service to review the Selective Service policies before the system's renewal later in the year. One of the claims the committee reviewed was a charge by Hayden Covington, Ali's lawyer, that the minuscule presence of blacks on Kentucky's draft boards "violated the original concept of neighborhood boards." Ali's board was in a neighborhood where African Americans were in the majority. "If the champ's board were a neighborhood board, you can bet there would be a lot of black men on it," Covington insisted.[112] After the Supreme Court declined to hear Ali's appeals, he refused to take the oath of induction. In early May 1967, a federal grand jury indicted him. As state boxing committees stripped Ali of his titles, state draft boards came under increasing scrutiny. Civil rights activists argued that states like Mississippi had no blacks on their boards *and* civil rights workers were drafted at disproportionate rates. Charles Evers noted that "until Negroes are appointed to these boards, the draft will continue to be used in Mississippi as a weapon to punish civil rights leaders and undermine the civil rights movement."[113] As Ali's case ricocheted between the Louisville draft board, the Justice Department, federal appeals courts, and the Supreme Court, America learned about the high enlistment rates of black men and their equally high casualty rates.

By the time Ali said "no" in May 1967, he joined a growing number of other young black men who had made similar decisions since the war's escalation. As young men resisted the draft, editors of black newspapers remonstrated them to do their civil rights duty and register or heed the draft notice. To be disloyal, the *Chicago Defender* argued, cast a "stain [on] this record of unstinted loyalty." Draft dodging gave "ammunition to those who are still fighting to keep the Negro race pinned down to second-class citizenship." The future of the civil rights movement rested on blacks' willingness to accept the draft. "We cannot afford to be draft dodgers and deserters. It places us in the indefensible contradiction of opposing expansion of American democracy at the very time we are engaged in a mighty struggle for extension of democratic rights at home." Instead, the editorial suggested, black men needed to sacrifice for civil rights and the "present social order of freedom and equality."[114]

As Ali questioned the draft board policies, increasing numbers of African Americans questioned the racial and class inequalities of the Selective Service System. Many men, for example, discovered that a draft card made them undesirable workers. Registered for the draft and declared fit for service, teenager James Daly discovered how "many prospective employers just weren't about to hire someone with a 1-A classification." Daly found low-waged clerical work in a New York City department store. Another teenager, Terry Whitmore, quickly learned that with a 1-A status he did not find work either.[115] Blacks' increasing unrest caught the attention of David Parks, photographer Gordon Parks's son. Home from basic training in mid-July 1966, he noticed that "people seem to have more gripes against the war now than they did when I left the first time. More guys are burning their draft cards and refusing to step forward. Lots of my buddies are getting married."[116]

In the first years of the war, Whitmore and his friends ignored the draft. Maybe the street bravado of young men who bragged about women and sports overshadowed the reports about blacks' particularly high combat death toll. For Whitmore and his friends, the "military after high school was still a big joke to us." Instead, the men "jived about it. People are dying in Vietnam? Not our problem." The summer after his graduation, he served as a pallbearer for a friend who died in Vietnam. He thought then about the war, but only for a moment. Maybe the precariousness of young black men's lives inured them to the daily news about the war. In the newspapers, fifteen guys "died in the Nam today. And the next day, fifteen guys were killed in car accidents. So what's the difference?"[117]

Whitmore and his friends knew about their brothers' and older friends' experiences with failing either the mental or the health exam. Many of these young men did not think "Sam" wanted them for the military. Whitmore considered himself "just another poor-ass black on the block. Sam doesn't even know I'm alive." Some of Whitmore's friends hoped to escape receiving a draft notice. The men changed their 1-A status to 4-F status on their draft cards. The draft notices arrived anyway.[118] As blacks' draft rates soared in late 1966, many men believed they had little chance to escape the "call-up." When Whitmore's induction notice arrived and he was ordered to report for a physical, he thought "maybe just maybe Sam will see that I have bad lungs and send me home." After he passed the physical exam, Whitmore calculated that if he got drafted, he would be drafted into the army and certain combat. After a Marine recruiter came to his home and promised the teenager only two years of service, he chose the Marines and hoped for a better assignment.[119]

Isaac Witter had more optimism about evading induction than Whitmore did. Witter registered for the draft and then calculated his chances. Four of his older brothers had failed the entrance exam, and he expected to do the same. Still, Witter relied on the general practice other black men used to distance themselves from the draft: He left South Carolina for New York and did not inform the draft board. Unlike the other black women in her neighborhood, his mother forwarded her son's draft notice, and Witter felt bound to report. Because so many of his friends had already enlisted or had been drafted, he returned home and "join[ed] his buddies."[120]

Anxious about the draft, James Daly went to the Selective Service office in Brooklyn and applied for CO status. A lifelong Jehovah's Witness, Daly did not believe in killing anyone under any circumstances. He planned to be a minister, but the Selective Service agent told him only full-time ministers qualified for CO status. The man in the office advised him to enlist, and then he could apply. An army recruiter confirmed what Daly heard in the Selective Service office and encouraged him to enlist in the Regular Army for two years. "A big draft was coming up in January 1967," the recruiter warned. Daly enlisted. Neither the Selective Service agent nor the recruiter informed Daly that in order to apply for CO status and receive a noncombat job, he had to enlist for an additional year. Over the next months Daly repeatedly applied for CO status, and at each step he was denied. He did not learn of the decisions until after it was too late for him to appeal or reapply. After his unit received orders for Vietnam, Daly again sought advice. He appealed to a Catholic priest in the military who encouraged him to go AWOL. For Daly and other poor black men like him in outsider religions, CO status was not available. Ali, too, found out that the Selective Service did not consider the Nation of Islam a valid religion. Ministry in the Jehovah's Witnesses was voluntary, and Daly needed to work to provide for his family. Going AWOL or going to prison were not options for the Jehovah's Witnesses because breaking the law also violated their beliefs.[121]

As the national press focused on the racial and economic inequalities of the draft after Ali refused induction, and as many more African Americans questioned not only the draft but the war, too, the Johnson administration moved to reclaim blacks' support. White House advisor Louis Martin and John Sengstacke, editor of the *Chicago Defender*, attempted to establish the presence of blacks in the war as a civil rights gain and thought the experienced correspondent Ethel Payne would provide a "unique" perspective as a woman who had also reported about the Korean War and the civil rights movement. Payne agreed. After her initial briefing with other correspondents at the Pentagon, she thought that the military "was very anxious" for her and other correspondents from the black press "to get some favorable stories." In turn, she "liked the idea of finding out what was happening to the black troops in Vietnam." One of two black women correspondents reporting about the war—the other was Philippa Schuyler—and the only black woman on the front line, Payne joined other black correspondents, including Jesse W. Lewis, who wrote for the *Washington Post*, and Mike Davis, who reported for the *Baltimore Afro-American*. All three left for Vietnam in late December 1966 intent on telling a war story about black pride and professionalism on the battlefield.[122]

Once "in country" as an official war correspondent, Payne became bound to a military that obstructed her efforts to write full reports. First, the military required that she and the other correspondents rely on the

U.S. Mission Press for information about military operations. Every day she went with hundreds of other reporters to the headquarters to hear what the press called the "Five O'clock Follies." Barry Zorthian, head of the Joint U.S. Public Affairs Office, "fed the usual, carefully orchestrated and sanitized" news. Payne recoiled at "the casual way" the press secretary announced "the body counts, so many dead. It was numbers; it was just numbers." Then she received particular clearance to visit the Da Nang headquarters of the Marine operations and board the carrier *Enterprise*. Accompanied by heavily armed military escorts in jeeps and a military photographer, Payne reported from sites carefully selected by the U.S. military. Despite the military's near-control of her every move, the indefatigable Payne interviewed hundreds of black soldiers and Marines.[123]

Payne attempted to balance popular skepticism about the war, pressure from her editors to detail blacks' important gains in the military, and the raw anger she saw and heard from soldiers. She continued reporters' habits in World War II and Korea where articles in the black weeklies relayed greetings and family affiliations. At the same time, Payne attempted to describe life in Vietnam from the perspective of black Marines, and GIs increasingly resistant to the U.S. "mission." Black reporters in Korea had rarely mentioned the work of killing on the battlefield, but Payne made it integral to her stories. The country "bristles with arms," she reported, and she saw "no peace on earth here, nothing but the deadly business of kill, kill, kill."[124]

Payne chafed at the efforts to filter the news from the front lines, but her articles nonetheless hewed to U.S. policy. The war was, she determined days into her trip, a U.S. and South Vietnamese struggle against communists' efforts "to control the hearts and minds and lives of all the people of Asia."[125] Omitting any discussion of the oppressive control of South Vietnamese leaders Ngo Dinh Diem and Nguyen Cao Ky that appeared in *Freedomways* and other journals that questioned U.S. policy, Payne argued that North Vietnam instigated a "campaign of 'national liberation' and embarked on an aggressive program of wholesale violations of the Geneva agreements." The Viet Cong terrorized villages, she wrote, and they used "tactics and methods of gang mobs."[126] The South Vietnamese peasants were "popular forces of local people who are paramilitary in purpose, something like our militia." She observed that "it is hard sometimes to tell where their loyalties lie, with the government or with the Viet Cong."[127]

Along with articles that invoked the military's efforts to change the "hearts and minds" of peasant communists, Payne included articles about humanitarian efforts that obscured the aggressive combat tactics of black troops. Nineteen-year-old Marine Lance Corporal Lorenzo Forest was assigned to the Combined Action Platoon (CAP) in Tuy Lodn, a village of 2,000 five miles south of Da Nang. Forest and nine other Marines reported they planned to help villagers build sewers and purify water. Forest, Payne concluded, was a young ambassador in khaki who dispensed medicine "and soap in quantities." Rather than using bullets, Forest fought the war through personal contact and humanitarian aid. He and the other Marines, she concluded, intended to "rehabilitate" the village through their "mercy mission."[128]

Payne either did not know or chose not to report that the Marines and the local Viet Cong, along with other guerilla groups, engaged in daily skirmishes in Tuy Lodn. Heavily armed, the Marines set up the CAP in these villages because they considered the local militias ineffective against the Viet Cong. The Marines arrived from nearby Da Nang and occupied the village to "clear" the area of Viet Cong. After these battles, the Marines returned to Da Nang and left the villagers to fend for themselves. The villagers, the majority of whom were children, feared angering the Viet Cong and the Americans. Those who appeared to support the Americans faced immediate danger. Many of the Vietnamese despised the Americans, their use of tear gas in the marketplaces, and their roundups of young men. The South Vietnamese army terrorized the population and frequently raped the women.[129]

Alongside the increasingly disturbing policies and politics of the war, Payne and the other African American correspondents emphasized blacks' military professionalism and skill. "The colored soldier understands why he is here," Major Beauregard Brown told *Afro-American* reporter Mike Davis. A career army officer, Brown insisted Vietnam gave black men unlimited opportunities "for individual achievement and accomplishment." He claimed it bothered the men that African Americans did not value the struggle in Vietnam.[130] African American GIs, Davis discovered, did not share a similar enthusiasm for the war or the individual mobility it might promise. "I've had enough," said one man from Special Forces. After losing more than twenty-eight men in combat—"all of them young boys"—the soldier did not think the war worth the men's deaths. "Why the hell are they dying?"[131] While black officers had a greater tendency to endorse the war against communism generally, support for or critiques of the Vietnam War did not break along rank. Black officers in the air force readily discussed with Ethel Payne their unease about "black [people] fighting against people of color," but she chose not to report it. In their descriptions of their work—the flying and bombing—she "got the feeling that it was not pleasant for them to go out on bombing missions or strafing missions, to bomb people that, as they said, they were kind of kindred to." They also "said 'We are military people and we have a job to do and that's what we have to do.'" Familiar with the criticisms of and stereotypes about black personnel in World War II and Korea, the men stressed they did "a better than average job."[132] Black women in the military, too, expressed similar perspectives. In military intelligence, Lucki Allen considered the war as "working every day and that's all it was. It's just a job. It wasn't a matter of we're at war, it was a matter of do your job."[133]

These reports about blacks' expertise in war did little to alter readers' plummeting support for the war. As riots erupted in 1967, the popular media's earlier assessment of black support for the war as "solid" changed. "Negro supporters of the war are tortured by wry twists of racial logic," *Newsweek* observed. "Should the black man help the white kill the yellow?"[134] Critic Clyde Taylor explained the earlier support as the distortions common in black life. "The appeal of the military to Black youth has to be recognized," he conceded. "The Army is obviously an alternative to the disorientations of the Black community. Juvenile courts often make the alternative clear: the Army or jail, a kind of modern Shanghai recruitment. The choice may also be the Army or unemployment rolls, boredom, futurelessness, collisions with the police, or an uncongenial, woman-dominated household." When black parents used "unreflecting words, 'I thought, at least the Army will make a *man* out of him,'" they lent support to this "warped logic."[135]

As rioters were depicted as hostile young black men engaged in urban warfare and the war was referred to as a "quagmire," the media's portrayals of poor black soldiers increasingly described them as "naturally" fitted for the chaos of "jungle warfare." This new representation of the black soldier as ideally suited to guerilla warfare combined images from previous wars, which variously depicted black men as cheerful soldiers or black savages, and was coincident with Americans' dissatisfaction with the war. A 1967 *Time* article followed the experiences of twenty-four-year old Alabamian Staff Sergeant Clyde Brown, a member of a long-range reconnaissance patrol in the 173rd Airborne. Brown was at once a "cool" professional and a natural soldier "itching to destroy" the enemy. Wearing "tiger suits" and camouflage paint, Brown easily blended into the "jungle heartland." This "naturalistic" performance, the reporter concluded, "reaffirms the success—and diversity—of the American experiment. Often inchoate and inconsistent, instinctively self-serving yet naturally altruistic, the Negro fighting man is both savage in combat and gentle in his regard for the Vietnamese." This description departed from earlier portrayals of frightened black soldiers who ran from battle during the Korean War. This new stereotype presented an innate "Negro warrior" who chose war to escape the ghetto.[136]

The growing perception that black men went into combat out of choice instigated a broad public response. The Left and liberals alike no longer viewed these men as victims and instead described them as "Black Hessians," a "ghetto dweller" making financial calculations for the best pay. This soldier chose "hazardous duty pay on top of combat pay on top of regular pay, which he considers not bad to begin with." He went to war "largely without the preconceived notions of world politics that the more fortunate pick up in school or the press, the Black Hessian is ready to accept the army version—so long as the 'benefits is good.'" Such a man, some on the Left argued, was not a victim of a "diabolical racist plot, as some super-militants of the civil rights movement suggest." Rather, he came from a "socially isolated group," a "ghetto man."[137]

Black GIs in Vietnam offered their own responses to these popular claims of their satisfaction with the military and combat. The most immediate and dramatic response to the war appeared in black reenlistment rates, which plunged from 66.5 percent in 1967 to 31.7 percent a year later. Inside the military, African Americans engaged in a variety of daily resistances that disrupted military discipline. As early as spring 1967, rumors circulated in the press that black soldiers refused to fight, "telling officers 'Let your mother do it.'" Others, correspondent William Worthy claimed, were "actually shooting cracker-type officers in the back."[138] Reports about fragging—enlisted men shooting officers—persisted throughout the war. Soldiers argued that the "DMZ and the Mekong Delta are poor places to go hunting for freedom when the soul brothers are stalking it in the streets of urban America." Soldiers' rates of going AWOL skyrocketed. Reportedly by 1970, one soldier went AWOL every three minutes. For many soldiers, "Saigon and Harlem" were "two fronts of one same war."[139]

But the vivid association between the riots and other unrest in the United States with the racial politics of Vietnam was complicated by black men's experiences in combat and their shared and differing understandings of who were their enemies. David Parks flunked out of college and immediately faced the consequences when he received a draft notice. He surveyed his circumstances when he reported to "Uncle Samuel" at the Mt. Vernon draft board near his home in White Plains, New York. Should he "refuse to take the oath"? Parks did not have the "guts" to say no. He "felt trapped." Assigned to Fort Riley, Kansas, Parks quickly discerned that the orderliness and sparse integration of the camp hid a far more complicated confrontation with what he had to do—learn to kill "the other" in Vietnam. Drill instructors shouted daily that he and the other recruits would "learn to kill or the VC would blow your ass to hell." Bullying, misogynistic harassment, and racial epithets accompanied this repeated warning that he had to kill to stay alive.[140]

Terry Whitmore, too, learned from drill instructors who goaded the men with racial taunts and physical brutality. His Parris Island black drill instructor ridiculed him through an aggressive patter that merged military claims of a nonracial combat brotherhood, misogyny, and the compunction to "kill" for one another. "This is brother to brother! It ain't going to be no big happy family." The only color in the Marines, he screamed, was green. "Your mother is a whore. I fucked her." Whitmore knew that "if any fool said that back on the block, he'd be looking at a switchblade before he could finish." If a recruit fought back, the instructor "hoped for an excuse to kick that boot's ass bloody. Street stuff just wouldn't work in boot camp." Fierce competition accompanied the verbal assaults and physical confrontations. In training, platoons were turned against platoons. And racial abuse of the "Asian other" was part of this acculturation. White, Mexican American, Native American, and Puerto Rican Marines received the same training. Drill instructors showed "souvenir" photographs of "Charlies with their guts hanging out. Their legs, arms, heads blown off."[141]

Once in Vietnam, Parks learned quickly that the other men in his squad had no moral squeamishness about killing Vietnamese. "Everyone has killing on their mind," he wrote his father, photographer Gordon Parks. Unable to escape from combat or put down his M-16, Parks determined that all he wanted to do was "get it over with." American soldiers faced friendly fire, inept commanders, and a depleted sense of purpose. Men stepped on mines laid by U.S. troops, while Parks and others were nearly killed by mortar rounds fired by another squad. Confronted with the mounting malaise and danger he and others faced by the "goofs" of one squad or another, Parks noted, "There is death all around us. I hate being in this place, but there is a job to be done. It's our job, so they tell us, but I don't know the whole story—nobody seems to be explaining it to us, at least so it makes sense." He wondered with all the death precipitated by the United

States "if we are helping or hurting these poor people." Increasingly, he became depressed as friends died and he was ordered into frequent search-and-destroy missions. Eventually he became acclimated to combat, and he no longer feared using his weapons.[142]

The acclimation to the chaos of war appeared to increase the unit's use of indiscriminate violence. Soldiers in Parks's company began mutilating bodies they claimed were the enemy; one of the commanding NCOs wore "a pair of dried-out VC ears around his neck on a string." Looting and burning became regular features of patrol. One company in Parks's unit placed five corpses on their tracks (a military armored vehicle that used tracks instead of wheels) and rode through villages. Parks thought the display "a bad scene, those bloody corpses turning gray from the heat and paddy mud."[143] Soldiers' growing indifference to the indiscriminate violence of war escalated into a rising racial fury toward Vietnamese civilians. "Someone throws a piece of bread on the road. The kids go for it like a pack of wolves. Often one of them gets hit by a track, or several get hurt in the scramble. You never see a soul do anything like that."[144]

Parks, too, succumbed to the intensity of the violence. When his unit came under fire, a friend died. The commander ordered Parks to "dismount and pursue." He immediately complied. "As we hit the water, we flushed out about fifteen Charlies hiding in the reeds. We shot them up like fish in a barrel—and I got my third kill." He recounted this event in a letter home, and his father noted his son's changed tone: "He had written about taking three lives—in a manner that was cold and swaggering. And this from a son who had once told me he could never be able to kill. But now he had done it, and with a feeling of triumph."[145]

Some black GIs' and Marines' participation in the brutality against the Vietnamese that Parks witnessed appeared months later in the charges against soldiers who participated in the My Lai Massacre. African Americans and Latinos made up half the company. Few came into the military through Project 100,000, and the majority of Charlie Company had finished high school. At the outset, the company appeared to be made up of disciplined and well-trained soldiers who volunteered for combat. Trained in similar ways, the men nonetheless viewed the "enemy" in very different ways. Varnado Simpson, a rifleman, thought "all [the Vietnamese] looked the same." He and Harry Stanley observed the rising callousness among the company months before they entered My Lai. Some of the soldiers used the "search and destroy" missions to "prey" on the women. Harry Stanley heard the men brag about "the rape and gang bangs." No one in the company ever faced punishment, and it "continued unchecked." In this atmosphere of brutality, many of the younger black and Latino soldiers admired Stanley because he repeatedly refused to participate. Others capitulated. Simpson participated in the later massacre of civilians in the village, "shooting, cutting their throats, scalping them, or cutting off their hands and cutting out their tongues." He killed twenty-five or more. Horrified at the slaughter, Harry Stanley and Herbert Carter refused Lieutenant William Calley's orders, even though they faced the possibility of courts-martial.[146]

Terry Whitmore described the complicated racial camaraderie in combat as a sharp distinction between jiving and killing. "In the Nam we blacks pretty much kept to ourselves, no matter how close we were to our squads. The real bullshitting was always done with other blacks. Jiving about our blocks. Sometimes gambling a little." But the erratic demands of combat created an environment for intense intraracial and cross-racial solidarities and conflicts. "In combat the squad was the more important group. No matter what kinds of guys and colors were in the squad, it had to run smoothly if we're to stay alive."[147] Whitmore's squad was "a groovy squad, really tight when it came to combat. Rarely any bullshit jive then. Just fighting."[148] On the front line, men squelched hard feelings about race, but it also stoked racial conflict. Killing communists was all about killing Viet Cong, and men tended to describe them in racially derogatory ways. In this confluence of two charged moments—combat and racial denigration—Whitmore's platoon always had their .45s half-cocked "for Charlie." One day, Whitmore nearly pulled it on a white soldier who taunted him with a racial epithet. For many men, the episodic violence over integration and the hundreds of urban uprisings in the United States created a distant echo, but in the context of horrific battle, the men chose the needs of the squad over individual racial identities. In a particularly devastating ambush, Whitmore saved the man he had nearly shot weeks earlier; moments later, an unknown white Marine saved his life, jived with him, and kept him out of shock.[149]

The racial conflict targeted at the Vietnamese had its counterpart in the violence that flared with regularity in the diverse population of rear units. Intraservice rivalries erupted everywhere. The intricate web of military culture that encouraged rivalry and camaraderie through misogyny and shared racial perceptions of the enemy also encouraged racial conflict within the military. In rear units, with their fluid population, men's interracial combat camaraderie and service affiliations quickly eroded. Racial remarks tolerated in combat instigated quarrels, brawls, and riots in the rear. While combat demanded physical proximity in spite of racial animosity, GIs and Marines in the rear asserted their identities in highly segregated and racialized ways. Black men created and lived in a "different world" shaped by solidarities of race and geography. "After work 'Chuck' goes his way and I go mine," said Michael D. Kelley. Raised in Detroit, Kelley described the bars and brothels in Saigon that catered to American GIs as "just like Mississippi. It's segregated." Saigon was not unique. Black sailors reported similar patterns in the Philippines, where blacks went to a section in Subic Bay called "the Jungle." Everywhere in these bars and back alleys where soldiers and sailors congregated, racial epithets and antiblack graffiti in latrines were common.[150]

As the rapid troop escalation and Project 100,000 brought many more black soldiers, sailors, and Marines into contact, these men responded to the racist outbursts and the uncertainty of combat with a new racial pride informed by Black Power. They greeted new and old friends with the dap, an intricate and lengthy handshake. New arrivals learned these elaborate handshakes, which involved slapping of hands, finger-snapping, and "pounding" of the upper body of another man, as they were welcomed into a shifting community of black men who managed to survive another day in Vietnam. As the men refused to use the deferential and hierarchical military salute and chose to dap instead, they challenged the hierarchies that rank and service demanded. Considered "hip," the dap also displayed the menace of a collective black male power enhanced by combat. Dozens of men at any one time congregated in combat fatigues, and they meant to convey a threat as they held up mess lines and crowded the entrances and aisles of PXs. Black GIs, sailors, and Marines understood that when they dapped, whites balked at the disruption and watched with a mixture of "consternation, curiosity, and resentment." Many commanders considered the dap and the abandonment of military deference as a display of mass insubordination; others saw it as a sign of racial militancy; others considered it nonsensical and disruptive. When commanders attempted to restrict or ban the dap, blacks responded through resisting the order or rioted.[151] Not all the soldiers eschewed the salute. In the 82nd Airborne, troops continued to shout "All the way, sir!" and men in the 173rd shouted "airborne," which conveyed "the fierce pride" of paratroopers, regardless of race.[152]

Steve Dant described how his unit of mostly white infantry arrived for a break in the rear and became immediately entangled in a brawl with black soldiers. Dant's commander loaded his men up and headed them back to combat. Out of combat, he recalled, the "men were tightly wound" and the tension took racial forms of expression. He also felt it was because of "what was going on then in the States." Black Marines, GIs, and sailors greeted one another with upraised fists. Dant and other whites considered the salute, like the dap, as a threat.[153] Others, whites and some blacks, rightly understood the salute "as an insolent challenge to authority."[154] Black soldiers grew Afros, wore dashikis, and replaced military headgear with black berets. Since the Airborne and Special Forces wore berets as designations of skill, blacks who wore black berets acquired a more ominous presence as a segregated paramilitary within the military. The symbols of Black Power signaled a widespread fear that the Black Panther Party had organized secret cells in the military.

Blacks' organization within the military also responded to white GIs, Marines, and sailors who organized and repeatedly intimidated blacks. Southern white soldiers wore Confederate flags or hoisted them on their trucks and jeeps. At bases in the United States, especially in the South, some white soldiers taunted black soldiers by announcing plans to burn crosses.[155] While many commanders correlated the rise in black militancy with tensions over integration in the United States, they also perceived racial conflicts in Vietnam as disruptive to combat cohesion. Black Power, they argued, created "dangerous tensions." They blamed the frequent riots, clubbings, shootings, and stabbings on black and white soldiers "who brought their prejudices and tendencies toward violence with them when they were drafted."[156] Commanders insisted Black Power differed little from White Power displayed through racist symbols. Others insisted it was a reaction to white soldiers who flew Confederate flags, sprayed racial epitaphs on buildings and latrines, and burned crosses; they played "hillbilly" music meant to provoke black troops.[157]

Experienced in reporting the shifts within the civil rights leadership and the rank and file, Ethel Payne observed the changes among black troops. By late 1966, she noted, a "new breed of black soldier [had] arrived. Younger, with an average age of 18–19 years old, more aggressive, more militant, more confident," these soldiers replaced an older generation "resigned to the system" and with "a more subdued view." In contrast, these "young, Negro blades" arrived from the "concrete jungles of the big cities and the civil rights battlegrounds of the South." Some had spent time in jail because of their participation in civil rights struggles. Many, she concluded, had "a flair for adventure."[158] These men did not see themselves as professional, career soldiers and instead considered themselves draftees and "short timers"; they did not see the military as an opportunity.

This vocal population arrived from communities occupied by National Guard and military units, and they increasingly viewed themselves as colonized people. Many came from communities, especially schools, where integration created charged spaces. In this milieu, chants, attacks, and physical resistance were all part of the "informal ways in the psychological process of resistance." This behavior, Jeffrey Ogbar concludes, "represented a clear rejection of the general ethos of peace from the civil rights movement." While these shifts in tone, attitude, and tactics of young blacks alarmed those committed to nonviolence, this resistance "affirmed [the young people] in ways that the [nonviolent civil rights] movement did not."[159] Many had lived in cities where the police targeted young black men for particular surveillance and harassment. Then they trained in and served in a military that consistently used its forms of power against them and against the Vietnamese.

Commanders and other observers blamed "racial tensions" in the United States on the blacks' growing militancy in Vietnam, but the politicization and radicalism of blacks deepened in Vietnam because of the menacing and brutal context of combat. Ordered to kill, bomb, and assault Vietnamese, black GIs and Marines participated in or witnessed the military power of the United States unleashed on civilian populations. As some white troops had commanders' consent to enter combat with Confederate flags, black troops watched how the symbols and practices of white supremacy framed and fueled battles. African Americans disagreed with the conflation of their protests against the war and the military culture as simply displays of radical racial symbols imported from America. Instead, they used Black Power as a form of self-defense within a racialized military and to understand the U.S. violence and the North Vietnamese struggles. From the letters they sent to newspapers and black journals, to correspondent Wallace Terry's interviews later released on a spoken-word album, blacks in Vietnam used Black Power's critical analysis of race, power, and violence to frame their experiences with the work of killing in Vietnam.[160]

Native American soldiers also rejected the white military commanders' repeated comparison of killing Vietnamese to killing Indians. These soldiers found the units that called themselves the cavalry—and the First Cavalry Division was an airmobile regiment—to be particularly problematic. These references to nineteenth-century massacres of Native Americans and the rhetoric of military officials, which typically characterized

U.S. troops as American cowboys capturing Viet Cong savages, pushed many Native American troops to identify with the Vietnamese. In the United States, American Indian activists considered the indigenous freedom struggles waged by the Viet Cong to be important models for their own struggles against colonialism.[161]

Increasingly, black troops meant to stop the war through their resistances against the military. As early as 1966, on military bases in the United States and Europe black GIs and Marines refused orders to Vietnam. Black GI newspapers, some organized and staffed by drafted SNCC workers and Black Panthers, revealed this growing consciousness, rebelliousness, and militancy. *Black Unity* addressed black men and women in the various services. It included articles about the Black Panther Party and other radical political activities in the United States and elsewhere. While these newspapers expressed a radical racial consciousness, they also evinced a class sensibility. The articles and comments in these and other underground papers helped soldiers "interpret their place within the military—and by association—their living conditions exclusively as a consequence of class." Men and women for whom the military was a career especially received a sustained critique in both the white and black GI newspapers. These "lifers" were "Uncle Toms" in *Black Unity*, *Rap*, and other black newspapers; they participated in the oppression of all black people. The editor of *Black Unity* urged GIs to "abandon the military en masse" and "help unite the people of your own communities."[162]

As some soldiers critiqued the military, others came to comprehend the war as part of the larger genocide against nonwhite people. Terry Whitmore's unit was ordered to "burn. Kill the adults. Shoot the livestock." After he shot and killed an old woman and a child in a "friendly village," Whitmore "got sick. Sick to my stomach." Unable to comprehend these orders as necessary yet unwilling to disobey the commands, he and the other black Marines strongly reacted to the "green-assed lieutenants who ordered them around." Whitmore considered his new lieutenant loud, an officer who "let everybody in the whole jungle know." When the officer ordered the platoon into an open space and the men were ambushed, Whitmore determined the war—and its use of inexperienced officers—to be a travesty.[163]

Increasingly, young men's disruptions of the war on the front lines extended to the rear, on ships, and on bases. By 1968, riots, protests, and disorder erupted with regularity and quickly acquired an organized character. The most sustained struggles appeared in the stockades in Long

Binh and on the ships in the Mediterranean and the South China Sea. Between 1969 and 1972, thousands of clashes occurred on ships and in prisons. Investigators insisted that drugs and alcohol inflamed many of these battles, but Black Power ideology and the horrible and de facto segregated conditions created the environment for their eruptions. In the crowded Long Binh stockade—which held nearly double its capacity—black prisoners comprised nearly half of the 719 residents. Understaffed, many of the inexperienced MPs brutalized the prisoners to maintain order. They waterboarded and beat prisoners; strip searches were intended to reduce the influx of drugs brought in by local Vietnamese and MPs. These tactics, along with the general conditions, sparked a riot in late August 1968. Feeling especially targeted, black prisoners organized and stockpiled lumber and pipes. They then attacked the prison's commander and other white inmates. The riot became a month-long siege.[164] Less explosive riots led by black prisoners erupted at military bases in Vietnam, including one in Da Nang in October 1968. Frequent and protracted race riots flashed through installations in Asia, Europe, and the United States. At Camp Lejeune, black and white Marines assaulted one another for a variety of reasons, but most frequently because of racial antagonism. Only after a white Marine was killed did authorities step in and stop the attacks. Frequently, black guards and officers sympathized with the men. Others refused to intervene and left the men to their struggles.[165] In 1970, more than 1,000 racial incidents took place in the Marine Corps, including in many of the units in Vietnam.

Many men chose to leave combat by going AWOL. Terry Whitmore honed his criticism of the war in the daily discipline and racism of his unit, but it was the terrible work of killing Vietnamese women and children that informed his decision to go AWOL. "Sam" had ordered him to help "in his dirty work" and ordered him to "haul" his "black ass back to that jungle. The man doesn't dig Charlie, so *you* shoot some gooks for him and if you get shot doing it, sorry 'bout that shit—maybe we'll give you another medal for it. You're one hell of a lucky nigger to have a second chance to do all this for your country!"[166] For Whitmore and other black men in combat, the issue became whether or not they "had the brains and the balls to tell Sam to take his goddamn war and shove it." With the help of sympathetic Japanese and blacks in Japan, Whitmore went AWOL and entered an international underground that helped him go to Sweden.[167]

As black men shaped their radical critical consciousness about their roles in the war, they also reconsidered blacks' long struggle "for the right to fight" and the military as steady employment. Faced with few opportunities for work elsewhere, many black men reluctantly enlisted because the military was a job; they volunteered for combat because of the extra pay. While they increasingly viewed the war "as not right," African Americans encountered a draft that favored wealthy, mostly white young men. Blacks' high draft and combat rates gruesomely revealed how the military benefited from their economic marginalization. At the same time, the military had done little to advance black America's social and economic stability. Informed by the horrors of combat and the camaraderie of a black critical consciousness, many black soldiers, sailors, and Marines considered themselves to be oppressed people pressed into service for colonial powers. Their experiences of war, and their resistances to the violence in the military, accelerated and fueled African Americans' critiques of the war into a powerful social and racial justice movement at home.

6

Sing No More of War

Black Freedom Struggles and Antiwar Activism, 1960–1973

When antiwar activists pressed him to denounce the Vietnam War in 1965, Langston Hughes refused. After deflecting accusations of procommunism in the previous decade, he feared any public statement against the war might disrupt his recent civil rights activities. His suspicions were not unfounded. Later that year, anticommunist protesters heckled him at a Kansas City lecture. At an appearance in Oakland, conservatives branded his newly published *Pictorial History of the Negro* as Communist propaganda and demanded that the local library remove its copies. Again, Hughes distanced himself from the charges, insisting, "I have never been a Communist, am not now a Communist, and don't intend to be a Communist in my natural life." The series of incidents reinforced Hughes's public silence about Vietnam, but he did not participate when friends at a dinner party criticized the antiwar statements of the Reverend Martin Luther King Jr.[1]

Although Hughes declined to make public statements against the Vietnam War, his poetry and essays tied black rebellion in Watts and Chicago to anticolonial movements in South Africa and Saigon. Since 1960 he had read his work about colonial violence, poverty, segregation, and apartheid to crowds at jazz festivals. In these and other settings he delivered "impudent interjections" that anticipated the oppositional tone heard in later black antiwar performances.[2] For years critics claimed his poetry had

"Is this America, the land of the free and the home of the brave?" Fannie Lou Hamer speaking on behalf of the Mississippi Freedom Democratic Party at the Democratic National Convention, Atlantic City, N.J., August 22, 1964. Photo by Warren K. Leffler; Library of Congress, Prints & Photographs Division, U.S. News & World Report Magazine Collection.

grown careless and lacked complexity, but Hughes's new work captured African Americans' growing dissent about the Vietnam War draft that inducted young black men at twice the rate of whites.[3] Simple, the alter ego he created to urge blacks' assent to World War II, agitated for black rebellions and dissent against America's new war. "We have got to think up new ways of agitating," said Simple, "because the old ways is worn out. Speech making is not enough. Marching is not enough. Martin Luther King is not enough." Always prescient, Simple warned that blacks' dissent against the poverty they faced in Watts and Harlem would be turned against the draft and the war. "The young Negroes is impatient. Now, if they have to go in a draft to Viet Nam, who knows what is going to happen? The young Negroes is liable to say, 'Gimme my gun right here in Harlem and Selma and Chicago and Cambridge, Maryland.'"[4]

After another summer of uprisings in northern cities, Hughes honed a poem that captured blacks' outrage over the nation's resistance to their

calls for racial and economic justice and the draft's inequities that disproportionately placed them in combat.

> Mister Backlash, Mister Backlash,
> Just who do you think I am?
> You raise my taxes, freeze my wages,
> Send my son to Vietnam.
> You give me second class houses, second class schools,
> Do you think colored people are second class fools?[5]

Hughes immediately sent Nina Simone the poem, and she composed
music, making it the collaboration they had sought since their appearances at the 1960 Newport Jazz Festival.[6] With a political voice unloosed
in "Mississippi Goddam," Simone performed "The Backlash Blues" as
an antiwar anthem in late 1966 in New York and Chicago; early the next
year, she included the piece in her European performances.[7] By the time
Simone recorded "The Backlash Blues" months later, the song's tone and
rhythm had become menacing. Onstage and in subsequent recordings,
Simone snapped each word: "Second class houses, second class schools /
Do you think all colored people are second class fools?" Simone's cascade
of treble chords and riotous tone sounded the subterranean rage from
people compelled to war while the nation resisted their calls for full and
equal citizenship.

"The Backlash Blues" tapped a hidden but deep vein of blacks' resistances to their overrepresentation in the military draft, "police actions,"
and wars since World War II. Since World War II, African Americans had
resisted the nation's wars and the draft. Simone and Hughes used the stage
to foment blacks' dissent toward the Vietnam War.[8] Their aural protests
formed the leading edge of public protests launched by African Americans in the 1960s as they linked America's suppression of their freedom
struggles in the United States and their impressments into the military "as
an armed gendarme" with the anticolonial struggles in Vietnam and elsewhere.[9]

Blacks who spoke out against American wars received fierce and immediate retaliation for stepping out of their "place" in American political
discourse.[10] As large numbers of American troops arrived in Vietnam, the
NAACP insisted that the integrated military remained the most successful
of its civil rights gains. As blacks' support for the war plummeted, some
in the mainstream movement viewed agitation against the war as separate from the civil rights struggles. Others considered the war misguided

and terrible, but they feared the antiwar movement might divert support for civil rights and wreak havoc on already strained relationships with the Johnson administration. As the administration repudiated prominent African Americans and activists who denounced the war, including the Reverend Martin Luther King Jr., conservative civil rights leaders called any critique of American foreign policy a "serious tactical mistake."[11]

Compelled to send their "sons to Vietnam," increasing numbers of African Americans disagreed, and as civil rights activists organized for blacks' voting and economic rights, they encountered southern and northern communities in rebellion against U.S. draft policies. These activists were soon galvanized by African Americans' myriad protests against the draft and the war, including soldiers' protests, which linked their everyday inequities *and* their significant presence in the military. For decades, black antiwar dissent had been relegated to the margins of civil rights discourse, but these communities soon challenged civil rights leaders and organizations to make critiques of the war integral to the movement for racial justice and black freedom.

Black Critical Consciousness and Cold War Civil Rights

After World War II, mainstream civil rights leaders and organizations tied blacks' long struggle for full citizenship to the nation's new Cold War militarism, but other pacifist civil rights activists insisted such associations aligned blacks' aspirations for equal rights at home with American imperial interests abroad. But speaking out against U.S. foreign policy proved dangerous, and those African Americans who critiqued war and militarism or who dared advocate peace experienced imprisonment, deportation, and economic reprisals.[12]

At the same time, African Americans traveled an ever-widening geography in the 1940s and 1950s where they investigated and wrote about American militarism and racial violence that also challenged the national rhetoric of universalism and democracy.[13] Journalists, writers, and musicians reinforced African Americans' perspective on the great chasm between the nation's rhetoric of democracy and its unequal and violent practices against nonwhites at home and abroad. Simone and Hughes's late 1961 tour through Nigeria followed the violence of the Freedom Rides and the assassination of Patrice Lumumba, the newly elected president of the Congo. It prompted Louis Armstrong, who performed in the Congo just months before Lumumba's death, to produce the critical "Real Ambassadors"; Langston Hughes's satirical *Ask Your Mama* enunciated "impudent interjections" against U.S. foreign policy.[14] With the contradictions of racial inequality in the United States framed and reframed "in the shadow of world events," many African Americans questioned an American democracy whose rhetoric simultaneously justified or ignored systematic violence against black people. Though the deportation of Claudia Jones and the public harassment of Paul Robeson and W. E. B. Du Bois in the 1950s meant few other antiwar activists mounted such public campaigns for peace at the decade's close, many others, including Bayard Rustin, William Worthy, and James Lawson, remained active in international peace efforts. A new generation of black women joined the Women's International League for Peace and Freedom (WILPF).[15]

While mainstream civil rights organization muted the associations between racial inequalities in the United States and militarism abroad, African Americans' cultural performances and writings of the late 1950s and early 1960s wrestled with the links between local and global racial violence.[16] The stage not only provided an important platform for documenting and expressing the hidden critiques of racial and class inequalities, but it also revealed blacks' vision for racial justice. Frequently surveilled and reviled at home, black writers, intellectuals, and performers used the page and the stage to mount a critical analysis of American racial and foreign policies. Jazz composers like Charlie Mingus produced sonic critiques about the limits of American democracy in black life. Gwendolyn Brooks's *Annie Allen* and *Maude Martha* and Langston Hughes's *Ask Your Mama* incorporated vernacular critiques in poetry that became counterpoints to the Cold War rhetoric of abundance that glossed over class, gender, and racial inequalities.[17] In the aftermath of the anticommunist purges, these cultural critiques were at odds with prominent civil rights rhetoric, especially in assessing African Americans' inclusions in America's social and cultural life. Instead, black literature and music captured what Duke Ellington called "the dissonance" of everyday black life in a "nation within a nation."[18]

Black popular culture, especially, mounted covert resistances to Cold War militarism. Louis Jordan regaled audiences with tales of thieves in the henhouse stealing the farmer blind: "It's easy pickin's, ain't nobody here but us chickens." George Lipsitz notes that in this popular song, which appeared in "the age of anticommunism and countersubversion, covert struggles could continue among people whose public posture insisted 'ain't nobody here but us chickens.'"[19] The song's repeated refrain slyly referenced the ongoing debates about black elites who pushed to put young black men into combat. Critiques of the atom bomb were considered off the grid in mass culture, but it nonetheless remained a worthy subject for some blues performers. In the 1946 "Atomic Bomb Blues," Homer Harris, with Muddy Waters on guitar, signified on civil rights rhetoric that demanded black soldiers be included in combat. Their positions on the front lines, Harris suggested, increased the possibility they would be harmed by atomic weapons. "Wrote my baby, I was behind the risin' sun, / I told her: 'Don't be uneasy, because I'm behind the atomic bomb.'"[20] Black troops in Korea joked that Truman never intended to use the bomb; he planned to send more black men to the front lines instead.[21]

The rejection of racial and military violence as especially targeting poor black men remained a key theme in black folk blues music. J. B. Lenoir's "Eisenhower Blues" attracted the attention of the FBI. This music flourished in southern and northern black communities and provided liniments for the upheavals of black life after the Korean War: migration; the constant search for work and dignity; the episodic struggles for racial, gender, and class justice; and the increased presence of blacks in the nation's "police actions."[22] By the 1960s, Willie Dixon, J. B. Lenoir, and Odetta had inspired a new generation of folk singers who led the way to a very articulated antiwar music. Hardly a "folk revival," these singers carried on a critical tradition that had its origins in the Popular Front of the 1930s and 1940s and had quietly flourished in the 1950s.

The constant threat of war in the 1950s and blacks' participation in the Cold War military influenced an emerging generation of writers. Amiri Baraka, Haki Madhubuti (Don Lee), Walter Dean Myers, and James Stewart spent time in the newly integrated army and air force. All were drafted or enlisted after the Korean War, but all of these men trained in a military that had unevenly desegregated. While in the service, many of these writers found themselves isolated in barely integrated units. The compulsion to enlist or the threat of draft, in the context of the dynamics of war and desegregation, propelled each into new understandings of race, class, and nation.[23]

"Embarrassed" after he flunked out of Howard University in 1954, Amiri Baraka—then LeRoi Jones—enlisted in the air force. He soon considered his decision a mistake that landed him in the "Error Farce." In basic training, he joined "bloods from South Jersey mostly. Dudes from Camden and Trenton, mostly black dudes looking for a way off the streets. Trying to keep out from under the final bust. Seeing in that Air Force blue some trace of sky that they might get away in." Baraka was the only African American assigned to a meteorological unit as a weather gunner. In the isolation, he became a voracious reader; he soon found a collective of "aspiring intellectuals" who studied jazz, the graphic arts, and literature of all sorts. His reading list, which included a variety of Left magazines and publications, resulted in an anonymous accusation that he belonged to the Communist Party. Labeled "undesirable," Baraka was relieved of duty and given a dishonorable discharge.[24] Over the next decade, he transformed, first, into a highly regarded writer in Greenwich Village and then into an uptown Harlem black revolutionary poet. In the late 1950s and early 1960s, Baraka published poetry in liberal journals and magazines; he wrote *Blues People*, a well-received meditation on the role of music in black history, and created incendiary plays, including the award-winning *Dutchman*. By 1964, Baraka, Madhubuti, Dudley Randall, founder of Broadside Press, and other veterans launched the Black Arts Movement.[25]

Black Antiwar Activism and SNCC

In the late 1950s, neither the NAACP nor the new SCLC explicitly endorsed antimilitarism, but FOR and CORE remained key to African Americans committed to racial justice *and* pacifism. While battered by the anticommunist purges of the late 1940s and early 1950s, these organizations sustained antiwar activism under the rubric of civil rights. After 1955, members of these groups energized the new civil rights organizations. Many of these activists mediated African Americans' competing philosophies of and approaches to civil rights, which included direct action, self-defense, and nonviolence. Between 1955 and 1957, activists from FOR and CORE provided knowledge and resources about nonviolence to the burgeoning mass civil rights movement. During the Montgomery Bus Boycott, Bayard Rustin, Ella Baker, William Worthy, James Farmer, and James Lawson, all of whom were conscientious objectors and radical pacifists, joined activists in Montgomery, and they encouraged and informed the mass nonviolence. Familiar with the anticolonial struggles in Asia and Africa, these activists brought a global perspective to local struggles.[26]

Young men and women joined these organizations, but compelled by their own experiences with resistances to school integration and the incessant pull of the military draft, they soon created an influential nonviolent organization of their own, the Student Non-Violent Coordinating

Committee. After *Brown*, these young blacks were thrust knowingly, and sometimes unwittingly, into the epicenter of the earthquakes created by the massive movements for and against integration. At the same time, the draft military interrupted young men's lives. By 1958, these students formed a critical mass at black colleges, particularly the four colleges in Nashville. James Lawson, a CO from the Korean War and a field secretary for FOR, organized weekly workshops on nonviolence. These workshops in Nashville and elsewhere provided the forum where students debated war, militarism, and colonialism. Across the central and Deep South, these women and men organized SNCC in 1960 to execute the ideology of nonviolence and create their "beloved community." Along with a cadre of white students committed to racial justice, they crafted a disciplined nonviolent activism that heightened the exposure of the organized anti-integration violence.[27]

They learned, too, from an assortment of veterans of the 1930s Popular Front and labor struggles and men and women from antiwar struggles of the previous wars. These teachers included Bayard Rustin, James Farmer, and James Lawson. Bob Moses, a northerner influenced by the pacifist American Friends Society, declared himself a CO. Ella Baker, Coretta Scott King, and Septima Clark, all members of WILPF, exemplified pacifism and nonviolence. This cadre of activists demonstrated the long history of black antiwar thought and practices shaped by both domestic and international concerns. James Lawson, who taught nonviolence in workshops at Fisk in 1959, blended a black Christian radicalism that emphasized love with the philosophy of nonviolence. Having endured threats and assaults as a CO in a federal prison during the Korean War, Lawson traveled to India as a Methodist missionary. His embrace of Gandhianism was inspired by its complex struggle against colonialism. Lawson returned to the United States and organized workshops to show participants how to challenge Cold War consensus politics through a mixture of Christian theology and nonviolence.[28] A Harvard student and a CO, Bob Moses became an important leader, and younger pacifists, including John Lewis, Julian Bond, Diane Nash, and Gwen Patton soon joined him. Some of these new members were military veterans, COs, or children of veterans. Lucretia Collins, one of the 1961 Freedom Riders, had lived on integrated military bases in the 1950s.[29] Nurtured by this older generation of activists, many in SNCC considered nonviolent civil rights activism as a response to imperialism, militarism, and racial injustice. Lawson helped draft SNCC's founding statement, and Ella Baker, a veteran of grassroots organizations, nurtured the group's independent practices of nonviolent direct action.[30]

WILPF and Civil Rights

As these new civil rights organizations with an avowed nonviolent philosophy focused on the war against integration in the South, a core of activists in WILPF believed the nonviolent civil rights movement provided the opportunity to launch an integrated antiwar movement in the South. Key members of WILPF were also visible activists in civil rights, including Coretta Scott King, Sadie Mays, Diane Nash, Erna P. Harris, Septima Clark, and Virginia Durr. Though the charges that the civil rights struggles in the South had ties to the Communist Party eroded some older southern white women's commitment to WILPF, organizers hoped SNCC's efforts to register black voters in the South might attract younger white women, including women from southern churches.[31]

Longtime WILPF member and stalwart civil rights activist Virginia Durr hoped the two energized movements might combine in the South. The few branches that had been integrated in the South after World War II atrophied. Many white and black women in the South who were sympathetic to and participated in both efforts feared that WILPF might be considered "an outside agitator" and a front for the Communist Party. Well-educated and middle-class black women in the Tuskegee branch of WILPF felt vulnerable, as did women in the larger cities of Birmingham and Montgomery. Some of these women had presented themselves as "conservative," and they feared that WILPF might weaken the support for blacks' voting rights. They encouraged strategic organizing. During the Birmingham struggles in 1963, Dorothy Manley, wife of Spelman College president Albert Manley, wrote WILPF executive director Mildred Olmsted and suggested she send statements of support for the agreements to integrate stores. WILPF, she urged privately, should use its international stature to "encourage," "praise," and "support" integration. When she asked Olmsted not to use her name, Manley revealed the strains she faced in Alabama if she and other black women associated with WILPF.[32]

Along with some longtime white members, including Durr, younger and newer members insisted that the organization needed to organize against the war *and* for civil rights. Their commitment to both causes attracted younger black women from SNCC and from local black communities. The majority of older white members in and outside the South did not share their enthusiasm or vision for a united struggle.[33] As WILPF allied itself with civil rights, including SNCC, Durr anticipated older white members in the South would resign because of these associations. "Peace forces have made some headway in their protests" against the war, she noted to WILPF president Annalee Stewart, but she feared President Johnson "will trade off support for the Negroes for the Southern support for his war policies." She remained optimistic about interracial and inter-organizational efforts when older black women in the South continued to support WILPF even with the charges of communism. At a meeting one member announced, "We Negroes have been called everything in the world and being called a 'Communist' is just one more word to us."[34]

WILPF organizers arrived in Mississippi in July 1964 and found a heightened violence against SNCC. As they listened to the long "list of security instructions," the women quickly learned the anti-black vigilantes numbered in the thousands, maybe tens of thousands. For decades, blacks in the area faced violence and intimidation; when blacks pursued the right to vote, or claimed economic rights, they lost their jobs, or they were removed from their tenants. Vigilantes bombed and burned their homes, businesses, and churches. Now this vigilantism extended to attacks against black and white volunteers. In many areas of the state, activists did not dare to travel or organize. Still, black families — especially the poorer families — housed and fed the SNCC volunteers. "And more than this," one WILPF organizer reported, "they are prepared to protect us. When a young man from Phila[delphia] was beaten up, some 40 farmers appeared with guns that evening in Holly Springs and formed a cordon around the Freedom House. In many cases, farmers stand guard with guns over the various Freedom Centers at night." A minister housed four members of WILPF. He reassured the women of their safety and showed them his 16-gauge shotgun he kept beside his bed. "The swift progression from God to guns was almost too much for us," one WILPF member reported.[35]

In this onslaught of daily violence, WILPF organizers observed how increasing numbers of SNCC volunteers found nonviolence impractical. "COFO (Council of Federated Organizations) has held to non-violence only by a slim thread. Several times they have almost given up nonviolence, and when one hears the tales of beatings, brutality, harassment and bombings that SNICK and COFO workers have undergone, one realizes that their decision that no guns (or anything that could be possibly considered as a weapon) be carried is a brave step." Over the next weeks, one WILPF organizer heard rumbling through the communities that "violence may be necessary now to offset the previous brutality against Negroes." Local people knew that many of the white sheriffs and deputies belonged to the local Klan or the Citizens' Councils. At the very least, these local police allowed white vigilantism and rarely ensured blacks' safety.[36]

As WILPF members attempted to encapsulate the struggles for racial justice in the South within the organization's activism for peace, they also considered Alabama and Mississippi as a war zone. The work of peaceful integration in the South, they insisted in their reports, was as pressing as, if not more so than, peace abroad. In the report of the Mississippi voting project, WILPF activists suggested the organization stood to lose opportunities by not understanding the daily barriers blacks faced in the Deep South. "Voting, education, integration of schools," WILPF organizer Kitty Arnett stressed in her memo, were the "real needs" that also required "new modes of operation."[37] If the South was a war zone, then these women considered their association with the black freedom struggles as part of WILPF's efforts to broker global peace.

Wars in Mississippi

Young blacks opposed to militarism led SNCC; they entered a war zone in Mississippi, but they did not come south to organize an antiwar movement. Yet in McComb County, SNCC organizers immediately encountered a population of poor and young black men who were more vulnerable to the draft than young white men. The violence and coercion used to enforce blacks' political oppression also ensured black men's compliance with the draft. But Mississippi's draft boards, all of which were staffed by whites, used the local police and the courts to make sure blacks reported for induction. Local SNCC activists were especially vulnerable.[38]

SNCC organizers also found a local population influenced by the militarism that had been in the area since World War I. Camp Shelby in Hattiesburg, the largest base in the state during World War I, had been deactivated in 1919 and then redesignated as a training camp in 1940. By 1943 it was the largest base in the state, training 50,000 troops at a time. After World War II, Camp Shelby became the largest training base in the nation. Keesler Army Air Field in Biloxi rapidly grew to equal size. By 1943, more than 69,000 personnel were stationed at the camp, including 7,000 Tuskegee Airmen. Camp Van Dorn housed large all-black units, including the 364th Infantry Regiment. The camp and the nearby town of Centerville—just thirty-four miles from McComb County—became the epicenter of blacks' struggles against the military's segregation. Prior to the regiment's arrival, dozens of men in the unit reportedly formed a Double V club to challenge the military's segregation. First stationed in Arizona, the unit rioted in 1942, and the military moved the men to the South. When they arrived in Centerville, the men reportedly vowed to rid the area of white supremacy. Black soldiers were assaulted and murdered when they went off base, but the men refused to yield. Soldiers in the unit stole rifles—white soldiers carried sidearms—and they vowed to defend themselves. Dozens of soldiers went AWOL and reportedly disappeared into nearby towns.[39] Camp Van Dorn closed after World War II, but by 1960, airborne units and infantry brigades trained for Vietnam at Keesler and Shelby bases. While the draft was intrusive, the integrated military appeared to provide black Mississippians with economic independence and an opportunity to escape segregation.

World War II created some employment opportunities for blacks in and around McComb County, though the new jobs required that they migrate. Blacks in the county departed for war industries and the military at higher rates than populations elsewhere in the state. Some left permanently; others found temporary work in railroads and lumber camps. While some veterans left the state, others returned determined to live, work, and vote with a measure of equality. Veterans who returned to the state after the war found that Mississippi remained a violent place for African Americans, especially for those who served in the military. Despite the lull in lynchings during the 1930s, the Mississippi Klan remained strong, and its supporters were "mean" in the southwest hill counties of the state. The NAACP also took root in these counties. Chapters that sprang up in the 1940s remained active during the political and economic repression of the 1950s. People worked on small subsistence farms, and far fewer blacks and whites grew cotton. The combination of military experience, a separate organizational life based in the churches, and their wartime experiences informed a palpable black pride.[40]

When Bob Moses began the search for places in the area to organize for civil rights after the 1961 Freedom Rides, he found older black activists, many of whom were veterans, who were eager to have SNCC lead a voter registration effort. By August 1961, Moses and local organizers, including high school students, opened the first voter registration school in the area.[41] The arrival of SNCC for voter registration added to the tensions in the area. As voter registration gained momentum, the assaults against SNCC workers began. In response, more volunteers arrived to hold workshops on direct-action nonviolence. These workshops attracted older black activists and a cadre of young people. That fall, two young recruits began a sit-in at the local Woolworth. They got arrested and spent over a month in jail. The arrests and convictions of teenagers working with SNCC, along with the assaults and murders of organizers, nearly derailed the efforts in McComb County. The organization's attempts to desegregate the county were not wholly defeated. As Charles Payne notes, "SNCC learned that merely the process of trying to organize a town would attract young people, a few of whom were willing to identify completely with the organization's work." SNCC built a movement in Mississippi "largely around these home-grown organizers."[42]

As younger men joined SNCC in the Delta, they also registered for the draft, received draft notices, or faced an imminent "call-up." Bob Moses, who received CO status in the late 1950s, remained attuned to the ebbs and flows of the draft. As draft calls increased in the local communities, Moses argued that SNCC needed to link the black struggle with the antiwar struggle. Like William Patterson a decade earlier, Moses and John Lewis connected the violence against SNCC with the escalating war. Three SNCC organizers, Michael Schwerner, Andrew Goodman, and James Chaney, disappeared the day of the Gulf of Tonkin Bay incident, which President Johnson then used to justify sending troops into Vietnam. Days later, four members of the Georgia Ku Klux Klan murdered Lemuel Penn, a lieutenant colonel in the army reserve, as he drove home to Washington, D.C., following two weeks of training at Fort Benning. The four men later indicted for Penn's murder claimed they heard rumors about the SCLC's plan to "make Georgia a testing ground for the civil rights bill." James S. Lackey, one of the four men indicted for Penn's murder, said they "intended scaring off any out-of-town colored people before they could give us any trouble." After seeing Penn's car with Washington, D.C., plates outside Athens, James H. Sims announced, "I'm going to kill me a nigger."[43] These four men and the four men charged with killing Viola Liuzzo after the Selma march in 1965 all belonged to the United Klans of America, and they reportedly trained as "killer squads in shoot-and-run technique."[44]

As the pace of the draft quickened, Moses argued for SNCC to address the war. He insisted black people's struggle for justice included full participation in American life. The ability to critique the war was part of this full participation. Students for a Democratic Society held a protest against the war in April, and Moses spoke. John L. Lewis, James Bevel, and Diane Nash made individual protests, and Julian Bond, who was running for state representative in Georgia on an antiwar platform, "disassociate[ed] himself from the organization" whenever he critiqued Johnson and the war.[45] SNCC remained silent and Bond won his race, but he then faced a protracted—and ultimately unsuccessful—effort to unseat him.[46]

As SNCC members discussed how best to address the war, they could not ignore its effect on the organization or the communities it organized. By summer, John Lewis observed that black men filled the front and rear lines of combat units in disproportionate numbers, and many men in SNCC received draft notices. Increasing numbers were inducted. He surmised that a startling majority of the young men in SNCC—close to 85 percent—"were eligible and exposed to the draft." Many of the men had graduated from college or were no longer taking classes. He and Moses realized that "most of our people didn't qualify for student deferments and they certainly couldn't expect their draft boards, most of them in the South, to give them a sympathetic ear."[47]

SNCC's debates about whether or not to make a public statement dragged on, but blacks in McComb County, Mississippi, called for a boycott of the draft after John D. Shaw, a local rights activist, died in combat. Unable to vote and prevented from being seated at the Democratic National Convention, MFDP member Fannie Lou Hamer addressed the Credentials Committee and recounted the brutal treatment she and others faced when they attempted to register to vote. She alluded to the only right black Mississippians had in 1964—sending sons to the military. Mocking the demand for blacks' martial fidelity and the denial of their rights as citizens, she asked from the podium in Atlantic City, "Is this the land of the free and home of the brave?" Still unable to vote freely in 1965, activists in McComb County distributed a circular listing five reasons "why Negroes should not be in any war fighting for America." Activists argued that "until all the Negro people are free in Mississippi," blacks "should not honor the draft here in Mississippi. Mothers should encourage their sons not to go." Obeying a draft call, activists insisted, did not bring full citizenship. Rather, Mississippi blacks "will gain respect and dignity as a race only by forcing the U.S. Government to come with guns, dogs and trucks to take our sons away to fight and be killed protecting Mississippi, Alabama, Georgia, and Louisiana." Activists implored blacks in the military to resist as well.

Last week a white soldier from New Jersey was discharged from the Army because he refused to fight in Vietnam; he went on a hunger strike. Negro boys can do the same thing. We can write and ask our sons if they know what they are fighting for. If he answers Freedom, tell him that's what we are fighting for here in Mississippi. And if he says Democracy, tell him the truth—we don't know anything about Communism, Socialism, and all that, but we do know that Negroes have caught hell right here under this American Democracy.[48]

Individuals in civil rights organizations had questioned the war, but the statement from McComb County, later printed in the newsletter of the MFDP of McComb, was the first from a civil rights organization to denounce the war and call for community and military activism. Southern congressional representatives labeled the statement incendiary. Lawrence Guyot, chair of the MFDP executive committee, and the Reverend Ed King, another member, insisted the executive committee did not issue the statement but added that they "under[stood] why Negro citizens of McComb, themselves, the victims of bombings, Klan-inspired terrorism, and harassment arrests, should resent the death of a citizen of McComb while fighting for 'freedom' not enjoyed by the Negro Community of McComb." Since its organization, members in the MFDP, particularly Fannie Lou Hamer, had challenged the political rhetoric that allowed terrorism against blacks, justified their political exclusion, and drafted them.[49]

While the MFDP response to the antidraft activism in McComb County increased the pressure on SNCC to oppose the war, the accelerated draft of SNCC members forced the issue. For several years, the draft affected SNCC's day-to-day operations across its northern and southern locales. But the draft in the Deep South spurred SNCC into action. The murder of SNCC member and navy veteran Sammy Younge on December 31, 1965, solidified the organization's denouncement of the war. SNCC released its statement on January 6, 1966, the day after Younge's funeral. Ignoring the MFDP's earlier statement and the many statements from individuals in SNCC, the media cast the organization's opposition as the first from a civil rights organization. Linking black freedom struggles in the South with independence movements around the world, SNCC's statement also equated the suppression of blacks' political rights and the continued violence in the South as part of the larger U.S. war against nonwhites, including in Vietnam. The statement advocated resistance against the draft for the Vietnam War and urged a "draft for the Freedom fight in the United States."[50]

Peace activists and organizations applauded the statement, while the NAACP and the Urban League chastised SNCC. The furor over SNCC's public opposition came just as the organization fiercely debated its future and commitment to nonviolence. Influenced by both the violence it faced and the violence it witnessed in other communities, SNCC undertook an intense examination of nonviolence as many black communities organized themselves around the long history of black self-defense. After local and federal authorities refused to protect African Americans against rising Klan activity in parts of the Deep South, blacks organized their own protection in groups such as the Deacons for Defense and the Revolutionary Action Movement. Some members of these self-defense groups were veterans, and they brought their skills and discipline learned in the army and Marines to the defense of their communities. Attuned to the political events abroad and agitated by the violence in the South and his own repeated arrests, Stokely Carmichael called for Black Power during the 1966 march for James Meredith, an air force veteran who sued for and won admission to the University of Mississippi four years earlier. Bill Ware, another SNCC activist, called for other black organizations to separate from whites and focus on their communities. Over the next months, SNCC dissolved its ties to interracial activism, while many in the organization left for the new Black Power movement.[51]

A cadre of SNCC members remained committed to nonviolent direct-action efforts against the war and the draft. John Lewis immediately sought ways to combine civil rights and interracial peace activism. Replaced as chair of SNCC by Carmichael, Lewis cofounded the Southern Coordinating Committee to End the War in Vietnam. James Bevel worked with the SCLC and advocated a sit-in on the battlefield in the Mekong Delta.[52] In April 1967 he directed the Spring Mobilization Committee to End the War, which organized mass rallies against the draft in New York and San Francisco. Along with Dave Dellinger and Cleveland Robinson, Bevel encouraged students to burn their draft cards during the rallies. As white antiwar activists organized teach-ins about the war, Bevel agitated for a broader community-based involvement in these efforts, and he taught the direct action tactics of SNCC. These activists responded with street theater, the showing of antiwar films, and direct appeals to young men who opposed the war.[53]

Before SNCC issued its statement against the war, its activists observed that a growing number of black soldiers and draftees resisted orders for combat duty. In late 1965, four black soldiers refused to follow their units into combat, and they rejected inoculations. Other soldiers went on hunger strikes.[54] Here were examples of direct action within the ranks. In 1969, Marine Corporal William Harvey was accused, tried, and then convicted for inciting "a wildcat strike" when he preached disobedience to other black Marines. Agitating against the war, Marine Corps officials insisted, violated the military codes. Increasingly, black soldiers aired their grievances against the war in highly public and disciplined ways. Such efforts led to punishment, including courts-martial. At Fort Jackson, the interracial GIs United Against the War in Vietnam held outdoor meetings and published a variety of antiwar material. The army arrested eight members and quickly pushed several to accept dishonorable discharges. Others faced charges of "violent overthrow of the government."[55]

SNCC splintered as Project 100,000 accelerated, and the remaining members committed to the antiwar efforts became "alarmingly aware" of the need to launch an antidraft program within black communities. "Realizing how the draft is taking more and more of our Bro[thers] from the Freedom Struggle and from our Black Communities, we sense the urgency of our having begun yesterday." The peace movement, SNCC argued, did not provide black men with "a viable program of resistance to the draft." The organization needed to create a "resistance which will prevent this country from dealing with each Bro[ther] as an individual and cause them to know that the induction of each Bro[ther] will bring the fury of the Black Community down on their heads."[56] As SNCC considered its future, activists focused on providing direct aid to young men faced with the draft. SNCC members also refined their opposition to the draft and the war within the twined ideas of racial and class oppression. In this equation, they argued, black men were forced into the role of mercenaries, a claim John Lewis made in SNCC's January statement. These activists went further, anticipating charges William Peterson would use several years later in a new introduction to *We Charge Genocide*. SNCC noted, "The country has devised a way of killing two birds with one stone, i.e. brutalizing and murdering people of color around the world and exterminating Black men of this country in the process. We are the ever-growing army of mercenaries that this country will send to slaughter year after year to continue the slaughter of our Bros. in Africa, Asia, and Latin America."[57]

Using tactics honed in the Freedom Schools, SNCC informed men about their draft rights and urged their communities into direct action against the war by opposing the draft.

YOU DO NOT HAVE TO BE DRAFTED IF—
you are supporting a family
you have one of over 150 different physical disabilities
you can qualify for any one of 13 legal deferments to the draft

Along with ignoring or evading draft notices, local SNCC offices urged black men to challenge their 1-A status. If a man had at least one of the listed qualifications, he had the right to file an appeal within ten days of the board's decision. "If your draft board turns your appeal down, *you can ask the Appeals Board to hear your case.*" Activists gave black men information that the segregated southern draft boards refused to provide. "Every day, many men are drafted who could have stayed out of the Army if they had realized how many ways there are to get a legal deferment." Many men feared their chances for an appeal had passed, but SNCC insisted that "*it's not too late.*"[58]

Through flyers, pamphlets, counseling, and workshops, SNCC showed men how to file for CO status. Schooled by a series of questions and statements, men learned what CO status meant, how it was defined, and how they might file for it. Draft boards refused to consider the overwhelming majority of CO applications, especially those from black men. Still, SNCC urged, "Find out about how American soldiers are ordered to bomb villages with women and children in them, and about the thousands of colored people who have been killed or horribly burnt by the U.S. Army." SNCC warned men that in order to file for and obtain CO status, they had "to fill out papers [and] some of the questions are very tricky." Get expert advice, SNCC urged. "Find out about your right not to be drafted." And SNCC members were willing to provide counsel. At the bottom of flyers, SNCC provided the address and phone number of an office where men could seek advice and aid.[59] By 1967, Howard University students were some of the most organized antiwar activists from the black colleges and universities.

Along with local efforts, SNCC proposed national antidraft resistance and pushed for an immediate action against the October 1967 draft call of 46,000 men. Launching a national resistance program to the draft presented a dilemma to the organization as its own members faced particular pressure from Project 100,000. As Muhammad Ali came under attack for refusing his induction notice, more vulnerable men in SNCC feared accusations of treason or anti-Americanism might lead to indictments. Instead of a "frontal attack" on the draft, SNCC proposed mass action to inform black communities about the racial and class inequities of the draft. These grassroots efforts coordinated community awareness of the global impact of U.S. militarism and how the military trained black men to kill populations of color in other nations. SNCC locals organized protests at induction centers, which included efforts to prevent young men from being pulled into the military. Other locals had black veterans stop young men as they entered draft offices or induction centers. They organized veterans to testify about their experiences in war. Some locals organized petitions to allow black men to choose where to fight for freedom, Vietnam or Harlem.[60]

By 1966, King and others in the SCLC deliberated over the nation's continued intransigence against civil rights and its willingness to spend billions each month on a war and a fraction on the poor. Reluctant to make public critiques of the president's war policies, King turned his attention to broadening the civil rights struggles to include mass protests against poverty. After he moved to Chicago in 1965, King and the SCLC struggled to create a strategy that would allow the use of mass action honed in the segregated South in the more subtle but widespread segregated North. In Chicago, Mayor Richard Daley opposed the war in Vietnam, but city officials turned to the Johnson administration for ways to stall or thwart King in exchange for support for the war. Along with the city administration's obfuscations, antiblack organizations proudly resisted jobs programs and school desegregation. Despite Supreme Court rulings, real estate agents used legendary efforts to keep blacks out of better housing, and the city boasted the least-integrated neighborhoods of any city in the nation. Efforts by King and the Chicago SCLC to integrate housing and jobs met hostile counterdemonstrators carrying Confederate flags and signs scrawled with racial epithets. At a particularly violent confrontation in early August 1966, crowds rushed at King and pelted him with rocks and debris. Similar displays of violence had created international sympathy for civil rights demonstrators in 1963, but the mass demonstrations in Chicago dissolved into charges that King created the mayhem. He later told a phalanx of reporters that he had "never seen such hate. Not in Mississippi, or Alabama."[61]

Chicago had some of the oldest and largest Black Nationalist organizations in the nation. The Nation of Islam had one of its largest mosques in the city, and its newspaper, *Muhammad Speaks*, published articles that denounced racism and imperialism. While the *Chicago Defender* claimed the integrated military was a civil rights gain and chastised black men to obey their induction notices, *Muhammad Speaks* kept up an incessant critique of the war. Before Elijah Muhammad ousted him, Malcolm X regularly denounced the war. This resistance in Black Chicago and the Nation of Islam grew as African Americans in Chicago had the highest draft rates, enlistment rates, and casualty rates in the nation. And when black men (or their mothers) protested, the Selective Service found the men and worked to draft them. By 1965, Korean and Vietnam War veterans radicalized local black freedom struggles through the Black Arts Movement. Haki Madhubuti had served in the army in the 1950s, and he returned to Chicago, where he became a Black Arts activist and published his first volume of poetry in 1966.[62] The succession of antiwar and antidraft statements from the MFDP, SNCC, and Muhammad Ali further radicalized northern black communities.

Like SNCC, the SCLC experienced the reverberations of this activism within its membership. King and Fred Shuttlesworth had already delivered private critiques of the war. At its April 1966 meeting, as a body the SCLC concluded that "the gangrene of Vietnam has played havoc with our domestic destinies. The promises of the Great Society top the casualty list of the conflict. The pursuit of the widened war has narrowed domestic welfare programs, making the poor, white and Negro, bear the heaviest burdens both at the front and at home." Members concluded they "must condemn this war on the grounds that war is not the way to solve social problems. Mass murder can never lead to constructive and creative government or to the creation of a democratic society in Vietnam." The SCLC urged withdrawal and the pursuit of peace.[63]

When representatives from the Urban League, the SCLC, CORE, and the NAACP attended a "rights conference" sponsored by the White House in early June 1966, moderates worked to squelch a resolution against the war put forward by CORE. As these struggles disrupted the conference, news circulated that the national cemetery in Alabama refused to bury paratrooper and Vietnam casualty Private First Class Jimmy Williams. The statement from CORE and the publicity from Williams's funeral alarmed Johnson administration officials who did not want civil rights organizations to reject their foreign policy or denounce Project 100,000. Administration advisor Louis Martin; Roy Wilkins, executive director of the NAACP; and Whitney Young, executive director of the Urban League, aided the administration's machinations. Reluctant to create dissent, King left the conference. Floyd McKissick, new director of CORE and Black Power advocate, described the gathering as a "hoax."[64]

Pressure from black antiwar activists continued as SNCC cofounder Diane Nash Bevel visited Vietnam in late 1966. Her trip received extensive coverage in the black press. She described the war as part of a longer history of U.S. violence "toward 'coloreds'" at home and abroad. "Economic interests are at stake in Viet Nam," she observed, "the same interests that overcame the Indians and led to the enslavement of Negroes." She drew parallels between the exploitation of Vietnamese villagers and black soldiers. "Negro Americans are going to have to decide whether they want to be murderers of other colored people."[65] Her claims induced a rebuke. Chicago civil rights activist Donald Mosby charged Bevel "was had by the Commies in Hanoi." Black people, he insisted, needed to avoid racializing the war and stay out of U.S. foreign politics. Black Americans, *Defender* columnist Arletta Claire insisted, should not get involved in "extraneous issues like Vietnam." Besides, she concluded, the idea of redemption through battle "still thrives in other corners of black thought."[66] Despite these criticisms, polls showed a rising black opposition to the war.

As increasing numbers of African Americans questioned the war, King supported SNCC's call to end the war in early 1966, and over the next year he questioned the war and its impact on black communities. He issued his first formal call for the civil rights movement to focus on ending the war in a late March 1967 address in Chicago, arguing for a "peace movement that combined the fervor of the civil rights movements." Speaking in Riverside Church in early April 1967, King framed his opposition in sharp and critical terms that addressed the racial and class inequities in the draft. As more of the nation's resources went for the war and away from critical care of the poor, King described America as a "society gone mad on war." He described how he came to "see the war not only as a moral outrage but also as an enemy of the poor." Young black men "crippled by our society" went thousands of miles "to guarantee liberties in Southeast Asia which they had not found in southwest Georgia and east Harlem." He watched the "cruel irony" of "Negro and white boys on TV screens as they kill and die together for a nation that has been unable to seat them together in the same schools. We watch them in solidarity burning the huts of a poor village, but we realize that they would never live on the same block in Detroit."[67]

King called for civil rights activists to act not only against the war that impressed poor men into Vietnam but also against U.S. foreign policy that bred economic and racial injustice. He called for an immediate halt to the bombing, a unilateral cease-fire, a cessation of the military's buildup in the region, negotiation with the South Vietnamese National Liberation Front, and a removal of all troops in accordance with the 1954 Geneva agreement. He pressed for all Americans to intercede in this and other wars—from Venezuela to Mozambique and South Africa—where the United States chose to suppress, and not aid, efforts to end oppressive governments. "We must continue to raise our voices if our nation persists in its perverse ways in Vietnam. We must be prepared to match actions with words by seeking out every creative means of protest possible." He urged young men to resist the draft. If men found "the American course in Vietnam a dishonorable and unjust one," he urged them to seek CO status.[68]

King's Riverside address aired over radio stations in the Northeast and on the SCLC-sponsored *Martin Luther King Speaks* in southern markets. Mainstream civil rights advocates were immediately forced to counter his call for Americans to end the war and for African Americans to resist the draft. For several years the NAACP ignored pleas from branches to take a stand against the war, and the national office periodically reminded branches that participated in "war and peace" efforts that the association "had not passed any resolution opposing U.S. policy in Vietnam." Now forced to respond, Roy Wilkins had the NAACP concentrate on King's statement, and the sixty-member board unanimously voted for a resolution rejecting any efforts to merge the civil rights and peace movements. "We are not a peace organization nor a foreign policy association," the NAACP board declared. "Civil rights battles will have to be fought and won on their own merits, irrespective of the state of war or peace in the world."[69] Nobel Prize recipient Ralph Bunche agreed and insisted that the civil rights movement and the peace movement "had too little in common." He hoped King would see that speaking out about the war threatened the progress of the civil rights movement, and he acknowledged that during the association's board meeting he urged representatives to repudiate the minister's call for a civil rights and peace movement as a "serious tactical mistake."[70]

In public addresses, NAACP executive director Roy Wilkins lashed out at King. Since the War of 1898, he argued, African Americans had attempted to leverage their participation in wars abroad into civil rights gains at home. In a stunning display of amnesia, Wilkins insisted that during World War II blacks gave "all out support" for the war and kept separate their push against discrimination. "One of their prized dividends was the abolition of racial segregation in the armed services." The NAACP, he declared, did not consider the drive for civil rights entwined with, "for, or against the United States policy and procedures in South Vietnam." If the association's members had thoughts on U.S. policy in Kashmir, Pakistan, and India, he argued, they would join other organizations. Wilkins insisted that the NAACP did not have the time or resources to consider much beyond the school cases in Boston. Instead, "we think we should stick to our knitting." Ultimately, Wilkins ignored the deep concerns of NAACP members about the Johnson administration's advance of violence abroad and its use of violence against African Americans at home. Yet, Wilkins's rejection also exposed the NAACP's unease with the philosophy of nonviolence. King, Wilkins argued, put peace over civil rights. "Civil rights is number one." Unlike King and SNCC, he "preferred not to commit himself on Vietnam." He disagreed with King and thousands of black soldiers: "When an American colored soldier kills a Viet Cong, he is not killing a colored brother. Why should we consider the Viet Cong our colored brothers?"[71]

Wilkins's criticism of King, which was also a criticism of the black antiwar efforts and the growing antiwar activism of black soldiers, elicited immediate and protracted rebuke from the association's members. In the weeks following Wilkins's statements, the association's membership dropped by tens of thousands, and hundreds resigned from local branch boards. Many simply returned their membership cards. Some members expressed incredulity at Wilkins's "point of view"; others sharply criticized him for refusing to see the connections between the staggering cost of the war and diminishing support for antipoverty policies. "It is very clear that war in Vietnam is being used as an excuse to cut the plans and progress of the Great Society," Addie Weber wrote. She suggested Wilkins might read the newspapers for more evidence of her points. Joseph Ford wondered why Wilkins had not publicly denounced the expenditures of "two billions per month on the war and a meager 1.6 billion per year on anti-poverty. You are not telling Senator Javits that he is wrong in saying that the government can not do justice to the Negro and fight the war at the same time." Ford suggested Wilkins come to Patterson, New Jersey, and meet its residents "who feel immediately and directly the results of Federal cutbacks in domestic spending for the purpose of waging war in Vietnam. Tell them, if you will, that there is no relationship between the two."[72]

Association members called Wilkins's remarks "shameful" in the rejection of peace. Peace and racial justice, they argued, were linked. His "tactical shrewdness" abandoned a key principle in the association's history: human rights. One woman, who lived in the South and only signed her initials, felt that the association had abandoned her son on the battlefield. He went into the service, she informed Wilkins, because for "the Negro boy, that is all that is left." In her four-page letter to Wilkins, she argued she "knew what Dr. King had been doing these past years. I'm sorry I can't say the same for the NAACP." M. Franklin, a Cleveland resident, agreed. "I am glad Dr. King spoke out and said what so many of us little people believe. I wish you would grow up while some of our black sons are still living." One member demanded to know why Wilkins saw no relationship between civil rights and Vietnam. "Or will you go along with the view that Negroes will best find equality and economic security in the armed forces?" Wilkins, some members charged, lacked any outrage about the high black casualties. A. J. de Witte believed Wilkins missed a fundamental point in the disproportionate number of black men in Vietnam. "This means that Negro GIs also do a disproportionate amount of the killing in Vietnam. This double outrage does not seem to concern you." He asked, "Do you believe that civil rights consists only in the American Negro getting his share of the loot, no matter how ill gotten?"[73]

Other members were more explicit in the moral and political costs of the war for African Americans' pursuit of racial justice. When Wilkins disavowed criticism of the war, he reaffirmed "the view that the black American has a *place* and it's best that he keep in that place," Clyde Taylor wrote.

> You have confused salvation with effective tactical policy. You have abandoned "soul" for boardroom expediency. You have failed to understand Negro. Negro is not a suffering that wants at any cost to be put out of its misery. Negro is an anguish that safeguards the obligations of its miscry, that having won its human wisdom at such cost, refuses to sell the promise of that pain cheaply, for the conditional support of influential white bureaucrats, refuses to trade that pain for anything less than a noble humanity as expensive as the pain has been deep. Negro is a cool wager, exhibiting grace under pressure, and refusing to diminish that pressure until the pot that has been won holds the totality of human values. Negro *is*, not hopes to profit.

Taylor wondered how the NAACP could combat racism "by avoiding giving offense to racists."[74] Virginia and Robert Chute offered a brief description of what the association should represent. "We oppose lynching and beating in Mississippi—Napalm and crop destruction in Vietnam and believe that they stem from the same disregard for human rights. Moral opposition to the one is undermined by tacit or actual approval of the other."[75] In these letters, members reminded the association of its history as an organization that fought for justice for all human beings, regardless of color.

Since its inception, the association had supported America's wars, including the war in Vietnam, for both tactical and ideological reasons. Wilkins was keenly aware that the Vietnam War had drained resources from the civil rights efforts; but he had been with the association since World War II, and like others of his generation, he considered American wars as opportunities to make civil rights advances. Privately, Wilkins worried that any denunciation of the war would unleash an assault against the association. With the NAACP's long history of support for wars and Wilkins's concerns about a backlash, he reminded critics of the association's support for the war. In a letter sent to its 440,000 members (now down by 60,000), Wilkins insisted that they held "a wide range of views on Viet Nam and it would be immoral to impose upon them any stand at all regarding the war."[76]

Despite the NAACP's efforts to reassure the Johnson administration of black America's martial fidelity, African Americans no longer embraced statements that suggested they collectively supported the war as a "civic responsibility" or considered their participation a civil rights imperative. As the many letters to the NAACP revealed, increasing numbers of African Americans considered the war inimical to their values and aspirations for racial justice. The enormous resources and horrific power of the U.S. military, many declared, were turned against women and children. As sailors' riots on ships and soldiers' rebellions on bases escalated, many compounded by the riots in the United States, Wilkins and others in the national office quietly recognized they knew very little about the experiences of black Marines, soldiers, and sailors. By 1970, the association's investigations revealed the trends others had tracked. Only the army had a discernible cadre of black officers, but even these percentages were low. Instead, the rates of the courts-martial and dishonorable discharges against African Americans soared. A chastened Wilkins finally questioned the war.

Antidraft Black Power

The rhetoric and philosophy of Black Power, which stressed black self-determination and anticolonialism, precipitated SNCC's severing ties to the interracial civil rights movement, but these differences accelerated African Americans' involvement with the antiwar movement. SNCC defined Black Power as black communities determining their own destinies and forming their own economic, social, political, and cultural institutions. Solutions, advocates argued, must address blacks' interests, needs, and problems.[77] Abandoning the rhetoric and symbols of an interracial and nonviolent civil rights organization, Stokely Carmichael articulated radical alternatives about how best to achieve black self-determination. He insisted black people had the right—the obligation—to demand their right to self-defense. "For once, black people are going to use the words they want to use—not just the words whites want to hear."[78] Carmichael articulated black militancy in language and action as mass self-defense to determine blacks' destiny, and as part of the larger struggle against colonialism. As Carmichael and others advocated black self-determination, they goaded and encouraged white activists to return to their own communities and confront violence that made racism possible, including American foreign policy. Carmichael insisted black men must refuse the draft for an "immoral" war.[79]

The succession of riots in 1967 amplified the call for black self-determination and connections between the war and racial inequality. The Kerner Report, which was released the next year by the president's National Advisory Commission on Civil Disorders, described these uprisings as blacks' reaction to racial oppression, including terrible housing, underfunded schools, and police brutality. Significant portions of African Americans involved in the riots—39.9 percent in Detroit and 52.8 percent in Newark—reported that the "U.S. was not worth fighting and dying for" in a war. African American activists argued that the riots were more than simply a reaction to white racism and racial inequalities in U.S. institutions. Amiri Baraka declared the five-day riot in Newark as the "next stage of the revolutionary uprising."[80] As more riots occurred that summer, the new Black Panther Party described the uprisings as part of the global upsurge of colonized people in search of political and economic liberation. While the party endorsed this global rebellion, its efforts also focused on the local. In Newark, Kevin Mumford argues, "the broad swath of Black Power was characterized by black-led coalitions and strategic pragmatism, rather than by ideology and revolution." Those activists who organized in a black public sphere and called for black empowerment tended to "believe in democratic values of community and (both physical and political) representation."[81]

The July 1967 conference in Newark, which occurred after the six-day riot in the city where twenty-three people died, drew over 1,300 people who represented more than forty organizations. These delegates met in more than a dozen workshops to discuss and consider the state and "future of the black struggle." Discussions included the creation of a black militia; the establishment of black universities; the election of more blacks to local, state, and national offices; and cultural and educational exchanges with African nations. Representatives debated establishing a separate homeland in the United States, and they strategized about how to achieve equality and Black Power.[82]

They also criticized the antiwar movement, describing it as mostly white and unresponsive to their concerns. Correlating the violence in Vietnam with violence in the black neighborhoods of Newark, CORE director Floyd McKissick charged that antiwar activists found "it too easy to look thousands of miles away from home and with much indignation, see the extermination of the Vietnamese. On the other hand, they cannot see ten blocks away, where many Black People are the Walking Dead—dead in mind and spirit, because of the lack of hope and lack of chance." Despite the harsh critique, the body voted to support the antiwar effort and participate in the October 21 mobilization against the war, in Washington, D.C. They expressed support for the National Liberation Front and called for the immediate withdrawal of U.S. troops.[83]

For many radical black antiwar activists, the riots signaled a new black critical consciousness at the grassroots level, which the white peace movement was unable to organize. Black activists determined that the rhetoric and practices of the peace movement were not expansive enough to include the broader political concerns and experiences of black communities. Sit-ins at universities and large rallies in white communities did not acknowledge the differing experiences of African Americans. In their day-to-day activities, antiwar black activists were aware that some communities continued to give President Johnson strong support, and many blacks viewed the military as an opportunity to find work, even as they questioned the war. White activists interpreted these complex views as indifference to the peace movement and the power of blacks' pride in military service. Others argued that blacks' economic vulnerability in the South made antiwar activities too dangerous. Some whites argued that the peace movement was white because "black people don't understand the war." SNCC activist and pacifist Gwen Patton argued that a black antiwar effort had to address the impact of the war *within* and not just outside their communities. She and other antiwar activists pointed to Muhammad Ali's challenge to the segregated draft board and the racial inequities of Project 100,000. Many African Americans correlated their high draft rates and casualty rates not just with their poverty but also with their limited political power generally.[84]

While Stokely Carmichael used the national media attention to make statements about Black Power and black separatism that alarmed many whites, he also drew attention to the stark differences between blacks' defense against police brutality and the U.S. practices of war that insisted on using black men as murderers. He made equally incendiary remarks to black audiences skeptical about the merits of Black Power. "There is nothing wrong with violence. It is just who is able to control it. That's what counts," Carmichael insisted. Challenging an audience of men vulnerable to the draft, Carmichael asked, "Do you not have the guts to say: 'Hell no.' Do you not have the guts to say, 'I will not allow anyone to make me a hired killer.'" Going further, Carmichael charged, "When McNamara says he is going to draft 30 per cent of the black people out of the ghettoes, baby, that is nothing but urban removal." With Vietnam, Carmichael argued, "the choice is very clear. You either suffer or you inflict suffering. Either you go to the Leavenworth federal penitentiary in Kansas or you become a killer. I will choose to suffer. I will go to jail. To hell with this country."[85] Over the next months, he escalated his rhetoric.

At a conference in New York City after King's murder, 700 black activists gathered to discuss "the survival of blacks in America" and "solidarity with the Vietnamese struggle." Carmichael's speech tied the success of a black rebellion at home with stopping the war in Vietnam. The black movement, he argued, differed "from the white left because the white left is not fighting for its survival. . . . They want to save America. We have to burn America down. In order for black people to survive America must be destroyed." Adding to the charged rhetoric, Huey P. Newton's 1970 letter to the National Liberation Front of South Vietnam pledged "international revolutionary solidarity" and "an undetermined number of troops" to assist in the "fight against American imperialism." And black activists encouraged black soldiers not to fight against the Vietnamese—a stance many soldiers practiced or considered as early as 1966.[86]

The ideology of Black Nationalism, Robert F. Williams insisted, was antiwar. While some believed the violent rhetoric from Black Power advocates and the Black Panther Party undermined the peace movement, others argued Black Power provided a new vocabulary and a new analysis of racism and colonialism. The Black Panther Party worked to regenerate communities, and antiwar activities played a prominent role in these daily and local activities. Most important, Black Power activists challenged what made the military's recruitment of poor black men possible—their high unemployment and the misinformation they received about the draft. As black antiwar activists and Black Panthers created strategies to stop the war by organizing communities to protest the draft and recruitment, they introduced ordinary African Americans to Black Nationalism that called for political self-determination. Integral to self-determination was the right to question the impact of war on black communities.[87]

As Carmichael and others in the Black Power movement urged black men to avoid the draft, Gwen Patton turned to black communities and mounted an antidraft movement that transcended the divisive debates about antiwar, the draft, and black American's agitation to participate in the military. Born and raised in Detroit, Patton was the child of Alabama migrants; she moved to Montgomery after her mother's death. She joined the Montgomery Improvement Association in 1962; organized Freedom Schools in Macon County, Georgia; and participated in the 1965 Selma-to-Montgomery voting rights march. She later worked in the Lowndes Freedom organization. As a key figure in teaching SNCC's ideologies and tactics of nonviolence, Patton nurtured the organization's shift to an antiwar movement. She called for the establishment of a grassroots, direct-action antidraft and antiwar effort. Along with John Wilson, another SNCC veteran, Patton organized the National Black Antiwar Antidraft Union in late January 1968. Compelled by the unwillingness of peace movement organizations to see the war as part of a wider struggle against the global color line—she and others believed the antiwar efforts needed to work with antiracist and anticolonial struggles—Patton wanted to make clear the racism of the war and address the particular impact of the draft on African Americans. A separate organization that focused on challenging the draft would address concerns ignored by white antiwar efforts. The large marches of the peace movement and the burning of draft cards, Patton observed, did not "change the lot of black men who were being drafted into the racist genocidal war."[88]

The black antidraft effort intended to stop the ready availability of men for the war. Efforts were focused on disruption of official activities and realignment of community support. Hoping to stop men's participation in combat, activists encouraged GI resistance campaigns. Local antiwar activists were especially focused on organizing black women's antidraft efforts. While the national antiwar movement cordoned off recruitment and induction centers, the National Black Antiwar Antidraft Union worked to inform men before they arrived to register. Such counter-recruitment happened in churches and living rooms and around kitchen tables. Activists made direct appeals to black women, who were urged to provide "refuge" to black men "when the man is after them." In preparation, women were encouraged to raise funds for legal expenses, take classes on the draft, and counsel men to resist enlistment. These activists connected the antidraft efforts to black self-defense. Women confronted the daily intrusions of military police doing house-to-house searches for draft evaders, so activists urged them to prepare their communities for self-defense for "when the shit hits the fan." Men with guns threatened communities, and women needed knowledge of "judo, karate, with the realization that this may not work when the man has a .38 revolver."[89]

Backlash Blues

Surveys conducted throughout the 1960s suggested that as increasing proportions of African Americans called for racial and economic justice to end the draft and stop the war, the majority of white Americans objected to their demands, even those made through nonviolent demonstrations. Although a slim majority of whites expressed some sympathy for blacks' aspirations in voting rights, the majority opposed integrated housing and "social contact" in everyday life, including in stores, restaurants, and interracial dating. Most whites insisted blacks had "looser morals" and "welcomed handouts" from the government. Overall, whites' intolerance for demonstrations rose from 51 percent disapproval in 1963 to 63 percent in 1966, with the overwhelming majority of working-class whites and white southerners expressing strong objections to blacks' "demonstrations." Three-quarters of those interviewed noted that riots "harmed the Negro cause," and many "felt crowded" by blacks' calls for equal access to all parts of American life, including jobs. Seventy percent reportedly believed "the Negro is moving too fast."[90]

In 1964, Republican presidential candidate and Arizona senator Barry Goldwater hoped to corral these opinions into momentum for his campaign, which he framed as the "white backlash" against the demands of civil rights. After the riots in Harlem, Elizabeth, Chicago, and Philadelphia, the idea of a backlash against civil rights gained momentum. Goldwater lost in a landslide, but when numerous other urban uprisings erupted the following year, including in Watts, moderate and liberal voters expressed declining sympathy and support for blacks' demands. White politicians and political consultants, columnist Tom Wicker noted, believed "that while people may talk more about Vietnam and inflation, they worry more about Negroes moving into the block, taking over their jobs, and making their streets a battleground." White politicians openly courted this "backlash vote."[91]

Over the next half-decade, harnessing the "white backlash" became a political strategy for a rising conservative movement, though Democratic candidates, too, sought to sway voters by making similar appeals to whites angered by blacks' demands for equal rights.[92] Ronald Reagan's rhetoric of "law and order" during his successful 1966 campaign for California governor drew from the language of massive resistance to school integration, voting rights, and the 1961 Freedom Riders. The violent venom of massive resistance remained alive in anti-civil-rights backlash politics. Johnson, conservative critics argued, had lost the war at home to the rioters and in Vietnam against the Viet Cong. In deft claims, 1968 presidential candidate Richard M. Nixon promised to suppress the guerillas in Harlem and in Saigon. White voters in the South and white ethnic voters in the North abandoned the Democratic Party in droves, seeing their votes as a counter to black voters. Powerful segregationist Democrat Strom Thurmond left the party for the GOP in 1964. White conservatives who abhorred the virulent displays of southern white racism and blacks' calls for civil rights equally—including conservatives like William F. Buckley, *National Review* editor and *Firing Line* host, and Tom Charles Houston, president of Young Americans for Freedom—helped reframe the overt racism of white backlash into a nationwide conservative crusade under the charge of "law and order."[93]

By early 1967, liberals and members of mainstream civil rights organizations worried that voters embraced this rhetoric in response to Black Power's call for African Americans' full participation in political power. But African Americans had witnessed "backlash" against their appeals for the right to vote and for the end to job and housing discrimination. King considered the rise of black political power and white backlash as "independent phenomena," and he "rejected common theories that one justified or propped up the other." King "described backlash as coded resistance to structural changes beyond free access to a bus or a library." The wave of backlash in the 1960s, he observed, was like the segregation laws that followed black political activism and economic independence after the end of slavery. It "served notice that white men were determined to retain tangible privilege from jobs to neighborhoods."[94] Nina Simone, who commanded considerable international attention from her music, publicly agreed that blacks' demands for freedom and political power evoked a systematic response. Backlash, she told one interviewer, arose from a historical dynamic given contemporary leverage by blacks' demands to turn their right to vote into full participation in politics. "Every time we try to get our rights and we do something that displeases [whites], they take it out on us in different ways. They may take away our jobs tomorrow to get back at us. Or they may induct a lot of guys into the Army deliberately to punish us, for whatever steps we've made to try and get some freedom. Every time we do something and they disapprove, they hit us, and it gets worse the more aggression we have, that is white backlash."[95]

African Americans from every social group pressed their claims for political rights and economic justice, though making such demands carried enormous consequences, even for the famous. Actress Eartha Kitt became involved in a number of antipoverty efforts in 1966, but she had avoided public criticism of the Vietnam War even as she saw the resources needed to end poverty drained from communities. Like King, Kitt heard young black men associate their marginal status as poor and disfranchised black men with their higher draft rates. In early 1968 she received an invitation from Lady Bird Johnson to participate in a discussion on juvenile delinquency.[96] Asked at the gathering of women what she thought about the rise in youth crime rates, Kitt responded, "You send the best of this country off to be shot and maimed. They rebel in the street. They will take pot and they will get high. They don't want to go to school because they're going to be snatched off from their mothers to be shot in Vietnam." Ignoring the immediate opprobrium in the room, Kitt continued with her assessment. Young men, she insisted, "are angry because there is a war going on that they don't understand, that they don't know why. . . . Mothers feel they raise sons and [the administration] sends them to war."[97]

A chilled silence followed Kitt's remarks, but several women quickly rebuked her. Elizabeth S. Hughes, the wife of New Jersey Democratic governor Richard J. Hughes, prefaced her reply to Kitt with the assertion that she intended to defend "the war." She argued against relating youthful "rebellion" to the administration's draft and war policies. Lady Bird Johnson, "pale, . . . her voice trembling and tears welling up in her eyes," also insisted that the war, riots, and antiwar protests were unrelated. "Just because there is a war on—and I pray there will be a just and honest peace— that still doesn't give us a free ticket not to try to work for better things such as against crime in the streets, better education, and better health for our people."[98]

Kitt's criticism of Johnson's war and its impact on antipoverty programs elicited a flood of responses in the national press from those who supported the administration and others who denounced its policies. An editorial in the *New York Times* described Kitt's remarks "as a rude confrontation with the First Lady" that "did not add significantly to the national dialogue on juvenile delinquency, the war, taxes, poverty, or race." Supporters disagreed, arguing that Kitt voiced what was "vigorously aired in homes throughout America" and she tapped into widespread anger at the Johnson administration's squandering of resources on a war "with questionable ends." Several portrayed Kitt's response as "a last resort for those who have exhausted other avenues."[99] The criticism against Kitt continued, and CBS replaced her as Catwoman on the popular TV show *Batman*. The Johnson administration launched an intensive campaign of harassment against her, similar to the government's campaign against Josephine Baker after she critiqued segregation in the early 1950s. For the next decade, Kitt found little work in the United States.[100]

As individuals and civil rights organizations faced severe consequences for denouncing the war in public forums, ordinary African Americans looked to alternative forms, including popular music, to express their dissent against the war. Until 1967, most black commercial music released by corporations did not openly address the growing antiwar movement in black America or soldiers' increasing militancy. Even as increasing numbers of black Americans questioned the war and demanded music that reflected their interests, producers of popular black music resisted. Commercial music sidestepped the debates within the civil rights movement about the war, and singles voiced a martial pride and heroic dignity even in the face of death. As riots continued and black support for the war plummeted, Eddy Giles's 1967 "While I'm Away" included the plaintive insistence "I'm fighting for my country / I'm doing the best I can." His plea typified the commercial music created to appeal to a population perceived as supportive of the war and proud of black men's presence in the integrated military.[101]

James Brown, described as the "Godfather of Soul," testified to a black America that still claimed such pride in the integrated military. Supportive of Nixon, Brown also possessed an incomparable political force among black Americans. While he supported Cold War civil rights and emphatically endorsed black economic pride and bootstrap black capitalism, he also denounced the urban uprisings. His concert in Boston was rumored to have quashed a riot in the city. While Brown worked to dampen support for rebellions in the United States, he also agreed to lend support for the war. After many black performers refused to perform for the USO, Brown put on two to three daily shows for troops when he toured Vietnam in 1968. In Long Binh, he sang "My Country 'tis of Thee" to thousands of black and white soldiers and Marines. The son of a navy veteran, Brown refrained from using the Black Power salute onstage, but he hoped his performance of "Papa's Got a Brand New Bag" prepared men for battle.[102]

Brown's USO tour commenced when black commercial music openly addressed the growing black resentment against the war. John Lee Hooker's insistence in 1968 that "[we] got so much trouble at home, we don't need to go to Vietnam" and Curtis Mayfield and the Impressions' "Don't Cry My Love" signaled the shift in popular music from support for black martial fidelity to resistance. The Impressions' "Don't Cry" featured the group's signature mix of personal dignity, social critique, and blacks' struggle for racial justice. "I'm off to war and I'm long overdue for human rights," Mayfield sings.

> I can see no reason for our fighting this time
> So many have gone
> So much wrong going here
> I pretend not to see
> But it makes me wonder,
> Everybody's free here but me.

This song and others released between 1968 and 1970 weighed the disparate claims mainstream civil rights leaders made about the opportunities in the military and the Cold War against the experiences of African American soldiers and their communities. The military understood the subversive impact of this music that called for black pride and questioned the work of killing. Such music launched riots in the rear areas of Vietnam and stoked soldiers' resistance.[103]

When Jimi Hendrix stood on the Woodstock stage dressed in fringed white leather on that hazy morning in late August 1969, his Afro held back by a blue bandana, he demonstrated the power of black public performance to rebuke a nation's violent martial history. Richie Havens launched the event with "Freedom (Motherless Child)," and Sly and the Family Stone ended their early Sunday morning set with "Stand!" Hendrix launched Sunday's performances when he and his new band took to the stage. The former paratrooper prodded the bedraggled audience to "come alive, come alive now." One of the last acts to perform after two days of drenching rain, Hendrix's new band, Gypsy Sun and Rainbows, included bassist Billy Cox, a friend Hendrix met during his year in the army. The hastily formed band started its 140-minute set with "Message to Love / Message to the Universe," which opened with a thrumming march tempo. With the old Experience recently disbanded, the Woodstock band relied primarily on Hendrix's well-known pieces from his earlier years. Late in the set, they played the new "Izabella," and Hendrix reminded the audience about the men who did the work of killing. Hendrix's guitar morphed into a machine gun and displayed the grim reality many poor young men faced:

> Izabella I'm dreamin' about ya every night
> Hey girl you know we gotta war
> Yeah, we got a war to fight.[104]

Hendrix led the band through several more songs, and he segued into an extended solo of distorted sounds that slowly shaped into the opening notes of "The Star-Spangled Banner." Dismantled and reassembled, Hendrix's chords became shrill planes, whizzing parachutes, and exploding bombs. These were the sounds he knew paratroopers heard and experienced as they fell out of planes and began their work of killing. Hendrix included distorted bars of "The Battle Hymn of the Republic" and "Dixie," two martial tunes in the nation's long race war at home that now accompanied troops in Vietnam. Then Hendrix reordered these rallying cries for America's double war into electrified shrieks of mourning and outrage. With the national anthem now reassembled into a horrific soundscape of war, Hendrix played "Taps" as an extended howl for the dead. In his sonic shredding of "The Star-Spangled Banner," it was as if he had burned the flag.[105]

As Hendrix offered an aural interrogation of the nation's master narrative of war and race embedded in the national anthem, his barrage of sound also questioned the festival's antiwar rhetoric. The former paratrooper from the 101st Airborne rarely referenced the war in Vietnam, and even when he did, his comments appeared ambiguous. "Of course, war is horrible," he observed in early 1967, "but at present it's still the only guarantee to maintain peace." His perspective was not uncommon among African American veterans who came of age in the early Cold War. Between 1967 and 1968, he did not make public remarks about the war, and his stage dedications to "soldiers fighting in Detroit" seemed mumbled afterthoughts. Yet these remarks referenced the scores of black soldiers in the stockades after they refused to spray tear gas on blacks during the riots at the 1968 Democratic National Convention.[106] By 1968, he had begun reordering the national anthem into a chaos of sound. He performed at Woodstock just three months after forty-six men in the 101st Airborne—many of them African Americans—died at Hamburger Hill. Compounding this horror, *Life* magazine's late June 1969 issue showed images of one week's combat deaths; the majority were barely nineteen years old. His brother, Leon, was then AWOL.[107] Like Hughes at Newport in 1961, Hendrix found a largely young and affluent white audience more privileged than other groups to consume leisure. "We've got a war to fight," he admonished his audience, but the "we" did not include the bedraggled listeners. Like these young men gathered in the mud, Hendrix did not want to go to war, but he understood that others did go, some because the military provided work, while others were conscripted because of the draft's racial and class inequalities. His performance was as much a critique of the thousands of young white men gathered there—many of whom were opposed to the war but whose race and class protected them from the draft—as it was a critique of the Vietnam War.[108]

Hendrix later commented on the class politics of Woodstock. In an interview after the weekend performance, noted talk show host Dick Cavett asked the musician why so few African Americans attended Woodstock. He replied that perhaps many lacked the money to travel to or pay for the show.[109] At Woodstock he aligned his music with a black protest politics that expressed the triple consciousness of black men at war. He sounded the thoughts of black men conscious of their race and class inequality, their understanding of oppressed people's global fight against colonialism, and the particular pride black people had when they served in the military. The martial precision that Hendrix infused into "Izabella" and "The Star-Spangled Banner" claimed that pride, but he also participated in a critical black performance and cultural history, as each song presented to an international audience the implosion of the mellifluous black voice acquiescing to the nation's racial inequality and U.S. foreign policy.

Along with black musicians, writers and artists associated with the Black Arts Movement allied the radical impulses of the grassroots antidraft struggles with Black Pride, Black Freedom struggles, and the Black Power movement. Black writers and artists examined "the meaning of African American popular culture and its relation to revolutionary black art" that hoped to address black pride and self-determination.[110] Amiri

Baraka and others had "an almost obsessive concern with the theorizing of the relationship of the African American artist and his or her formal practices to the black community or (nation). It was one of the distinguishing features of the [Black Arts] movement." This new art rooted itself in black vernacular, and while artists considered their work outside mass culture, they were deeply informed by its political possibilities.[111] This new generation of writers considered popular black music in particular as the location for struggle. Many Black Arts poets looked to blues and jazz as sources for their writing, but they did not overtly tie their work to contemporary commercial music. By the mid-1960s, some began to see soul as a source, too. Without ignoring its commercialism, Baraka found that black music "reflected the rising tide of the people's struggles. Martha and the Vandellas' 'Dancing in the Streets' was like our national anthem."[112] By the late 1960s, Black Arts writers addressed how their art might affect politics in their grassroots efforts. Oral performances, music festivals, and independent clubs provided new venues and opportunities for collaboration between writers and musicians. On these stages, many in abandoned buildings, or out in the streets of neighborhoods under siege because of the riots, black poets, many military veterans, considered the overlapping violences in their communities and abroad.[113]

Like the antiwar blues music of the 1950s, the Black Arts Movement produced within and in response to the experiences of black communities also spoke to, and out of, a radical perspective about black history. As poets and musicians considered "black art" and black history, they also asked how a revolutionary black art might "shove" U.S. "history off of its violent course."[114] This art with force, Larry Neal argues, arose from a "profound ethical sense that makes a Black artist question a society in which art is one thing and the actions of men [sic] another."[115] By 1966, the Black Arts Movement responded to contradictions in a black culture that had long viewed the military as critical to black masculinity and full citizenship; poets interrogated a war that required poor black men to kill in nonwhite nations.

Even as it interrogated violence, the language and imagery in Black Arts poetry, theater, and art drew on the militaristic and masculinist overtones of Black Power and Black Nationalism. Older stereotypes, especially the images of compliant blacks, gave way to a valorization of a black revolution.[116] This creative work announced itself as a new black aesthetic characterized as resistance. This militant and resistant creative activity became critical to the larger political struggles for Black Power. Poets, writers, and artists turned to the images of black resistance across space and time. Robert Hayden's "Runagate Runagate," for example, described Harriet Tubman leading slaves to freedom with a pistol in her hand: "Armed and known to be Dangerous."[117] In these revisions, poets questioned the efficacy of nonviolence when faced with bombings, fire hoses, and police dogs. At the same time, Wahneema Lubiano argues, "black feminist[s] critique[d] a black nationalist ideology" that did not adequately sever its ties to "patriarchal modes of economic, political, cultural (especially familial), and social circulations of power that mimic Euro-American modes."[118] Gwendolyn Brooks's image of a "weaponed woman" who "fights with semi-folded arms, / her strong bag, and the stiff / Frost of her face (that challenges 'when' and 'if')" imagined a radical yet nonviolent response to oppression.[119]

But many poets questioned the efficacy of wars abroad to advance black freedom struggles. Robert Hayden's haunting and graphic poem "Words in the Mourning Time" underscored this point:

> as the victories are tallied up
> with flag-draped coffins, plastic bodybags,
> what can my sorrow anger pity say
> but this, this:
> We must not be frightened nor cajoled
> into accepting evil as deliverance from evil.
> We must go on struggling to be human,
> though monsters of abstraction
> police and threaten us.[120]

For Hayden, assent to violent nationalism undermined racial justice.

In her poetry and public performances, June Jordan consistently challenged war as the path to black freedom. Jordan was one of the younger poets to participate in the Black Arts Movement. In "LBJ: Rejoinder," Jordan warned that those who waged war against people had no moral ability to critique calls for Black Power:

> He lost the peace so
> he can keep the peril he
> knows war is nothing like please.[121]

"Last Poem for a Little While" described a cityscape where statues hide the grief of the victims of American imperialism. The narrator cannot cross a bridge draped in an American flag. Instead,

Got to underslide the lying spangled banner.
. . . The massacre of sorrow songs.
Songmy. Songmy. Vietnam.
Goddamn. Vietnam.

In a reference to the myth of national regeneration and liberation born from war played out in national music, such as Julia Ward Howe's "Battle Hymn of the Republic," the narrator sits before the Thanksgiving feast and prays:

Please pass the ham.
I want to show
Vietnam how we give thanks
around here.
Pass the ham.
And wipe your fingers on the flag.[122]

Jordan's juxtaposition of national symbols—flags, memorials, and Thanksgiving—challenged an equally long national narrative of freedom made from war's destruction elsewhere.

Black Arts poets directly addressed soldiers. The Last Poets' 1970 "The Black Soldier" signaled contempt for black men who acquiesced to the draft notice—"the draftees and the volunteers"—and who chose Vietnam over the revolution in Harlem. In a parody of soldiers' cadence call, the Last Poets simultaneously parodied national pride derived from military experiences and African Americans' historical critiques of war:

Hep two left hop
I don't know what I've been told
We'll be jumping from the iron bird
Stand up and shuffle to the door.

The Poets irreverently opined,

Here's to you black soldier
fightin' in Vietnam
Helping your oppressor
oppress another man.[123]

But no one was spared from the Poets' scathing critique. The Last Poets' "When the Revolution Comes" and Gil Scott-Heron's "The Revolution Will

Not Be Televised" leveled charges of complicity and collaboration on all sides—those who conformed and those who decided to "party" instead of working for a lasting black freedom.[124] The poets heaped equal scorn on the obedient soldier and the stoned loafer.

William Patterson, former head of the Civil Rights Congress, joined this growing critique of blacks' complicity in the war's violence. In a new introduction to *We Charge Genocide*, the 1951 report he and others submitted to the United Nations on the systematic racial violence and discrimination against African Americans, Patterson noted in 1970 that "profound changes have taken place in the world since 1951," but new evidence demonstrated that "racism has grown consistently more vicious." He noted that nearly two decades later, the United Nations still refused to address the human indignity of racial inequality and violence in the United States even as it "leveled the charge of criminality at the South African Republic." For Patterson, the charges he and the committee made nearly two decades earlier had "materially enlarged," based on the reports from the civil rights commissions of the administrations of three presidents. These reports, amplified by a wide array of other statistical data and evidence, demonstrated that blacks remained systemically confined to "the squalor of slums" where discrimination, poverty, unemployment, disease, crime, and police brutality significantly shortened their life spans. He described the deaths of hundreds of black men, women, and children during the four years of urban riots in "ghettoes in which they are forced to live, [and] the use of state troopers to suppress their democratic demonstrations seeking enjoyment of the inalienable and constitutional rights" as "murderous brutality toward 'colored' citizens." The rhetoric of white supremacy had justified the violence against blacks after World War II. Now, Patterson charged, "force and violence systematically and consistently employed to quell the righteous anger of blacks is justified by calling murder an exercise of 'law and order.'" This pattern of violence in blacks' neighborhoods was "coupled with the increasing use of black nationals as armed gendarme to force America's murderous brand of democracy upon foreign peoples. Korea, Vietnam and Cambodia are proof of the last allegation." The wars in Southeast Asia and the shootings of black demonstrators in Chicago and at Jackson State University in Mississippi were "inseparably related." Young black men "determin[ed] not to accept racism or be intimidated by its force and violence" were branded criminals, just as "the 'crimes' of 'our' foreign foes are that they want control of their own destinies." In 1951,

Patterson and Robeson hoped the United Nations would take up their appeal. In 1970, Patterson harbored no such illusion. Instead, he hoped his new charge might "mobilize worldwide action against genocide."[125]

Antiwar Politics, 1968–1972

By the late 1960s, many African Americans considered electoral politics the route to change U.S. foreign policy. After Julian Bond successfully ran for state representative in Georgia as an antiwar candidate, activists determined that African Americans could elect other antiwar candidates. Many black community activists who had engaged in both antipoverty and antiwar activities a decade earlier turned to local politics to effect change in housing, schools, and employment. In many communities, including the District of Columbia, black activism shifted from the streets and storefronts to the voting booth. Elected to Congress in 1968, New York Democrat Shirley Chisholm defeated CORE activist James Farmer. She quickly became one of the most vocal antiwar critics in the House of Representatives. During her first months in office as representative from Brooklyn, she remained optimistic that Nixon would bring about "a quick end to an unjust war we had drifted into, and a redirection of our nation's wealth and energy to the attack on hunger, poverty, ignorance, and the other evils that flourish in this country."[126] Chisholm quickly discerned that Nixon did not intend to withdraw troops and instead planned to end or diminish important social and economic programs, particularly antipoverty programs, in favor of military spending.

Rather than concentrating on the administration's Vietnam agenda, Chisholm's first criticisms of Nixon's policies focused on his decision to curtail spending for social programs. While "ending the war had not been a major theme" of her campaign, her perspective shifted markedly when Nixon "announced on the same day that the United States would not be safe until we started an ABM system, and that the Head Start program in the District of Columbia was to be cut back for lack of money." In her first speech on the House floor, Chisholm vowed to vote against military spending when the Nixon administration slashed funding for social programs. Nixon's defunding of social programs and the war's escalation accelerated Chisholm's antiwar critiques.[127] From her perspective, the war in Vietnam was "neither just nor unavoidable; it was an unnecessary war into which we stumbled, led by shortsighted, stubborn men who . . . concealed their mistakes by systematically lying to the country about the nature of the war and the prospects of ending it."[128]

In late March 1969, Chisholm delivered a blistering critique of the war in her first speech on the House floor. She charged that the Nixon administration used resources for the war at the expense of antipoverty programs, and it failed to plan for an immediate end to the conflict. As she lambasted the administration's declared goal of establishing "freedom" in Southeast Asia, Chisholm also appropriated the administration's rhetoric of "order" at home. For Chisholm, such order included money for social programs in the United States:

> I am deeply disappointed at the clear evidence that the number one priority of the new administration is to buy more and more and more weapons of war, to return to the era of the Cold War and to ignore the war we must fight here, the war that is not optional. . . . Congress must respond to the mandate that the American people have clearly expressed. They have said, "End this war. Stop the waste. Stop the killing. Do something for our own people first."[129]

She vowed "to vote 'no' on every money bill that comes to the floor of the House" until the country "use[d] its strength, its tremendous resources, for people, for peace, not for profits and war. . . . Nowhere has the conflict between official policy and what the public wants been more bitter and prolonged than it has over the Southeast Asian war and its relation to domestic priorities." As cofounder of the Congressional Black Caucus, she used her high visibility to support antiwar critics. Along with Ron Dellums, a former Marine who came to Congress in 1971 as a representative from California, Chisholm sharpened her critiques of the war and support for soldiers who resisted the war.[130] And she decided to launch a bid for the Democratic presidential nomination.

Chisholm's campaign for the 1972 nomination was more than historic. As a feminist and an outspoken critic of the war and Nixon, she had the potential to reach and unite young people, progressive workers and women of all races, African Americans, and Latinos/Latinas. Since the Voting Rights Act of 1965, these groups had become active in local politics, and many had resisted their exclusion from the national electoral process. Chisholm was well aware of the daunting challenge she faced, not just from the Republican Party and the Nixon administration, but from the Right and Center factions of the Democratic Party. The powerful politicians in both parties ascribed to the doctrine of American dominance through economic and military assertiveness. Even as the Vietnam War divided Americans, the belief in American military power held many in its thrall. At the same time, many Americans believed that the social and cultural transformations taking place, especially the challenges to racial and sexual hierarchies, made the nation vulnerable to attack. Claiming to speak for the "silent majority" who ascribed to law and order at home and abroad, Nixon tied grassroots challenges to racial, class, and gender inequality with weakened national security. By implication, class, racial, and gender hierarchy and war made the nation stronger. Legal remedies, not radical or even nonviolent activism, would allow for measured change. Conservatives massaged these fears of mass and unreasonable changes in the "social fabric" and included the eroded confidence in traditional religious, military, and political leaders in a politics of coercion, fear, and secrecy. This political and rhetorical mix appeared in various combinations in the 1972 election as Nixon argued for a full use of the state to ensure "law and order" in Harlem and Saigon.[131]

Paradoxically, while the rhetoric of "law and order" persuaded Americans to vote for a president deeply invested in winning in Vietnam and suppressing dissent at home, more African Americans and women ran and won in local, state, and congressional races on the idea of political change. African Americans, many of them former community organizers, civil rights activists, and antiwar activists, won an unprecedented number of local and state offices, including in the South. Andrew Young, Yvonne Braithwaite Burke, Cardiss Collins, and Barbara Jordan joined Chisholm, Dellums, and Louis Stokes in the House of Representatives. For Chisholm, the 1972 campaign ultimately solidified her stature in the House and the party as she won 87 percent of the vote in her district. Yet the new coalition of voters that reelected Chisholm and elected others in local, state, and congressional races could not halt the rise of a New Right. While Nixon would resign nearly two years later, his "southern strategy" united disparate groups that had advocated militarism, anticommunism, and antiintegration in the 1950s into a powerful conservative movement in the 1970s that manipulated Americans' fears of communism, immigration, integration, gender equity, and workers' rights.[132]

Sing No More of War

Weeks after his reelection, Nixon abandoned his rhetoric to take immediate steps to end the Vietnam War. In mid-December, he launched a brutal weeklong bombing campaign. During these "Christmas Bombings," U.S. pilots flew more than 4,000 sorties over Hanoi and Haiphong; nearly a quarter of these raids were carried out by B-52 bombers. Targeted at civilian population centers of North Vietnam, the relentless bombardment shocked supporters and critics of the war alike. And Nixon's decision to escalate and expand the war into Cambodia and Laos elicited a new wave of antiwar activism.

Diverse communities who opposed the war considered Nixon's second inauguration an opportunity to protest both the war and his presidency. Energized by the horrible bombings, an interracial peace effort emerged. Black congregations offered their buildings and members' homes to house antiwar demonstrators. The Metropolitan African Methodist Episcopal Church—the oldest AME church in Washington, D.C.—became a "mini-Pentagon for peace" as its members trained others in tactics of nonviolent protest.[133] On Nixon's inauguration day, a diverse crowd of 60,000 arrived in Washington, D.C., prepared to protest.

June Jordan re-created this broad-based public outrage over Nixon's actions and reelection in a poem that addressed jazz singer Ethel Ennis, who sang the national anthem at the president's inauguration. Jordan's "Poem to My Sister, Ethel Ennis, Who Sang 'The Star-Spangled Banner' at the Second Inauguration of Richard Milhous Nixon, January 20, 1973," signified on Ennis's performance of the national anthem, and she rebuked the horrific December bombing campaign.

> on his 47th inauguration of the killer king
> my sister what is this song
> you have chosen to sing?
> *and the rockets' red glare*
> *the bombs bursting in air*
> my sister
> what is your song to a flag?[134]

Describing Nixon's decision to bomb Cambodia "homicidal holiday shit" aimed at women and children, Jordan delivered a series of percussive rebukes to Ennis:

can you see
my sister
is the night
and the red glaring blood clear at last
say
can you see
my sister
and sing no more of war.[135]

Jordan's "To Ethel Ennis" simultaneously questioned blacks' complicity in and support for war, whether as soldiers, artists, or voters. After more than half a century of demanding "the right to fight," Jordan's poetic harangue drew its righteous tone from people who understood that while they struggled for their own freedom, they were also compelled to turn their collective power to demand justice for others. Speaking out against war had become a fundamental part of the struggle for racial justice. And as they struggled for this justice, they would "*sing no more of war.*"

An

EPILOGUE

about the United States and Wars in Medias Res

Live from the Front Lines

Military Policy and Soldiers' Rap from Iraq

Bernice Murray watched her grandson Brad Gaskins "strut inside New Hope Baptist Church" in East Orange, New Jersey, wearing his new green uniform. The army recruiter told him the military offered a career, a chance to help his family, and an opportunity to "serve his country." Assigned to the 10th Mountain Division, 2nd Brigade, Gaskins left for Kosovo in 1999. By April 2003, newly promoted Sergeant Gaskins arrived in Iraq just after the "shock and awe" bombing campaign. As the Bush administration declared "Mission Accomplished," soldiers bulldozed the badly decomposed Iraqi bodies into mass graves and then continued the war that had not ended. Gaskins returned to New York in late 2004, and within nine months his division deployed to Iraq as waves of violence surged through the cities. Gaskins's squad searched for and dismantled the improvised explosive devices (IEDs). Sometimes soldiers died, and many Iraqis, including children, were blown up. In early 2006 his unit returned to Fort Drum, New York, where he prepared for another deployment in the spring. By then, he could not sleep. His head reverberated with the chatter of boots and the click of the safety on his M-16. He repeatedly recalled what the children wore before they died. As his distress increased, he hit Amber Gaskins, his wife, and he threatened to kill her. Alarmed and fearful the army might send him back to Iraq, his family helped him go AWOL in 2007.[1]

Demonstration organized by antiwar organizations ANSWER and United for Peace and Justice, October 25, 2003, Washington, D.C., drew tens of thousands of participants who protested the U.S. war and the occupation of Iraq. This demonstration attracted a visible and vocal population of veterans and families with soldiers in Iraq. © Eleanor Bentall/Corbis.

Despite the Bush administration's promise of swift victory, the U.S. wars in Afghanistan and Iraq are now two of the longest American wars fought by a volunteer military. There are stark differences between these wars and the draft war in Vietnam, but U.S. officials have drawn comparisons between the wars, both to dispel criticisms of the new wars and to lure Americans' support. According to Christian G. Appy, "American officials and policy makers in both wars used broad, abstract threats (global Communism/global terrorism) to justify wars against forces that posed no direct challenge to U.S. security." These officials created "lies and distortions (the Gulf of Tonkin incident/weapons of mass destruction) as pretexts for war," and they made "routine claims of progress in the face of ongoing resistance." And, he notes, the United States has sent a largely working-class military.[2] But the Pentagon has sent a very different volunteer military to these recent wars, one staffed by volunteers in units with significant populations of African Americans, Latinos, and women of all races for whom the military has become their career.

Though enlistment numbers for African Americans rose and fell over the past four decades of successive recessions and wars, on the eve of the Iraq invasion in 2003, blacks comprised more than 25 percent of the overall military force, nearly twice their portion of the U.S. population overall. As the military shifted to diminished occupations and covert wars between 1975 and 1991, the need for volunteers contracted, but African American enlistment rates remained high. When the military downsized in the mid-1980s, and again after the 1992 Gulf War, blacks shifted to reserve and National Guard units. Enlistment rates for blacks in the active-duty military rose again during the erratic economy of the next decade, then fell in response to the tight labor market in the late 1990s. Their volunteer rates rose sharply with the demand for troops in Bosnia and the recession in 2000. By then, African Americans made up slightly more than 31 percent of the military, but both the recession in the first year of the new century and recruitment for the war in Iraq increased the pace of their enlistments.[3]

African Americans have not only provided a disproportionate portion of the army's foot soldiers, but they have served as architects of these new wars. As chairman of the Joint Chiefs of Staff, General Colin Powell shaped the military strategy against the Iraqi army in the Persian Gulf War of 1991. Calling for a massive and decisive force, Powell's "short war" left Saddam Hussein in power. Nonetheless, Powell articulated future criteria for the military's "efficient and decisive action" in a war, criteria that quickly became known as the Powell Doctrine. Military action, he argued, should be used only as a last resort and only if the United States faced a clear risk to its national security; force, when used, should be overwhelming and disproportionate to the force used by the enemy; there must be strong support for the campaign by the general public; and there must be a clear exit strategy from the conflict in which the military is engaged. Though President George W. Bush's 2002 war in Iraq met only one of the criteria—disproportionate force—Colin Powell, now secretary of state, invoked this plan. Drawing on their considerable stature and presentation of "irrefutable" evidence, both Powell and national security advisor Condoleezza Rice attempted to assure a very skeptical America that al-Qaeda in Iraq had planned the horrific bombing of the World Trade buildings in 2001 and Saddam Hussein had amassed "weapons of mass destruction" that now posed a grave threat to U.S. security. Millions around the world questioned this link, since Osama bin Laden, the mastermind of 9/11, was believed to be in Afghanistan. Nonetheless, only a minority of Americans disapproved of the war in Iraq. The Bush administration sent a comparably smaller cadre of troops into Afghanistan and launched its mass invasion of Iraq.[4]

Although volunteer rates for blacks in the military rose after 2002, nearly twice as many—close to 59 percent—disapproved of the war, more than any other group in the United States. Since the 1960s, the majority of African Americans have typically objected to war as a way to resolve international conflicts. Regardless of class, gender, age, or region, black Americans have not supported invasions of other nations. And high percentages have expressed extreme skepticism when the United States has invaded small, nonwhite nations.[5] Harlem resident Dolores Jackson drew from a history of African Americans' dissent expressed since the Korean and Vietnam wars when she asked, "Why should African Americans fight Iraqis? They never did anything to me, or mine." Despite Powell's and Rice's testimony under oath, most blacks did not think Iraq was responsible for the attacks on the World Trade Center. Instead, they believe the president went to war for oil; he went to war to upstage his father. In the disdain for the war in Iraq, African Americans expressed their overall disapproval of the president. He suppressed the black vote and stole two elections; his war and "cowboy demeanor" damaged American prestige abroad. African Americans considered his foreign and domestic policies as inimical to their values and indifferent to America's needs.[6] Informed by the Bush administration's failures in Louisiana and Mississippi after Hurricane Katrina and the news from family on the front lines, by 2006 the percentage of African Americans opposed to these wars climbed to 85 percent, a full 25 percent higher than any other group in the nation.

African Americans across all social groups have expressed a diverse and widespread dissent. Black journalists in mainstream and online journals have written extensively against the war. In contrast to the overwhelming support from representatives in the House and Senate, all but four of thirty-one African American Democrats voted against the 2002 Iraq War Resolution that allowed the president power to attack Iraq unilaterally. Congresswomen Barbara Lee (D-California) and Maxine Waters (D-California) have been the most vocal antiwar opponents in the House. At the start of the war in Iraq, Lee proposed an alternative resolution calling for continued support for the efforts of the United Nations. In music and print and on the World Wide Web, African Americans have provided alternative information to the prowar mainstream media and agitated against the war. Across the media, including websites like Root.com and Salon.com, African Americans have questioned the moral and ethical reasons for the nation's use of such overpowering military aggression to encourage democracy in Iraq and Afghanistan. They have asked, What are America's real intentions? Why did the United States fail to stop genocide in Rwanda or make a vital difference in Haiti and Sudan? Through numerous blogs, African Americans have helped organize and sustain a virtual antiwar movement. Though generally supportive of President Barack Obama, increasing numbers of African Americans have criticized his escalation of the war in Afghanistan.[7] In the face of their resistance to these wars, why has the all-volunteer military continued to attract African Americans?

African Americans have historically enlisted and reenlisted at high rates, not because of any oversized sense of nationalism or patriotism, but because the military remains a steady job. Since the Vietnam War, the armed forces have served as a de facto jobs program for black Americans and a symbol of a gain in their long struggle for full citizenship. In a postindustrial economy of the late twentieth century, the military has provided steady work and important benefits, including health care, child care, and education. For increasing numbers of black immigrants, military service has provided a step toward legal citizenship. Dispossessed from the machines for a peace economy, black people remain—as Lucius Brockway told the Narrator in Ralph Ellison's *Invisible Man*—"the machines inside the machines." Like their grandfathers and their fathers in the Cold War military, young blacks serve as the machines inside the machines of the "War against Terror." In a decade when few decent jobs are available to working-class Americans, the military's promises of decent entry pay, bonuses, job training, and financial assistance for college seem remarkable. For many working-class blacks in the twenty-first century, the military remains one of the most important—for many the *only*—step onto the economic ladder. Despite the protracted wars, many have stayed in the military to sustain some economic equilibrium.

The military has touted its heterogeneity to working-class blacks *because* it perceives them as living on the fringes of middle-class mobility. The volunteer military emerged as much in response to the availability of large numbers of economically vulnerable men and women as it did in response to the nation's discontent with the draft during the Vietnam War. The racial diversity of the military reflects the continued economic vulnerability that working-class blacks and Latinos have faced in America. The generation of African Americans now in the military has been at the epicenter of a profound loss of manufacturing and service sector jobs. After some initial gains in the tight labor market of the mid-1990s, increasing numbers of African Americans live in neighborhoods, attend schools, and participate in sports and leisure that are profoundly segregated. Unable to afford or be prepared for college, many of these young men and women have found few options beyond low-wage employment.[8] Some are children of veterans and active-duty military, so enlistment has provided a familiar, even expected path toward economic independence. Even during months when the military missed its monthly recruitment quotas, it neither pursued nor desired the poorest of the poor. This accounts, then, for the still-high unemployment rate among black and Latino men and the high number of these men with high school diplomas who volunteer for the military.[9]

Despite a worsened economy since 2001, black men and women have shown their skepticism about the invasion of Iraq and Afghanistan in their defection from the military. In 2000, African Americans made up 31.3 percent of the army, and they comprised 14.6 percent of the air force, 16.1 percent of the Marines, and 16.3 percent of the navy. Between 2000 and 2005, blacks' enlistments in the military services declined by 40 percent, lowering the overall presence of blacks in the military to 25 percent. By the end of 2006, blacks' presence fell to 19.25 percent; by 2008, black enlistment rates fell another 20 percent. Despite the perilous streets of many black neighborhoods, potential recruits expressed no interest in "going overseas with guns and fighting other people's wars."[10] And despite the limited job opportunities in many sectors of the labor market, many African Americans with high school diplomas saw no benefits in a military bogged down by two protracted wars.

Observers insist that the declines in African Americans' enlistment and reenlistment rates were attributable to the conflicts in Iraq and Afghanistan, not the military more generally.[11] Recruiters grew frustrated as counter-recruiters—many veterans—and parents, especially mothers, actively *discouraged* teenagers and young adults from enlisting. Departing from post-9/11 ads that emphasized patriotism and national sacrifice, the army launched new ads that portrayed a young black man begging his mother to listen while he explained the army's merits. In the summer of 2007, the army offered $20,000 signing bonuses to potential recruits if they enlisted before the end of September.[12] But a recession became the recruiters' best marketing tool, including among African Americans. With employment slack elsewhere, all active-duty and reserve forces met or exceeded their recruitment goals by late 2008. The army met its quota during the last four months of the year. As it now has waiting lists, "the

Army hopes to decrease its roster of less qualified applicants" and attract younger, smarter men and women who have postponed going to college or cannot find other work.[13]

Despite the fluctuating enlistments, military analysts remain watchful of black casualty rates and combat participation. During Vietnam, blacks' concentration in combat positions and their high casualty rate between 1966 and 1968 created a political backlash. In these new wars, analysts insist that fewer blacks serve in frontline troops and fewer are killed in combat. They have compared the 2006 combat fatality rate of 9 percent for blacks to the murder rate of young black men in Philadelphia, which was at 11 percent. In other words, black men have a better chance of survival in Baghdad. Making meaning from such claims is disingenuous, as the overall U.S. military casualty rate doubled between late 2006 and mid-2007. And these claims ignore the high casualty rate of black women, which reached 30 percent in 2006 even as the military claimed few women were in combat units. The military has not released complete fatality rates since 2006. Moreover, the number of wounded, including black wounded, remains relatively high. More soldiers are treated, perhaps for the rest of their lives, for amputations and other catastrophic injuries. The repeated deployments, the widely used stop-loss policy, the intense urban fighting that has largely targeted civilians, and the rise of an invisible insurgency precipitated by American military policy have produced untold stress on soldiers and, eventually, on their families. Increasing numbers of troops meet the criteria for depression, anxiety, or post-traumatic stress disorder (PTSD). Ignoring the complex of fatalities, high numbers of wounded, high civilian casualty rates in Iraq and Afghanistan, and PTSD leads to misapprehension of the overall devastation of this war on African Americans.[14]

Women make up more than 15 percent of the services, and 11 percent have served in Iraq and Afghanistan. African American women serve in greater numbers, comprising 20 percent of women in uniform (25 percent in the army). By 2010, more than 121 women have died in combat, and one-third—30 percent—were women of color. Hundreds have been wounded, and nearly as many women have suffered from PTSD. None of these female soldiers served in an official combat unit but in units attached to combat troops, where they have patrolled streets and participated in house-to-house raids. Most of the women killed or injured were harmed by IEDs while out on patrol, but a significant proportion died under mysterious circumstances. Reports indicate that one in three women in the military have experienced sexual assault; the numbers are higher in Iraq and Af-ghanistan. Pentagon and congressional officials agree that women face as great a danger from their male comrades as they do from battle. Yet, the unwillingness to acknowledge women's presence in combat roles has had equally devastating consequences. Because the military has not officially recognized women's combat roles, which are described as participation in "irregular warfare," women have been denied a range of services given to men in combat, including combat pay and access to recognition and pro-motions for combat service. Many women have found it difficult to receive support and care for combat-related illnesses and traumas.[15]

"Fuck 'em"

While the full histories of these wars have yet to be written, accounts from the military and political analysts, war zone intellectuals, and soldiers themselves, including black soldiers' rap from the front lines, tell a story of American hubris that has created a calamity of epic proportions. Most, if not all, American wars since World War II have been chaotic and marked by extreme and disproportionate violence, but no previous war has pro-duced such an outpouring of information comparable to that from sol-diers about their participation in the indiscriminate violence that became commonplace in Iraq. Strained by more than eight years of combat in two wars, soldiers have been ordered to engage in terror in the war on terror that has ultimately sparked a fierce counterinsurgency and has drawn ex-tremists from other countries.

Since 2003, soldiers have been engaged in the tactics of "Fuck 'em," a military command widely used in Iraq for troops to beat, assault, shame, and use weapons to frighten Iraqis. For many black and Latino soldiers, these tactics feel alarmingly familiar. Indeed, police have used these tac-tics in urban neighborhoods where they have confronted blacks and Lati-nos or kept them under surveillance on a regular basis.[16] Trained by the military, Los Angeles police began using these aggressive tactics in 1966. Conceived in 1966 as paramilitary units to combat radicals, these counter-insurgency units then focused on poor black and Latino neighborhoods perceived as loci of gang and drug activities. Over the next decades, military personnel trained urban SWAT (Special Weapons and Tactics) teams. After 1990, these units became part of everyday policing in many cities, and since 2003, these units have targeted young men considered gang members. More recently, police have included suspected radicals and terrorists, including African American Muslims. Supplied by the Department of Defense, these units have used combat helicopters, automatic assault rifles, armored personnel carriers, military-inspired "blunt trauma" projectiles, and military-trained attack dogs. In communities identified as aiding and abetting suspects, police patrols have used blanket warrants and regularly cordoned off black and Latino neighborhoods, forced young men to the ground, and ran warrant checks. As police became trained and equipped like the military, their use of deadly force, indiscriminate attacks on neighborhoods, and false arrests increased dramatically. Ron Hampton, who served as executive director of the National Black Police Association, argued that by the 1990s — before the wars in Iraq and Afghanistan — "policing [had become] a war. This aggressive, military-style policing is misguided policy, misguided political leadership, and misguided police leadership."[17] First trained by the military, these urban police forces began to train the military. These practices in Iraq, then, did not emerge in the "fog of war" but are a deliberate export of U.S. urban policing.

African American soldiers and Marines, many from neighborhoods that resemble war zones, have both witnessed and participated in the military's systemic use of urban tactics in Iraqi prisons and communities. The beatings and other abuses at Abu Ghraib—the big prison west of Baghdad— were part of the army's "missteps."[18] Javal Davis was a reservist in the 372nd MPs, perhaps one of the most diverse units in the army. African Americans, Asian Americans, Latinos, and women of all races served in the unit. Assigned to "Ghetto Abu," each night Davis helped coordinate the music— from rap and country to Britney Spears—used to terrorize prisoners. Commanders told Davis and the other soldiers that loud music and other forms of torture "softened them up" for questioning and "saved American lives." He helped with the water torture and helped elevate the noise levels. "Make hell for them," he thought. Still, Davis wondered, "what's with all the nakedness?" Along with many other soldiers, Davis took pictures of the naked prisoners and emailed them to others. He pummeled the prisoners and "found that whaling on men toward whom he had no personal animus could work him into a mounting, generalized rage." He did not work alone or on his own initiative, but the army's investigation never went beyond a few soldiers who took pictures on the night shifts. Photographs that captured the systematic torture of prisoners were reframed as pornography. Davis, six other low-enlisted soldiers, and one officer were charged with and convicted of violating the Geneva Conventions.[19]

Yet the policy of "fuck 'em" continued, and troops in the First Cavalry

Division followed it as they arrived in Sadr City in April 2004. This impoverished Shiite enclave on the eastern edge of Baghdad is the size of the Bronx. Days after the division's arrival, units encountered the city's Mahdi Army. Eight soldiers were killed and fifty-one were wounded. Hundreds of Iraqi civilians and soldiers were killed. Soldiers heard the daily command from senior officers and NCOs: Go "fuck 'em," because "it's war, ain't no rules here." At checkpoints, on patrols, and during home invasions, troops either did not have or ignored the "rules of engagement." Over the next two years, commanders and units tolerated, first, "acts of terror" against and, then, open war on all Iraqis. These tactics, an unwarranted war, IEDs, and an "elusive enemy" precipitated a widespread attitude among American troops that "a dead Iraqi is just another dead Iraqi." Many soldiers came to believe that all Arabs were enemies, and "haji," which denotes someone who has made the pilgrimage to Mecca, was "used in the same way 'gook' was used in Vietnam." They also use terms like "camel jockeys, Jihad Johnny," and "sand nigger." In Afghanistan, troops use "raghead." Such terms, soldiers acknowledge, "dehumanize the enemy."[20]

This racialism, attitudes, fears, and training have fueled the military's endless raids into the homes and compounds of Iraqi civilians. Patrols arrived at an address, believing they would find nothing, but they blew out the doors with missiles, held the families at gunpoint, and destroyed the households. Some commanders reportedly ordered troops to plant evidence, especially when they accidentally killed women and children. Since most soldiers were unable to communicate with Iraqis, checkpoints and neighborhood patrols became deadly encounters between well-armed soldiers and unarmed civilians. By late 2004, killing unarmed civilians became common and accepted. Without clear rules of engagement and with policy that differed "from service to service, base to base, and year to year," soldiers made split-second decisions and decided to shoot to kill. Even as Abu Ghraib taught them that the lowest-ranked soldiers were also the most vulnerable, the "prevailing attitude among them was 'better to be tried by twelve men than carried by six.'" Despite several high-profile investigations, few soldiers have experienced a court-martial for killing civilians.[21]

Rap in Iraq

Soldiers and Marines have not been silent about military tactics that make them scapegoats for the indiscriminate violence that formed the heart of

U.S. policies in Iraq. These wars stand as the most-chronicled by soldiers and Marines on the front lines, but besides soldiers' rap CDs, few African Americans in the military have produced memoirs or films about the war.[22] Despite the paucity of wartime storytelling produced by African Americans overall, rap music created by soldiers and Marines on the front lines has attempted to understand their "work of killing." With its fractured and reassembled sounds, its sampling, and its social defiance, rap is the quintessential music to critique life lived in what rap historian Jeff Chang describes as a "locked down" and militarized nation.[23] Rap about the front lines replaces the sonic barrage and drama of urban life with the soundscape and mayhem of war—gunfire, exploding IEDs, the drone of helicopters, screaming civilians, and the harsh commands. Rap, like other American music, has been pervasive in these wars. It has been used to terrorize prisoners and "pump up" troops for patrols. Streaming from Humvees and played on ipods, rap turns a soldier's fear into rage, and it encourages lethal force to become reflexive.

Yet black soldiers' rap also has become the ideal music to interrogate the American war in Iraq. Ordered to "hunt" terrorists and "soften them up," these soldiers have ruminated about military policy that required *them* to inflict a horrific terror that had its origins in American cities and prisons. Soldiers are acutely aware of the pervasiveness of rap, that it has a peculiar "Americanness" to it even as it is now heard around the world, and its presence in these wars allows them to consider the differences and similarities between the "slaughter" in the streets from Compton to Baghdad.[24] For troops, rap about Iraq arises from the silences about the common terrorized experiences of nonwhite lives in various war zones, urban and military, and their own participation in and experiences of this indiscriminate violence. What is a soldier's duty, they ask, "when there ain't no rules," when

> I hear his momma cryin'
> But I still scream fuckem
> Unload my magazine on this buster
> That's how I say fuckem
> You know we don't trust em
> Let them all lie dead in a dirt bed
> With a bullet in his head.[25]

Soldiers' frontline hip hop re-creates war's tones and the vicious lyrics question its legality, but it simultaneously articulates the shared experiences of hypermasculinity, fear, and rage. From their low rank, to the violence and torture they inflict, to the suppression of their individual morality for the good of the unit, troops repeat "fuck 'em" to highlight their paradoxical role as subjugated soldiers and subjugators of the "enemy." In Iraq, the orders to "soften up prisoners" and harass civilians frequently come from commanders who were trained by or worked as civilian police. In Iraq, black soldiers have re-appropriated the "fuck 'em" used by SWAT teams—first chronicled in rap of the early 1990s—that perceived them as criminals in America but now reposition their actions as men "doing a soldier's duty." At the same time, these soldiers use the term to address one another, their commanders, and Iraqis of unequal power, including women and children. Did these rap tracks reveal soldiers' fantasies or were they unofficial after-action reports? The men have insisted that they put their anger into the lyrics and not toward the people they encountered while on patrol, but official reports and anecdotal evidence now reveal the widespread and indiscriminate violence used against Iraqi civilians. Some soldiers insisted that making music with such violent lyrics calmed them. For others, the lyrics articulated ideas and emotions they were unable to express to family and friends "back home."[26]

As they recite their experiences with and fantasies about killing, soldiers also interrogate the vocabulary of hip hop that has variously reviled, commodified, and glorified violence. Since its inception, hip hop has been critically engaged with the multimedia fascination of war, especially war against "the other." Soldiers' rap draws on the violent and graphic language of popular rap; it also mines a rap activism ignored by consumers and critics.[27] Crafted in the aftermath of battle, in the tedium of patrols, and in the wake of dead "brothers and sisters in arms," rap on the front lines has much in common with literature produced in response to modern war—it both sympathizes with the civilians who are killed and maimed and identifies with the soldiers who have killed and harmed. These rap performances, too, appear in the interstices between the antiwar critiques in soldiers' own communities and the values of unit cohesion that yield to the military's demand that they remain silent about the tactics of killing. These rap performances, then, provide an anti-soundtrack to a nation that has used music to mediate its antiwar sentiments and its collective acceptance of the violence in Iraq, whether against civilians or against soldiers.

Even as black soldiers and Marines translate their experiences with war into sound and language that others might understand, they do not provide conclusions about why they have volunteered for the military in disproportionate numbers. In the mid-twentieth century, African Americans embraced "the right to fight" as an effort to claim full citizenship. In the twenty-first century, they serve as architects of these wars, as policymakers, dissenters, and proud or reluctant soldiers. The carnage imagined and recounted in rap from the front lines demands that the nation reckon with the consequences when it asks some people to do the work of killing for others. Despite their silence on their own motivations for joining the military, African Americans soldiers' rap demands that the nation grapple with why poor young people turn to the military, especially during times of war, for steady work and health care. And they demand that we understand the implications of their participation in an American nationalism hell-bent on eradicating terrorism abroad through tactics long used in Compton. These soldiers and Marines craft their rap as they patrol the streets, their voices part of the din and the chaos. In their recitation of graphic, violent, and nasty language about the work of war, they challenge a military rhetoric that this war is peace and soldiers with M-16s are its ambassadors out to "win hearts and minds."[28] Walking point and chanting, they offer a counterpoint.

Notes

Introduction

1. Edwin Starr, "War" (MOT-464, 1970); U.S. National Advisory Commission on Civil Disorders, *Report of the National Advisory Commission on Civil Disorders* (New York: Dutton, 1968), 109–12, 229–32; L. Deckle McLean, "The Black Man and the Draft," *Ebony*, August 1968, 61; Morris J. MacGregor, *Integration of the Armed Services, 1940–1965* (Washington, D.C.: Center of Military History, 1981).

2. The Temptations first recorded "War!," written by Norman Whitfield, a veteran, and Barrett Strong, as a salve to audiences demanding that Motown address the Vietnam War, but the company refused to release it as a single out of a fear that it might alienate fans who supported the war. The Funk Brothers, many of whom were veterans, provided the distinctive rhythm for Starr's version. See Temptations, "War," *Psychedelic Shack* (GS947, 1970), and Starr, "War." On Motown's concerns, see Suzanne E. Smith, *Dancing in the Street: Motown and the Cultural Politics of Detroit* (Cambridge: Harvard University Press, 1999), 235–36. On Motown's general process of "do-overs," see Brian Ward, *Just My Soul Responding: Rhythm and Blues, Black Consciousness, and Race Relations* (Berkeley: University of California Press, 1998), 376.

3. "Machine Gun," *Band of Gypsys* (Columbia, 1970). Discussions of Hendrix's guitar techniques usually focus on sexual imagery and ignore his myriad representations of war's violence. See Steve Waksman, *Instruments of Desire: The Electric Guitar and the Shaping of Musical Experience* (Cambridge: Harvard University Press, 1999), 167–206.

4. Charles R. Cross, *Room Full of Mirrors: A Biography of Jimi Hendrix* (New York: Hyperion, 2005), 82–89; "Machine Gun," *Band of Gypsys*; David Cortright, *Soldiers in Revolt: GI Resistance during the Vietnam War* (1975; reprint, Chicago: Haymarket Press, 2005), 74–75, 88–89.

5. Jimi Hendrix, *Jimi Hendrix Live at Woodstock* (Seattle: Hal Leonard, 1995), 115. For a discussion of the long history of America's "regenerative militarism," see Jackson Lears, *Rebirth of a Nation: The Making of Modern America, 1877–1920* (New York: Harper, 2009), 1–11, and Stephen E. Feinberg, "Randomization and Social Affairs: The 1970 Draft Lottery," *Science* 22 (January 1971): 255–61.

6. Anders Stephanson, *Manifest Destiny: American Expansion and the Empire of Right* (New York: Hill and Wang, 1996); Clive Webb, *Rabble Rousers: The American Far Right in the Civil Rights Era* (Athens: University of Georgia Press, 2010).

7. Scholarship on race and war generally includes David J. Silbey, *A War of Frontier and Empire: The Philippine-American War, 1899–1902* (New York: Hill and Wang, 2008), and John Dower, *War without Mercy: Race and Power in the Pacific War* (New York: Pantheon, 1986). On African Americans in the military, see Gerald Astor, *The Right to Fight: A History of African Americans in the Military* (New York: Da Capo Press, 2001); Charles C. Moskos and John Sibley Butler, *All That We Can Be* (New York: Basic Books, 1997); and Bernard C. Nalty, *Strength for the Fight: A History of Black Americans in the Military* (New York: Free Press, 1986). The literature on Native Americans and the military includes Dennis Banks, *Ojibwa Warrior: Dennis Banks and the American Indian Movement* (Norman: University of Oklahoma Press, 2004); Al Carroll, *"Medicine Bags and Dog Tags": American Indian Veterans from Colonial Times to the Second Iraq War* (Lincoln: University of Nebraska Press, 2008); and Paul C. Rosier, *Serving Their Country: American Indian Politics and Patriotism in the Twentieth Century* (Cambridge: Harvard University Press, 2009). On Japanese Americans, see Eric L. Muller, *Free to Die for Their Country: The Story of the Japanese Draft Resisters in World War II* (Chicago: University of Chicago Press, 2001). The recent history of Latinos in the military includes Ernesto Cien-Fuegos, "La Raza: The 'Grunts' of the U.S. Armed Forces," *La Voz de Aztlan*, September 9, 2002, www.aztlan.net/grunts.htm (accessed November 15, 2010); Maggie Rivas-Rodriquez and Emilio Zamora, eds., *Beyond the Latino World War II Hero: The Social and Political Legacy of a Generation* (Austin: University of Texas Press, 2009); Lorena Oropeza, *¡Raza Si! ¡Guerra No!: Chicano Protest and Patriotism during the Viet Nam War Era* (Berkeley: University of California Press, 2005); and David L. Leal, "It's Not Just a Job: Military Service and Latino Political Participation," *Political Behavior* 21 (June 1999): 153–74.

8. Mae M. Ngai, *Impossible Subjects: Illegal Aliens and the Making of Modern America* (Princeton: Princeton University Press, 2004), 7.

9. Karl Jacoby, *Shadows at Dawn: A Borderlands Massacre and the Violence of History* (New York: Penguin, 2008); Dower, *War without Mercy*; Mary A. Renda, *Taking Haiti: Military Occupation and the Culture of U.S. Imperialism* (Chapel Hill: University of North Carolina Press, 2001); Ronald Takaki, *Double Victory: A Multicultural History of America in World War II* (Boston: Little, Brown, 2000). On race and imperial rule, see Ann Laura Stoler, "Tense and Tender Ties: The Politics of Comparison in North American History and (Post) Colonial Studies," in *Haunted by Empire: Geographies of Intimacy in North American History*, ed. Ann Laura Stoler (Durham: Duke University Press, 2006), and Ann Laura Stoler, *Carnal Knowledge and Imperial Rule: Race and the Intimate in Colonial Rule*, 2nd ed. (Berkeley: University of California Press, 2010).

10. Over the past decade, new studies about the participation of Mexican Americans, Puerto Ricans, Native Americans, Japanese Americans, and other nonwhite groups in the military have emerged. These histories demonstrate experiences different from and similar to those of African Americans in the military, and they raise questions different from and similar to those that I have raised in this book. While a history of how these groups' understandings of military service and citizenship shaped expanding civil rights and antiwar movements deserves its own study, wherever possible, I note the similarities of experiences, the parallel efforts to combat racial inequality in the military, and the cross-fertilization between each group's civil rights and antiwar activism. See Banks, *Ojibwa Warrior*; Carroll, *"Medicine Bags and Dog Tags"*; Rosier, *Serving*

Their Country; and Muller, *Free to Die for Their Country*. The recent history of Latinos in the military includes Cien-Fuegos, "La Raza"; Rivas-Rodriquez and Zamora, *Beyond the Latino World War II Hero*; Oropeza, *¡Raza Sí! ¡Guerra No!*; and Leal, "It's Not Just a Job," 153–74.

11. Mary L. Dudziak, *Cold War Civil Rights: Race and the Image of American Democracy* (Princeton: Princeton University Press, 2000), 79–90; Thomas Borstelmann, *The Cold War and the Color Line: American Race Relations in the Global Arena* (Cambridge: Harvard University Press, 2001); Carol Anderson, *Eyes off the Prize: The United Nations and the African American Struggle for Human Rights, 1944–1955* (New York: Cambridge University Press, 2003).

12. Melani McAlister, *Epic Encounters: Culture, Media, and U.S. Interests in the Middle East, 1945–2000* (Berkeley: University of California Press, 2001), 123.

13. Works that consider anticolonialism and militarism after World War II include Penny M. Von Eschen, *Race against Empire: Black Americans and Anticolonialism, 1937–1957* (Ithaca: Cornell University Press, 1997), 109–21; Nikhil Pal Singh, *Black Is a Country: Race and the Unfinished Struggle for Democracy* (Cambridge: Harvard University Press, 2004); Brenda Gayle Plummer, *Rising Wind: Black Americans and U.S. Foreign Affairs, 1935–1960* (Chapel Hill: University of North Carolina Press, 1996); James Forman, *The Making of Black Revolutionaries* (New York: Macmillan, 1972); and Timothy B. Tyson, *Radio Free Dixie: Robert F. Williams and the Roots of Black Power* (Chapel Hill: University of North Carolina Press, 1999), 26–53.

14. Nalty, *Strength for the Fight*; Ulysses Lee, *The Employment of Negro Troops* (Washington, D.C.: Office of the Chief of Military History, 1966).

15. Willard B. Gatewood Jr., *Black Americans and the White Man's Burden, 1898–1903* (Urbana: University of Illinois Press, 1975); Willard B. Gatewood Jr., *"Smoked Yankees" and the Struggle for Empire: Letters from Negro Soldiers, 1898–1902* (Urbana: University of Illinois Press, 1971); Theodore Roosevelt, *The Rough Riders: An Autobiography* (New York: Library of America, 2004), 144–45.

16. W. E. B. Du Bois, "Close Ranks," *Crisis* 16 (July 1918): 111; Adriane Lentz-Smith, *Freedom Struggles: African Americans and World War I* (Cambridge: Harvard University Press, 2009); Richard Slotkin, *Lost Battalions: The Great War and the Crisis of American Nationality* (New York: Henry Holt, 2005); Stephen L. Harris, *Harlem's Hell Fighters: The African-American 369th Infantry in World War I* (Washington, D.C.: Brassey's, 2003).

17. Langston Hughes, "Jim Crow's Last Stand," in *The Collected Poems of Langston Hughes*, ed. Arnold Rampersad (New York: Knopf, 1994), 299; Daniel Kryder, *Divided Arsenal: Race and the American State during World War II* (New York: Cambridge University Press, 2000); Philip A. Klinkner, *The Unsteady March: The Rise and Decline of Racial Equality in America* (Chicago: University of Chicago Press, 1999), 161–201; Joyce Thomas, "The 'Double V' Was for Victory: The Black Soldiers, the Black Protest, and World War II" (Ph.D. diss., Ohio State University, 1993).

18. "Draft Exemption on Segregation Grounds Denied," *Baltimore Afro-American*, January 11, 1941, 1; Rayford W. Logan, "The Negro Wants First-Class Citizenship," in *What the Negro Wants*, ed. Rayford W. Logan (Chapel Hill: University of North Carolina Press, 1944), 11–12; "The Work-But-Not-Fight Policy," *Chicago Defender*, February 10, 1945, 10.

19. George Gallup, "The Gallup Poll," *Washington Post*, August 28, 1943, 5; Logan, "Negro Wants First-Class Citizenship."

20. Harry S. Truman, "Executive Order 9981," in *Documentary History of the Truman Presidency: The Truman Administration's Civil Rights Program*, ed. Dennis Merrill (New York: University Publications of America, 1996), 741; Walter White, *How Far the Promised Land?* (New York: Viking, 1955), 87–103; "New Army Upsets South's Traditions," *Ebony*, September 1954, 16–20; Charles C. Moskos, "Has the Army Killed Jim Crow?," *Negro History Bulletin* 21 (November 1957): 27–29.

21. Glenda Elizabeth Gilmore, *Gender and Jim Crow: Women and Politics of White Supremacy in North Carolina, 1896–1920* (Chapel Hill: University of North Carolina Press, 1996), 111–14.

22. Carroll, *"Medicine Bags and Dog Tags"*; Takaki, *Double Victory*; Renda, *Taking Haiti*; Lane Ryo Hirabayashi and James A. Hirabayashi, "A Reconsideration of the United States Military's Role in the Violation of Japanese-American Citizenship Rights," in *Ethnicity and War*, vol. 3, Ethnicity and Public Policy Series (Milwaukee: University of Wisconsin System American Ethnic Studies, 1984).

23. W. E. B. Du Bois, *Black Reconstruction in America: An Essay toward a History of the Part Which Black Folk Played in the Attempt to Reconstruct Democracy in America, 1860–1880* (New York: Harcourt, Brace, 1935; reprint, New York: Touchstone, 1995), 104, 110.

24. See Langston Hughes's "Memo to Non-White People" and "Expendable," both published in 1957, in *Collected Poems of Langston Hughes*, 456–57. On the increasing presence of nonwhite men in the military after 1945, see Rosier, *Serving Their Country*; Banks, *Ojibwa Warrior*; and Rivas-Rodriquez and Zamora, *Beyond the Latino World War II Hero*.

25. James Baldwin, *The Fire Next Time*, in *The Price of the Ticket: Collected Non-Fiction, 1948–1985* (New York: St. Martin's Press, 1985), 337–79.

26. James Baldwin, *No Name in the Street*, in *Price of the Ticket*, 517.

27. Ibid., 458–59.

28. Pettis Perry, *White Chauvinism and the Struggle for Peace* (New York: New Century, 1952), 6–7; William Worthy, "Korean Debacle Bound to Open Eyes of US GIs," *Baltimore Afro-American*, August 22, 1953; Nikhil Pal Singh, *Climbin' Jacob's Ladder: The Black Freedom Movement Writings of Jack O'Dell* (Berkeley: University of California Press, 2010), 1–27; Clive Webb, ed., *Massive Resistance: Southern Opposition to the Second Reconstruction* (New York: Oxford University Press, 2005); Glenn Feldman, ed., *Before* Brown*: Civil Rights and White Backlash in the Modern South* (Tuscaloosa: University of Alabama Press, 2004); Jeff Woods, *Black Struggle, Red Scare: Segregation and Anti-Communism in the South, 1948–1968* (Baton Rouge: Louisiana State University Press, 2004); Pete Daniel, *Lost Revolutions: The South in the 1950s* (Chapel Hill: University of North Carolina Press for Smithsonian National Museum of American History, 2000).

29. Civil Rights Congress, *We Charge Genocide: The Historic Petition to the United Nations for Relief from a Crime of the United States against the Negro People* (New York, 1951; reprint, New York: International Publishers, new ed., 1970), 3, 7–8. This petition, which was delivered to the United Nations and published in 1951, documented the widespread violence systematically used against African Americans between World War II and the Korean War.

30. John D'Emilio, *Lost Prophet: The Life and Times of Bayard Rustin* (New York: Free Press, 2003); Martin B. Duberman, *Paul Robeson* (New York: Knopf, 1989); Gerald Horne, *Communist Front? The Civil Rights Congress, 1946–1956* (Rutherford: Associated University Presses, 1988); Carole Boyce Davies, *Left of Karl Marx: The Political Life of Black Communist Claudia Jones* (Durham: Duke University Press, 2007); Barbara Ransby, *Ella Baker and the Black Freedom Movement: A Radical Democratic Vision* (Chapel Hill: University of North Carolina Press, 2005).

31. Singh, *Black Is a Country*, 69.

32. *Victory without Violence: The First Ten Years of the St. Louis Committee of Racial Equality (CORE), 1947–1957* (Columbia: University of Missouri Press, 2000), 28; D'Emilio, *Lost Prophet*; August Meier and Elliot Rudwick, *CORE: A Study in the Civil Rights Movement, 1942–1968* (New York: Oxford University Press, 1973).

33. Horace Cayton, "Fighting for White Folks," *Nation*, September 26, 1942.

34. Forman, *Making of Black Revolutionaries*, 50.

35. Michael Ferber and Staughton Lynd, *The Resistance* (Boston: Beacon Press, 1971), 31. For an objection to these resistances, see Ed Emanuel, *Soul Patrol* (New York: Ballantine Books, 2003), 121–22.

36. Men of the 857th, "Pertinent GI Questions," and George F. Baynham, "Hear Our Lord Amen?," *Baltimore Afro-American*, August 4, 1951, 4.

37. Civil Rights Congress, *We Charge Genocide*, 121–25; Steven F. Lawson, ed., *To Secure These Rights: The Report of President Harry S. Truman's Committee on Civil Rights* (Boston: Bedford/St. Martin, 2004).

38. Neil R. McMillen, *The Citizens' Councils: Organized Resistance to the Second Reconstruction, 1954–64* (Urbana: University of Illinois Press, 1971).

39. Marvin Harris, "Brothers in Arms: Refusal to Take Action in Chicago," *Nation*, October 28, 1968, 421–22; Elizabeth Hillman, "Guarding Women: Abu Ghraib and Military Sexual Culture," in *One of the Guys: Women as Aggressors and Torturers*, ed. Tara McKelvey (Emeryville, Calif.: Seal Press, 2007), 111–24; Sean Michael Flynn, *The Fighting 69th: One Remarkable National Guard Unit from Ground Zero to Baghdad* (New York: Viking, 2007); Christian Parenti, *Lockdown America: Police and Prisons in the Age of Crisis* (New York: Verso, 2008); Leal, "It's Not Just a Job," 153–74; Cien-Fuegos, "La Raza."

40. John Ditmer, *Local People: The Struggle for Civil Rights in Mississippi* (Urbana: University of Illinois Press, 1994); Charles M. Payne, *I've Got the Light of Freedom: The Organizing Tradition and the Mississippi Freedom Struggle* (Berkeley: University of California Press, 1995); Jacquelyn Dowd Hall, "The Long Civil Rights Movement and the Political Uses of the Past," *Journal of American History* 91 (September 2005): 1233–63; Laurie B. Green, *Battling the Plantation Mentality: Memphis and the Black Freedom Struggle* (Chapel Hill: University of North Carolina Press, 2007), 6; Martha Biondi, *To Stand and Fight: The Struggle for Civil Rights in Postwar New York City* (Cambridge: Harvard University Press, 2003).

41. Kimberley L. Phillips, "'War! What Is It Good For?': Vietnam, Conscription, and Migration in Black America," in *Repositioning North American Migration History*, ed. Marc S. Rodriguez (New York: University of Rochester Press, 2004), 265–83.

42. Timothy B. Tyson, "Robert F. Williams, 'Black Power,' and the Roots of the African American Freedom Struggle," *Journal of American History* 85 (September 1998): 541; Ossie Davis, preface to Civil Rights Congress, *We Charge Genocide*, 3.

43. Quoted in *Victory without Violence*, 28; see also D'Emilio, *Lost Prophet* (2003), and Meier and Rudwick, *CORE*.

44. Martin Luther King Jr., "A Time to Break Silence" (1967), in *A Testament of Hope: The Essential Writings and Speeches of Martin Luther King, Jr.*, ed. James Melvin Washington (San Francisco: Harper, 1986), 231–44; Thomas F. Jackson, *From Civil Rights to Human Rights: Martin Luther King, Jr., and the Struggle for Economic Justice* (Philadelphia: University of Pennsylvania Press, 2007), 308–27; Robin D. G. Kelley, "'But a Local Phase of a World Problem': Black History's Global Vision, 1883–1950," *Journal of American History* 86 (December 1999).

45. Truman, "Executive Order 9981," 741; Nalty, *Strength for the Fight*; Richard M. Dalfiume, *Desegregation of the U.S. Armed Forces: Fighting on Two Fronts, 1939–1953* (Columbus: University of Missouri Press, 1969); Richard J. Stillman, *Integration of the Negro in the U.S. Armed Forces* (New York: Praeger, 1968); Lee Nichols, *Breakthrough on the Color Front* (1954; reprint, Colorado Springs: Three Continents Press, 1993).

46. Mississippi Freedom Democratic Party, "Program of the Mississippi Freedom Democratic Party, 1968," 8–9, Digital Civil Rights, digilib.usm.edu/cdm4/document .php?CISOROOT=/manu&CISOPTR=443&CISOSHOW=434.

47. Quoted in Clayborne Carson, *In Struggle: SNCC and the Black Awakening of the 1960s* (Cambridge: Harvard University Press, 1981), 185; see also "Anti-Draft Circular," reprinted in *Black Protest: History Documents and Analyses, 1619 to the Present*, ed. Joanne Grant (New York: St. Martin's Press, 1968), 415–16.

48. George W. Bush, "Remarks at West Point: New Threats Require New Thinking," in *The Iraq War Reader: History, Documents, Opinions*, ed. Micah L. Sifry and Christopher Cerf (New York: Touchstone, 2003), 250–52; Amp Prophet, "Intro," *Voices from the Frontline* (Crosscheck Records, 2006).

49. 4th25, *Live from Iraq* (4th25.com Entertainment, 2005).

Chapter 1

1. "NAACP Asks for Hero Medal for Mess Attendant," *Pittsburgh Courier*, January 2, 1942, 1.

2. Amalia K. Amaki, "Flash from the Past: Hidden Messages in the Photographs of Prentice Herman Polk," in *A Century of African American Art: The Paul R. Jones Collection*, ed. Amalia K. Amaki (New Brunswick, N.J.: Rutgers University Press, 2004), 73.

3. "Where Are Our Soldiers?," *Pittsburgh Courier*, March 7, 1942, 2.

4. Susan D. Moeller, *Shooting War: Photography and the American Experience of Combat* (New York: Basic Books, 1989), 213–47.

5. George H. Roeder Jr., *The Censored War: American Visual Experience during World War Two* (New Haven: Yale University Press, 1993), 44.

6. L. D. Reddick, "The Negro Policy of the United States Army, 1775–1945," *Journal of Negro History* 34 (January 1949): 9–11, 23–29. Reddick noted in 1949 that this policy was not explicitly written before or during the war. Yet key elements had been established as early as World War I. See Chad L. Williams, *Torchbearers of Democracy: African American Soldiers in the World War I Era* (Chapel Hill: University of North Carolina Press, 2010), 50–62, 67–69.

7. Reddick, "Negro Policy of the United States Army"; Ulysses Lee, *The Employment of Negro Troops* (Washington, D.C.: Office of the Chief of Military History, 1966).

8. "Integration of Both Races in Army Units Highly Unlikely," *Baltimore Afro-American*, December 13, 1941, 1; Walter White, "N.A.A.C.P. Opposing Army Jim Crow," *Baltimore Afro-American*, March 28, 1942, 2.

9. James Baldwin, *Notes of a Native Son* (Boston: Beacon Press, 1955), 100–101; Thurgood Marshall, "Negro Discrimination and the Need for Federal Action: William H. Hastie and Thurgood Marshall Lawyers Guild Review, November 1942," in *Thurgood Marshall: His Speeches, Writings, Arguments, Opinions, and Reminiscences*, ed. Mark V. Tushnet (Chicago: Lawrence Hill Books, 2001), 80–81.

10. Robert Hill, ed., *The FBI's RACON: Racial Conditions in the United States during World War II* (Boston: Northeastern University Press, 1995), 7; "Nashville, Man on the Street," December 1941, AFS 6361B, Cut B2, "Day of Infamy," Library of Congress, memory.loc.gov/cgi-bin/query/r?ammem/afcpearltext:@field(DOCID+@lit(afcpearlsr056361b).

11. John Hope Franklin, *Mirror to America: The Autobiography of John Hope Franklin* (New York: Farrar, Straus and Giroux, 2005), 103.

12. Roi Ottley, *New World A-Coming* (Evanston, Ill.: Northwestern University Press, 1943; reprint, New York: Literary Classics, 1968), 288; Adam C. Powell Jr., "Is This a 'White Man's War'?," *Common Sense* 11 (April 1942): 111–12; Roi Ottley, "A White Folk's War?," *Common Ground* 2 (Spring 1942): 28–31.

13. Kenneth B. Clark and James Barker, "The Zoot Effect in Personality: A Race Riot Participant," *Journal of Abnormal Psychology* 40 (Winter 1945): 143–48. For extended and expansive investigations into how African Americans' hostility toward and resentment of racial discrimination in the United States diminished their support for the war effort, see Hill, *FBI's RACON*, esp. 1–49, 306–26, and Robin D. G. Kelley, *Race Rebels: Culture, Politics, and the Black Working Class* (New York: Free Press, 1994), 55–77, 161–82.

14. Anne Brown, "Soldiers Object to Two Front Fight," and Willie Martin, "Asks Race to Help U.S. and Get Equal Rights," *Pittsburgh Courier*, January 31, 1942.

15. James G. Thompson, "Should I Sacrifice to Live 'Half-American'?," *Pittsburgh Courier*, January 31, 1942.

16. For a history of World War II imagery and propaganda, see William L. Bird Jr. and Harry R. Rubenstein, *Design for Victory: World War II Posters on the American Home Front* (New York: Princeton Architectural Press, 1998); Roeder, *Censored War*.

17. "Where Are Our Soldiers?," 2.

18. "Messman Hero Identified," *Pittsburgh Courier*, March 14, 1942, 1.

19. Judith Weisenfeld, *Hollywood Be Thy Name: African American Religion in American Film, 1929–1949* (Berkeley: University of California Press, 2007), 163–64; André Bazin, "On *Why We Fight*: History, Documentation, and the Newsreel," *Film and History* 31 (Winter 2001): 60–62; Roeder, *Censored War*, 46; Richard W. Steele, "News of the 'Good War': World War II News Management," *Journalism Quarterly* 24 (Fall 1985): 707–16, 783.

20. Nicholas Natanson, *The Black Image in the New Deal: The Politics of FSA Photography* (Knoxville: University of Tennessee Press, 1992).

21. Barbara Dianne Savage, *Broadcasting Freedom: Radio, War, and the Politics of Race, 1938–1948* (Chapel Hill: University of North Carolina Press, 1999), 124–35; Beth T. Bates,

"'Double V for Victory' Mobilizes Detroit, 1941-1946," in *Freedom North: Black Freedom Struggles Outside the South, 1940-1980*, ed. Jeanne Theoharis and Komozi Woodard (New York: Palgrave Macmillan, 2003); Maureen Honey, ed., *Bitter Fruit: African American Women in World War II* (Columbia: University of Missouri Press, 1999); Lee Finkle, *Forum for Protest: The Black Press during World War II* (Rutherford: Fairleigh Dickinson University Press, 1975); Ottley, *New World A-Coming*.

22. Images of war and its violence can both galvanize and subvert support. See Alan Trachtenberg, *Reading American Photographs: Images as History, Mathew Brady to Walker Evans* (New York: Hill and Wang, 1989); Laura Wexler, *Tender Violence: Domestic Visions in an Age of U.S. Imperialism* (Chapel Hill: University of North Carolina Press, 2000); Susan Sontag, *Regarding the Pain of Others* (New York: Picador, 2003); and Moeller, *Shooting War*.

23. Allan Winkler, *The Politics of Propaganda: The Office of War Information, 1942-1945* (New Haven: Yale University Press, 1978); Maureen Honey, *Creating Rosie the Riveter: Class, Gender, and Propaganda during World War II* (Amherst: University of Massachusetts Press, 1984); Branford W. Wright, *Comic Book Nation: The Transformation of Youth Culture in America* (Baltimore: Johns Hopkins University Press, 2001), 30-55; Bill Mauldin, *Up Front* (New York: Norton, 1945).

24. Moeller, *Shooting War*, 213.

25. Roeder, *Censored War*, 43-44.

26. Wright, *Comic Book Nation*, 37-54.

27. Memorandum for John C. McCloy, Assistant Secretary of War, from Truman K. Gibson Jr., Civilian Aide to the Secretary of War, August 8, 1945, in *Blacks in the United States Armed Forces: Basic Documents*, ed. Morris J. MacGregor and Bernard C. Nalty (Wilmington, Del.: Scholarly Resources, 1977), 7:16-20; Walter White, *A Rising Wind* (Westport, Conn.: Negro Universities Press, 1945), 15-32.

28. Winkler, *Politics of Propaganda*, 67-68.

29. Ibid., 68.

30. Quoted in Roeder, *Censored War*, 79.

31. Lauren Rebecca Sklaroff, "Constructing G.I. Joe Louis: Cultural Solutions to the 'Negro Problem' during World War II," *Journal of American History* 89 (December 2002): 959; Savage, *Broadcasting Freedom*.

32. Graham Smith, *When Jim Crow Met John Bull: Black American Soldiers in World War II Britain* (New York: St. Martin's Press, 1988); Jane Dailey, "Fighting Hitler and Jim Crow," *Berlin Journal*, Fall 2005, 27-30.

33. Nicholas Natanson, "From Sophie's Alley to the White House: Rediscovering the Visions of Pioneering Black Government Photographers," *Prologue Magazine* 29 (Summer 1997), www.archives.gov/publications/prologue/1997/summer/pioneering-photographers.html (accessed February 1, 2011).

34. Carl Fleischhauer and Beverly Brannan, eds., *Documenting America* (Berkeley: University of California Press, 1988), 228-29; Gene Roberts and Hank Klibanoff, *The Race Beat: The Press, the Civil Rights Struggle, and the Awakening of a Nation* (New York: Vintage, 2006).

35. Quoted in Kathleen A. Hauke, *Ted Poston: Pioneer American Journalist* (Athens: University of Georgia Press, 1998), 104.

36. Gordon Parks, *Half Past Autumn: A Retrospective* (Boston: Bull Finch Press, 1997), 66-70; Hauke, *Ted Poston*, 102-4, nn. 81-84, 239-40.

37. Hauke, *Ted Poston*, 101-2; Studs Terkel, "Alfred Duckett," in *The Good War: An Oral History of World War II* (New York: Pantheon, 1984), 366-72.

38. Natanson, *Black Image in the New Deal*, 39-42, quote on 258.

39. William M. Banks, *Black Intellectuals: Race and Responsibility in American Life* (New York: Norton, 1996), 78-80; Chandler Owen, *What Will Happen to the Negro if Hitler Wins!* (1941), 6.

40. Owen, *What Will Happen to the Negro*, 16.

41. William H. Hastie to Chandler Owen, letter, May 1, 1942, NAACP Papers, pt. 9 (Discrimination in the U.S. Armed Forces, 1918-1955), series A (General Office Files on Armed Forces' Affairs, 1918-1955), reel 7.

42. Theodore Berry to Walter White, letter, December 17, 1942, NAACP Papers, pt. 9, series A, reel 7.

43. Chandler Owen, *Negroes and the War* (1942); Wendy Kozel, *Life's America: Family and Nation in Postwar Photojournalism* (Philadelphia: Temple University Press, 1994); Maren Stange, "Photographs Taken in Everyday Life: *Ebony*'s Photojournalistic Discourse," in *The Black Press: New Literary and Historical Essays*, ed. Todd Vogel (New Brunswick, N.J.: Rutgers University Press, 2001), 207-27; Adam Green, *Selling the Race: Culture, Community, and Black Chicago, 1940-1955* (Chicago: University of Chicago Press, 2007).

44. Owen, *Negroes and the War*, 71.

45. Walter White to Milton MacKaye, letter, January 25, 1943, NAACP Papers, pt. 9, series A, reel 7.

46. *New York Herald Tribune*, January 31, 1943.

47. Lorena Oropeza, *¡Raza Si! ¡Guerra No!: Chicano Protest and Patriotism during the Viet Nam War Era* (Berkeley: University of California Press, 2005), 22-32; Luis Alverez, *The Power of the Zoot: Youth Culture and Resistance during World War II* (Berkeley: University of California Press, 2008); Baldwin, *Notes of a Native Son*, 93-101.

48. Baldwin, *Notes of a Native Son*, 99, 100, 101.

49. "Calls for Federal Action," *New York Amsterdam News*, August 14, 1943, 1; Christopher Moore, *Fighting for America: Black Soldiers, the Unsung Heroes of World War II* (New York: One World Press, 2005), 148-49.

50. Franklin, *Mirror to America*, 105-9, 128.

51. Malcolm X, with the assistance of Alex Haley, *The Autobiography of Malcolm X* (New York: Grove Press, 1965), 194, 196.

52. Robert L. Allen, *The Port Chicago Mutiny* (New York: Warner Books, 1989); Langston Hughes, "Fifty Young Negroes," in *Langston Hughes and the Chicago Defender*, ed. Christopher C. De Dantis (Urbana: University of Illinois Press, 1995), 151-52.

53. Shawn Michelle Smith, *Photography on the Color Line: W. E. B. Du Bois, Race, and Visual Culture* (Durham: Duke University Press, 2004), 25.

54. Henry Louis Gates Jr., "The Face and Voice of Blackness," in *Facing History: The Black Image in American Art, 1710-1940*, ed. Guy C. McElroy (San Francisco: Bedford Arts, 1990), xxix; Wexler, *Tender Violence*, 2-3.

55. Bill V. Mullen, *Popular Fronts: Chicago and African-American Cultural Politics,*

1935–46 (Urbana: University of Illinois Press, 1999), 44–75; Penny M. Von Eschen, *Race against Empire: Black Americans and Anticolonialism, 1937–1957* (Ithaca: Cornell University Press, 1997), 118–20; Hayward Farrar, *The Baltimore* Afro-American (Westport, Conn.: Greenwood Press, 1998); Charles A. Simmons, *The African American Press* (Jefferson, N.C.: McFarland, 1998), 9–68; Claude A. Barnett, "The Role of the Press, Radio, and Motion Picture and Negro Morale," *Journal of Negro Education* 12 (Summer 1943): 474–89.

56. Mullen, *Popular Fronts*, 50–55.

57. George Lipsitz, *Time Passages: Collective Memory and American Popular Culture* (Minneapolis: University of Minnesota Press, 2001), 5.

58. Carl Murphy, introduction to *This Is Our War* (Baltimore: Afro-American Company, 1945).

59. Farrar, *Baltimore* Afro-American, 170–73; Simmons, *African American Press*, 69–90; Harry McAlpin, "Two Negroes among 450 Invasion Correspondents," *Chicago Defender*, June 14, 1944, 1.

60. According to standard histories of the campaign, black elites began and sustained it. See Farrar, *Baltimore* Afro-American, 168; Earl V. Patterson, "Now after Race Enemies," *Pittsburgh Courier*, March 7, 1942; and Beyden A. Steele, "Praises 'Double V' Design!," *Pittsburgh Courier*, March 14, 1942.

61. "Immortalizes General MacArthur in Song," *Pittsburgh Courier*, March 14, 1942; "Endorses 'Double V' Campaign!," *Pittsburgh Courier*, March 7, 1942; quoted in RJ Smith, *The Great Black Way: L.A. in the 1940s and the Lost African American Renaissance* (New York: Public Affairs, 2006), 53.

62. W. Brower, "Soldier Slain, 1 Hurt at Army Camp in Miss[issippi]," *Baltimore Afro-American*, June 12, 1943, 1.

63. "Messman Hero Identified," *Pittsburgh Courier*, March 14, 1942, 1; Richard E. Miller, *African Americans in the Navy, 1932–1943* (Annapolis: Naval Institute Press, 2004), 286–91.

64. "Mess Attendant Turned Machine Gun on Japanese," *Pittsburgh Courier*, March 7, 1942, 1, 4. Mamie Till Bradley has received important attention for taking an active role in letting the "whole world see what happened to my boy." She was part of a community where such activism was commonplace. See Ruth Feldstein, *Motherhood in Black and White: Race and Sex in American Liberalism, 1930–1965* (Ithaca: Cornell University Press, 2000), 86–110.

65. Hill, *FBI's RACON*, 633; Patrick S. Washburn, *Question of Sedition: The Federal Government's Investigation of the Black Press during World War II* (New York: Oxford University Press, 1986).

66. Hill, *FBI's RACON*, 633.

67. Ottley, *New World A-Coming*; Gordon Parks, *A Choice of Weapons* (New York: Harper and Row, 1966).

68. Bell hooks, "In Our Glory: Photography and Black Life," in *Picturing Us: African American Identity in Photography* (New York: New Press, 1994), 48, 50.

69. Susan V. Donaldson, "Whiteness Visible" (unpublished essay in my possession), 5–6. On the role of art and the black countergaze in the Harlem Renaissance, see Caroline Goeser, *Picturing the New Negro Harlem Renaissance: Print Culture and Modern Black Identity* (Lawrence: University of Kansas Press, 2007); Amy Kirschke, *Art in Crisis:*

W. E. B. Du Bois and the Struggle for African American Identity (Bloomington: Indiana University Press, 2007); David Margolick, *Beyond Glory: Joe Louis vs. Max Schmeling, and a World on the Brink* (New York: Vintage, 2006); "Stay out of the Olympics," *Baltimore Afro-American*, December 14, 1935, 23.

70. During the 1940s, blacks in Virginia used photographs to challenge national park directors' claims that Shenandoah National Park did not post Jim Crow signs. See Erin Kruko Devlin, *"Under the Sky All of Us Are Free": African American Travel, Visitation, and Segregation in Shenandoah National Park* (National Park Service, forthcoming).

71. Baldwin, *Notes of a Native Son*, 93-10.

72. Richard Powell, *Homecoming: The Art and Life of William H. Johnson* (New York: Norton, 1991), 156-58.

73. See americanart.si.edu/images/1967/1967.59.1120R_1b.jpg (accessed February 1, 2011).

74. Neil A. Wynn, *The Afro-American and the Second World War*, rev. ed. (New York: Homes and Meier, 1993), 74-75; Darlene Clark Hine, *Black Women in White: Racial Conflict and Cooperation in the Nursing Profession, 1890-1950* (Bloomington: Indiana University Press, 1989), 171-72; Patricia Sullivan, *Days of Hope: Race and Democracy in the New Deal Era* (Chapel Hill: University of North Carolina Press, 1996), 136-38.

75. Richard Powell describes Johnson's use of doubling as one of opposing and complimentary elements. See Powell, *Homecoming*, 156-58.

76. "The Negro at War," *Fortune*, June 1942, 77.

77. On the use of text and images, see W. T. J. Miller, *Picture Theory Essays on Verbal and Visual Representation* (Chicago: University of Chicago Press, 1994); Martha Nadell, *Enter the New Negroes: Images of Race in American Culture* (Cambridge: Harvard University Press, 2004), 28.

78. Harlan Phillips, oral history interview with Charles Alston, September 28, 1965, Smithsonian Archives of Art, http://www.aaa.si.edu/collections/oralhistories/transcripts/alston65.htm (accessed April 4, 2011).

79. Lemoine D. Pierce, "Charles Alston—An Appreciation," *International Review of African American Art* 19 (Fall 2004): 29.

80. Albert Murray, oral history interview with Charles Alston, October 19, 1968, Smithsonian Archives of Art, http://www.aaa.si.edu/collections/interviews/oral-history-interview-charles-henry-alston-11460 (accessed April 4, 2011).

81. Deborah Willis-Thomas, "Visualizing Memory: Photographs and the Art of Biography," *American Art* 17 (Spring 2003): 21; Pierce, "Charles Alston."

82. *New York Amsterdam News*, August 28, 1943, 1.

83. Charles Alston Papers, Manuscript Department, Wilson Library, University of North Carolina, Chapel Hill, #4931, box 1, folder 13.

84. Robert B. Westbrook, "I Want a Girl Just Like the Girl That Married Harry James: American Women and the Problem of Political Obligation in World War II," *American Quarterly* 42 (December 1990): 588.

85. Sherrie Tucker, *Swing Shift: "All-Girl" Bands of the 1940s* (Durham: Duke University Press, 2000), 246.

86. "Letters from Amsterdam News Readers," *New York Amsterdam News*, March 18, 1944.

87. Quoted in Tucker, *Swing Shift*, 239.

88. Letter to the editors, *New York Amsterdam News*, July 22, 1944.

89. Ibid., January 20, 1945.

90. "Pin-Up Girl," *Baltimore Afro-American*, May 6, 1944, 10.

91. My discussion here has been influenced by Karla Holloway, *Codes of Conduct: Race, Ethics, and the Color of Our Character* (New Brunswick, N.J.: Rutgers University Press, 1995), esp. 15–72.

92. Marshall, "Negro Discrimination and the Need for Federal Action"; Langston Hughes, "Gall and Glory," October 23, 1943, in *Langston Hughes and the* Chicago Defender, 149; Wynn, *Afro-American and the Second World War*; Sean Brawley and Chris Dixon, "Jim Crow Downunder? African American Encounters with White Australia, 1942–1945," *Pacific Historical Review* 71 (Fall 2002): 607–32; Arnold Rampersad, *Jackie Robinson: A Biography* (New York: Knopf, 1998).

93. *Baltimore Afro-American*, March 4, 1944.

94. Laurie B. Green, *Battling the Plantation Mentality: Memphis and the Black Freedom Struggle* (Chapel Hill: University of North Carolina Press, 2007), 47–95, esp. 89–93.

95. Hughes, "Gall and Glory," 149.

96. Green, *Battling the Plantation Mentality*, 89–93.

97. Ted Shearer, "Next Door," *Pittsburgh Courier*, March 20, May 8, October 2, 1943.

98. Ted Shearer, "Around Harlem," *New York Amsterdam News*, November 6, 1943.

99. Ibid., August 7, 1943.

100. Tucker, *Swing Shift*, 47.

101. Kate Scott phone interview with Jessie Ada Richardson, June 22, 2005, Women's Memorial Foundation Oral History Collection, Women's Memorial Foundation, Arlington, Va.; Jacqueline Bobo, *Black Women as Cultural Readers* (New York: Columbia University Press, 1995), 33–59.

102. Brenda L. Moore, *To Serve My Country, to Serve My Race* (New York: New York University Press, 1996), 53–66; Leisa D. Meyer, *Creating GI Jane: Sexuality and Power in the Women's Army Corps during World War II* (New York: Columbia University Press, 1996), 139–40.

103. Hine, *Black Women in White*.

104. Meyer, *Creating GI Jane*, 95.

105. Ermayne S. Faulk, "Brooklyn WAC Tells Reasons," *New York Amsterdam News*, March 17, 1945, B1.

106. *New York Amsterdam News*, August 26, 1944.

107. Moore, *To Serve My Country*, 133–37.

108. "Liked WAVE Stories," *New York Amsterdam News*, January 20, 1945.

109. "Newsreels 'Cut' Negro Fighters," *New York Amsterdam News*, January 8, 1944, A1.

110. Clayton Koppes and Gregory D. Black, "Blacks, Loyalty, and Motion-Picture Propaganda in World War II," *Journal of American History* 73 (September 1986): 400–402. Films that challenged racial stereotypes and caricatures, such as *Lifeboat* and *Casablanca*, were deemed too controversial and were not exported.

111. Manny Farber, "The Great White Way," *New Republic*, July 5, 1943, 20.

112. Koppes and Black, "Blacks, Loyalty, and Motion-Picture Propaganda."

113. Samuel A. Stouffer et al., *The American Soldier: Adjustment during Army Life*

(Princeton: Princeton University Press, 1949), 495–97; Lee, *Employment of Negro Troops*, 417–49, 591–643.

114. Lee, *Employment of Negro Troops*, 428–44; Emiel W. Owens, *Blood on German Snow: An African American Artilleryman in World War II and Beyond* (College Station: Texas A&M University Press, 2004), 65–66.

115. George Padmore, "All Colored Troops in Africa 'Labor Battalions,'" *Pittsburgh Courier*, November 28, 1942.

116. The military claimed black troops had high rates of venereal disease and they posed a threat to local women; thus the troops needed to be removed from the Congo. State Department reports indicated another reason. For the first version, see Lee, *Employment of Negro Troops*, 437–38, and "Army Policy Unchanged," *Pittsburgh Courier*, October 16, 1943, 1. For the second, see Jonathan E. Helmreich, *United States Relations with Belgium and the Congo, 1940–1960* (Newark: University of Delaware Press, 1998), 38–41. I thank Ira Dworkin for bringing this information to my attention.

117. Arthur Miller, *Situation Normal* (New York: Reynal and Hitchcock, 1944), 91, 93.

118. Ibid., 116–19.

119. Stouffer et al., *American Soldier*, 514. These percentages include undecideds.

120. Ibid., 489–94, 504–6. Stouffer worked with Gunnar Myrdal on *The American Dilemma*, and he and the other researchers were significantly influenced by Myrdal's methods. As a result, they began to suspect the military's claim that black men were poorly educated and uneducable. "In evaluating the AGCT test scores of Negroes, caution is necessary. It may be noted that the atmosphere in which Negroes took the tests was not always satisfactory." Not only were the testers resistant, but "community morale and Negro soldier morale entered into the problem by creating non-cooperative attitudes on the part of registrants" (Stouffer et al., *American Soldier*, 493).

121. Stouffer et al., *American Soldier*, 505–6, 519–25, quote on 525.

122. Alston's images and Rogers's histories predate the historical reenactments in *The Negro Soldier*. Moss would have known about these drawings, as they were widely syndicated.

123. John T. McManus, "The Negro Soldier," *New York Newspaper PM*, April 23, 1944.

124. Archer Winstein, "The Negro Soldier," *New York Post*, April 22, 1944.

125. Bosley Crowther, "Documentary Picture Issued by War Department Opens in Broadway Houses," *New York Times*, April 22, 1944.

126. Michael Carter, "Preview of the Film 'The Negro Soldier,'" *Baltimore Afro-American*, March 4, 1944, 1, 12.

127. Quoted in Robert F. Jefferson, *Fighting for Hope: African American Troops of the 93rd Infantry Division in World War II and Postwar America* (Baltimore: Johns Hopkins University Press, 2008), 188.

128. Owens, *Blood on German Snow*, 56.

129. Ibid., 62–80, quote on 63.

130. Roeder, *Censored War*, 79.

131. Richard Durham, "Europe's Skies Prove Jim Crow's Graveyard," *Chicago Defender*, January 6, 1945, 1; "Dixie Prefers Nazis to Negroes," *Chicago Defender*, January 27, 1945, 2.

132. Sterling Brown, "Count Us In," in *What the Negro Wants*, ed. Rayford W. Logan (Chapel Hill: University of North Carolina Press, 1944), 313.

133. James C. Chinn, "Bilbo Warns about Racial Danger Here," *Washington Post*, March 23, 1944, 1; Roy Wilkins, "The Negro Wants Full Equality," in Logan, *What the Negro Wants*, 132.

134. George Gallup, "The Gallup Poll," *Washington Post*, August 28, 1943, 5; Chinn, "Bilbo Warns about Racial Danger Here," 4.

Chapter 2

1. Letter from James P. Stanley to Walter White, July 19, 1945, Camp Conditions, NAACP Papers, pt. 9 (Discrimination in the U.S. Armed Forces, 1918–1955), series A (General Office Files on Armed Forces' Affairs, 1918–1955), reel 8; Cpl. Harold T. Pinkett, letter to the editor, *New York Amsterdam News*, August 4, 1945; Walter White, *A Rising Wind* (Westport, Conn.: Negro Universities Press, 1945).

2. For example, see David Brion Davis, "The Americanized Mannheim of 1945–46," in *American Places: Encounters with History*, ed. William E. Leuchtenburg (New York: Oxford University Press, 2000), 90–91; Philip McGuire, *Taps for a Jim Crow Army: Letters from Black Soldiers in World War II* (Santa Barbara, Calif.: ABC-Clio, 1983), 240–41; Ollie Stewart, "Failure to Provide Adequate Recreation Held Reason Installation Is One of the Worst," *Baltimore Afro-American*, June 5, 1946; Washington Davis, "Finds Americans, Not Germans His Enemy," *Chicago Defender*, September 1, 1945, 12; "M.P.'s Stop Manila G.I. White-Negro Skirmish," *Los Angeles Times*, January 9, 1946, 1.

3. Langston Hughes, "Here to Yonder: North, South, and the Army," *Chicago Defender*, October 27, 1945, 12.

4. Earl Conrad, "The Negro Press Fights On," *Chicago Defender*, March 2, 1946, 15. See the NAACP files marked "Soldier Complaints," "Soldier Troubles," and "Soldier Killings," NAACP Papers, pt. 9, series A and series B (Armed Forces' Legal Files, 1940–1950).

5. Walter Mosley, *What Next: A Memoir toward World Peace* (Baltimore: Black Classic Press, 2003), 10.

6. Conrad, "Negro Press Fights On," 15; James Wolfinger, *Philadelphia Divided: Race and Politics in the City of Brotherly Love* (Chapel Hill: University of North Carolina Press, 2007); Martha Biondi, *To Stand and Fight: The Struggle for Civil Rights in Postwar New York City* (Cambridge: Harvard University Press, 2003); Emilio Zamora, *Claiming Rights and Righting Wrongs in Texas: Mexican Workers and Job Politics during World War II* (College Station: Texas A&M University Press, 2009); Cletus Daniel, *Chicano Workers and the Politics of Fairness: The FEPC in the Southwest, 1941–1945* (Austin: University of Texas Press, 1990).

7. The literature on the role of black veterans in the post–World War II struggles for civil rights includes Christopher S. Parker, *Fighting for Democracy: Black Veterans and the Struggle against White Supremacy in the Postwar South* (Princeton: Princeton University Press, 2009); Horace Huntley and David Montgomery, eds., *Black Workers' Struggle for Equality in Birmingham* (Urbana: University of Illinois Press, 2004); Biondi, *To Stand and Fight*; Charles D. Chamberlin, *Victory at Home: Manpower and Race in the American South during World War II* (Athens: University of Georgia Press, 2003), 181–201; Charles M. Payne, *I've Got the Light of Freedom: The Organizing Tradition and the Mississippi Freedom*

Struggle (Berkeley: University of California Press, 1995); John Dittmer, *Local People: The Struggle for Civil Rights in Mississippi* (Urbana: University of Illinois Press, 1994).

8. James F. Scott to the NAACP, Soldier Complaints, August 13, 1945, NAACP Papers, pt. 9, series C (Veterans Affairs Committee, 1940–1950), reel 1.

9. For other examples, see McGuire, *Taps for a Jim Crow Army*, and Mosley, *What Next*, 9–10.

10. Christopher Moore, *Fighting for America: Black Soldiers, the Unsung Heroes of World War II* (New York: One World Press, 2005), 204–5, 276; Jack Hamann, *On American Soil: How Justice Became a Casualty of World War II* (Chapel Hill: Algonquin, 2005).

11. Mary A. Renda, *Taking Haiti: Military Occupation and the Culture of U.S. Imperialism* (Chapel Hill: University of North Carolina Press, 2001). For racial policies used for Asian Americans, see Lucy E. Salyer, "Baptism by Fire: Race, Military Service, and U.S. Citizenship Policy, 1918–1935," *Journal of American History* 91 (December 2004): 847–76.

12. Letter from Walter White to Wayne Morse, April 14, 1948, National Committee to Abolish Segregation in the Armed Forces, NAACP Papers, pt. 9, series A, reel 7; Grace Elizabeth Hale, *Making Whiteness: The Culture of Segregation in the South, 1890–1940* (New York: Pantheon, 1998); John Dower, *War without Mercy: Race and Power in the Pacific War* (New York: Pantheon, 1986).

13. "Army Bans Jim Crow PXs, Theaters," *Chicago Defender*, August 12, 1944, 1.

14. Letter from Roy Wilkins to Pvt. Charley Hanley, August 26, 1944, Soldier Complaints, NAACP Papers, pt. 9, series C, reel 1.

15. From the 10th Company 2nd Battalion to the NAACP, September 7, 1944, and letter from John J. McCloy, Assistant Secretary of War, to Walter White, November 13, 1944, Soldier Complaints, NAACP Papers, pt. 9, series C, reel 1.

16. Letter from Leland Jones to the NAACP, April 30, 1945, Soldier Complaints, NAACP Papers, pt. 9, series C, reel 1.

17. Satterfield to Dedmon, May 28, 1945, Camp Investigations, NAACP Papers, pt. 9, series C, reel 1; Leslie S. Perry to Walter White, memorandum, November 24, 1944, Camp Investigations, General File, NAACP Papers, pt. 9, series C, reel 2.

18. Private Brewington Kish to Virginia Kish, Baltimore NAACP, January 29, 1945, Camp Investigations, General File, NAACP Papers, pt. 9, series C, reel 1; Leslie S. Perry to Walter White, memorandum, November 24, 1944, Camp Investigations, General File, NAACP Papers, pt. 9, series C, reel 2.

19. Letter from Herman Recht to Esther Recht, March 20, 1945, Unprocessed Collection, Herman Recht Paper, Swem Special Collections, College of William and Mary, Williamsburg, Va. Thanks to Arthur Knight for bringing this collection to my attention.

20. Pvt. David Icheson, letter to *Yank*, ca. Spring 1945, Southern Regional Council Papers, series 7, reel 192 (University Microfilms International, 1984).

21. Langston Hughes Papers, box 209, folder 3544, James Weldon Johnson Collection, Beinecke Library, Yale University, New Haven, Conn. Hereafter cited as JWJ Collection.

22. Jackson to Hughes, June 3, July 27, 1945, box 209, folder 3550, JWJ Collection.

23. J. Hollingsworth to Leslie Perry, May 1, 1945, Camp Investigations, General File, NAACP Papers, pt. 9, series C, reel 1.

24. Letter from the Bomber Group to the NAACP, April 10, 1945, Camp Investigations, General File, NAACP Papers, pt. 9, series C, reel 1; Alan L. Gropman, *The Air Force Integrates, 1945-1964* (Washington, D.C.: Smithsonian Institution Press, 1998), 11-18.

25. R. H. Hines to Roy Wilkins, May 5, 1945, and letter from Pvt. Bernard Perry to Roy Wilkins, April 28, 1945, Camp Investigations, General File, NAACP Papers, pt. 9, series C, reel 1; Roy Wilkins, memorandum to Walter White, re: Senator Wayne Morse Wire on [A. Philip] Randolph, April 9, 1948, National Committee to Abolish Segregation in the Armed Forces, NAACP Papers, pt. 9, series A, reel 7.

26. Leslie S. Perry to Walter White, memorandum, November 24, 1944, Camp Investigations, General File, NAACP Papers, pt. 9, series C, reel 2.

27. Tentative Data for Army, November 24, 1944, Camp Investigations, General File, NAACP Papers, pt. 9, series C, reel 2.

28. Minutes of Meeting of Committee on Administration of the NAACP, November 27, 1944; letter from Walter White to Branches, December 26, 1944; Gregory Hawkins to Leslie Perry, April 3, 1945; and report, n.d., all in Camp Investigations, General File, NAACP Papers, pt. 9, series C, reel 2.

29. Walter White, memorandum to Jesse O. Dedmon, Leslie Perry, and William H. Hastie, June 13, 1945, Camp Investigations, General File, NAACP Papers, pt. 9, series C, reel 2.

30. Jesse O. Dedmon, Report of Army Camp Investigation Tour, Camp Investigations, 3-4, NAACP Papers, pt. 9, series B, Jesse O. Dedmon, 1944-1949, reel 7.

31. Ibid., 5-6.

32. Ibid., 8-9.

33. White did not notify the War Department about Dedmon's findings until December 1945. See Dedmon to Robert P. Patterson, Secretary of War, September 12, 1946, and Howard C. Petersen to Jesse O. Dedmon, October 31, 1946, Soldier Complaints, General File, NAACP Papers, pt. 9, series C, reel 1.

34. "Brutality to Negro GIs Hard to Crack," *Chicago Defender*, May 24, 1947.

35. Ellen Herman, *The Romance of American Psychology: Political Culture in the Age of Experts* (Berkeley: University of California Press, 1995), 73-74; Samuel Stouffer, *Studies in Social Psychology in World War II*, vol. 1 (Princeton: Princeton University Press, 1949).

36. Langston Hughes, "Hey Doc! I Got Jim Crow Shock!," *Chicago Defender*, February 26, 1944, 12.

37. Archie Gittens to the Commanding Officer, Drew Field, Tampa, Florida, July 10, 1944, Soldier Complaints, General File, NAACP Papers, pt. 9, series C, reel 11.

38. "Soldier, Tired of Jim Crow, Attempts Suicide," *Chicago Defender*, April 22, 1944.

39. Letter from Thurman Dillard to Langston Hughes, May 1, 1944, Langston Hughes Papers, box 209, folder 3547, JWJ Collection.

40. "South Whipping Negro Soldiers Report Says," *Chicago Defender*, April 29, 1944, 1.

41. "Negro Troops Called Injured by Segregation," *Washington Post*, May 31, 1946, 4; Stouffer, *Studies in Social Psychology in World War II*.

42. Quoted in Timothy B. Tyson, *Radio Free Dixie: Robert F. Williams and the Roots of Black Power* (Chapel Hill: University of North Carolina Press, 1999), 46, 47.

43. On efforts to defend black soldiers and sailors, see Kenneth Janken, *White: The Biography of Walter White and the NAACP* (New York: New Press, 2003).

44. Ulysses Lee, *The Employment of Negro Troops* (Washington, D.C.: Office of the Chief of Military History, 1966), 421–23; "WACs Barred from Overseas," *Chicago Defender*, July 20, 1946. Black women comprised 25 percent of the total Women's Army Corps strength, and the army refused to admit many more women.

45. "Urge More Mixed Combat Units," *Chicago Defender*, May 5, 1945; "Congressmen Join Fight for Mixed Army Units," *Chicago Defender*, June 2, 1945, 3.

46. "U.S. Occupation Forces in Germany 10.4% Negro," *Chicago Defender*, June 23, 1945, 1; Jesse Johnson, *Ebony Brass: An Autobiography of Negro Frustration amid Aspiration* (New York: William-Frederick Press, 1967), 71–75.

47. "Negro Troops Fail, Eastland Asserts," *New York Times*, June 30, 1945, 9.

48. "Defends Negro GIs," *New York Times*, July 13, 1945, 9; "The National NAACP and Dozens of Branches Hits Reports on Negroes," *New York Times*, July 1, 1945, 13.

49. "General's Praise for Negro Troops Cited by Virginia Editor," *Washington Post*, July 3, 1945, 3; "Congressmen Join Fight for Mixed Army Units," *Chicago Defender*, June 2, 1945, 3.

50. "Mr. Gibson's Chickens," *Chicago Defender*, July 21, 1945, 12; Truman K. Gibson, *Knocking Down Barriers: My Fight for Black America* (Evanston, Ill.: Northwestern University Press, 2005), 165; Moore, *Fighting for America*, 263. For a full account of the 92nd Division, see Moore, *Fighting for America*, 259–74.

51. "White Y Raps Senator," *Chicago Defender*, July 21, 1945, 5; quoted in "Dixie Rips Eastland's Slur on Negro GIs," *Chicago Defender*, July 28, 1945, 11.

52. "White Dixie Editors Hit Slander on Negro Troops," *Chicago Defender*, September 1, 1945, 8.

53. Helen Gahagan Douglas, "Negro Soldier Attains Fine Record in War Despite His Handicaps," *Washington Post*, February 10, 1946, 8; "Representative Douglas Cites Negro GI Heroism," *Chicago Defender*, February 2, 1946, 3; Ingrid Winther Scobie, *Center Stage: Helen Gahagan Douglas* (New York: Oxford University Press, 1992).

54. John Robert Badger, "The Negro's War History," *Chicago Defender*, February 16, 1946, 15; Gibson, *Knocking Down Barriers*, 153–67, 170–72. Gibson made these charges when he investigated the training program of the 92nd at Fort Huachuca in 1943. Gibson described the training program at Fort Huachuca as "ground zero for the collision of the conflicting demands of a war to save democracy and American society's commitment to segregation" (153). For information about receiving little training, see Robert L. Carter, *A Matter of Law: A Memoir of Struggle in the Cause of Equal Rights* (New York: New Press, 2005).

55. Paul Sann, "War Department Is Probing Army's Negro Policy," *New York Post*, October 24, 1945, 2B.

56. Testimony of Walter White before a Special War Department Board, October 15, 1945, NAACP Papers, pt. 9, series A, Gillem Report on the Utilization of Negro Manpower in Postwar Army, 1944–1947, reel 11.

57. Memorandum from Leslie Perry to Walter White, October 23, 1945, NAACP Papers, pt. 9, series A, Gillem Report, reel 11.

58. Leslie Perry to Walter White, November 1, 1945, NAACP Papers, pt. 9, series A, Gillem Report, reel 11.

59. Venice T. Spraggs, "Army to End Jim Crow!," *Chicago Defender*, December 1, 1945, 1, 4; "Eisenhower Studies Army Non-Bias Plan," *Chicago Defender*, December 15, 1945, 1.

60. Anthony Leviero, "Army Maps Plan for Negro Troops," *New York Times*, March 4, 1946, 25; "Negro Troops to Get Larger Role in Army," *Chicago Tribune*, March 4, 1946, 28.

61. Memorandum for John C. McCloy, Assistant Secretary of War, from Truman K. Gibson Jr., Civilian Aide to the Secretary of War, August 8, 1945, in *Blacks in the United States Armed Forces: Basic Documents*, ed. Morris J. MacGregor and Bernard C. Nalty (Wilmington, Del.: Scholarly Resources, 1977), 7:16-20.

62. Gillem Report, "Utilization of Negro Manpower in the Postwar Army Policy," War Department, April 27, 1946, in MacGregor and Nalty, *Blacks in the United States Armed Forces*, 7:394-95; "Analysis of the Gillem Report," memorandum from William H. Hastie to Walter White, March 26, 1946, NAACP Papers, pt. 9, series A, Gillem Report, reel 11.

63. Gillem Report, 7:394.

64. Ibid., 7:395.

65. "Analysis of the Gillem Report," memorandum from William H. Hastie to Walter White, March 26, 1946; Dedmon to White, memorandum, "Analysis of the Gillem Report," March 26, 1946; Leslie Perry to Walter White, "Comments on the Gillem Report," March 26, 1946, all in NAACP Papers, pt. 9, series A, Gillem Report, reel 11.

66. Soldier's letter, May 21, 1944, Camp Investigations, NAACP Papers, pt. 9, series C, reel 2.

67. Johnson, *Ebony Brass*, 75; quoted in Tyson, *Radio Free Dixie*, 46.

68. Robin D. G. Kelley, *Race Rebels: Culture, Politics, and the Black Working Class* (New York: Free Press, 1994), 57.

69. Johnson, *Ebony Brass*, 47–50.

70. Kelley, *Race Rebels*, 55; Howard W. Odum, *Race and Rumors of Race: The American South in the Early Forties* (1954; reprint, Baltimore: Johns Hopkins University Press, 1997), 113–26.

71. Arnold Rampersad, *Jackie Robinson: A Biography* (New York: Knopf, 1998), 102–9.

72. Interview with Herbert B. Gross, Rutgers University, New Brunswick, N.J., History Department, Oral History Archives of World War II, conducted by G. Kurt Piehler and Travis Richards, Princeton, N.J., October 26, 1994.

73. Kelley, *Race Rebels*; Sterling Brown, "Count Us In," in *What the Negro Wants*, ed. Rayford W. Logan (Chapel Hill: University of North Carolina Press, 1944); Raymond Arsenault, *Freedom Riders: 1961 and the Struggle for Racial Justice* (New York: Oxford University Press, 2006), 11–14.

74. Isaac Woodard, "Sworn Testimony for Civil Lawsuit," November 1947, NAACP 1940–1955 Legal File, Isaac Woodard, 1943–1950, NAACP Papers, pt. 8 (Discrimination in the Criminal Justice System, 1910–1955), series B (Legal Department and Central Office Records, 1940–1955), reel 30; "Medical Evaluation," August 15, 1946, NAACP 1940–1955 Legal File, Isaac Woodard, 1943–1950, NAACP Papers, pt. 8, series B, reel 28. Local police later claimed Woodard "was drunk and disorderly on the bus." Woodard stayed in the VA hospital for two months.

75. Franklin H. Williams to James C. Evans, May 6, 1949, Soldier Killings, NAACP Papers, pt. 9, series B, reel 14.

76. "Five Courts-Martialed WACs Beaten by Cop in Kentucky," *New York Amsterdam News*, August 4, 1945, 11B; Civil Rights Congress, *We Charge Genocide: The Historic Petition to the United Nations for Relief from a Crime of the United States against the Negro People* (New York, 1951; reprint, New York: International Publishers, new ed., 1970), 81.

77. Carl Ranse to Thurgood Marshall, April 15, 1946; Corrine Trotter to Thurgood Marshall; Thurgood Marshall to Tom C. Clark, Assistant Attorney General, Department of Justice, Edward Green File, Soldier Killings, 1940–1949, NAACP Papers, pt. 9, series B, reel 14. Though reported to the FBI in 1946, the brutal assault of Isaac Woodard only received attention from the Justice Department in late 1947.

78. Kelley, *Race Rebels*, 71; Civil Rights Congress, *We Charge Genocide*, 62.

79. "Lynch Toll Soars to 12 since Monroe Slaughter," *Chicago Defender*, August 31, 1946, 1.

80. *The People of the State of New York v. Richard A. Ferguson*, Freeport Police Court, February 5, 1946, and Statement of Joseph A. Ferguson, February 6, 1946, both in NAACP Papers, pt. 9, series B, Soldier Killing, Ferguson, Charles and Alfonso, February–March, 1946, reel 14; Biondi, *To Stand and Fight*, 61–66.

81. "Four Brothers Having Fun at Reunion," *New York Amsterdam News*, February 9, 1946, 25.

82. *People of the State of New York v. Richard A. Ferguson*; Statement of Joseph A. Ferguson, NAACP Papers, pt. 9, series B, Soldier Killing, Ferguson and Alfonso, reel 14.

83. Ibid.

84. Press release, American Youth for Democracy, February 8, 1946, and "Metropolitan Digest," February 1946, vol. 2, no. 1, p. 1, in NAACP Papers, pt. 9, series B, Soldier Killing, Ferguson and Alfonso, reel 14.

85. "Metropolitan Digest," 3.

86. Public announcement, Committee for Justice in the Ferguson Case, February 10, 1946, NAACP Papers, pt. 9, series B, Soldier Killing, Ferguson and Alfonso, reel 14.

87. Letter from Franklin H. Williams to Harold Cowan, Anti-Defamation League, February 27, 1946, and SWP Flyer, Ferguson Killings, SWP Press Release, February 28, 1946, NAACP Papers, pt. 9, series B, Soldier Killing, Ferguson and Alfonso, reel 14.

88. Agnes E. Meyer, "The Untold Story of the Columbia, Tenn[essee,] Riot," *Washington Post*, May 19, 1946, B1; Oliver W. Harrington, *Terror in Tennessee: The Truth about the Columbia Outrages* (pamphlet published by the NAACP, 1946), 3–4.

89. Meyer, "Untold Story," 2; George Streater, "Insists Tennessee Is 'Fair' to Negro," *New York Times*, April 25, 1946, 12.

90. Harrington, *Terror in Tennessee*, 4–6.

91. W. E. B. Du Bois, "The Winds of Time," *Chicago Defender*, March 30, 1946, 15.

92. "America's Year of Decision," *Ebony*, May 1946, 5.

93. "Letter from Charles Lohman to Madison Jones," March 2, 1946, Ferguson Killings, NAACP Papers, pt. 9, series B, Soldier Killing, Ferguson and Alfonso, reel 14.

94. Vincent Sheean, "Tennessee Race Riot Trial Like Lidice, Says Sheean," *Washington Post*, September 27, 1946, 1.

95. J. Wayne Dudley, "'Hate' Organizations of the 1940s: The Columbians, Inc.," *Phylon* 42 (Summer 1981): 263; "Mania Grips Dixie," *Chicago Defender*, August 10, 1946, 1.

96. "Chaplain Arrested Leading Alabama Vets in Vote Protest," *New York Amsterdam News*, February 9, 1946; "Riot at the Polls," *Washington Post*, August 3, 1946, 6.

97. "Training to Ease Racial Bias Urged," ca. 1947, Southern Regional Council Papers, reel 189; C. Alvin Hughes, "We Demand Our Rights: The Southern Negro Youth Congress, 1937–1948," *Phylon* 47 (Winter 1987): 38–50.

98. Civil Rights Congress, *We Charge Genocide*, 94; Dittmer, *Local People*, 2–9; Payne, *I've Got the Light of Freedom*, 24–25.

99. "Unmasked Band Massacres 2 Negroes, Wives in Georgia," *Washington Post*, July 27, 1946, 1; "Georgia Mob of 20 Men Massacres 2 Negroes, Wives; One was Ex-GI," *New York Times*, July 27, 1946, 1; "Georgia Jury Can't Identify Lynchers of 4," *Washington Post*, December 20, 1946, 1; Philip Dray, *At the Hands of Persons Unknown: The Lynching of Black America* (New York: Modern Library Paperbacks, 2003), 379–82.

100. "Klan Boasts of Murder, Say Secret Agents," *Washington Post*, June 8, 1946, 5.

101. Quoted in Dudley, "'Hate' Organizations of the 1940s," 262.

102. Civil Rights Congress, *We Charge Genocide*, 92.

103. Dudley, "'Hate' Organizations of the 1940s," 264–69; "Georgia Fascists," *Life*, December 23, 1946, 28; Harold B. Hinton, "Klan in South Keeps under Cover," *New York Times*, September 1, 1946, 65; Civil Rights Congress, *We Charge Genocide*, 92. Others disputed a growth in the postwar KKK, while also acknowledging that it remained powerful. See "Many in the South Seen Cool to Klan," *New York Times*, September 6, 1946, 23.

104. John E. Rousseau Jr., "LA Joins Dixie Lynch War," *Chicago Defender*, August 24, 1946, 1; "Sheriff Blamed in Minden Death; Hint Oil Motive," *Chicago Defender*, September 14, 1946, 1; "Chief of Police Exonerated in Lynching Case," *Washington Post*, November 28, 1946, 1.

105. "Silent March in Mourning and Protest," *Chicago Defender*, August 24, 1946, 12; "12,000 Attend Anti-Lynch Rally in Detroit," *Chicago Defender*, August 31, 1946, 13; "1,500 Protest Mob Lynching of 4 in Georgia," *Chicago Defender*, August 17, 1946, 3; "Protests Grow as Hate Shock Grips Nation," *Chicago Defender*, August 10, 1946, 1; Benjamin J. Davis, *Communist Councilman from Harlem* (New York: International Publishers, 1969), 161–64.

106. "Seaman Beaten at Gun Point for Asking Question in Texas," *Chicago Defender*, August 17, 1946, 20; "Protests Grow as Hate Shock Grips Nation," 1, 4.

107. "Lynching Hit in London," *New York Times*, August 19, 1946, 4; "Lynching Protests Issued Here," *New York Times*, July 31, 1946, 48; "3 Meetings Protest Cruelty to Negroes," *New York Times*, July 30, 1946, 13.

108. "Two Murdered Mysteriously in Texas," *Chicago Defender*, August 31, 1946, 1; *Chicago Defender*, September 21, 1946.

109. "To Open Crusade against Lynching," *New York Times*, September 23, 1946, 16; Drew Pearson, "How Robeson Sounded Wrong Key," *New York Times*, September 29, 1946, B5; George H. Copeland, "White House Pickets," *New York Times*, December 22, 1946, 120; "Lynchings Rose in '46," *New York Times*, December 29, 1946, 7.

110. Janken, *White*, 305; Patricia Sullivan, *Lift Every Voice: The NAACP and the Making of the Civil Rights Movement* (New York: New Press, 2010), 322–32; Mary L. Dudziak, *Cold*

War Civil Rights: Race and the Image of American Democracy (Princeton: Princeton University Press, 2000), 79–80; Steven F. Lawson, ed., *To Secure These Rights: The Report of President Harry S. Truman's Committee on Civil Rights* (Boston: Bedford/St. Martin, 2004), 15.

111. Lawson, *To Secure These Rights*, 82.

112. Ibid., 83.

113. Ibid., 84.

114. Ibid.

115. "Borough Attorney Elected to American Veteran Post," *New York Amsterdam News*, May 25, 1946.

116. Carter, *Matter of Law*, 37–53.

117. Letter, Organizing Appeal, April 5, 1945, Papers of A. Philip Randolph (Bethesda, Md.: University Publications of America, 1990), reel 1.

118. Roger Baldwin to A. Philip Randolph, May 23, 1945, Papers of A. Philip Randolph, reel 12.

119. Meeting minutes, October 1945, Papers of A. Philip Randolph, reel 12.

120. Statement, "Committee against Jimcrow in the Military," ca. July 1947, NAACP Papers, pt. 9, series A, reel 7.

121. "A Proposal for a Civil Disobedience Campaign against Military Jim Crow," from George M. Houser, Executive Secretary, Congress of Racial Equality, to A. Philip Randolph, February 14, 1948, in Papers of A. Philip Randolph, reel 12; Paula Pfeffer, *A. Philip Randolph: Pioneer of the Civil Rights Movement* (Baton Rouge: Louisiana State University Press, 1990), 136.

122. Grant Reynolds and A. Philip Randolph, letter to Walter White, November 14, 1947; letter to Reynolds from White's secretary, November 19, 1947; memo from Marshall to White, December 4, 1947, NAACP Papers, pt. 9, series A, reel 7.

123. Randolph testimony, reprinted in McGregor and Nalty, *Blacks in the United States Armed Forces*, 7:237.

124. Ibid.

125. Letter to branches from Walter White, April 1, 1948; telegram from Walter White to Wayne Morse, April 1, 1948, NAACP Papers, pt. 9, series A, reel 7.

126. Telegram from Wayne Morse to Walter White, April 7, 1948, NAACP Papers, pt. 9, series A, reel 7.

127. Draft of letter from White to Morse, April 7, 1948. It is not clear that White sent this letter, but it became the foundation for subsequent letters that he and Wilkins sent to Morse. See White to Morse, April 22, 1948, NAACP Papers, pt. 9, series A, reel 7.

128. John A. Ward to Walter White, April 5, 1948; Marie G. Barker to Walter White, April 1, 1948, NAACP Papers, pt. 9, series A, reel 7.

129. Letter, Lenore G. Marshall to Walter White, April 13, 1946, and A. A. Heist to Walter White, April 15, 1948, NAACP Papers, pt. 9, series A, Committee against Jim Crow in Military Service and Training, reel 7.

130. Wilkins's memo to White, April 9, 1948, and Wilkins to Current, Moon, and Dudley, April 13, 1948, NAACP Papers, pt. 9, series A, Committee against Jim Crow, reel 7.

131. Wilkins memorandum to Walter White, re: Senator Morse wire on Randolph, April 9, 1946, NAACP Papers, pt. 9, series A, Committee against Jim Crow, reel 7.

132. White to Morse, Apri1 14, 1948, NAACP Papers, pt. 9, series A, Committee against Jim Crow, reel 7.

133. Morse to White, April 20, 1948, NAACP Papers, pt. 9, series A, Committee against Jim Crow, reel 7.

134. "The Open Forum, ACLU, Southern California Branch," May, 1, 1948, NAACP Papers, pt. 9, series A, Committee against Jim Crow, reel 7.

135. Memo from Madison Jones to White, May 3, 1948, NAACP Papers, pt. 9, series A, Committee against Jim Crow, reel 7.

Chapter 3

1. George Lipsitz, *A Life in Struggle: Ivory Perry and the Culture of Opposition*, rev. ed. (Philadelphia: Temple University Press, 1995), 39–41. For a similar perspective, see Charles Rangel, *And I Haven't Had a Bad Day Since: From the Streets of Harlem to the Halls of Congress* (New York: Thomas Dunne/St. Martin's, 2007), 52–74, and James Forman, *The Making of Black Revolutionaries* (New York: Macmillan, 1972), 59.

2. Willie Ruff, *A Call to Assembly: An American Success Story* (New York: Viking, 1991), 104–85.

3. Milton A. Smith, "Frequently Shot GI Nearly Dies Trying to Keep Shoes," *Baltimore Afro-American*, January 13, 1951, 1, 2.

4. Harry S. Truman, "Executive Order 9981," in *Documentary History of the Truman Presidency: The Truman Administration's Civil Rights Program*, ed. Dennis Merrill (New York: University Publications of America, 1996), 741; Bernard C. Nalty, *Strength for the Fight: A History of Black Americans in the Military* (New York: Free Press, 1986); Richard M. Dalfiume, *Desegregation of the U.S. Armed Forces: Fighting on Two Fronts, 1939–1953* (Columbus: University of Missouri Press, 1969); Richard J. Stillman, *Integration of the Negro in the U.S. Armed Forces* (New York: Praeger, 1968); Lee Nichols, *Breakthrough on the Color Front* (1954; reprint, Colorado Springs: Three Continents Press, 1993).

5. Edward H. Humes, *Over Here: How the G.I. Bill Transformed the American Dream* (New York: Harcourt, 2006), 96–96, 125–26; David H. Onkst, "'First a Negro . . . Incidentally a Veteran': Black World War II Veterans and the G.I. Bill of Rights in the Deep South, 1944–1948," *Journal of Social History* 31 (Spring 1998): 517–43.

6. Charles S. Johnson, "Social Changes and Their Effects on Race Relations in the South," *Social Forces* 23 (March 1945): 343–44.

7. James N. Gregory, *The Southern Diaspora: How the Great Migrations of Black and White Southerners Transformed America* (Chapel Hill: University of North Carolina Press, 2005).

8. Sue E. Berryman, *Who Serves? The Persistent Myth of the Underclass Army* (Boulder, Colo.: Westview Press, 1988), 6; Manning Marable, *How Capitalism Underdeveloped Black America* (Boston: South End Press, 1983), 1–133. On trends in industries, see William Jones, *The Tribe of Black Ulysses: African American Lumber Workers in the Jim Crow South* (Urbana: University of Illinois Press, 2005), and Gregory, *Southern Diaspora*.

9. Gregory, *Southern Diaspora*, 96.

10. Marable, *How Capitalism Underdeveloped Black America*, 33; Berryman, *Who Serves?*, 1–18.

11. Leo Bogart, ed., *Project Clear: Social Research and the Desegregation of the United States Army* (New York: Markham, 1969; reprint, New Brunswick, N.J.: Transaction, 1991); Nalty, *Strength for the Fight*; Ruff, *Call to Assembly*, 111–85; Dalfiume, *Desegregation of the U.S. Armed Forces*; "The Fahy Committee," in *Blacks in the United States Armed Forces: Basic Documents*, ed. Morris J. MacGregor and Bernard C. Nalty (Wilmington, Del.: Scholarly Resources, 1977), 9:388–400.

12. On the diplomatic tensions, see Mary L. Dudziak, *Cold War Civil Rights: Race and the Image of American Democracy* (Princeton: Princeton University Press, 2000), and Michael J. Krenn, ed., *Race and U.S. Foreign Policy during the Cold War* (New York: Garland, 1998). For eyewitness accounts of the segregated occupation army, see David Brion Davis, "The Americanized Mannheim of 1945–46," in *American Places: Encounters with History*, ed. William E. Leuchtenburg (New York: Oxford University Press, 2000), 90–91.

13. William Smith, "Chopped Off by Army: Half of Tan GIs Leaving Germany," *Pittsburgh Courier*, December 21, 1946, 1, 4.

14. "Ex-GI Starts Haiti Airline," *Ebony*, February 1948, 28–30; "GI Business Wizard," *Ebony*, December 1948, 39–42; "Chicken Farm: A GI Dream Come True," *Ebony*, February 1949, 62–65.

15. Wilbert L. Walker, *We Are Men: Memoirs of World War II and the Korean War* (Chicago: Adams Press, 1972), 53–64.

16. James L. Hicks, "If You're within Draft Age Don't Wait, Join Up Now," *Baltimore Afro-American*, July 31, 1948; James L. Hicks, "Army Offers New Course to Train Newspapermen," *Baltimore Afro-American*, October 23, 1948.

17. James L. Hicks, "Army Uses 5 Words to Teach a Man How to Be a Killer," *Baltimore Afro-American*, July 17, 1948, 8.

18. "Opportunities in Navy ROTC," *Baltimore Afro-American*, July 24, 1948.

19. "Navy Day," *Baltimore Afro-American Magazine*, 5, October 23, 1948; "Submarine Men," *Ebony*, May 1950, 15.

20. "The Air Force Goes Interracial," *Ebony*, September 1949, 15–17.

21. Quoted in "Ahead of the Country," *Time*, June 5, 1950, 18; Stillman, *Integration of the Negro in the U.S. Armed Forces*, 57–59.

22. "Submarine Men," 16.

23. Douglas Hall, "Tan Yanks Nation's Best Good Neighbor Envoy," *Baltimore Afro-American*, June 24, 1950.

24. William C. Berman, *The Politics of Civil Rights in the Truman Administration* (Columbus: Ohio State University Press, 1970), 124.

25. Ibid., 118, 119.

26. Monroe Billington, "Freedom to Serve: The President's Committee on Equality of Treatment and Opportunity in the Armed Forces, 1949–1950," *Journal of Negro History* 51 (October 1966): 262–74; "Two Negroes Heard in High Court on 'Job Bias' in Rail Union Pact," *New York Times*, November 15, 1944, 19.

27. Donald R. McCoy, *Quest and Response: Minority Rights and the Truman Administration* (Lawrence: University of Kansas Press, 1973), 221.

28. Quoted in ibid., 222.

29. On the organization and structure of the Fahy Committee, see Sherie Mershon

and Steven Schlossman, *Foxholes and Colorlines: Desegregating the U.S. Armed Forces* (Baltimore: Johns Hopkins University Press, 1998), 187–93. On Fahy's approach, see McCoy, *Quest and Response*, 222.

30. L. D. Reddick, "The Negro Policy of the American Army since World War II," *Journal of Negro History* 38 (April 1953): 204.

31. Alan L. Gropman, *The Air Force Integrates, 1945–1964* (Washington, D.C.: Smithsonian Institution Press, 1998).

32. McCoy, *Quest and Response*, 225.

33. Kenneth C. Royall testimony to the President's Committee on Equality of Treatment and Opportunity in the Armed Services, March 28, 1949, in MacGregor and Nalty, *Blacks in the United States Armed Forces*, 9:505.

34. Ibid., 9:510–11, 517.

35. Reddick, "Negro Policy of the American Army," 12.

36. Royall testimony, 9:517.

37. Reddick, "Negro Policy of the American Army," 12–14.

38. Royall testimony, 9:507.

39. Ibid., 9:527.

40. Ibid., 9:542.

41. Ibid., 9:551.

42. McCoy, *Quest and Response*, 228. The president's agreement to let the army reinstate a quota system if it viewed it necessary appeared to be done without the knowledge of or input from the Fahy Committee. See ibid., 231.

43. "Army's Trying," *Chicago Defender*, January 21, 1950, 6; "Other Papers Say," *Chicago Defender*, April 22, 1950, 7.

44. Willard Townsend, "Harry Truman to Congress: Armed Forces Are Solving Racial Bias," *Chicago Defender*, July 22, 1950, 7.

45. Jesse Johnson, *Ebony Brass: An Autobiography of Negro Frustration amid Aspiration* (New York: William-Frederick Press, 1967), 77–81; Max Hastings, *The Korean War* (New York: Simon and Schuster, 1987), 23–127.

46. "24th Infantry to Police Japan," *Chicago Defender*, February 1, 1947, 7.

47. Selika Marianne Ducksworth, "What Hour of the Night: Black Enlisted Men's Experiences and the Desegregation of the Army during the Korean War, 1950–1" (Ph.D. diss., Ohio State University, 1994), 112–15; Hastings, *Korean War*, 18.

48. Clay Blair, *The Forgotten War: America in Korea, 1950–1953* (New York: Times Books, 1987), 151; Eiji Takemae, *Inside GHQ: The Allied Occupation of Japan and Its Legacy* (New York: Continuum, 2002), 130; Dale E. Wilson, "Recipe for Failure: Major General Edward M. Almond and Preparation of the U.S. 92nd Infantry Division for Combat in World War II," *Journal of Military History* 56, no. 3 (July 1992): 473–88.

49. Yuki Tanaka, *Japan's Comfort Women: Sexual Slavery and Prostitution during World War II and the U.S. Occupation* (New York: Routledge, 2002), 133–36; Yukiko Koshiro, *Trans-Pacific Racisms and the U.S. Occupation of Japan* (New York: Columbia University Press, 1999), 55–56; John W. Dower, *Embracing Defeat: Japan in the Wake of World War II* (New York: Norton, 1999), 130–31. Dower argues that the women believed the men had "been socialized to regard them as 'whites.'" Other evidence suggests that black soldiers sympathized with the Japanese. Many heard, of course, the racial epithets and

attitudes expressed toward the Japanese by white Americans. See Takemae, *Inside GHQ*, 131.

50. Ethel Payne, "Says Japanese Girls Playing GIs for Suckers," *Chicago Defender*, November 25, 1950, 12; Forman, *Making of Black Revolutionaries*, 67; Yasuhiro Okada, "Gendering the 'Black Pacific': Race Consciousness, National Identity, and the Masculine/Feminine Empowerment among African Americans in Japan under U.S. Military Occupation, 1945–1952" (Ph.D. diss., Michigan State University, 2008). Other nonwhite American soldiers adopted similar sensibilities. See Dennis Banks, *Ojibwa Warrior: Dennis Banks and the American Indian Movement* (Norman: University of Oklahoma Press, 2004), 44–48.

51. Tanaka, *Japan's Comfort Women*, 31–32, 146–47; Walker, *We Are Men*, 74.

52. Payne, "Says Japanese Girls Playing GIs for Suckers," 12.

53. Rangel, *And I Haven't Had a Bad Day Since*, 62–63.

54. "Retreat Held Rout," *New York Times*, July 5, 1950, 2.

55. Lindesay Parrot, "Foe Is Regrouping," *New York Times*, July 6, 1950, 1.

56. "U.S. Companies at the Kum Won More Time with Lives," *New York Times*, July 19, 1950, 1.

57. "Korean Foe Held Wily in Retreats," *New York Times*, August 13, 1950, 4; quoted in Hastings, *Korean War*, 81.

58. Marguerite Higgins, "The Terrible Days in Korea," *Saturday Evening Post*, August 19, 1950, 26–27, 110–12.

59. Hastings, *Korean War*, 20.

60. Quoted in ibid., 16; Parrot, "Foe Is Regrouping," 1. For overall combat conditions, see Blair, *Forgotten War*, 151.

61. "War Footing," *New York Times*, July 23, 1950, E1; Steven Casey, *Selling the Korean War: Propaganda, Politics, and Public Opinion in the United States, 1950–1953* (New York: Oxford University Press, 2010).

62. "114 Prisoners Named by Korean Red Radio," *New York Times*, July 19, 1950, 3; "Battle Front," *New York Times*, July 30, E1.

63. Photo caption, "Tan Yanks Land," *Baltimore Afro-American*, July 8, 1950, 1.

64. This biography of Hicks appeared in "Hicks off to Korea," *Baltimore Afro-American*, July 22, 1950, 1.

65. James Hicks, "AFRO Man One of 25 Missing," "The Situation Very Grave in Korean Fighting," and "Tan Lads in 14 Days of Continuous Battle," *Baltimore Afro-American*, August 5, 1950.

66. James Hicks, "24th Hit Hard," *Baltimore Afro-American*, August 19, 1950, 1, 19.

67. Ibid.

68. James Hicks, "Army Passes Buck," *Baltimore Afro-American*, August 26, 1950, 1–2, and "24th Hit Hard," 1, 19.

69. James Hicks, "Fight or Die," *Baltimore Afro-American*, August 12, 1950, 19.

70. Yvonne Latty and Ron Traver, eds., "Charles Armstrong," in *We Were There: Voices of African American Veterans from World War II to the War in Iraq* (New York: Harper Paperbacks, 2005), 58.

71. "Robert Yancy," in Latty and Travers, *We Were There*, 69–70.

72. Ducksworth, "What Hour of the Night," 115–16.

73. Curtis James Morrow, *What's a Commie Ever Done to Black People? A Korean War Memoir* (Jefferson, N.C.: McFarland, 1997).

74. L. Alex Wilson, "Generals Trace High Casualties among Troops to Army Jim Crow," *Chicago Defender*, February 10, 1951, 1.

75. Morrow, *What's a Commie Ever Done to Black People?*, 10.

76. James Hicks, "24th Quickly Learns New-Style Fighting," *Baltimore Afro-American*, August 5, 1950, 1.

77. Lyle Rishell, *With a Black Platoon in Combat: A Year in Korea* (College Station: Texas A&M University Press, 1993), 40–41; "Robert Yancy," 71.

78. Morrow, *What's a Commie Ever Done to Black People?*, 9 and 4–45; Lipsitz, *Life in the Struggle*, 53–55, quote on 53.

79. Gregory H. Winger interview with James Milton Harp, May 16, 2003, Veterans' Oral History Project, Library of Congress; Morrow, *What's a Commie Ever Done to Black People?*, 12.

80. Hicks, "Tan Lads in 14 Days of Continuous Battle," 2.

81. James Hicks, "24th Soldiers Do Impossible," *Baltimore Afro-American*, August 12, 1950, 2.

82. Hicks, "Army Passes Buck," 1–2.

83. Thurgood Marshall, *Report on Korea: The Shameful Story of the Courts-Martial of Negro GIs* (New York: National Association for the Advancement of Colored People, 1951), 1–2; Carl Rowan, *Dream Makers, Dream Breakers: The World of Thurgood Marshall* (Boston: Little, Brown, 1993), 165; Blair, *Forgotten War*, 162n.

84. James Hicks, "Courts-Martial Hasty," *Baltimore Afro-American*, February 24, 1951, 1–2; Juan Williams, *Thurgood Marshall: American Revolutionary* (New York: Times Books, 1998), 170.

85. Williams, *Thurgood Marshall*, 170.

86. Ibid., 171; Rowan, *Dream Makers, Dream Breakers*, 164.

87. "Marshall's Trip Home Is Delayed," *Baltimore Afro-American*, February 17, 1951. This aide's suggestion to Marshall was most interesting. When Marshall arrived, American troops were again in retreat.

88. Williams, *Thurgood Marshall*, 172; "Marshall's Trip Home Is Delayed."

89. Marshall, *Report on Korea*, 13.

90. Hicks, "Courts-Martial Hasty," 1–2; Blair, *Forgotten War*, 445.

91. Marshall, *Report on Korea*, 13–15, quote on 16.

92. Ibid., 17.

93. Ibid., 5; Thurgood Marshall, "Summary Justice—The Negro GI in Korea," *Crisis* 58 (May 1951): 297.

94. Matthew Ridgway, *Soldier: The Memoirs of Matthew Ridgway* (New York: Harper, 1956), 192.

95. Ibid.

96. Harold H. Martin, "How Do Our Negro Troops Measure Up?," *Saturday Evening Post*, June 16, 1951, 30–31, 139, 141, quote on 139. For similar perspectives, see William T. Bowers, *Black Soldier, White Army: The Twenty-Fourth Infantry Regiment in Korea* (Washington, D.C.: Center for Military History, 1996). Many military and academic historians

argue that this report used racially biased statements and after-action reports. It should be read with care. See Blair, *Forgotten War*, 152–53 and n. 28.

97. Blair documents these anti-Korean sensibilities. See Dower, *Embracing Defeat.*

98. My thinking about this diverse rhetoric and discourse has been shaped by Homi Bhabha, *The Location of Culture* (New York: Routledge, 2004), esp. 66–83, and Blair, who notes that too many histories have relied on Appleman's "sneering account" and that the accounts of the 24th Infantry have suffered from numerous retellings, erasures, and obliterations from the official record. In addition, too many of the advocates for segregation were given authority in the telling, including General Ned Almond. See Blair, *Forgotten War*, 152–53 and n. 28.

99. Bogart, *Project Clear*, 11–12.

100. Ibid., 17, 20.

101. Blair, *Forgotten War*, 150.

102. These surveys were undertaken in early 1951 and republished in 1991. See Bogart, *Project Clear. Clear*, Bogart recalled, "was the code name for the research that led to the official desegregation of the U.S. Army" (ix).

103. Ibid., 13–14.

104. Ibid., 16, 18–19.

105. Ibid., 29.

106. Ridgway, *Soldier*, 192, 193.

107. L. Alex Wilson, "Wilson Tells Story of Decision to Bring Democracy to Battlefield," *Chicago Defender*, October 28, 1950, 4.

108. Wilson, "Wilson Tells Story of Decision to Bring Democracy to Battlefield"; Wilson, "Generals Trace High Casualties among Troops to Army Jim Crow," 1.

109. "L. Alex Wilson to Air Korean War on Radio," *Chicago Defender*, December 2, 1950; "Bombs, Brass, and Brotherhood: Integration Is Forced to Test by War in Korea," *Chicago Defender*, February 3, 1951; Mary Whittaker, letter to the editor, "A Life for a Cause," *Chicago Defender*, April 28, 1951.

110. Bogart, *Project Clear*, 20; Blair, *Forgotten War*, 868.

111. Walker, *We Are Men*, 68–69.

112. Ibid., entries dated March 1, 1952, 89; March 11, 1952, 90; March 13, 1952, 91.

113. "Charles Armstrong," 60; Johnson, *Ebony Brass*, 92–100.

114. Forman, *Making of Black Revolutionaries*, 73.

115. "Charles Armstrong," 77–78.

116. Walter White, *How Far the Promised Land?* (New York: Viking, 1955), 93–102.

117. This point has received too little attention. In World War II, 1.7 million men, a population disproportionately African American, were charged with military crimes. Since World War II, the military has used the court-martial system in unequal ways. See Elizabeth Lutes Hillman, *Defending America: Military Culture and the Cold War Court-Martial* (Princeton: Princeton University Press, 2005), esp. 92–101, and Lipsitz, *Life in the Struggle*, 69–72.

118. Edward Suchman, Robin Williams Jr., and Rose K. Goldsen, "Student Reaction to Impending Military Service," *American Sociological Review* 18 (June 1953): 293–304.

119. David R. Segal, *Recruiting for Uncle Sam: Citizenship and Military Manpower*

Policy (Lawrence: University Press of Kansas, 1989), 32; Stillman, *Integration of the Negro in the U.S. Armed Forces*, 49-55, 66.

120. "Notes and Comments: The Selective Service," *Yale Law Journal* 76 (November 1966): 160-99; "Systematic Exclusion of Negroes from Selective Service Boards: Some Proposals for Reform," *Michigan Law Journal* 67 (February 1969): 756-811.

121. Paul T. Murray, "Blacks and the Draft: A History of Institutional Racism," *Journal of Black Studies* 2 (September 1971): 69.

122. Bernard C. Karpinos, *Draftees: Disqualifications for Military Service for Medical Reasons: An Analysis of Trends over Time* (Alexandria, Va.: Human Resources Research Organization, 1972), 55.

123. "Notes and Comments," 177-78.

124. Malcolm X, with the assistance of Alex Haley, *The Autobiography of Malcolm X* (New York: Grove Press, 1965), 194, 196, 234.

125. Johnson described how Coleson planned to "play dumb" and get out of the army; see Johnson, *Ebony Brass*, 12.

126. Rubin "Hurricane" Carter, *The 16th Round: From Number 1 Contender to Number 45472* (New York: Penguin, 1974), 106, 116, 131.

127. Forman, *Making of Black Revolutionaries*, 65.

128. Walter Dean Myers, *Bad Boy: A Memoir* (New York: HarperTempest, 2001), 183.

129. Ibid., 183.

130. See Mary Kaldor, *New and Old Wars: Organized Violence in a Global Era*, 2nd ed. (Stanford: Stanford University Press, 2007), 27-32; Gabriel Kolko, *A Century of War: Politics, Conflicts, and Society since 1914* (New York: New Press, 1994).

131. Judith Kent interview with James W. Allen, December 20, 2002, American Folklife, Library of Congress.

Chapter 4

1. "New Army Upsets South's Traditions," *Ebony*, September 1954, 16-20.

2. Roi Ottley, *No Green Pastures: The Negro in Europe Today* (New York: Scribner's Sons, 1951), 1; Walter White, *How Far the Promised Land?* (New York: Viking, 1955), 96, 102.

3. Lee Nichols, *Breakthrough on the Color Front* (1954; reprint, Colorado Springs: Three Continents Press, 1993), 5; James Forman, *The Making of Black Revolutionaries* (New York: Macmillan, 1972); Civil Rights Congress, *We Charge Genocide: The Historic Petition to the United Nations for Relief from a Crime of the United States against the Negro People* (New York, 1951; reprint, New York: International Publishers, new ed., 1970), 3-4.

4. White, *How Far the Promised Land?*, 103.

5. Patricia Sullivan, ed., *Freedom Writer: Virginia Foster Durr, Letters from the Civil Rights Years* (New York: Routledge, 2003), 83.

6. Ibid., 223.

7. Men of the 857th, "Pertinent GI Questions," *Baltimore Afro-American*, August 4, 1951, 4.

8. William Worthy, "Korean Debacle Bound to Open Eyes of US GIs," *Baltimore Afro-American*, August 22, 1953.

9. William Worthy, *Our Disgrace in Indo-China* (Cambridge, Mass.: American Friends Service, 1954), 5. This also appeared in the *Crisis* as "Our Disgrace in Indo-China," *Crisis* 62 (February 1954): 77-84.

10. Civil Rights Congress, *We Charge Genocide*, 3; Pettis Perry, *White Chauvinism and the Struggle for Peace* (New York: New Century, 1952), 6-7, 8-9.

11. Worthy, *Our Disgrace in Indo-China*; William L. Patterson, "The Third Great Crisis," *Baltimore Afro-American*, July 28, 1951, 4; "We're on the Wrong Side," *Baltimore Afro-American*, July 26, 1958, 4.

12. Willard Townsend, "Columnist Says Negro Has Stake in South Korean War," *Chicago Defender*, August 19, 1950, 7.

13. Brenda Gayle Plummer, *Rising Wind: Black Americans and U.S. Foreign Affairs, 1935-1960* (Chapel Hill: University of North Carolina Press, 1996), 104; Ralph Matthews, "What's Wrong with Paul Robeson?," *Baltimore Afro-American*, August 20, 1949, 7.

14. "This Is No Race War," *Los Angeles Sentinel*, August 31, 1950, A8.

15. "Says Red Propaganda Misses Mark in Korea," April 25, 1953, *Chicago Defender*, 12; "Case of the Exiles," *Chicago Defender*, October 10, 1953, 11; White, *How Far the Promised Land?*, 24-25.

16. Bill V. Mullen, *Afro-Orientalism* (Minneapolis: University of Minnesota Press, 2004), 64-68.

17. Jeff Woods, *Black Struggle, Red Scare: Segregation and Anti-Communism in the South, 1948-1968* (Baton Rouge: Louisiana State University Press, 2004), 49-52.

18. Quoted in Penny M. Von Eschen, *Race against Empire: Black Americans and Anti-colonialism, 1937-1957* (Ithaca: Cornell University Press, 1997), 117.

19. Quoted in ibid., 118. For the NAACP's shift in civil rights, see ibid. and Carol Anderson, *Eyes off the Prize: The United Nations and the African American Struggle for Human Rights, 1944-1955* (New York: Cambridge University Press, 2003).

20. W. E. B. Du Bois, "No Progress without Peace," *National Guardian*, October 4, 1950, reprinted in *Newspaper Columns by W. E. B. Du Bois*, comp. and ed. Herbert Aptheker, vol. 2, *1945-1961* (White Plains, N.Y.: Kraus-Thompsen, 1986), 873.

21. W. E. B. Du Bois, "I Take My Stand," in *The Oxford W. E. B. Du Bois Reader*, ed. Eric Sundquist (New York: Oxford University Press, 1996), 469; W. E. B. Du Bois, "U.S. Needs No More Cowards," from the *National Guardian*, October 25, 1950, reprinted in *Newspaper Columns by W. E. B. Du Bois*, 2:874 (quote), 878-79.

22. W. E. B. Du Bois, "There Must Be a Vast Social Change in the United States," *National Guardian*, July 11, 1951, reprinted in *Newspaper Columns by W. E. B. Du Bois*, 2:882, 884.

23. W. E. B. Du Bois, "We Cry Aloud," *National Guardian*, July 10, 1952, reprinted in *Newspaper Columns by W. E. B. Du Bois*, 2:892, 894, includes keynote address to the Progressive Party convention.

24. Arnold Rampersad, *The Life of Langston Hughes*, vol. 2, *1941-1967, I Dream a World* (New York: Oxford University Press, 1988), 186-95, 209-21; Robbie Lieberman, "'Another Side of the Story': African American Intellectuals Speak Out for Peace and Freedom during the Early Cold War Years," in *Anticommunism and the African American Freedom Movement*, ed. Robbie Lieberman and Clarence Lang (New York: Palgrave, 2009), 17-50.

25. Carole Boyce Davies, *Left of Karl Marx: The Political Life of Black Communist Claudia Jones* (Durham: Duke University Press, 2007); James Edward Smethurst, *The Black Arts Movement: Literary Nationalism in the 1960s and 1970s* (Chapel Hill: University of North Carolina Press, 2005), 29-38; Bill V. Mullen and James Smethurst, eds., *Left of the Color Line: Race, Radicalism, and Twentieth-Century Literature of the United States* (Chapel Hill: University of North Carolina Press, 2003), 1-12; Mary Helen Washington, "Alice Childress, Lorraine Hansberry, and Claudia Jones: Black Women Write the Popular Front," in Mullen and Smethurst, *Left of the Color Line*, 183-200.

26. W. E. B. Du Bois, "The World Peace Movement," in *Against Racism: Unpublished Essays, Papers, Addresses, 1867-1961*, ed. Herbert Aptheker (Amherst: University of Massachusetts Press, 1985), 238.

27. Civil Rights Congress, *We Charge Genocide*, 3; Perry, *White Chauvinism and the Struggle for Peace*, 6-7; Gerald Horne, *Communist Front? The Civil Rights Congress, 1946-1956* (Rutherford: Associated University Presses, 1988), 163-81.

28. Civil Rights Congress, *We Charge Genocide*, 9; Horne, *Communist Front?*, 169.

29. Civil Rights Congress, *We Charge Genocide*, 5-6, 132-53.

30. Ibid., 7-8.

31. Quoted in Martin B. Duberman, *Paul Robeson* (New York: Knopf, 1989), 395; Kenneth Janken, *White: The Biography of Walter White and the NAACP* (New York: New Press, 2003), 319-21.

32. Davies, *Left of Karl Marx*, 147-58.

33. Worthy, *Our Disgrace in Indo-China*, 5-6; on Worthy's work as a war intellectual in the late 1950s and 1960s, see Peniel E. Joseph, *Waiting 'til the Midnight Hour: A Narrative History of Black Power in America* (New York: Henry Holt, 2006), 44-51.

34. Worthy, *Our Disgrace in Indo-China*.

35. Ibid.

36. William Worthy, "Of Global Bondage," *Crisis* 61 (October 1954): 469.

37. St. Clair Drake, "The International Implications of Race and Race Relations," *Journal of Negro Education* 20 (Summer 1951): 261-64; Hugh H. Smythe and Mabel M. Smythe, "Report from Japan: Comments on the Race Question," *Crisis* 59 (March 1952): 159. On St. Clair Drake's political and cultural activism in the 1950s, see Kevin K. Gaines, *American Africans in Ghana: Black Expatriates and the Civil Rights Era* (Chapel Hill: University of North Carolina Press, 2006), 44-51.

38. Drake, "International Implications," 278.

39. Forman, *Making of Black Revolutionaries*.

40. Kathleen Currie, interview with Ethel Payne, August 25, September 8, 1987, Women in Journalism, Washington Press Club Foundation, http://www.wpcf.org/oralhistory/payn.html; Von Eschen, *Race against Empire*, 172.

41. Richard Wright, *Color Curtain*, in *Black Power: Three Books from Exile: Black Power, The Color Curtain, and White Man, Listen!* (1957; reprint, New York: HarperPerennial, 2008), 437-40; Hazel Rowley, *The Life and Times of Richard Wright* (Chicago: University of Chicago Press, 2001), 462-68. On the Bandung Conference, see Mullen, *Afro-Orientalism*, 59-63; Von Eschen, *Race against Empire*, 167-73; Cary Fraser, "An American Dilemma: Race and Realpolitik in the American Response to the Bandung Conference,

1955," in *Window on Freedom: Race, Civil Rights, and Foreign Affairs, 1945–1988*, ed. Brenda Gayle Plummer (Chapel Hill: University of North Carolina Press, 2003), 115–40; and Currie interview with Payne, September 22, 1987, 63–84.

42. Von Eschen, *Race against Empire*, 173.

43. Currie interview with Payne, September 22, 1987, 71–73.

44. Forman, *Making of Black Revolutionaries*, 279–80.

45. "NACW Calls for Probe of Mississippi Killing," *Baltimore Afro-American*, July 2, 1955, 20; David T. Beito, *Black Maverick: T. R. M. Howard's Fight for Civil Rights and Economic Power* (Urbana: University of Illinois Press, 2009), 108–10. In December 1955, Courts was shot. See James Hicks, "Mob Shoots Leader," *Baltimore Afro-American*, December 3, 1955, 1.

46. "3rd Lynching of the Year Shocks Nation," *Baltimore Afro-American*, September 10, 1955, 1; Beito, *Black Maverick*, 115–50.

47. "NAACP Urges U.S. Action in Miss. 'Reign of Terror,'" *Baltimore Afro-American*, September 17, 1955, 14.

48. Alice Kaplan, *The Interpreter* (New York: Free Press, 2005), 173.

49. "'Were Never into Meanness' Says Accused Men's Mother," *Memphis Commercial Appeal*, September 2, 1955, in *The Lynching of Emmett Till: A Documentary Narrative*, ed. Christopher Metress (Charlottesville: University of Virginia Press, 2002), 34–37; Gene Roberts and Hank Klibanoff, *The Race Beat: The Press, the Civil Rights Struggle, and the Awakening of a Nation* (New York: Vintage, 2006).

50. Metress, *Lynching of Emmett Till*, 37–45.

51. Sam Johnson, "Jury Hears Defense and Prosecution Arguments as Testimony Ends in Kidnap-Slaying Case," *Greenwood Commonwealth*, September 23, 1955, reprinted in Metress, *Lynching of Emmett Till*, 99.

52. Roberts and Klibanoff, *Race Beat*, 19.

53. Olive Arnold Adams, *Time Bomb: Mississippi Exposed and the Full Story of Emmett Till* (Mound Bayou: Mississippi Regional Council of Negro Leadership, 1956), 17.

54. Metress, *Lynching of Emmett Till*, 246; Roberts and Klibanoff, *Race Beat*, 101–2.

55. Ruth Feldstein, *Motherhood in Black and White: Race and Sex in American Liberalism, 1930–1965* (Ithaca: Cornell University Press, 2000), 86–110.

56. Aldon D. Morris, *The Origins of the Civil Rights Movement: Black Communities Organizing for Change* (New York: Free Press, 1984), 51–55; Steven Hahn, *The Political Worlds of Slavery and Freedom* (Cambridge: Harvard University Press, 2009), 149–50. On Parks, see Jeanne Theoharis, "'A Life History of Being Rebellious': The Radicalism of Rosa Parks," in *Want to Start a Revolution? Radical Women in the Black Freedom Struggle*, ed. Dayo F. Gore, Jeanne Theoharris, and Komozi Woodard (New York: New York University Press, 2009), 115–37; Marisa Chappell, Jenny Hutchinson, and Brian Ward, "'Dress Modestly, Neatly . . . as if You Were Going to Church': Respectability, Class, and Gender in the Montgomery Bus Boycott and the Early Civil Rights Movement," in *Gender and the Civil Rights Movement*, ed. Peter Lin and Sharon Monteith (New Brunswick, N.J.: Rutgers University Press, 2004), 69–100. For African Americans' interest in South Africa, see Francis Njubi Nesbitt, *Race for Sanctions: African Americans against Apartheid, 1946–1994* (Bloomington: Indiana University Press, 1994), 31; "Defiance in S[outh]

Africa," *Baltimore Afro-American*, September 13, 1952, 4; Bayard Rustin, "Africa Looks to Colored America," *Baltimore Afro-American*, November 29, 1952, A6; and Samuel Perry, "South Africa Set Anti-J. C. Strike," *Baltimore Afro-American*, April 18, 1953, 2.

57. Reverend Martin Luther King Jr., *Stride toward Freedom*, reprinted in *A Testament of Hope: The Essential Writings and Speeches of Martin Luther King, Jr.*, ed. James Melvin Washington (San Francisco: Harper, 1986), 425-27, 438-50; Bayard Rustin, "Montgomery Diary," in *Time on Two Crosses: The Collected Writings of Bayard Rustin*, ed. Devon W. Carbado and Donald Weise (San Francisco: Cleis Press, 2003), 58-65.

58. Christopher B. Strain, *Pure Fire: Self-Defense as Activism in the Civil Rights Era* (Athens: University of Georgia Press, 2005), 36-48; Rustin, "Montgomery Diary," 58; John D'Emilio, *Lost Prophet: The Life and Times of Bayard Rustin* (Chicago: University of Chicago Press, 2004), 237-46.

59. Rustin, "Montgomery Diary," 58.

60. Ibid. On Rustin's work in writing chapter 4 of *Speak Truth to Power*, see D'Emilio, *Lost Prophet*, 219-22.

61. Rustin, "Montgomery Diary," 60.

62. William Worthy, "Worthy Finds Montgomery Is Moscow," *Baltimore Afro-American*, March 6, 1956; "Tale of Two Cities," *Baltimore Afro-American*, March 20, 1956, 8; "None Are So Blind," *Baltimore Afro-American*, October 30, 1956, 11.

63. Reverend Martin Luther King Jr., "Nonviolence and Racial Justice," in *Testament of Hope*, 7-8.

64. Forman, *Making of Black Revolutionaries*, 105.

65. Richard M. Weaver, "Integration Is Communization," *National Review*, July 13, 1957, 67.

66. Pete Daniel, *Lost Revolutions: The South in the 1950s* (Chapel Hill: University of North Carolina Press for Smithsonian National Museum of American History, 2000), 251-57.

67. Ibid.

68. "Integration Help Seen in Bombing of School," *Los Angeles Times*, September 16, 1957.

69. "U.S. Troops Put Down Little Rock Outbreak," *Los Angeles Times*, September 26, 1957, 1, 10.

70. See http://rcarterpittman.org/images/Little_Rock.jpg (accessed February 9, 2011), and R. Carter Pittman, "The Federal Invasion of Arkansas: In Light of the Constitution," *American Mercury*, February 1958, 117-22.

71. "Reds Backing Integration, Senator Says," *Los Angeles Times*, September 29, 1957, 14; George Gallup, "Nation Backs President on Troops' Use," *Los Angeles Times*, October 4, 1957, 2; Holmes Alexander, "If Little Rock Were a Foreign Adventure," *Los Angeles Times*, October 8, 1957, B4.

72. "Satchmo Ready to Take Golden Horn to Russia," *Los Angeles Times*, October 11, 1957, 5.

73. Strain, *Pure Fire*, 7.

74. Julian Mayfield, "Challenge to Negro Leadership: The Case of Robert Williams," in *Reporting Civil Rights*, pt. 1, *American Journalism, 1941-1963* (New York: Library of America, 2003), 558.

75. Ibid., 564.

76. Robert F. Williams, *Negroes with Guns* (New York: Marzani and Munsell, 1962; reprint, Chicago: Third World Press, 1973), 40.

77. Forman, *Making of Black Revolutionaries*, 105.

78. Scott H. Bennett, *Radical Pacifism: The War Resisters League and Gandhian Nonviolence in America, 1915–1963* (Syracuse: Syracuse University Press, 2003), xv–xvi; D'Emilio, *Lost Prophet*, 223–48; William Worthy, "Worthy Views Group as Custodians of Democracy," *Atlanta Daily World*, May 8, 1957, 6.

79. Washington, "Alice Childress, Lorraine Hansberry, and Claudia Jones," 185.

80. Rampersad, *Life of Langston Hughes*, 2:181, 196.

81. Frederick Glaysher, ed., *Collected Prose: Robert Hayden* (Ann Arbor: University of Michigan Press, 1984), 136; Paule Marshall, *Triangular Road: A Memoir* (New York: Basic Books, 2009), 20–21.

82. See Hughes's writings about the efficacy of war in freedom struggles, in Langston Hughes, "Democracy, Negroes, and Writers," in *Essays on Art, Race, Politics and World Affairs*, ed. Christopher De Santis (Columbia: University of Missouri Press, 2002), 211–12.

83. Langston Hughes, "Memo to Non-White Peoples," in *The Collected Poems of Langston Hughes*, ed. Arnold Rampersad (New York: Knopf, 1994), 456; William Worthy, "Laughing to Keep from Crying!," *Baltimore Afro-American* (magazine section), July 1, 1967, 5. Hughes's "Memo" was originally published in *Africa South*, April–June 1957, 99.

84. John Oliver Killens, *And Then We Heard the Thunder* (New York: Knopf, 1962; reprint, 1970).

85. For important discussions of Afro-Asian encounters through World War II, see Marc Gallicchio, *The African American Encounter with Japan and China: Black Internationalism in Asia, 1895–1945* (Chapel Hill: University of North Carolina Press, 2000), 182–83, 203–7.

86. Killens, *And Then We Heard the Thunder*, 314–85, quote on 331. Killens provides a fictional account of a ten-day riot that the military has yet to acknowledge. Anecdotal accounts and Killens's novel offer the only evidence of this brutal battle between black and white troops in the streets of Brisbane. See Yuki Tanaka, *Japan's Comfort Women: Sexual Slavery and Prostitution during World War II and the U.S. Occupation* (New York: Routledge, 2002), 102–3, and Kay Saunders, "In a Cloud of Lust: Black GIs and Sex in World War II," in *Gender and War: Australia at War in the Twentieth Century*, ed. Joy Doumasi and Marilyn Lake (Melbourne: Cambridge University Press, 1995), 178–90.

87. Killens, *And Then We Heard the Thunder*, 485.

Chapter 5

1. Charles R. Cross, *Room Full of Mirrors: A Biography of Jimi Hendrix* (New York: Hyperion, 2005), 82–89.

2. Rick St. John, *Circle of Helmets: Poetry and Letters of the Vietnam Years* (Bloomington, Ind.: 1st Books, 2002); Merrill Roff, "Juvenile Delinquency and Military Service," in *Selective Service and American Society*, ed. Roger W. Little (New York: Russell Sage Foundation, 1969), 111–12.

3. Tony Brown, *Jimi Hendrix: In His Own Words* (London: Omnibus Press, 1994), 15.

4. Cross, *Room Full of Mirrors*, 75–82.

5. Brink Lindsey, *The Age of Abundance: How Prosperity Transformed America's Politics and Culture* (New York: Collins/HarperCollins, 2007).

6. Lizbeth Cohen, *Consumer Republic: The Politics of Consumption in Postwar America* (New York: Vintage, 2003), 137–46; Mark R. Grandstaff, "Making the Military American: Advertising, Reform, and the Demise of an Antistanding Military Tradition, 1945–1955," *Journal of Military History* 60 (April 1996): 299–324.

7. Quoted in Nikhil Pal Singh, *Black Is a Country: Race and the Unfinished Struggle for Democracy* (Cambridge: Harvard University Press, 2004), 166, 167.

8. "The Great Society—in Uniform," *Newsweek*, August 22, 1966, 68.

9. Kathleen Currie, interview with Ethel Payne, September 24, 1987, Women in Journalism, Washington Press Club Foundation, 94, http://www.wpcf.org/oralhistory/payn .html.

10. Clyde Taylor, "Then and Now," in *Vietnam and Black America: An Anthology of Protest and Resistance*, ed. Clyde Taylor (Garden City, N.Y.: Anchor, 1973), 20; Mike Marqusee, *Redemption Song: Muhammad Ali and the Spirit of the Sixties* (New York: Verso, 1999), 178–79.

11. William Peterson, foreword to Civil Rights Congress, *We Charge Genocide: The Historic Petition to the United Nations for Relief from a Crime of the United States against the Negro People* (New York, 1951; reprint, New York: International Publishers, new ed., 1970), viii–xi; John McDonald to John A. Morsell, August 24, 1967, NAACP Papers, pt. 28, series B, reel 13, Vietnam Correspondence, 1966–1967.

12. "Tan Worker Hit Hardest in Economic Downturn," *Baltimore Afro-American*, March 11, 1961, 3; Louis Lautier, "What's to Be Done about Job Problem?," *Baltimore Afro-American*, March 18, 1961, 18.

13. James Baldwin, "Sonny's Blues," in *Going to Meet the Man* (New York: Vintage, 1995), 104; originally published in *Partisan Review* 24 (Summer 1957): 327–58.

14. Ibid., 113.

15. *Congressional Record*, June 1, 1960, 11563.

16. Morton Puner, "What the Army Taught Us about Integration," *Coronet*, June 1960, 107.

17. Kimberley L. Phillips interview with Don Phillips, March 31, 2007, Williamsburg, Va., in author's possession; RJ Smith, *The Great Black Way: L.A. in the 1940s and the Lost African American Renaissance* (New York: Public Affairs, 2006), 235–53; Stephen Grant Meyer, *As Long as They Don't Move Next Door: Segregation and Racial Conflict in American Neighborhoods* (New York: Rowman and Littlefield, 2000), 75–78, 115–16, 127–29; Gerald Horne, *Fire This Time: The Watts Uprising and the 1960s* (Charlottesville: University Press of Virginia, 1995), 31–36.

18. Phillips interview.

19. Ibid. Their fear was widely shared. See Jean Carper, *Bitter Greetings: The Scandal of the Military Draft* (New York: Grossman, 1967), 59.

20. Colin L. Powell, *My American Journey* (New York: Random House, 1995), 23.

21. Ibid., 28.

22. "Four Draft Registrants Allege Bias," *Washington Post*, October 17, 1961, A1.

23. Ethel L. Payne, "The U.S. Armed Forces and Integration," *Chicago Defender*, November 16, 1957, 11.

24. Morris J. MacGregor, *Integration of the Armed Services, 1940–1965* (Washington, D.C.: Center of Military History, 1981); Elizabeth Lutes Hillman, *Defending America: Military Culture and the Cold War Court-Martial* (Princeton: Princeton University Press, 2005).

25. For an important analysis of the role of southern migrants in postwar racial politics outside the South, see James N. Gregory, *The Southern Diaspora: How the Great Migrations of Black and White Southerners Changed America* (Chapel Hill: University of North Carolina Press, 2005), esp. 302–20.

26. Steve Maxner interview with Joe Powell, December 27, 2000, Vietnam Archive Oral History Project, Texas Tech University, http://www.vietnam.ttu.edu/index.php.

27. Letter from H. M. McCowen to Roy Wilkins, December 7, 1960, General Files, 1956–1964, NAACP Papers, pt. 24, series C, reel 38.

28. Memorandum, Major General H. D. Ives, Headquarters, Fort Jackson, June 15, 1961, and memorandum, Secretary of Defense, "Availability of Facilities to Military Personnel," June 19, 1961, both in General Files, 1956–1964, NAACP Papers, pt. 24, series C, reel 38.

29. Brown, *Jimi Hendrix*, 13; "Ballad of the Green Beret" (RCA Victor, 1966).

30. "4,000 'Chutists Jump," *New York Times*, August 12, 1961, 42; "Paratroopers Fly to Turkey for War Games," *Chicago Daily Tribune*, September 10, 1961, 3.

31. Tom Wicker, "President Warns of Long Struggle with Communism," *New York Times*, October 13, 1961, 1.

32. Cross, *Room Full of Mirrors*, 94–95.

33. Stanley Karnow, *Vietnam: A History* (New York: Penguin, 1997), 270; Phillips interview.

34. Marvin Gaye's "Soldier's Plea" first appeared on his 1962 album, *That Stubborn Kinda Fella* (Tamla, 1962).

35. "Diggs Asks 'Honorable' Chance in Defense Plans," *Baltimore Afro-American*, September 9, 1961, 3.

36. "Time Out for a Smoke," *Baltimore Afro-American*, September 9, 1961, 4.

37. "Worthy Warns against U.S. Troops in Cuba," *Baltimore Afro-American*, May 6, 1961, 15.

38. Quoted in Clarence R. Wyatt, *Paper Soldiers: The American Press and the Vietnam War* (Chicago: University of Chicago Press, 1995), 91.

39. Karnow, *Vietnam*, 340–41.

40. "Negro Writer Slated for State Department Job," *Chicago Daily Defender*, January 26, 1961, 1.

41. "Keep Press Free, Rowan Tells Group," *Chicago Daily Defender*, May 9, 1961, 11.

42. Wyatt, *Paper Soldiers*, 92; Karnow, *Vietnam*, 312; Louis Martin, "The Negro Decision Makers," *Chicago Defender*, April 21, 1962, 8.

43. Martin, "Negro Decision Makers."

44. Quoted in William M. Hammond, *Reporting Vietnam: Media and Military at War* (Lawrence: University Press of Kansas, 1999), 22.

45. Tobias Wolff, *In Pharaoh's Army: Memories of the Lost War* (New York: Vintage, 1995), 28–29. Wolff determined that the Vietnamese preferred white over black military advisors. "The Vietnamese had added our bigotries to their own, and now looked down on blacks along with Chinese, Montagnards, Lao, Cambodians, and other Vietnamese" (29). See also Phillips interview. Between 1964 and 1966, Phillips helped plan Operation Junction City for the 173rd, which was the first major invasion of U.S. paratroopers.

46. Carper, *Bitter Greetings*, 37.

47. Phillips interview; "Maryland U. Star Tamburello Files Suit to Beat Draft," *Chicago Daily Defender*, October 2, 1956, 18.

48. Quoted in Carper, *Bitter Greetings*, 76.

49. "Draft to Stay," *Chicago Daily Defender*, August 6, 1956, 2; "Army Cuts Draft Call by 2,000," *Chicago Daily Defender*, June 25, 1957, 2; Louis Cassels, "Questions and Answers on Getting Caught in the Draft Are Numerous," *Chicago Daily Defender*, August 31, 1961, 9.

50. "Hits Misuse of Draft Exams," *Chicago Daily Defender*, April 6, 1961, 8.

51. "There's a Career for You in WAC," *Chicago Defender*, September 4, 1954, 15; "Draft Board in New Quarters," *Chicago Daily Defender*, February 4, 1957, 13; "Recruiting at the Theater," *Washington Post*, March 15, 1962, C20.

52. "Convict Moslem Leader's Son," *Chicago Defender*, May 21, 1958, A2; "Black Muslim Faces Term on Draft Charge," *Chicago Defender*, July 28, 1962, 3.

53. "Draft Boards Sound Warning," *Chicago Defender*, November 25, 1961, 4; "Selective Service Lists Chicago Delinquents," *Chicago Defender*, December 23, 1961, 5.

54. "24 Draft Delinquents Warned to Report," *Chicago Defender*, September 24, 1962, 8.

55. See "Draft Boards List Delinquent Registrants," *Chicago Defender*, July 8, 1963, 16; "Draft Boards List Delinquent Youths," *Chicago Defender*, October 1, 1963, A6.

56. "Know Your Negro History," *Chicago Daily Defender*, April 16, 1964, 5.

57. Carper, *Bitter Greetings*, 32, 48.

58. Pete Daniel, *Lost Revolutions: The South in the 1950s* (Chapel Hill: University of North Carolina Press for Smithsonian National Museum of American History, 2000), 251–83.

59. Thomas Sugrue, *Sweet Land of Liberty: The Forgotten Struggle of Civil Rights* (New York: Random House, 2008), 325–35, 351–52; Suzanne E. Smith, *Dancing in the Street: Motown and the Cultural Politics of Detroit* (Cambridge: Harvard University Press, 1999), 171–88.

60. Gregory, *Southern Diaspora*; Sugrue, *Sweet Land of Liberty*, 356–80.

61. Annelise Orleck, *Storming Caesars Palace: How Black Mothers Fought Their Own War on Poverty* (New York: Beacon Press, 2005), 81; Deborah Gray White, *Too Heavy a Load: Black Women in Defense of Themselves, 1894–1994* (New York: Norton, 1999), 198–200.

62. Taylor Branch, *At Canaan's Edge: America in the King Years, 1965–68* (New York: Simon and Schuster, 2006), 371–72.

63. Sue Cronk, "Way Out of Poverty for a Man Is a Job," *Washington Post*, February 26, 1964, D1.

64. Daniel P. Moynihan, "Who Gets in the Army?," *New Republic*, November 5, 1966, 21.

65. President's Task Force on Manpower Conservation, *One Third of a Nation: A Report on Young Men Found Unqualified for Military Service* (Washington, D.C., 1964), 2–5.

66. David R. Segal, *Recruiting for Uncle Sam: Citizenship and Military Manpower Policy* (Lawrence: University Press of Kansas, 1989), 91.

67. Moynihan, "Who Gets in the Army?," 22; Segal, *Recruiting for Uncle Sam*, 91–92.

68. Robert S. McNamara, *The Essence of Security: Reflections in Office* (New York: Harper and Row, 1968), 123.

69. "Project One Hundred Thousand, Department of Defense, 1963–1969, Manpower," in *Civil Rights, the White House, and the Justice Department, 1945–1968*, vol. 3, *Integration of the Armed Forces*, ed. Michael R. Belknap (New York: Garland, 1991), 463–64.

70. Segal, *Recruiting for Uncle Sam*, 91; second quote in Christian G. Appy, *Working-Class War: American Combat Soldiers and Vietnam* (Chapel Hill: University of North Carolina Press, 1993), 32.

71. Howard H. McFann, *Progress Report on HumROO Research on Project 100,000* (Alexandria, Va.: George Washington University, 1969), 6.

72. Thomas C. Sticht, *Cast Off Youth: Policy and Training Methods from the Military Experience* (New York: Praeger, 1987), 45.

73. Amy E. Murrell, "The 'Impossible' Prince Edward Case: The Endurance of Resistance in a Southside County," in *The Moderate's Dilemma: Massive Resistance to School Desegregation in Virginia*, ed. Matthew D. Lassiter and Andrew B. Lewis (Charlottesville: University of Virginia Press, 1998), 134–66.

74. Neil Sheehan, "Military Ready to Absorb Influx of Former 'Rejects,'" *New York Times*, October 16, 1966, 9.

75. Gene Roberts, "Civil Rights: A Turning Point," *New York Times*, September 19, 1966, 1.

76. John Herbers, "Republicans Say President Leads U.S. to 'Failure,'" *New York Times*, January 20, 1967, 1; "Federal Budget Assailed by GOP," *New York Times*, February 3, 1967, 1.

77. "Abuse of the Draft," *Baltimore Afro-American*, January 15, 1966, 4; Whitney Young, "Democratizing the Draft," *Baltimore Afro-American*, June 18, 1966, 20.

78. Hanson W. Baldwin, "The Draft Is Here to Stay, But It Should Be Changed," *New York Times Magazine*, November 20, 1966, 99, 102.

79. Karl H. Purnell, "The Negro in Vietnam," *Nation*, July 3, 1967, 8.

80. "Armed Forces: The Integrated Society," *Time*, December 23, 1966, 22.

81. Phillips interview.

82. Currie interview with Payne.

83. Gene Grove, "The Army and the Negro," *New York Times Magazine*, July 24, 1966, 5.

84. Ibid., 48.

85. St. John, *Circle of Helmets*, 23.

86. David Parks, *GI Diary* (Washington, D.C.: Howard University Press, 1984), 50; Phillips interview. Don Phillips was on that road the morning Parks arrived. Phillips recalled that his company "cleared the road" so that the 56th Infantry could move into place.

87. Grove, "Army and the Negro," 48–51.

88. Julius Lester, *Revolutionary Notes* (New York: R. W. Baron, 1969), 83.

89. Ibid., 89.

90. L. Deckle McLean, "The Black Man and the Draft," *Ebony*, August 1968, 61–65.

91. Robert Lipsyte, "Fighter Charges Board with Bias," *New York Times*, February 18, 1966, 37; Marqusee, *Redemption Song*, 74.

92. Carper, *Bitter Greetings*, 40.

93. "Namath and Clay Cited as Draft Bill Is Backed," *New York Times*, February 10, 1966, 48.

94. Carper, *Bitter Greetings*, 46–49.

95. "Clay Says Draft Board Weighs His Reclassification," February 11, 1966, 25; "Cassius Nears Induction," *Chicago Daily Defender*, February 14, 1966, 28. For General Lewis Hershey's role in changing the status of other prominent antiwar critics, see Marqusee, *Redemption Song*, 231.

96. Lipsyte, "Fighter Charges Board with Bias," 37.

97. Robert Lipsyte, "Children Bring Joy to World-Weary Champion," *New York Times*, February 20, 1966, S3.

98. "Clay to Fight Induction," *Chicago Daily Defender*, February 21, 1966, 64. Mike Marqusee notes that Robert Lipsyte, the *New York Times* sportswriter, spent the day with Ali. Reportedly "disoriented," Ali "blurted out the fateful riposte: 'Man, I ain't got no quarrel with them Vietcong.'" The *New York Times* reported the statement as it appeared in the *Defender*, except for one difference: "Vietcongs." See "Clay Plans to Apologize in Chicago for Remarks about Draft Classification," *New York Times*, February 22, 1966, 17. By June, however, the *Defender* had reverted to quoting Ali as saying, "I ain't got no quarrel with them Viet Congs." See "Clay Deferment Rejected," *Chicago Defender*, June 9, 1966, 38. Latino and Mexican American activists made similar arguments to the draft board in this period. See Lorena Oropeza, *¡Raza Sí! ¡Guerra No!: Chicano Protest and Patriotism during the Viet Nam War Era* (Berkeley: University of California Press, 2005), 89–92. Native Americans identified with Asians more generally. See Dennis Banks, *Ojibwa Warrior: Dennis Banks and the American Indian Movement* (Norman: University of Oklahoma Press, 2004), 46–47.

99. "Ernie Terrell Blasts Clay," *Chicago Daily Defender*, February 23, 1966, 64.

100. Robert Lipsyte, "Instant Bile," *New York Times*, February 24, 1966, 42.

101. Carper, *Bitter Greetings*, 61, 103. In 1966, Hershey reclassified fifteen University of Michigan students who staged a sit-in at an Ann Arbor draft board.

102. Lipsyte, "Instant Bile."

103. "Clay Faces Reclassification to 1-A," *New York Times*, February 12, 1966, 41.

104. Lipsyte, "Instant Bile."

105. Robert Lipsyte, "Louisville Rejects Plans for a Clay-Terrell Title Fight," *New York Times*, March 2, 1966; "Coast Backs Boycott," *New York Times*, March 10, 1966, 37; "Denounces Clay," *Chicago Daily Defender*, March 29, 1966, 3.

106. Gladwin Hill, "Swift Action Is Pledged; Watts Area Tense in Wake of Riot," *New York Times*, March 17, 1966, 1.

107. Harry Golden, "Only in America," *Chicago Defender* (national ed.), March 19, 1966, 10.

108. "Cassius' Father Says Army 'May Straighten Out' Champ," *Chicago Defender*, March 22, 1966.

109. "Clay Deferment Rejected," *Chicago Daily Defender*, June 9, 1966, 38; "Cassius Hearing August 18," *Chicago Daily Defender*, August 9, 1966, 28.

110. Jackie Robinson, "An Open Letter to Dr. Martin L. King," *Chicago Defender* (national ed.), May 13, 1967, 10.

111. "Ali (Clay) Renews Action to Halt Army Induction," *Chicago Defender*, March 22, 1967, 25.

112. "Ali Has a Date to Enter Army," *Chicago Daily Defender*, March 30, 1967, 1. On Executive Order 11289, see Michael S. Foley, *Confronting the War Machine: Draft Resistance during the Vietnam War* (Chapel Hill: University of North Carolina Press, 2003).

113. Carper, *Bitter Greetings*, 145.

114. "Draft Dodging," *Chicago Defender*, August 5, 1965, 17.

115. James A. Daly, *Black Prisoner of War: A Conscientious Objector's Vietnam Memoir* (Lawrence: University of Kansas Press, 2000), 1; Terry Whitmore, *Memphis, Nam, Sweden: The Story of a Black Deserter* (1971; reprint, Jackson: University Press of Mississippi, 1997), 37.

116. Parks, *GI Diary*, 31.

117. Whitmore, *Memphis, Nam, Sweden*, 36.

118. Ibid., 37.

119. Ibid., 38.

120. Isaac Witter, *My Experience in Vietnam: An African American Perspective* (PublishAmerica, 2003), 7–8.

121. Daly, *Black Prisoner of War*, 2–3, 16, 20–36, 39.

122. Currie interview with Payne, 94–96.

123. Ethel L. Payne, "How the Press Works in Viet Nam," *Chicago Daily Defender*, January 4, 1967, 1.

124. Ethel L. Payne, "First Impressions in Vietnam," *Chicago Daily Defender*, January 3, 1967, 4.

125. Ethel L. Payne, "Vietnam: The History of an Abused People," *Chicago Defender* (national ed.), January 7, 1967, 28.

126. Ibid.

127. Ethel L. Payne, "Two Views of the Conflict in Vietnam," *Chicago Daily Defender*, January 23, 1967, 4.

128. Ibid., 8; Michael E. Peterson, *The Combined Action Platoons: The U.S. Marines' Other War in Vietnam* (New York: Praeger, 1989), 31–51.

129. Le Ly Hayslip, *When Heaven and Earth Changed Places: A Vietnamese Woman's Journey from War to Peace* (New York: Plume, 1990); Michael Bilton and Kevin Sim, *Four Hours in My Lai* (New York: Viking, 1992), 76–78, 297–98.

130. Mike Davis, "Your Decisions Have to Be Right," *Baltimore Afro-American*, August 5, 1967, 1–2; for similar statements, including some from Brown, see "Armed Forces: Democracy in the Foxhole," *Time*, May 23, 1967.

131. Mike Davis, "When You Go into Combat You Have to Hang Tough," *Baltimore Afro-American*, August 5, 1967, 8.

132. Currie interview with Payne, 95.

133. Ron Steinman, ed., "Doris Lucki Allen," in *Women in Vietnam: The Oral History* (New York: TV Books, 2000), 251–52.

134. Marvin Kupfer, "The Negro View: A Special Anguish," *Newsweek*, July 10, 1967, 34.

135. Clyde Taylor, introduction to *Vietnam and Black America: An Anthology of Protest and Resistance*, ed. Clyde Taylor (Garden City, N.Y.: Anchor, 1973), 17–18.

136. "Armed Forces: Democracy in the Foxhole."

137. Charles R. Eisendrath, "The Black Hessians," *Nation*, January 29, 1968, 148.

138. William Worthy, "GI Viet Mutiny Reported," *Baltimore Afro-American*, May 6, 1967, 4; Matthew Rinaldi, "The Olive-Drab Rebels: Military Organizing during the Vietnam Era," *Radical America* 8 (May–June 1974): 29–30.

139. "One War," *Nation*, October 14, 1968, 357.

140. Parks, *GI Diary*, 1–2, 10–13.

141. Whitmore, *Memphis, Nam, Sweden*, 41–45.

142. Parks, *GI Diary*, 71–75.

143. Ibid., 98–99.

144. Ibid., 71. On soldiers' escalating and indiscriminate violence and racial fury in Vietnam, see Bilton and Sim, *Four Hours in My Lai*, 39–41, 76–78, 297–98. The My Lai Massacre was part of a larger pattern of assaults.

145. Gordon Parks, *Voices in the Mirror: An Autobiography* (New York: Doubleday, 1990), 241. And on African Americans' participation and refusals to participate in the My Lai Massacre, see Bilton and Sim, *Four Hours in My Lai*, 19–21, 117, 298–99. The soldiers, including the black soldiers, felt powerless to stop the events. See Herbert Carter's trial testimony, 298–99.

146. Bilton and Sim, *Four Hours in My Lai*, 19–21, 82–83, 372–73; "Remember My Lai," Frontline Broadcast, original broadcast, May 23, 1989. Transcript is available online: www.pbs.org/wgbh/pages/frontline/programs/transcripts/714.html.

147. Whitmore, *Memphis, Nam, Sweden*, 52.

148. Ibid., 53–54.

149. Ibid., 79; "Armed Forces: Democracy in the Foxhole."

150. Whitmore, *Memphis, Nam, Sweden*, 103–5; Jesse W. Lewis Jr., "Off Duty We're in a Different Bag, Patrons of Soulsville Philosophize," *Washington Post*, April 4, 1967, A1; Steward Kellerman, "Swinging Counter-Culture Develops on Army's Vietnam Bases," *Baltimore Afro-American*, May 15, 1971, 22; Wallace Terry, *Guess Who's Coming Home: Black Fighting Men Recorded Live in Vietnam* (2006; originally released by Motown Records, 1972).

151. "Recommendation on Dapping," memo from Kermit D. Johnson, Lt. Colonel and Chaplain, to William R. Kraft Jr., August 12, 1971, copy in author's possession. I thank General (Ret.) Johnson for providing me a copy of his memo.

152. Herman Graham III, *The Brothers' Vietnam War: Black Power, Manhood, and the Military Experience* (Gainesville: University Press of Florida, 2003), 105–6; Grove, "Army and the Negro," 48; Ethel L. Payne, "173rd Airborne Brigade: The Heroes' Address," *Chicago Defender*, March 23, 1967, 4.

153. Richard Burks Veronne interview with Steve Dant, March 9, 2005, Steve Dant

Collection, Vietnam Archive Oral History Project, Texas Tech University, http://www
.vietnam.ttu.edu/index.php; Zalin B. Grant, "Whites against Blacks in Vietnam," *New Republic*, January 18, 1969, 15.

154. William Greider, "Black Ire Erupts on Military Posts," *Washington Post*, August 16, 1969, A5.

155. Grove, "Army and the Negro," 50.

156. John T. Wheeler, "Black Power Comes to Vietnam as Racial Tensions Increase," *Washington Post*, April 20, 1969, 20; Greider, "Black Ire Erupts on Military Posts," A5.

157. Grant, "Whites against Blacks in Vietnam."

158. Ethel L. Payne, "How Negro Troops See War," *Chicago Defender*, April 11, 1967, 1.

159. Jeffrey Ogbar, *Black Power: Radical Politics and African American Identity* (Baltimore: Johns Hopkins University Press, 2004), 139; Currie interview with Payne, 97.

160. "Viet War Not My Fight, Says GI," *Baltimore Afro-American*, June 18, 1966; Terry, *Guess Who's Coming Home*.

161. Al Carroll, *"Medicine Bags and Dog Tags": American Indian Veterans from Colonial Times to the Second Iraq War* (Lincoln: University of Nebraska Press, 2008); Paul C. Rosier, *Serving Their Country: American Indian Politics and Patriotism in the Twentieth Century* (Cambridge: Harvard University Press, 2009).

162. James Lewes, *Protest and Survive: Underground GI Newspapers during the Vietnam War* (Westport, Conn.: Praeger, 2003), 68, 110-14, quote on 122.

163. Whitmore, *Memphis, Nam, Sweden*, 62-69.

164. Graham, *Brothers' Vietnam War*, 29-33; Wheeler, "Black Power Comes to Vietnam," 20.

165. "War within War," *Washington Post*, October 25, 1968, A24; John Lengel, "Racial Animosity among Troops at Danang Worries U.S. Officers," *Washington Post*, November 7, 1968, F2; Greider, "Black Ire Erupts on Military Posts," A1; Phillips interview; Graham, *Brothers' Vietnam War*, 34; John Darrell Sherwood, *Black Sailor, White Navy: Racial Unrest in the Fleet during the Vietnam War Era* (New York: New York University Press, 2007), 193-226.

166. Whitmore, *Memphis, Nam, Sweden*, 120.

167. Ibid., 124-67.

Chapter 6

1. Arnold Rampersad, *The Life of Langston Hughes*, vol. 2, *1941-1967, I Dream a World* (New York: Oxford University Press, 1988), quote on 386, 417.

2. Langston Hughes, "Montage of a Dream Deferred," in *Montage of a Dream Deferred*, in *The Collected Poems of Langston Hughes*, ed. Arnold Rampersad (New York: Knopf, 1994), 387; Scott Saul, *Freedom Is, Freedom Ain't: Jazz and the Making of the Sixties* (Cambridge: Harvard University Press, 2003), 124. See *Collected Poems of Langston Hughes*, where Hughes's poems from the 1950s and 1960s are like dispatches from the anticolonial struggles from Harlem and Chicago to Brazzaville and Cape Town.

3. James Edward Smethurst, *The Black Arts Movement: Literary Nationalism in the 1960s and 1970s* (Chapel Hill: University of North Carolina Press, 2005), 27; L. Deckle McLean, "The Black Man and the Draft," *Ebony*, August 1968, 61-66.

4. "Simple Solution to Vietnam War: Draft All Older White Men First," *Muhammad Speaks*, August 20, 1965, 17. Hughes wrote this article before the Watts riot, which began on August 11, 1965.

5. First published in the *Crisis* (June 1967) and *The Panther and the Lash: Poems of Our Times* (New York: Knopf, 1967). *Panther* included a series of critical poems about war. Nina Simone began performing the song in November 1966. See Robert Sherman, "Nina Simone Casts Her Moody Spells," *New York Times*, November 23, 1966, 28.

6. This history is gleaned from the letters each wrote the other and Simone's prefatory dedications to "The Backlash Blues." See letter from Langston Hughes to Nina Simone, January 26, 1965, box 147, folder 2724, series 1, personal correspondence, James Weldon Johnson Collection, Beinecke Library, Yale University, New Haven, Conn.

7. Ruth Feldstein, "'I Don't Trust You Anymore': Nina Simone, Culture, and Black Activism in the 1960s," *Journal of American History* 91 (March 2005): 1350; Sherman, "Nina Simone Casts Her Moody Spells," 28.

8. Nina Simone, "Backlash," *Protest Anthology* (Artwork Media, 2008).

9. Civil Rights Congress, *We Charge Genocide: The Historic Petition to the United Nations for Relief from a Crime of the United States against the Negro People* (New York, 1951; reprint, New York: International Publishers, new ed., 1970), viii; on Hughes's jazz performances, see Saul, *Freedom Is, Freedom Ain't*, 124. For his controlled "outrage" in his responses to charges from black activists abroad that he "lacked militancy," see Paule Marshall, *Triangular Road: A Memoir* (New York: Basic Books, 2009), 20-21.

10. Fred Powderledge, "Vietnam Issue Divides Leaders of Rights Groups," *New York Times*, August 29, 1965, E4; "Viet Rebuke Stirs Storm," *Baltimore Afro-American*, January 22, 1966, 14.

11. "Celler Bids Rights Leaders Restrain Vietnam Criticism," *New York Times*, April 15, 1966, 60; John Herbers, "Rights Backers Fear a Backlash," *New York Times*, September 21, 1966, 1; "NAACP Decries Stand of Dr. King on Vietnam," *New York Times*, April 11, 1967, 1; "Dr. King's Tragic Doctrine," *Pittsburgh Courier*, April 15, 1967, 6.

12. Carole Boyce Davies, *Left of Karl Marx: The Political Life of Black Communist Claudia Jones* (Durham: Duke University Press, 2007); Timothy B. Tyson, *Radio Free Dixie: Robert F. Williams and the Roots of Black Power* (Chapel Hill: University of North Carolina Press, 1999).

13. William Worthy, "Of Global Bondage," *Crisis* 61 (October 1954): 469; Nikhil Pal Singh, *Black Is a Country: Race and the Unfinished Struggle for Democracy* (Cambridge: Harvard University Press, 2004), 17-18, 38-39; Roi Ottley, *No Green Pastures: The Negro in Europe Today* (New York: Scribner's Sons, 1951), 1-8.

14. Morris Kaplan, "U.S. Negro Artists Go to Africa to Join in Cultural Exchange," *New York Times*, December 14, 1961, 54; Langston Hughes, "Cultural Exchange," in *Ask Your Mama*, in *Collected Poems of Langston Hughes*, 527.

15. Joyce Blackwell, *No Peace without Freedom: Race and the Women's International League for Peace and Freedom, 1915-1975* (Carbondale: Southern Illinois University Press, 2004), 143-64.

16. For close readings of these instances, see George Lipsitz, *Rainbow at Midnight: Labor and Culture in the 1940s* (Urbana: University of Illinois Press, 1994), 303-6, and Saul, *Freedom Is, Freedom Ain't*. For the larger context, see Penny M. Von Eschen,

Satchmo Blows Up the World: Jazz Ambassadors Play the Cold War (Cambridge: Harvard University Press, 2004).

17. Numerous contemporary black critics and scholars of African American culture made this point. See Ralph Ellison, *Shadow and Act* (New York: Random House, 1964), and Langston Hughes, *Ask Your Mama: 12 Moods for Jazz* (New York: Hill and Wang, 1961). Scholars since have probed these interrogations into black cultural life more generally. See Robin D. G. Kelley, *Race Rebels: Culture, Politics, and the Black Working Class* (New York: Free Press, 1994); Angela Davis, *Blues Legacies and Feminism: Gertrude Ma Rainey, Bessie Smith, and Billie Holiday* (New York: Pantheon, 1998); and Saul, *Freedom Is, Freedom Ain't.*

18. Mark Tucker, ed., *The Duke Ellington Reader* (New York: Oxford University Press, 1993), 150.

19. Lipsitz, *Rainbow at Midnight*, 305.

20. Homer Harris, "Atomic Bomb Blues," 1946 (Testament LP 2207; CBS CD 467249 2).

21. Various artists, *Eisenhower Blues* (Empire Musicwerks, remastered 2006); Guido Van Rijn, *The Truman and Eisenhower Blues: African American Blues and Gospel Songs, 1945-1960* (New York: Continuum, 2006).

22. James N. Gregory, *The Southern Diaspora: How the Great Migrations of Black and White Southerners Transformed America* (Chapel Hill: University of North Carolina Press, 2005), 153-55. Few scholars have given soul music the larger political, cultural, and social context that blues and jazz have received. Notable exceptions include Amiri Baraka, *The Autobiography of LeRoi Jones* (New York: Freudlich Books, 1984), 202-29; Monique Guillory and Richard C. Green, eds., *Soul: Black Power, Politics, and Pleasure* (New York: New York University Press, 1998); and Suzanne E. Smith, *Dancing in the Street: Motown and the Cultural Politics of Detroit* (Cambridge: Harvard University Press, 1999).

23. Smethurst, *Black Arts Movement*, 33.

24. Baraka, *Autobiography of LeRoi Jones*, 94-123, quote on 97.

25. Ibid., 209-10; Smethurst, *Black Arts Movement*, 147-53, 179-249.

26. Raymond Arsenault, *Freedom Riders: 1961 and the Struggle for Racial Justice* (New York: Oxford University Press, 2006), 23-74, 82-179.

27. Charles M. Payne, *I've Got the Light of Freedom: The Organizing Tradition and the Mississippi Freedom Struggle* (Berkeley: University of California Press, 1995), 2-5; Pete Daniel, *Lost Revolutions: The South in the 1950s* (Chapel Hill: University of North Carolina Press for Smithsonian National Museum of American History, 2000); Arsenault, *Freedom Riders*, 86-97; Lynne Olson, *Freedom's Daughters: The Unsung Heroines of the Civil Rights Movement from 1830 to 1970* (New York: Touchstone, 2001), 151-61; Eric Burner, *And Gently He Shall Lead Them: Robert Paris Moses and Civil Rights in Mississippi* (New York: New York University Press, 1995); John Lewis with Michael D'Orso, *Walking with the Wind: A Memoir of the Movement* (New York: Simon and Schuster, 1998); Adam Mack, "No Illusion of Separatism: James L. Bevel, the Civil Rights Movement, and the Vietnam War," *Peace and Change* 28 (January 2003): 110.

28. David Halberstam, *The Children* (New York: Random House, 1998), 14-38, 64-82.

29. Arsenault, *Freedom Riders*, 185.

30. Payne, *I've Got the Light of Freedom*, 77-100.

31. Blackwell, *No Peace without Freedom*, 166-69.

32. Dorothy Manley to Mildred Olmsted, May 25, 1963, Miscellaneous Correspondence, Georgia, series C, box 75, Papers of the Women's International League for Peace and Freedom, Peace Collection, Swarthmore Library, Swarthmore, Pa. Hereafter referred to as WILPF Papers.

33. Virginia Durr to Mildred Olmsted, January 20, 1964, Correspondence, Montgomery, Alabama, Branch, series C, box 72, WILPF Papers.

34. Virginia Durr to Annalee Stewart, May 24, 1965, Correspondence, Montgomery, Alabama, Branch, series C, box 72, WILPF Papers.

35. "Memorandum to WILPF," July 8, 1964, Black Sash folder, series B, 2, box Y, Burlington County, N.J., Branch, WILPF Papers.

36. Ibid.

37. "WILPF Work in the South," April 7, 1965, General Correspondence, 1960–1969, series C correspondence, box 70, Selma Project, WILPF Papers.

38. SNCC, "Survey: Current Field Work, Spring 1963," 6, in SNCC Field Reports, http://www.crmvet.org/docs/snccrpts.htm; Desoto County, Mississippi, field reports, July 18–August 10, 1964, SNCC Papers, 1959–1972 (Sanford, N.C.: Microfilming Corporation of America, 1982), reel 6. These reports, which originated out of the SNCC office in Atlanta, provide a wealth of information about local volunteers, especially their ages.

39. "Negro Soldiers Threaten to Clean Out the State of Mississippi," *New York Amsterdam News*, June 12, 1943, 1; "Widespread Race Riots Feared over Abuse of Negro Troops," *New York Amsterdam News*, June 19, 1943, 1. Local and military officials denied the reports, but soldiers who witnessed the riots insisted otherwise. See Pvt. L. Y., "Another Miss[issippi] Riot," *Baltimore Afro-American*, July 17, 1943. Rumors circulated, with many continuing for decades, that the army systematically massacred hundreds of men in the 364th—maybe more than 1,200 men—and then secretly buried them. See Carroll Case, *The Slaughter: An American Atrocity* (Biltmore Corporation, 1998). Though its decision was considered controversial, the military agreed to reopen the investigation of the hundreds of men who seemingly disappeared from the regiment.

40. Payne, *I've Got the Light of Freedom*, 111–15.

41. Ibid.

42. Ibid., 119.

43. Penn was a well-known and highly regarded school administrator in Washington, D.C. See George Lardner Jr., "Scare Shots Killed Penn, Court Told," *Washington Post*, September 3, 1964, A1; "Confession Read in Penn's Slaying," *New York Times*, September 3, 1964, 18.

44. Drew Pearson, "The Klan and Its Terror Squads," *Los Angeles Times*, March 31, 1965, A6.

45. Quoted in Clayborne Carson, *In Struggle: SNCC and the Black Awakening of the 1960s* (Cambridge: Harvard University Press, 1981), 187.

46. Ibid., 185; Lewis, *Walking with the Wind*, 370; "Viet Rebuke Stirs Storm," 14.

47. Lewis, *Walking with the Wind*, 370; Carson, *In Struggle*, 183.

48. See Fannie Lou Hamer's address to the 1964 Democratic National Convention, http://www.youtube.com/watch?v=G-RoVzAqhYk; Charles Marsh, *God's Long Summer: Stories of Faith and Civil Rights* (Princeton: Princeton University Press, 1999), 33–43; and

"Anti-Draft Circular," reprinted in *Black Protest: History Documents and Analyses, 1619 to the Present*, ed. Joanne Grant (New York: St. Martin's Press, 1968), 415–16.

49. Grant, *Black Protest*, 415. See Hamer's address to the 1964 Democratic National Convention, and Marsh, *God's Long Summer*, 33–43.

50. Lewis, *Walking with the Wind*, 375–76; SNCC, "Statement on Vietnam, January 6, 1966," in Grant, *Black Protest*, 416–17; "SNCC Leader Urges Flock Avoid U.S. Draft," *Chicago Defender*, January 10, 1966, 6.

51. Carson, *In Struggle*; Lewis, *Walking with the Wind*.

52. Lewis, *Walking with the Wind*, 397.

53. "Letter to the Membership," November 26, 1966, SNCC Papers, reel 23; Lewis, *Walking with the Wind*, 372.

54. *Peace and Freedom News*, no. 6, October 1, 1965, 4, SNCC Papers, reel 62.

55. Bruce Galphin, "Ft. Bragg Restricts Antiwar Papers," *Washington Post*, May 6, 1969, A4.

56. SNCC Flyer, "When a Black Man Registers for the Draft and Passes the Tests," n.d., SNCC Papers, reel 62.

57. Ibid.

58. Ibid.; "You May Be a Conscientious Objector and Not Know It," n.d., SNCC Papers, reel 62, 1959–1972.

59. "You May Be a Conscientious Objector and Not Know It," n.d., SNCC Papers, reel 62, 1959–1972, and *"Hell No!," SNCC Antidraft Program*, vol. 1 (mimeograph, n.d.), SNCC Papers, reel 21.

60. Letter and proposal, National Anti-Draft Program, August 9, 1966, SNCC Papers, reel 72; "GI Says 4 SNCC Members Tried to Keep Him from Being Inducted," *Chicago Daily Defender*, September 14, 1967, 8.

61. James R. Ralph, *Northern Protest: Martin Luther King, Jr., Chicago, and the Civil Rights Movement* (Cambridge: Harvard University Press, 1993), 213–14; Taylor Branch, *At Canaan's Edge: America in the King Years, 1965–68* (New York: Simon and Schuster, 2006), 511; "Illinois Draft to Be Doubled," *Chicago Daily Defender*, August 5, 1965, 1.

62. Smethurst, *Black Arts Movement*, 33.

63. "Resolution of the Annual Board Meeting of the SCLC," April 13, 1966, SNCC Papers, reel 62.

64. Branch, *At Canaan's Edge*, 470–72; John Herbers, "Rights Conference Averts Showdown on War Policy," *New York Times*, June 3, 1966.

65. Betty Washington, "Diane Bevel Calls U.S. 'Aggressor,'" *Chicago Daily Defender*, January 23, 1967, 4.

66. Donald Mosby, "Mrs. Bevel Goes for Commie Bait," *Chicago Defender*, January 31, 1967, 10; Arletta Claire, "Arletta's Advice," *Chicago Daily Defender*, January 31, 1967, 18.

67. Martin Luther King Jr., "A Time to Break Silence" (1967), in *A Testament of Hope: The Essential Writings and Speeches of Martin Luther King, Jr.*, ed. James Melvin Washington (San Francisco: Harper, 1986), 232–33.

68. Ibid., 240.

69. NAACP Flint Branch, "Executive Board Resolution on Vietnam," April 10, 1965; memo, "Roy Wilkins to Branches and Youth Council Presidents," July 30, 1965; and

"Wilkin Warns NAACP Units against 'Peace' Assembly," August 4, 1965, all in NAACP Papers, Vietnam War 1964-65, pt. 24, series C, reel 38; "NAACP Decries Stand of Dr. King on Vietnam."

70. John Sibley, "Bunche Disputes Dr. King on Peace," *New York Times*, April 13, 1967, 1.

71. Roy Wilkins, speech, Yale University, April 18, 1967, NAACP Papers, Vietnam War 1966-69, pt. 28, series C, reel 14; Roy Wilkins, "Believes Most Americans Can't Follow King," *Afro-American*, April 22, 1967, 4; "Wilkins Attacks King's Peace Talk as 'hogwash.'" *Baltimore Afro-American*, April 29, 1967, 14.

72. Letter from S. G. Allen to Roy Wilkins, April 11, 1967; letter from Addie L. Weber to Roy Wilkins, April 11, 1967; and Joseph S. Ford to Roy Wilkins, April 17, 1967, all in NAACP Papers, General Files, pt. 28, series B, reel 13, Vietnam Correspondence, 1967.

73. Letter from ARB to Roy Wilkins, April 17, 1968; letter from M. Franklin to Roy Wilkins, April 21, 1967; and letter from A. J. de Witte to Roy Wilkins, April 23, 1967, all in NAACP Papers, General Files, pt. 28, series B, reel 13, Vietnam Correspondence, 1967.

74. Clyde R. Taylor to Roy Wilkins, April 17, 1967, NAACP Papers, General Files, pt. 28, series B, reel 13, Vietnam Correspondence, 1967.

75. Letter from Virginia Chute and Robert Chute to Roy Wilkins, April 20, 1967, NAACP Papers, General Files, pt. 28, series B, reel 13, Vietnam Correspondence, 1967.

76. John A. Morsell to Martin Kroll, April 27, 1967, NAACP Papers, General Files, pt. 28, series B, reel 13, Vietnam Correspondence, 1967.

77. Stokely Carmichael, "SNCC Position Paper: The Basis of Black Power," in *Takin' It to the Streets: A Sixties Reader* (New York: Oxford University Press, 1995), 152-59.

78. Ibid., 164.

79. Peniel E. Joseph, *Waiting 'til the Midnight Hour: A Narrative History of Black Power in America* (New York: Henry Holt, 2006), 153-59.

80. U.S. National Advisory Commission on Civil Disorders, *Report of the National Advisory Commission on Civil Disorders* (Washington, D.C.: United States GPO, 1968), 77; Kevin Mumford, *Newark: A History of Race, Rights, and Riots in America* (New York: New York University Press, 2007), 126.

81. Mumford, *Newark*, 193.

82. Simon Hall, *Peace and Freedom: The Civil Rights and Antiwar Movements in the 1960s* (Philadelphia: University of Pennsylvania Press, 2005), 110-11; Mumford, *Newark*, 126.

83. Hall, *Peace and Freedom*, 111.

84. Oswald Sykes, "Like Vietnam—Harlem," *Baltimore Afro-American*, August 1, 1964, 13; Julian Bond and T. G. Lewis, *Vietnam: An Antiwar Comic Book*, reprinted in *Putting the Movement Back into Civil Rights Teaching*, ed. Deborah Menkart, Alana D. Murray, and Jenice L. View (Washington, D.C.: Teaching for Change and PRRAC, 2004), 164.

85. Stokely Carmichael, "At Morgan State," in *Vietnam and Black America: An Anthology of Protest and Resistance*, ed. Clyde Taylor (Garden City, N.Y.: Anchor, 1973), 269-71.

86. Hall, *Peace and Freedom*, 144; Huey P. Newton, "In Defense of Self-Defense: Executive Mandate Number One," in *The Black Panthers Speak*, ed. Philip S. Foner (Cambridge, Mass.: Da Capo Press, 2002), 40; Michael L. Clemons and Charles E. Jones,

"Global Solidarity: The Black Panther Party in the International Arena," in *Liberation, Imagination, and the Black Panther Party*, ed. Kathleen Cleaver and George Katsiaficas (New York: Routledge, 2001), 31–32.

87. Hall, *Peace and Freedom*, 61–64; Tyson, *Radio Free Dixie*, 294–95; Vincent Harding, "The Religion of Black Power," in *African American Religious Thought: An Anthology*, ed. Cornel West (Louisville, Ky.: Westminster John Knox Press, 2003), 715–45.

88. Hall, *Peace and Freedom*, 143–44.

89. SNCC Papers, reel 62.

90. "Most Whites Found Opposed to Civil Rights Demonstrations," *New York Times*, August 16, 1966, 24.

91. Tom Wicker, "Is the Backlash Here at Last?," *New York Times*, September 7, 1966, 46.

92. Herbers, "Rights Backers Fear a Backlash," 1; "White Backlash Evident in Voting," *New York Times*, November 9, 1966, 31.

93. Rick Perlstein, *Nixonland: The Rise of a President and the Fracturing of America* (New York: Scribner and Sons, 2009), 164–66.

94. Branch, *At Canaan's Edge*, 554.

95. Simone, "Backlash."

96. First Lady Laura Bush's "indefinite postponement" of a gathering of poets scheduled for February 2003 after thousands of writers protested U.S. plans to invade Iraq recalled the encounter between Eartha Kitt and Lady Bird Johnson in January 1968. See www.poetsagainstthewar.org.

97. "Eartha Kitt Denounces War Policy to Mrs. Johnson," *New York Times*, January 19, 1968, 1.

98. Letter to the editor, *New York Times*, January 19, 1968, 46.

99. Ibid., January 20, 1968, 28; J. Russell Elkinton, "Miss Kitt Praised," letter to the editor, *New York Times*, January 24, 1968, 44.

100. Seymour Hersch, "C.I.A. in '68 Gave Secret Service a Report Containing Gossip about Eartha Kitt," *New York Times*, January 3, 1975. For a discussion of the surveillance against Josephine Baker, see Mary L. Dudziak, "Josephine Baker, Racial Protest, and the Cold War," *Journal of American History* 81 (September 1994): 543–70.

101. Eddy Giles, "While I'm Away" (1967) and other tracks available on *A Soldier's Sad Story: Vietnam through the Eyes of Black America, 1966–73* (Kent Records, 2003) and *Does Anybody Know I'm Here? Vietnam through the Eyes of Black America* (Kent Records, 2005). All lyrics in this text have been transcribed directly from the recorded music.

102. James Brown, "After They Got the Funk They Went Back and Reloaded," in *Patriots: The Vietnam War Remembered from All Sides*, ed. Christian G. Appy (New York: Penguin, 2003), 184.

103. The Impressions, "Don't Cry My Love," from *Does Anybody Know I'm Here?* Lyrics transcribed from the recorded music.

104. Jimi Hendrix, *Jimi Hendrix Live at Woodstock* (Seattle: Hal Leonard, 1995), 115.

105. My analysis focuses on his Woodstock performance. Earlier and subsequent versions were little more than fractured sound.

106. "Brothers in Arms: Refusal to Take Action in Chicago," *Nation*, October 28, 1968, 421.

107. Tony Brown, *Jimi Hendrix: In His Own Words* (London: Omnibus Press, 1994), 74.

108. For the association between race, privilege, and dissent, see Jeremi Suri, *Power and Protest: Global Revolution and the Rise of Détente* (Cambridge: Harvard University Press, 2003), 164–72.

109. Brown, *Jimi Hendrix*, 36.

110. Smethurst, *Black Arts Movement*, 57. See Hughes, *Panther and the Lash*.

111. Smethurst, *Black Arts Movement*, 68, 77–78, 244, quote on 68.

112. Baraka, *Autobiography of LeRoi Jones*, 210.

113. James D. Sullivan, *On the Walls and in the Streets: American Poetry Broadsides from the 1960s* (Urbana: University of Illinois Press, 1997), 27–53.

114. Ibid., 22.

115. Larry Neal, "And Shine Swam On," in *Black Fire: An Anthology of Afro-American Writing*, ed. Larry Neal and LeRoi Jones (New York: Morrow, 1968), reprinted in Jeffrey Louis Decker, *The Black Aesthetic Movement* (Detroit: Gale Research Group, 1991), 16.

116. Cheryl Clarke, *"After Mecca": Women Poets and the Black Arts Movement* (New Brunswick, N.J.: Rutgers University Press, 2005), 49, 53.

117. Robert Hayden, "Runagate Runagate," in *Collected Poems* (New York: Liveright, 1981), 59–61.

118. Wahneema Lubiano, "Black Nationalism and Black Common Sense," in *The House That Race Built: Black Americans, U.S. Terrain* (New York: Pantheon, 1997), 232 (first quote), 234 (second quote).

119. Gwendolyn Brooks, "A Catch of Shy Fish," in *Blacks* (Chicago: Third World Press, 1987), 398.

120. Robert Hayden, *Words in the Mourning Time* (New York: October House, 1970), 49.

121. June Jordan, *Directed by Desire: The Collected Poems of June Jordan* (Port Townsend, Wash.: Copper Canyon Press, 2005), 52.

122. June Jordan, "Last Poem for a Little While," in Jordan, *Directed by Desire*, 74, 75.

123. The Last Poets, "The Black Soldier," *The Very Best of the Last Poets* (SNAP 255, 2005).

124. The Last Poets, "When the Revolution Comes," *Very Best of the Last Poets*; Gil Scott-Heron, "The Revolution Will Not Be Televised," *Black Power: Music of a Revolution* (Shout Factory, 2004).

125. Civil Rights Congress, *We Charge Genocide*, viii–x.

126. Shirley Chisholm, *Unbought and Unbossed* (New York: Houghton Mifflin, 1970), 94.

127. Ibid., 94–95; Marjorie Hunter, "White House Pickets, House Speakers Score War," *New York Times*, March 27, 1969, 4.

128. Chisholm, *Unbought and Unbossed*, 96.

129. Ibid., 97.

130. Ibid.; Thomas A. Johnson, "Organized Servicemen Abroad Intensify Drive against Racism," *New York Times*, November 19, 1971, 14.

131. Perlstein, *Nixonland*, 447–65.

132. Ibid.

133. Marjorie Hyer, "Most Area Churches Protest," *Washington Post*, January 19, 1973, B19.

134. June Jordan, "Poem to My Sister, Ethel Ennis, Who Sang 'The Star-Spangled Banner' at the Second Inauguration of Richard Milhous Nixon, January 20, 1973," in Jordan, *Directed by Desire*, 166.

135. Ibid., 167-68.

Epilogue

1. Tom Shanker, "The Struggle for Iraq," *New York Times*, May 5, 2004, 19; Fernanda Santos, "A Sergeant Who Fled the Army but Not the War in His Head," *New York Times*, November 18, 2007.

2. Christian G. Appy, "Class Wars," in *Iraq and the Lessons of Vietnam*, ed. Lloyd C. Gardner and Marilyn B. Young (New York: New Press, 2007), 137.

3. President George W. Bush's plans to invade Iraq predated the bombing of the World Trade Center towers on September 11, 2001. On patterns of blacks' enlistments, see James E. Ellis, "Where Troop Cuts Will Be Cruelest: For Blacks, the Services Have Been the Best Employer Around," *Business Week*, June 8, 1992, 72-73; Kimberley L. Phillips, "'War! What Is It Good For?': Vietnam, Conscription, and Migration in Black America," in *Repositioning North American Migration History*, ed. Marc S. Rodriguez (New York: University of Rochester Press, 2004), 265-83; Sarah Abruzzesee, "Iraq War Brings Drop in Black Enlistees," *New York Times*, August 22, 2007.

4. Condoleezza Rice, "Why We Know Iraq Is Lying," and Colin Powell, "Presentation to the UN Security Council: A Threat to International Peace and Security," in *The Iraq War Reader: History, Documents, Opinions*, ed. Micah L. Sifry and Christopher Cerf (New York: Touchstone, 2003), 450-52, 465-78.

5. Christopher Marquis, "Blacks Counsel Caution on Liberia," *New York Times*, August 3, 2003, WK3.

6. Randy Kennedy and Diane Cardwell, "New Yorkers' Sharp Divisions Fall Roughly on Racial Lines," *New York Times*, March 27, 2003, B15; Derrick Z. Jackson, "Promises Abroad, While at Home Promises Go Forgotten," in Sifry and Cerf, *Iraq War Reader*, 495-96.

7. Carl Hulse, "The Dissent: Some in Congress, Recalling Vietnam, Oppose the War," *New York Times*, September 21, 2002, A9; see 2001-9 articles by Derrick Z. Jackson, who writes for the *Boston Globe*, and Bob Herbert, who wrote for the *New York Times* until 2011.

8. Algernon Austin, "Reversal of Fortune: Economic Gains of 1990s Overturned for African Americans from 2000-07," Economic Policy Briefing Paper, #220, September 18, 2008, www.EPI.org.

9. Lizette Alverez, "More Americans Joining Military as Jobs Dwindle," *New York Times*, January 19, 2009, A13; Lizette Alverez, "Army Efforts to Enlist Hispanics Draws Recruits, and Criticism," *New York Times*, February 9, 2006; Tim Weiner, "A Nation at War: Immigrant Marines; Latinos Give their Lives to a New Land," *New York Times*, April 4, 2003; Ernesto Cien-Fuegos, "La Raza: The 'Grunts' of the U.S. Armed Forces," *La Voz de Aztlan*, September 9, 2002, www.aztlan.net/grunts.htm (accessed November 15, 2010).

10. Abruzzesee, "Iraq War Brings Drop in Black Enlistees."

11. Derrick Z. Jackson, "For African Americans, Folly of This War Hits Home," *Boston Globe*, May 9, 2007; online edition: www.boston.com/news/globe/editorial_opinion/oped/articles.

12. Abruzzesee, "Iraq War Brings Drop in Black Enlistees."

13. Alverez, "More Americans Joining Military as Jobs Dwindle."

14. www4.1aw.cornell.edu/uscode/10/12305.html; see also the weekly index from the Brookings Institute on the costs of the wars to the United States, Iraq, and Afghanistan, www.brookings.edu/saban/iraq-index.aspx, and www.brookings.edu/foreign-policy/afghanistan-index.aspx.

15. As this book goes to press, the Military Leadership Diversity Committee and the Defense Advisory Committee on Women, two high-level military advisory panels, have recommended that the armed forces lift policies that bar women from combat. This recommendation followed the recent recommendation to repeal policies that denied gays and lesbians the right to serve openly and without punishment and harassment in the military. Women deployed to Iraq and Afghanistan have received "imminent danger" pay, but because they have been attached to combat units and were not assigned to or fully trained for combat positions, they do not receive all of the pay men in combat units receive. See Department of Defense, *Department of Defense Annual Report on Sexual Assault, CY 2006* (March 15, 2007); Steven Lee Meyers, "A Peril in the War Zones: Sexual Abuse by Fellow GIs," *New York Times*, December 27, 2009; and Lizette Alverez, "GI Jane Breaks the Combat Barrier," *New York Times*, August 15, 2009.

16. For an argument that the tactics emerged out of the chaos of the Iraq invasion, see Thomas E. Ricks, *Fiasco: The American Military Adventure in Iraq* (New York: Penguin, 2006), 290–97. For the links between paramilitary policing in the United States and policies in Iraq, see Major Andy J. Greer, "Negotiating with Pre-Terrorists: Police Tactics with Gangs Applied to Current Operations in Iraq" (master's thesis, Maxwell Air Force Base, 2008). Many reservists in the military also work in police departments, and their "expertise" has been widely sought, especially for Guantanamo and Abu Ghraib.

17. Christian Parenti, "Swat Nation: Paramilitary Policing Is on the Rise," *Nation*, May 31, 1999, 20.

18. Ricks, *Fiasco*, 272, 290–97.

19. Philip Gourevitch and Errol Morris, *Standard Operating Procedure* (New York: Penguin, 2008), 101; on Davis's role and conviction, see 71–105, 261–280; Kate Zernike, "The Struggle for Iraq: The Testimony," *New York Times*, May 14, 2004; "Head of U.S. Prisons in Iraq to Testify," *New York Times*, December 5, 2004. On the use of music in the military's interrogation and torture, see the very important article by Suzanne Cusick, "'You Are in a Place That Is out of This World . . .': Music in the Detention Camps of the 'Global War on Terror,'" *Journal of the Society for American Music* 2 (Winter 2008): 1–26.

20. Chris Hedges and Laila al-Arian, "The Other War: Iraq Vets Bear Witness," *Nation*, July 30, 2007; Bob Herbert, "Abusing Iraqi Citizens," *New York Times*, July 10, 2007, A21.

21. Hedges and al-Arian, "The Other War."

22. http://www.yesmagazine.org/multimedia/yes-film/i-know-im-not-alone. See Michael Franti, *Yell Fire!* (2006); 4th25, *Live from Iraq* (4th25.com Entertainment, 2005); and various artists, *Voices from the Frontlines* (Crosscheck Records, 2006).

23. Jeff Chang, *Can't Stop, Won't Stop: A History of the Hip-Hop Generation* (New York: St. Martin's Press, 2005), 437.

24. The literature on rap as a critique of violence against nonwhites is rich. See especially the essays in Tony Mitchell, ed., *Global Noise: Rap and Hip-Hop Outside the USA* (Middletown, Conn.: Wesleyan University Press, 2001), and Mitchell's introduction, 14.

25. "@uck#m," *Live from Iraq*.

26. http://www.blackmississippi.com/indexarticle.html?page=home&id=-1&fid=1133.

27. Chang, *Can't Stop, Won't Stop*, 453–65.

28. In 2008, American troops reportedly blasted music through an ipod as they distributed food. See www.crunchgear.com/2008/12/16/ipod-helping-to-win-hearts-and-minds-in-iraq/ (accessed June 8, 2011).

Index